Old Believers
in a CHANGING WORLD

Old Believers
in a Changing World

Robert O. Crummey

NORTHERN ILLINOIS UNIVERSITY PRESS *DeKalb*

Published by the Northern Illinois University Press, DeKalb, Illinois   60115

Design by Shaun Allshouse

Library of Congress Cataloging-in-Publication Data

Crummey, Robert O.

Old Believers in a changing world / Robert O. Crummey.

p. cm.

Includes bibliographical references and index.

ISBN 978-0-87580-650-1 (clothbound : alk. paper)

1. Old Believers. I. Title.

BX601.C79 2011

281.9'476dc22

2010053495

The Chronologic History of the Chapters (p. 265) provides both the history of and the permissions for the chapters in this volume.

Contents

Preface   vii

HISTORIOGRAPHY AND THEORY

1—Past and Current Interpretations of the Old Belief   5

2—Old Belief as Popular Religion
New Approaches   17

SEVENTEENTH-CENTURY ORIGINS

3—Ecclesiastical Elites and Popular Belief and Practice
in Seventeenth-Century Russia   31

4—Religious Radicalism in Seventeenth-Century Russia
Reexamining the Kapiton Movement   52

5—The Origins of the Old Believer Cultural Systems
The Works of Avraamii   68

6—The Miracle of Martyrdom
Reflections on Early Old Believer Hagiography   85

EIGHTEENTH- AND NINETEENTH-CENTURY COMMUNITIES

7—Old Believer Communities
Ideals and Structures   99

8—The Spirituality of the Vyg Fathers   119

9—The Historical Framework of the Vyg Fathers   129

10—The Cultural Worlds of Andrei Borisov   136

11—Interpreting the Fate of Old Believer Communities in
the Eighteenth and Nineteenth Centuries   157

OLD BELIEVER LIFE AND SCHOLARSHIP IN THE
LATE TWENTIETH CENTURY

12—The Novosibirsk School of Old Believer Studies   167

Afterword   190

Notes   195
Selected Bibliography   241
Index   259
Chronological History of the Chapters   265

Preface

Old Belief is a conservative offshoot of the Russian Orthodox Church. It began in the mid-seventeenth century in opposition to Patriarch Nikon's reforms of the liturgy and, over the following centuries, grew into a complex movement with many branches or accords, with widely differing forms of worship and conduct. In spite of their diversity, however, the Old Believers share the conviction that they are the last genuine Eastern Orthodox Christians on earth. Since they share the common Orthodox assumption that Western Christendom has fallen into error, they believe, by extension, that they must be the only remaining defenders of true Christianity.

Living as the Faithful Remnant is an enormous burden, for the adherents of the true faith must never waver in their convictions or fall into heresy. Because the stakes are so high, the Old Believers have conducted the debates among themselves and handled their confrontations with the officially sanctioned Russian Orthodox Church with profound determination, rigidity, bitterness, and at times outright fanaticism. The last defenders of the true faith must also separate themselves from the perishing world around them. Over the course of their history, Old Believers have set themselves apart by maintaining a radically distinct way of life. How they have done so has varied from one time and place to another. Nevertheless, each accord or local community has maintained customs and taboos that separate them from their non–Old Believer neighbors and often from one another. At the same time, they must take into account the changing world around them. Thus, disputes about appropriate personal grooming, dress, diet, and responses to modern technology are an ongoing feature of Old Believer life.

Most important of all, the Old Believers' conviction that they are the last defenders of authentic Christian faith leads inexorably to the conclusion that the End of the World is at hand. All Old Believers have shared a common apocalyptic language and lived with expectations of the End Time even though they have argued endlessly about the details. Some of them have found comfort in interpreting catastrophic events, from the Petrine reforms to the collectivization of agriculture in Soviet times, as the works of the Antichrist. The chapters that follow will examine these themes in greater detail.

How and why did a historian who is neither Russian nor Eastern Orthodox by background come to study the Old Believers? For, although I am a practicing Christian in the Western tradition and a lover of liturgy, I have always been a quintessential outsider in the Old Believers' world, and I admit, many features of all branches of Eastern Orthodoxy still seem exotic to me.

First, there were the intellectual attractions. For a historian of Russia, study of Old Belief is a gateway to many questions that scholars of religious movements in all societies must address. I will mention only a few obvious examples. As is already clear, the Old Believers are an excellent example of a religious community whose members believe that they are living in apocalyptic times. Moreover, their history provides an opportunity to explore the relationship between elite and popular belief and practice. To what extent do established religious and political authorities create and lead movements of revival, reform, or opposition? Or to what extent do such movements reflect first and foremost the discontents—spiritual, political, or social—of ordinary believers? As many historians of religious movements are discovering, any neat distinction between the beliefs, practices, and aspirations of the members of political and religious elites and those of ordinary men and women is very difficult to maintain. In addition, when a movement defines itself in part by the study and dissemination of a canon of religious writings, one is entitled to ask how these texts spread, how believers are trained to read or hear them, and what their contents might mean to the highly educated and the unlettered. In a word, Old Belief is an excellent example of the evolution of a "textual community."

Moreover, there were personal reasons for my decision that require some brief autobiographical comments to explain. Throughout my adult life I have had a deep interest in the Christian church and other religious organizations and their interactions with the larger community. In the graduate program at the University of Chicago, Leo Haimson's brilliant teaching convinced me to concentrate on Russian history. Then, when the time came to choose a dissertation topic, the late Oswald P. Backus urged me to study the church schism of the mid-seventeenth century and encouraged me to make Helsinki my research base since, for a citizen of Canada, there was no opportunity at that time to spend a year on an academic exchange in the USSR. When Michael Cherniavsky joined the faculty at Chicago and became my dissertation adviser, the Old Believers became the focus of my research.

To a remarkable degree, my mentors' advice bore fruit. While based in Helsinki, I spent two months early in 1963 as a "tourist" in Leningrad and met the legendary scholar of Old Belief, Vladimir Ivanovich Malyshev.

I no longer remember who provided the introduction to him. Even more mysterious are the reasons he was willing to provide protection and support to a confused and unfocused foreign graduate student with a weak command of Russian. Perhaps, in addition to his innate generosity of spirit, it was his knowledge that only foreign scholars could, in that time, publish work on the Old Belief as such. Whatever the reason, doors opened as if by magic. Access to the archival collections controlled by the Academy of Sciences, which could be granted locally, allowed me to study many of the fundamental sources on the Vyg community, the focus of my dissertation and subsequent book, *The Old Believers and the World of Antichrist.* If I can paste a label on my initial approach and methodology in studying Old Belief, it is "sociology of religion." While well aware of the cultural leadership of Vyg within the empire-wide networks of Old Believers, I concentrated on the structure of the community, its economic activities, and its complex relations with the imperial government.

Once I had completed the dissertation, I began the time-honored practice of turning it into a book. But as I worked on revising the manuscript, I became aware of tension between my own historical instincts and personal values and the approach of my mentor, Cherniavsky, whose best work, in my opinion, is his brilliant article on the Old Believers' "political theology" in the reign of Peter I. On a personal level, my relationship with Cherniavsky was cordial, especially during the period when we were both in Leningrad working in the same archival collections, where he concentrated on the Old Believers' political iconography and I focused on their monastic rules. Rather, my concerns lay not in his analysis of their political ideals and symbols but in his broader approach to the history of religious movements. The then-popular cocktail of Marxist and Freudian approaches to the study of history seemed to me to have led to two basic assumptions about the Old Believers—and other religious groups—that troubled me. Under the first, it was incumbent on a twentieth-century scholar to look for the overt or hidden political and social messages in religious texts rather than the theological and liturgical arguments to which the authors of the texts devoted the greatest attention. From this perspective, the fact that many Old Believers were convinced that Peter I was the Antichrist is highly significant, but the thousands of pages devoted to the two-finger sign of the cross and the other details of the Nikonian reforms are not. Similarly, the thinking went, since twentieth-century historians cannot possibly immerse themselves in the worldview of religious believers of an earlier time, they should concentrate on applying the concepts of their own day to make the subjects of their studies comprehensible to their contemporaries.

I had no trouble agreeing that I could not possibly enter the minds and hearts of seventeenth-century Russian dissenters. Still, I owed them the respect of taking their arguments and decisions with complete seriousness and trying to understand them in their own terms.

As work on *The Old Believers and the World of Antichrist* came to an end, my research interests turned in a completely different direction. As a reader and teacher of Russian history, I came to understand how much recent studies of the ruling elite in the fifteenth and sixteenth centuries had led to a thorough reevaluation of the workings of the Muscovite political system. For that reason, I joined the growing ranks of practitioners of collective biography (prosopographers) by undertaking a detailed study of the men who made up the boyar elite in the seventeenth century. Nevertheless, Malyshev and the Old Believers were not finished with me yet. While I was based in Moscow in 1969 on the newly established University of Toronto exchange program, a short research trip to Leningrad allowed me to study additional documents on the Vyg community. It also produced Vladimir Ivanovich's ultimate act of magic. He gently but firmly ordered me to go to Riga to visit the Grebenshchikovskaia Obshchina, one of the largest centers of priestless Old Belief in the USSR, and meet the legendary Ivan Nikiforovich Zavoloko. Over my protests that the notoriously unhelpful Foreign Students' Office of Leningrad University would never provide the paperwork, he simply told me to report there the following day. Somehow within twenty-four hours everything had been arranged!

My three days in Riga were among the highlights of my life. Zavoloko welcomed me with open arms. In the midsummer sun, I sat for three days at a small table in his garden reading manuscripts from his personal collection. The prize for me was an early eighteenth-century autograph copy of the Vyg rule (now in Pushkin House in St. Petersburg with the catalogue designation Zavoloko Collection number 3). As I took notes, he took care of my every need. He also gave me a few glimpses into his extraordinary life and difficult current circumstances—poverty and disability (he had lost a leg to gangrene in the Gulag)—which he regarded as conditions that would in no way limit his efforts to practice his faith and preserve the Old Believer tradition.

In 1983, after thirteen years of official Muscovite service registers, index cards, and computer printouts, *Aristocrats and Servitors*, the book on the boyar elite in seventeenth-century Russia, finally appeared in print. It was time for a change!

The Old Believers beckoned. Looking back on the Vyg project, the comments of two distinguished colleagues haunted me. In a kind and favorable review of *The Old Believers and the World of Antichrist*, Marc Raeff gently pointed out that the book had all but omitted the most significant accomplishment of Vyg, its leaders' creation and dissemination of a distinct Old Believer literary and artistic culture. Later, in a brief conversation, A. I. Klibanov expressed his dismay at my decision to do research on the ruling elite and his regret that I was abandoning study of "the spiritual treasures of the Russian people."

Moreover, the time was ripe. The so-called new cultural history called for historians to read familiar sources from new perspectives and to unearth new ones in order to deepen our understanding of the things that historical figures—including the marginal and obscure—said, wrote, and did. The essays in this book are the results of my attempt to apply this approach to the Old Believers.

Fortunately, like all historians I know, I am a pack rat. As a starting point, I still had the notes, photocopies, and rare editions from the Vyg project. In addition, in spite of the pressure of other commitments, I was able to spend January and February of 1991 in Leningrad. Work in all of the major collections of Old Believer manuscripts in the city blended almost seamlessly with the daily news broadcasts of political conflict and violence as the USSR began to fall apart. As we all juggled manuscripts and politics, I profited from the learning and enjoyed the friendship of Gleb Merkulov, Aleksandr Bobrov, and the late Aleksandr Amosov. At the turn of the 1980s and 1990s, I also made very short visits to Moscow, Novosibirsk, and Petrozavodsk. In retrospect, the importance of these trips lay in new or renewed contact with fellow Old Believer scholars, two of whom—Natal'ia Sergeevna Gur'ianova and Elena Mikhailovna Iukhimenko—have supported me in many ways. Without their advice and encouragement, including their copies of previously unknown texts that were crucial to my work, several of these essays could not have been written.

The purpose of this book, then, is to bring together a collection of scattered articles on the cultural history of the Old Believers into a single volume. Doing so is a long-established tradition of scholars late in their careers. Thanks, however, to modern word processing techniques, all of the articles have been printed in a consistent format. Two items, the comparative analysis of Old Believer communities (chapter 7) and the study of the Novosibirsk school of Old Believer studies (chapter 12) have never been published, nor have this Preface and the Afterword.

The reader should be aware that the chapters were originally published over a period of eighteen years. Most began life as conference papers. One (chapter 9) was originally published in Russian and appears for the first time in English. Moreover, in this book, the chapters appear in thematic order, not in the chronological sequence in which they were written. In order to avoid confusion, I have added to the table of contents a list of the chapters in chronological order. Given the circumstances of their initial publication, there is inevitably some repetition from one chapter to the next. I have, however, made minor editorial changes to eliminate the most obvious redundancies. Moreover, the notes reflect the state of the literature at the time of publication. For this edition, I have made no systematic attempt to update the endnotes except to add references to the published editions of works I cited in manuscript in the original version.

Since each article was originally written to stand alone, most require little additional commentary. The reader may find a few brief comments helpful. The first three chapters constitute an introduction to the more focused studies that follow. Chapter 1 is a brief survey of historical writing on Old Belief with particular emphasis on works published outside Russia. Chapter 2 discusses approaches to the study of the Old Believers in the context of the international debates about "popular religion." Chapter 3 is a survey of the early history of Old Belief in a comparative international context. It first appeared in a volume examining the relations between the early modern state, ecclesiastical hierarchies, and ordinary believers in a number of societies.

Several of the later chapters arose from my concern about the apparent reassertion of the old "populist" approach to Old Believer history as political and social protest in a religious guise. In retrospect, my worries appear exaggerated. Nevertheless, I wanted to carry out studies that would emphasize the theological, liturgical, and moral issues that preoccupied the Old Believers and other religious dissenters. For both theoretical and tactical reasons, I concentrated on four distinct areas—the so-called Kapiton movement of the mid-seventeenth century (chapter 4); Avraamii, a relatively neglected representative of the very first opponents of the Nikonian reforms (chapters 5 and 6); the spirituality and historical philosophy of the leaders of the Vyg community in the first half of the eighteenth century (chapters 8 and 9); and the writings and sermons of Andrei Borisov, the little known and complex figure who led Vyg in the late eighteenth century (chapter 10). With the wisdom of hindsight, I suspect that my enthusiasm for the new cultural history and symbolic anthropology may have led me to use the concepts and jargon of these disciplines too often or too loosely in the longer articles on Avraamii and Borisov. Finally, continuing my earlier work on the Vyg community, I have included a comparative survey of the structure and aspirations of the Old Believers' quasi-monastic communities throughout the Russian Empire (chapter 7) and their suppression by the government of Nicholas I (chapter 12).

Hindsight has also made clear the extent to which my views on Old Belief have changed over the course of the last two decades. Many of my basic assumptions have remained the same. The reader will note, however, a shift of emphasis in the discussion of the relative isolation of the Old Believers from the rest of Russian society. In the earliest two essays included in this volume —those on Vyg spirituality (chapter 8) and historiography (chapter 9)—I emphasized the radical separation of Old Believer culture from mainstream society. In more recent times, however, the discoveries of Russian scholars, particularly N. V. Ponyrko, Gur'ianova, and Iukhimenko, and my own studies of Avraamii (chapter 5) and Andrei Borisov (chapter 10) made me more acutely aware of the subtle ways in which the intellectual leaders of Old Belief remained in contact with official high culture and used its ideas and techniques to advance their cause.

In closing, I want to emphasize the obvious—that no historians can function without the foundation of their predecessors' writings, the inspiration and guidance of their mentors, and the encouragement and practical help of colleagues, librarians, and archivists. The autobiographical comments earlier in this preface give some indication of the number of individuals to whom I owe debts that I can never repay. It is to them that I dedicate this book of essays.

Old Believers
in a CHANGING WORLD

HISTORIOGRAPHY
and THEORY

Past and Current Interpretations of the Old Belief

IN THE LAST FEW YEARS, bibliographies of new books and articles and the agendas of scholarly conferences bear witness to an unprecedented surge of interest, in Russia and elsewhere, in the history and culture of the Old Believers. Not since the 1860s and 1870s and the interrevolutionary years, 1905–1917, has Old Belief attracted such wide interest among scholars and the general public. The reasons are not difficult to identify. As we are constantly reminded, in radically new political, social, and economic circumstances, Russians are seeking common values to replace the long-dead pieties of official Marxism-Leninism. The search leads in many directions, not least to Eastern Orthodox Christianity in its official and Old Believer variants. Indeed, in their enthusiasm for religiosity and religions of all kinds, Russians increasingly resemble Americans. Moreover, in struggling to create a new society on the ruins of the old, Russians are understandably searching for workable and culturally appropriate models of social organization and political action. For both practicing Old Believers and scholars of Old Belief, the past is an obvious place to look. In a broad sense, none of this is new. The earlier surges of interest in Old Belief also were responses to the social and political issues of the day.

The current flowering of Russian scholarship on the history and culture of Old Belief is the culmination of several decades of hard and careful work. Scholars published what the conditions permitted—studies on movements of religious heterodoxy as ideological reflections of popular resistance to political oppression and serfdom; editions and textological studies; and guides to manuscript collections. Annual summer expeditions combing remote regions for old books and manuscripts have long been a familiar feature of the academic landscape. Any work we undertake builds on these efforts. At the same time, as we all know, scholars like V. I. Malyshev cultivated a much deeper and more comprehensive scholarly understanding of Old Belief beneath the surface of the printed word. In the last few years, that which was hidden has been revealed: scholars in Russia can discuss any and all features of Old Belief without Aesopian language or intellectual gamesmanship. Their most serious problem now is a familiar one to their foreign colleagues—the economics of publishing.

A remarkable feature of the contemporary scene is the extent to which Old Believer studies has become a profoundly international enterprise. The prevailing currents in historical study are partly responsible for this situation. The "new history," as my younger colleagues call it, puts heavy emphasis on the study of cultural values or "mentalities" particularly of non-elite social groups. Many studies of popular religious culture have appeared in the last three decades.[1]

The close collaboration of historians, literary scholars, and ethnographers— long a feature of Old Believer studies in Russia—dovetails neatly with these scholarly agendas. Not surprisingly, then, in the last few years, important studies of Old Belief have appeared in several countries, Russian and non-Russian scholars alike have full access to unpublished written materials, the summer archeographical expedition has become a kind of international ecotourism and the international conference on Old Belief or traditional Russian culture a frequent occurrence. How we use this opportunity is surely our most important concern.

The core of this chapter will consist of observations on the history and current state of the literature on Old Belief. I make no claim to present a systematic survey of the historiography of Old Belief. Before offering my reflections, I have no choice but to raise issues of definition.

To begin with the most obvious question, what is Old Belief? From the mid-seventeenth century until today, officials, polemicists, and scholars alike have moved uneasily between two understandings of Old Belief— *staroobriadchestvo* and *raskol*—both well entrenched in serious scholarly writing. By *staroobriadchestvo*, scholars mean the groups of Eastern Orthodox Christians who have defined and identified themselves by their rejection of certain liturgical practices of the post-Nikonian Russian Orthodox Church such as the three-finger sign of the cross. This definition clearly includes members of the various accords of *popovtsy* (priestly) and *bespopovtsy* (priestless). Leaving aside its pejorative overtones, the word *raskol* (schism) logically encompasses a much wider variety of Russian Christians who reject their historical allegiance to the official Russian Orthodox Church, and thus it includes individuals and groups who have very little in common with Old Believers (*staroobriadtsy*) in the strict sense. These abstract distinctions can be very difficult to apply in practice. As Georg Michels has recently pointed out, the scattered inquisitorial and police sources of the late seventeenth century make it very difficult to distinguish Old Belief in the strict sense from more amorphous forms of heterodoxy.[2] Moreover, from that time until now, individuals—whether victims of early eighteenth-century inquisitors, sophisticated industrialists of the early twentieth century, or Karelian peasant women in recent years[3]—can be remarkably difficult to classify. How are we to categorize people who deny that they are Old Believers but adopt the identifying marks of that movement? Or how do we label individuals who identify themselves as Old Believers but whose lives show few signs of the movement's beliefs and practices?

Insofar as it is possible to maintain rigorous distinctions, this chapter will adopt the narrower definition of Old Belief and will give all who identify themselves with that label the benefit of the doubt. Two other caveats are also in order. The following reflections will center on the history of Old Belief, not contemporary ethnography. Moreover, the comments that follow will give relatively little emphasis to ongoing new work.[4]

In a sense, the historiography of Old Belief begins in the mid-seventeenth century for Old Belief is, by nature, a historical movement. The earliest polemics against the Nikonian reforms set forth a sacred history of Russian Orthodoxy to justify opposition to particular changes in liturgical practice, the theoretical justification for them, and the administrative style with which they were implemented.[5] The polemicists of the 1660s and early 1670s began with the premise that Russian Orthodoxy of the late sixteenth and early seventeenth centuries was the only authentic expression of the Christian faith left in the world. Thus any radical deviation from the fundamental patterns of Russia's recent ecclesiastical and cultural development automatically had to mean a fall into heresy and the beginning of the Apocalypse. Likewise Simeon Polotskii and later defenders of the reformed church had no choice but to present their countervailing vision of Orthodox history, which emphasized the ways in which the Muscovite church had strayed from the authentic Orthodox tradition. These fundamental assumptions underlay the polemics for and against the Old Belief for two centuries.

Thus, until the mid-nineteenth century, Old Believer apologetics and the polemics of the official Orthodox Church concentrated on the disputed issues of liturgical practice and the canonical and moral implications and consequences of those disputes. Moreover, for the first two centuries after the schism, the polemical exchange carried a subtext—more or less explicit depending on the time and circumstances—that Old Belief was subversive of good order in both church and state. In the reigns of Sophia (1682–1689) and Peter I (1689–1725) and again under Nicholas I (1825–1855), the civil government and ecclesiastical hierarchy shared a conviction that, far from being a harmless collection of eccentrics, the Old Believers actively fostered political subversion and moral anarchy.[6] For their part, the Old Believers saw themselves as the only true Christian community within a larger society that had lost its cultural and moral underpinnings.

The middle decades of the nineteenth century saw an explosion of public interest in Old Belief. Scholars often divide the resulting scholarly and polemical literature into two familiar categories, the works of ecclesiastical historians and of the populists.[7] The writings of the ecclesiastical historians arose from a missionary impulse supported by the imperial government, which, especially from the reign of Nicholas I, viewed the Old Believers both as schismatics and as politically and socially subversive. Beginning in the 1850s, Orthodox seminaries gave courses on the raskol to prepare future priests and missionaries. The instructors of these courses—the future Metropolitan Macarius and P. S. Smirnov, for example—wrote textbooks on the history and contemporary shape of Old Belief and other native forms of religious dissent in Russia.[8] Their objective—whether expressed militantly as N. I. Subbotin did or more gently in the manner of Smirnov—was the reintegration of all Eastern Orthodox Christians into the fold of the official church.[9] Their scholarly focus was equally specific: they concentrated on the liturgical, polemical, and canonical issues that separated the lost brothers and sisters from the Russian Orthodox Church and led to the division of Old Belief into innumerable contending branches or "accords." Their writings paid little, if any, attention to the political circumstances in which Old Belief developed and none at all to the social and economic circumstances in which it grew.

At the same time, it is all too easy to dismiss their achievements. The ecclesiastical historians deserve credit for taking the Old Believers' own writings seriously and concentrating on the issues that were of greatest importance to literate Old Believers themselves. Most of us have found the source publications of Subbotin and others indispensable.[10] The quality of their editorial work stands up remarkably well when measured by the more rigorous standards of contemporary textology.[11] Likewise, the best detailed analyses of the liturgical and polemical debates to which the Old Believers themselves devoted so much energy are to be found in the work of the seminary professors, particularly Smirnov.[12]

Finally, in their rigor and seriousness of purpose, the ecclesiastical historians sometimes advanced scholarly positions that were distinctly embarrassing to the Orthodox hierarchy. Although the author staunchly defended the official Orthodox position, E. E. Golubinskii's learned essays on the ecclesiastical conflicts of the seventeenth century suggested that both Greek and Muscovite Russian practices on disputed liturgical issues resulted from long, haphazard historical evolution and that neither, therefore, had any absolute claim to authenticity. Moreover, Golubinskii stated flatly that Patriarch Nikon and his allies made a disastrous error in arguing that earlier Russian practice was completely wrong and in anathematizing the two-finger sign of the cross, which was actually more ancient than the three-finger usage.[13] Going further, in his examination of the details of the Nikonian reforms, N. F. Kapterev emphasized the extent to which the reforming patriarch and his associates botched the editing of the disputed liturgical texts and ran roughshod over Russian Orthodox tradition as well as the sensibilities of many contemporaries. As Subbotin realized, Kapterev's work was far more subversive of the official Orthodox position than the most skillful Old Believer polemic.[14]

In the years of the Great Reforms, educated Russian society heard a compelling new voice, the populists. In his lengthy essays *Russkii raskol staroobriadstva* (1859) and *Zemstvo i raskol* (1862), A. P. Shchapov (1830–1876) expressed a radically new interpretation of the origins and spread of Old Belief and other forms of religious heterodoxy. Born in Siberia and educated in clergy schools, Shchapov wrote his first groundbreaking essays on the raskol while a teacher at the Kazan' Theological Academy and the local university. His passionate homily at the funeral of the victims of the government's repression of the peasant demonstrators at Bezdna in 1861 cost him his teaching positions. After three years of free-lance writing and political activity in St. Petersburg, he was exiled by the imperial government to Siberia where he spent the rest of his life.

In the first of his two programmatic statements, Shchapov interpreted Old Belief as the reassertion of the spiritual values and traditional religious practices of the Russian masses in opposition to the bureaucratizing reforms of the state and the ecclesiastical hierarchy. The Nikonian liturgical reforms, which Shchapov interpreted in the same way as the ecclesiastical historians, were not so much a cause as a pretext for the broad movement of popular opposition that emerged in the late seventeenth and early eighteenth centuries. In the jargon of our own day, Old Belief and other forms of dissent were the authentic expressions of popular religious culture in all its strengths and weaknesses. Once the movement of opposition took shape, it spread rapidly, thanks to the moral and organizational weaknesses of the Russian Orthodox Church, the energetic missionary work of its first leaders, and the oppressive policies of the Russian state. In short, Old Belief became a movement of democratic opposition to the administrative structure of the state.[15] By 1862, a more radical Shchapov stated bluntly that the raskol was the ideological justification for the opposition of the zemstvo (the spontaneous political, social, and economic forces in Russian society) to the bureaucratizing state and its ecclesiastical allies. Not surprisingly, his most telling evidence to support this view came from the most politically radical elements in Old Belief, the preachers and pamphleteers who denounced Peter I as the Antichrist and the later *beguny* (fugitives), and from the documentation on the great popular revolts of the period. It was Shchapov who first drew the connection between Old Belief and rebellion, between Avvakum and Stenka Razin, by arguing that the former provided the ideological justification and slogans for the latter.[16] Shchapov's essays set off a veritable avalanche of books and essays exploring Old Belief and other forms of dissent as expressions of popular initiative and forms of opposition and rebellion against imperial power. On a more practical level, radical activists in Russia and in emigration made futile attempts to enlist Old Believers for an active campaign of political opposition to the imperial government.

We owe a great debt to Shchapov and his successors. They examined Old Belief in the political, institutional, social, and cultural contexts in which it emerged and grew. Moreover, they posed questions that could never again be avoided: to what extent was the emergence of Old Belief really a reaction against the Nikonian reforms? And to what extent did political and social conditions and popular cultural traditions feed, shape, and sustain it? At the same time, the populist impulse contains pitfalls. Shchapov's own views were complex, and he knew and cared about the intellectual agendas and inner history of Old Belief.[17] In the writings of the later populists, however, we find an increasingly one-sided emphasis on the radical social content of Old Belief and, on occasion, a heavy-handed attempt to find geographical, sociological, or political explanations for the disputes and divisions within the movement.[18] In a more subtle sense, moreover, the populist approach contains the disturbing assumption that the Old Believers could not have meant what they wrote or said and could not have been interested in the issues to which they devoted so much energy, emotion, and paper. Instead (the assumption seems to be), the historian, as a modern man or woman, has the duty to deconstruct the Old Believers' statements in order to decipher the hidden, often unconscious, political and social messages in their words and actions.

In spite of these potential pitfalls, the populists' agenda retains its creative power. No serious historian can avoid the questions they asked. Moreover, in Marxist-Leninist rhetorical garb, their interpretation became the orthodox position in the official historiography of the Soviet period.[19]

In spite of the arbitrariness of the dichotomy, the ecclesiastical and the populist approaches remain the most useful polarities in interpreting the history of Old Belief. But must we, as Cherniavsky argued, make a radical choice to affirm the one and reject the other? I think not. An examination of the most important works published in recent decades outside of Russia suggests, rather, that the most fruitful approaches take seriously *both* the liturgical and canonical questions that define Old Belief *and* the social, political, and institutional conflicts that fed and shaped it. The very richness of recent writing on Old Belief comes from the fact that each historian establishes his or her own hierarchy of explanations and combines the liturgical and spiritual, political, social, and economic dimensions of the movement in his or her own way.

The rest of this chapter will briefly survey some high points in "Western" writing on Old Belief.[20] For many years, "foreigners" who studied Old Belief occupied a curious position. Given the political conditions in Russia, "Western" scholars had a virtual monopoly of publication on the history of Old Belief as such. At the same time, it makes no sense to speak of a "Western" or "foreign" historiography of Old Belief. Everyone who published outside of the Soviet Union wrote against the background of the Russian historiographical tradition and depended heavily on the source publications and practical help of colleagues, past and contemporary, within Russia. Until recently, moreover, "Western" scholars of Old Belief have been so few and have had so little in common that nothing like a "school" could develop. To mention only the most obvious distinction, some "foreign" scholars, like the late Serge Zenkovsky, were Russian and Orthodox; others, like Cherniavsky, were culturally Russian but most emphatically not Orthodox; still others are neither.

In my view, the most striking feature of most "foreign" publications on Old Belief is their rejection of monocausal explanations. In spite of Cherniavsky's advice, historians in the past eighty years have not followed either nineteenth-century school rigorously, including, I would argue, Cherniavsky himself in his brilliant analysis of Old Believer "political theology."[21]

One book towers over Old Believer studies in the twentieth century: Pierre Pascal's *Avvakum et les débuts du raskol.*[22] Consciously rejecting the extremes of both schools of interpretation, Pascal viewed the church schism as the clash of two profoundly different Christian understandings of society and the church. For Avvakum, whose biography is the central theme of the work, the objective of the church is to make all of society Christian. In the opinion of Nikon and his lay supporters, the church should exercise effective control over particular spheres of spiritual and cultural life and public and private morality: they were, however, willing, Pascal argued, to recognize the autonomy of many spheres of political, social, and cultural life with their own legitimacy and logic. In Pascal's view, the battle between these two irreconcilable visions of a Christian society was fought with particular ferocity in seventeenth-century Russia because of the apocalyptic expectations unleashed by the social and cultural devastation of the Time of Troubles.[23] Since the first edition appeared, Pascal's book has been the point of departure for most "Western" scholarship on Old Belief, not least because of its magisterial sweep, its literary brilliance, and the author's passionate empathy with his subject.

Although somewhat similar in its scope and goals, Serge Zenkovsky's comprehensive study of the origins of Old Belief had far less impact when first published.[24] In a sense, it appeared in the wrong place and time. Because Zenkovsky was determined to publish in Russian but could not do so in the Soviet Union, his work at first reached only a small group of specialists in the West, not the Russian audience for whom his neo-Slavophile approach would have had considerable appeal. Now, nearly twenty-five years later, we can better appreciate his achievement.

Zenkovsky saw Old Belief as a complex spiritual movement arising from a widespread religious awakening in seventeenth-century Russia to which the Orthodox hierarchy failed to respond adequately. In arguing this position, he adopted a very broad definition of Old Belief (closer to raskol than staroobriadchestvo, as I have outlined them): a wide variety of spiritual tendencies from the Zealots of Piety to the Kapiton movement converged in the battles over the Nikonian reforms, and resulting movements of opposition ranged from the most conservative Old Believers to the most radical of the sectarians. In elaborating this broad interpretative scheme, Zenkovsky, like Pascal, drew on both the ecclesiastical and populist traditions, stressing, among other things, the extent to which Old Belief grew out of the popular religious culture and practice of late Muscovy.

Perhaps the most controversial and striking of Zenkovsky's contributions is his argument that the Old Believers were Slavophiles *avant la lettre*. As he observed, Old Believer intellectuals cherished the earlier texts that speculated about Russia's unique role in Christian sacred history and integrated their messages into their own view of the world. Moreover, since the government and the ecclesiastical hierarchy had rejected true Orthodox Christianity, the Russian people alone could comprehend and achieve the nation's historical mission.[25] Although a superficial similarity to the teachings of the early Slavophiles is undeniable, the radical differences in philosophical presuppositions, cultural milieus, and political and social objectives make direct Old Believer influence on later nationalist thinking unlikely, in my view.

In a very different vein, my own study of the Vyg community began as an examination of early Old Believer economic activity and social organization and focused on understanding how a religious movement founded on the expectation that the Apocalypse is imminent organizes its life in this world when the End does not come. One thing, of course, led to another and my most recent work concentrates on the ideological and spiritual dimensions of Old Belief.[26]

The relationship between Old Belief and entrepreneurship in Russia recurs frequently in scholarly and popular literature on these subjects.[27] There is no question that Old Believers played a disproportionately important role in the development of industrial and commercial enterprise in late imperial Russia. It is the explanation of this phenomenon that arouses debate. Did the Old Believers hold beliefs or moral convictions not shared by other Russians, at least not with the same degree of rigor, that encouraged an entrepreneurial spirit? We might label this explanation the "Calvinist hypothesis." Or did Old Believer enterprise spring from the practical experience of living as members of a persecuted minority, as historians of Jewish life have argued?

Finally, any discussion of "Western" literature on the history of Old Belief, however fragmentary, should acknowledge the role of James Billington as advocate of the centrality of the church schism and Old Belief in Russian cultural history and his encouragement of scholarship on these themes.[28]

Now, in the early 1990s, the study of Old Belief is in remarkably good health. In addition to the ongoing work of well-established scholars, a younger generation that includes N. S. Gur'ianova, Manfred Hildermeier, Georg Michels, and Roy Robson has begun to make its mark. Their work addresses a remarkable variety of subjects and questions, including the spread and extreme diversity of opposition to the reformed church in the late seventeenth century;[29] the variety and complexity of Old Believer "political theology" and understandings of history;[30] the connection between Old Belief and commercial enterprise; and the role of public worship and its relation to other elements in Old Believer culture and daily life.[31]

Before closing, a few observations on the current scene are in order. The old and inevitable questions are still very much with us. First, like all historians, we must decide which sources help us most in explaining the origins and development of Old Belief. Should we continue to rely most heavily on the polemical and historical sources of the Old Believers themselves, as Pascal and Zenkovsky did? Or should we place greater faith in government documents and inquisitorial records? The choice, of course, is not one of mutual exclusion, but of comparative significance.

Second, we still face the eternal problem of defining what we mean by Old Belief. Is the definition with which I began adequate? Even if we agree that the so-called sectarians belong in a separate category, what are we to do with forms of heterodoxy such as the *Kapitonovshchina* that display some features of more conventional Old Belief and many that are radically different?[32] Are the bespopovtsy somehow more authentically Old Believer than the popovtsy?

Third, assuming that we choose to draw upon both the ecclesiastical and populist traditions, how do we order our hierarchy of explanations? What do we consider most important in explaining the origins of Old Belief and its subsequent spread and consolidation into a movement? The liturgical reforms and their broader symbolic and practical meanings? Politics on both the local and national scale? Administrative heavy-handedness in state and church? Social and economic oppression and resistance to them? In facing these interpretative choices, we continue a tradition more than a hundred years old.

If we share so much with our scholarly forbears, what is new in the contemporary scene? First, I believe, we are collectively more sensitive than ever before to the extreme diversity—chronological, regional, social, cultural, and canonical—within Old Belief. The work of scholars in Novosibirsk and Ekaterinburg has contributed greatly to our understanding of the conditions under which Old Belief spread to Siberia and the Urals and the characteristics of the movement in these regions.[33] Moreover, scholars have paid increasing attention to the ideas and practices of rank-and-file Old Believers and religious dissenters of other types.[34] We are asking—and must continue to ask—how well our generalizations about Old Believer culture, organizational structures, and economic and political activity fit this diversity.

Second, thanks to the effort of our colleagues in Russia, we can reap the fruits of the collaboration of historians and ethnographers. Indeed, participants in archeographical expeditions inevitably engage, to some degree, in both of these enterprises. Bringing history and ethnography together promises answers to a number of questions such as the ways in which ordinary Old Believers received and understood the often recondite texts of the sacred canon. At the same time, as our Russian colleagues are well aware, the marriage of history and ethnography has its moments of conflict. It is not easy to determine the extent to which contemporary Old Believer survivals preserve the beliefs, religious practices, and social customs of the past. Moreover, even if we answer this question positively, to which of the innumerable accords and subcultures within contemporary Old Belief do we look for these authentic remnants? For Old Belief, although a self-consciously conservative movement that sees itself as changeless, at least at the core of belief and practice, in fact has changed and continues to change in response to its own internal needs and the challenges of the outside world. The problem, from an Old Believer perspective, is to define what that core is and to defend it at all costs.

Third, the work of the newest generation demonstrates that there is still plenty of archival digging to do. Even the governmental and ecclesiastical archives of the late seventeenth century and the well-traveled manuscript collections of polemical and devotional materials still yield undiscovered treasures.[35] Long periods and major topics in the later history of Old Belief await their historian. And the history of Old Belief in the Soviet period is virtually untouched.

Fourth, in addition to the historians' tried and true weapons, the recent writings of historians of culture and cultural anthropologists provide us with new lenses through which to view Old Belief. In a stimulating recent essay, for example, Boris A. Uspensky uses his skills as a linguist and semiotician to analyze conflicting views of language and other cultural "signs" among literate Russians of the seventeenth century and the ways in which they shaped the Nikonian reforms and the first Old Believers' opposition to them.[36] A number of scholars have used the concepts and language of cultural anthropologists such as Clifford Geertz and Victor Turner in their studies of Old Believer literature and culture.[37] These new analytical tools should help us to understand and interpret the liturgical, canonical, and theological issues so dear to the hearts of the Old Believers themselves. We should at last be able to study their polemical statements and their liturgical culture sympathetically, but critically, and avoid either naively recapitulating their views and describing their practices or, at the other extreme, approaching their words and deeds with condescension either because, as sensible men and women, they could not have meant what they said or because the issues that most concerned them are of no interest to scholars at the end of the twentieth century.

Finally, although Old Belief is an intensely Eastern Orthodox and Russian phenomenon, we must avoid approaching it in a vacuum or as something entirely sui generis. The enormous literature on popular religious movements in other societies can, at the very least, suggest fruitful questions to ask and methods for finding answers. Moreover, comparative analysis of Old Belief and other Christian movements of popular piety or heterodoxy will undoubtedly deepen our understanding of both. The literature on religious movements in Western and Central Europe is especially rich and probably most helpful for our purposes. At the same time, we should not limit ourselves to Christian Europe: we may also have much to learn from studies of popular religious movements in Latin America and Africa, to mention only two obvious examples.

Comparative historical analysis consists, of course, of more than inspired free association, clever use of historical labels, or study of a few superficial characteristics that movements in different times or places may appear to share. Old Belief offers particularly exciting prospects for comparison. We should, for example, intensify the long-standing discussion of the roots of entrepreneurship among Old Believers and Calvinists, or Jews, overseas Chinese, and other ethnic and religious minorities. Other fundamental questions also emerge from comparative study. To what extent, for example, was Old Belief a spontaneous outpouring of popular piety and popular indignation against officialdom in church and state? Or, conversely, to what extent was it a top-down phenomenon like post-Tridentine Roman Catholicism, the creation of a clerical elite whose members set the standards for their followers and imposed discipline and order on their lives?[38] Comparative study will not produce simple answers to such basic questions but will provoke us to a continual reexamination of received wisdom and our own assumptions and interpretations.

To conclude, the study of Old Belief is in a condition of radiant good health. The quality of scholarly work is high, the range of approaches and interpretations broad, and the spirit of collaboration and mutual respect intense. In short, problems of funding aside, the prospects for stimulating and fruitful work are virtually limitless. Scholars of Old Belief in Russia and elsewhere must do all they can to take advantage of this extraordinary opportunity.

Old Belief as Popular Religion
New Approaches

IN RECENT DECADES, THE REDISCOVERY of historical ethnography in Western historiography has produced an extensive literature on "popular Christianity" in many European societies.[1] Until recently, however, this historiographical current has exercised very limited influence on historical study in the former Soviet Union. In one sense, Russian historians had no need for such influence; the populist tradition in Russian historiography and its continuation in Marxist-Leninist attire meant that the study of popular attitudes and beliefs was hardly the novelty it was in other countries in recent decades. At the same time, Russian scholars of that country's history had a very limited voice in the international debates on the nature and impact of popular Christianity for several reasons. For one thing, the extreme difficulty of openly studying the religious dimensions of popular culture placed severe limitations on the issues that they could discuss in print.[2] In addition, economic and political conditions have made access to contemporary Western European and American publications problematical at best.

For all of these reasons, scholars writing outside the former Soviet Union have made the most interesting recent attempts to characterize Russian popular Christianity.[3] Some of these essays present somewhat idealized re-creations of Russian Orthodox spirituality as epitomized, for example, by the neo-hesychast mystical revival of the late eighteenth and nineteenth centuries. Other authors concentrate on the syncretistic religious practices of ordinary believers who, in their daily lives, blended elements of Eastern Orthodox doctrine and practice with pre- or non-Christian folk beliefs and rituals. Their writings have as yet had little impact on broader discussions of popular religion on a European or worldwide scale.

On the other hand, Russian theoreticians and scholars of Western European traditions do play central roles in international discussions of popular culture. M. M. Bakhtin's theories (for example, the "carnivalesque" and "heteroglossia") inspire the works of many contemporary historians and literary scholars.[4] On a more concrete level, historians studying Western Europe in the Middle Ages praise the books of A. Ia. Gurevich, now available in translation, as among the most stimulating works on the history of European popular religion to appear in recent years.[5]

In this chapter I will reexamine the Old Believers in Russia in light of recent discussions of popular Christianity in Europe. The disparate groups that made up the Old Believer movement emerged in the second half of the seventeenth century in reaction against the liturgical reforms of Patriarch Nikon (1652–1667) and other changes in the church, state, and society.[6] Once they had codified their beliefs, established liturgical practices, and organized communities, they articulated a more conservative understanding of Eastern Orthodoxy than the established Orthodox Church; and they regarded themselves as the only true bearers of authentic Christian belief and practice and the Russian national tradition in faith and culture. Long persecuted by the imperial government and the official church, the Old Believers stubbornly defended their convictions and practices and, when given the opportunity, proved remarkably adept at surviving, coping, and prospering in a sinful world.[7] Although in this chapter I will concentrate on the Old Believers in the period between the mid-seventeenth century and the revolution of 1917, the main branches of the movement still survive in the former Soviet Union and in emigration and, like other religious confessions, are undergoing a revival in Russia thanks to recent political changes.[8]

The authors of the many recent works on the history of popular culture and beliefs in Western Europe have wrestled with a number of significant issues.[9] The very word "popular" both shapes and confuses the discussion: which "people" are meant? Many scholars use the term broadly to include peasants, the urban poor, and other lower-class groups.[10] Others, however, limit the "people" to the illiterate.[11] The latter distinction presents several serious difficulties: it fails to take into account the gradual extension of literacy in European societies in the "early modern" period, the differing levels of competency in reading and writing among the nominally literate, and the continual interaction between literate and illiterate members of many societies. To cite a Russian example, in Old Believer practice reading aloud was intended to introduce illiterate believers to complex written texts.[12]

Other scholars of "popular" religions make distinctions between the clergy and the laity: as they point out, nobles shared popular religious traditions with peasants.[13] This approach also poses difficulties, not least the fact that in many societies "clergy" is itself an abstraction, including men of widely varying social origins, levels of education, and styles of life. Some members of the clergy undoubtedly shared many of the convictions and practices of their lay followers.[14]

The nature of the relationship between "elite" and "popular" cultures is another subject of considerable dispute. Muchembled and others have tended to view popular culture as something radically distinct from and hostile to the culture of the elite.[15] But in more recent scholarship, the distinction between "high" and popular or folk religious cultures is proving to be less and less defensible. For one thing, many historians of popular culture in Western Europe have implicitly agreed that texts produced by educated men and women and distributed by entrepreneurs could be considered monuments of popular culture as long as members of the lower classes bought and read them. The studies of the "bibliothèque bleue" in eighteenth-century France provide particularly good examples.

Since high and popular culture can no longer be viewed as mutually incompatible categories, historians have offered two basic models of their interconnection. In charting the evolution of Christianity in Western Europe, some attempt to demonstrate how the ecclesiastical authorities gradually "Christianized" society and culture from the top down. This school of thought sees medieval religious culture as essentially a continuum, extending up and down the social hierarchy. Over the course of the Middle Ages, some of its representatives argue, the Roman Catholic clergy succeeded in extending its influence over the cultural elites of society and more thoroughly "Christianizing" elite culture.[16] Moreover, the Protestant Reformation and Catholic Counterreformation further codified, extended, and enforced the practice of elite religion, thus reducing syncretistic popular belief and practice to the margins of cultural and social life.[17] The argument that the leaders of Christendom gradually extended their influence more and more deeply into popular life has much to recommend it. One may question, however, whether this process and other forms of control marginalized popular piety or produced ever more subtle and ingenious forms of syncretism. Moreover, in the last few years historians have reaffirmed their awareness of the fact (which any ethnographer knows) that "popular religion" applies as well to the late twentieth century as to the late fourteenth, although the content of that popular tradition will, of course, be radically different.

The second model of the interconnections between high and popular cultures emphasizes the extent to which these cultures spontaneously influence and enrich each other.[18] In recent years, historians and ethnographers have amassed impressive evidence of their mutual interaction, and they increasingly use metaphors such as "osmosis" to describe their complex mutual relationship.[19] The work of a number of historians such as Carlo Ginzburg and N. N. Pokrovskii has revealed the thoughts of ordinary men who constructed cosmologies and philosophies of life from written texts, oral traditions, and their own creative reflections.[20]

Old Belief provides a particularly interesting and complex test of the categories that historians have used to analyze popular Christianity in Europe. This complexity springs from several sources: first of all, in the second half of the seventeenth century, the spread of Old Belief is very difficult to trace and appears to have been episodic, depending on local conditions of political, social, or ecclesiastical life. Historians have extensive documentation only of situations in which resistance to the new order in state and church flared into open revolt, as in the Solovetskii monastery, in the Don Cossack country, and in Moscow in 1682.[21] Second, it is legitimate to ask whether, in its first decades, Old Belief had mass support or was a top-down phenomenon, initially made up largely of dissenters within the clergy.[22] Third, from the beginning, Old Belief was far from monolithic; early in their history, the Old Believers split into two broad tendencies: the priestly (popovtsy) found ways to reestablish the priesthood and episcopate and maintain all of the liturgical observances of Eastern Orthodoxy; the priestless (bespopovtsy) regretfully concluded that the enforcement of the Nikonian reforms had broken the apostolic succession and that, as a consequence, the faithful remnant of true Orthodox Christians could maintain only those sacraments and forms of worship, such as baptism and the Ministry of the Word, that could in an emergency be celebrated by the laity. Finally, each of these groups, particularly the priestless who lacked a unifying institutional structure, gradually broke down into smaller sects or accords,[23] each defined by its position on particular liturgical or canonical issues, such as marriage, or by the charisma of individual leaders.

Moreover, Old Belief attracted the support of men and women of various social backgrounds. In spite of romantic attempts—past and present—to characterize Old Belief as the faith of the Russian peasantry and the continuation of medieval Russian popular religious culture,[24] the fact remains that the movement received very substantial support from other social groups, particularly merchants and the urban lower classes.[25] Indeed, at many junctures in Old Believer history, the well-being of the faithful depended on the collaboration of rich and poor, urban and rural adherents of the faith.

We must, moreover, be sensitive to the variations in conviction, organization, and social structure of Old Belief in different regions. During the first century of the schism, the most visible centers of the movement appeared on the periphery of the empire, distant from centers of state power. In the European north and in Siberia, Old Belief attracted considerable support among the free or state peasantry, the predominant group in those regions. In those areas, quasi-monastic centers, of which the Vyg community is the best-known example, took the lead in organizing local Old Believer populations and providing their members with the cultural weapons to defend traditional Orthodoxy as they understood it. These monastic communities perpetuated the tradition of the great Orthodox monasteries that had dominated the social, economic, and cultural life of the north for centuries. In the Urals, Old Belief drew adherents from the workers in the mines and metal factories, as well as from the peasantry among whom they were recruited. From the beginning, the Don Cossack communities, at once warriors and prosperous free peasants, joined the defense of traditional Orthodoxy. Many of their descendants remained Old Believer into the present century. Once Catherine II extended de facto toleration to the Old Believers, large and well-organized communities appeared in Moscow and St. Petersburg, building on what must have been extensive underground networks. Here Old Belief drew its leaders and followers from the merchantry and the lower orders of urban society (the *meshchane*). The most important centers of the various subgroups combined organizational features of normal Orthodox parishes, monastic communities, and charitable institutions.[26] In spite of the great distances that separated all centers and their differing social compositions, they remained in regular contact with one another; communities of the north, for example, maintained regular contact with their brothers and sisters in the cities and in the Urals and Siberia.

In spite of a recent revival of scholarly interest in the Old Believers, we badly need modern studies of their organization and historical development in a number of regions and in specific social strata. The most obvious lacunae lie in the areas most foreign to the categories of official Soviet historiography: the roles of merchant and, later, industrialist leaders, financiers, and protectors of Old Belief in the cities, and their relations with their scattered fellow believers in the countryside.[27]

Old Believer culture was varied and complex. From the beginning, the movement exhibited both an elaborate "high" book culture and complex systems of popular belief and practice, which are recorded in inquisitorial and police records.[28] As I have observed, the creators and transmitters of Old Believer culture came from a variety of social and cultural origins—the "black" and "white" clergy, merchants, déclassé nobles, and peasants. In addition, the political, social, and cultural features of diverse regions such as the European north, the Urals, Siberia, and the Cossack country influenced the ways in which Old Believers organized their spiritual and social lives. Finally, in spite of their belief that they lived in the End Time and that they preserved changeless, timeless traditions, the Old Believers responded—cautiously, to be sure—to the demands and stimuli of a rapidly changing world.

Thus, I would argue that, in view of the varieties of social origin and levels of education and cultural awareness among its adherents, we would be well advised to follow the suggestions of specialists on Western Europe and to think of Old Belief not as a single "cultural system" but as a multitude of interconnecting cultures.[29] The peculiarities of these cultures depended on the social and regional milieu, the historical moment, the level of education of the men and women who formulated and expressed them, and the branch of the movement from which they sprang. The various systems had synchronic and diachronic connections, and Old Believer cultures shared a devotion to pre-Nikonian Orthodoxy symbolized by such usages as the two-finger sign of the cross and a complex and shifting corpus of sacred writings and oral traditions that summarized their understandings of theology, liturgy, devotional life, and their own sacred history.[30]

In substantial measure, Old Belief was, in Brian Stock's phrase, a "textual community." As I have argued elsewhere, the first Old Believer cultural system was the creation of a group of learned men—a conservative "intelligentsia," if you like—whose rigorously traditional Orthodox Christian views distinguished them from the more cosmopolitan court intellectuals of the late seventeenth century. Theirs was a textual community in that their command of and dissemination of a limited repertoire of recondite writings both distinguished them from and united them with the ordinary peasant believers whom they led.[31] Later generations of Old Believer writers, like the Vyg "fathers" of the eighteenth century, extended, codified, and copied the canon of sacred texts that formed the cultural backbone of the movement. The fact that leaders and followers, teachers and pupils shared this repertoire of sacred writings made the distinction between them far from absolute. At the same time, recent studies of local Old Believer libraries and inquisitorial records demonstrate that, within broad limits, the selection of texts that made up the sacred canon varied significantly from one time, region, or branch of the movement to another.[32]

In any area, the Old Believers' textual community depended on middlemen and -women, peasant leaders of Old Belief in the villages who constituted a human bridge between the "high" canon of sacred texts and the ordinary believers. These local leaders preserved and copied the sacred texts and taught them to their followers, often adding their own interpretations, and used them as readers to teach children, especially boys, the skills they would need to maintain and pass on the tradition. Although ethnographic literature contains many descriptions of such local leaders, systematic study would greatly enhance our understanding of the sources of their authority and the practical ways in which they functioned.[33] Moreover, we have little idea of the significance of the complex and recondite classics of the Old Believer tradition for the ordinary villagers who treasured the books as sacred objects but may or may not have understood their contents. It will require the collaboration of theorists, historians, and ethnographers to study how ordinary believers understood these oft-copied writings.

At the village level, Old Belief may be considered "popular religion" by any reasonable definition. Living the "Old Faith" consisted of public worship and dietary taboos and other rules of life, all of which varied considerably from one branch of Old Belief to the next. Moreover, in addition to the texts of the "high" literary and polemical tradition, each community had its own oral tradition of music and literature as exemplified by the *dukhovnye stikhi* (spiritual verses).[34] The culture of uneducated urban believers in the last two centuries is a particularly complex and poorly understood issue. In all probability, Old Believers at the bottom of the urban social hierarchy reflected the rapidly changing milieus in which they lived. Although distinguished from their Orthodox neighbors by their distinct forms of worship and customs regarding diet and dress, they may well, in other respects, have shared with them a repertory of responses to the challenges of the city. At this stage of our understanding, my remarks can, at best, serve as hypotheses for future study.[35]

Finally, some recent ethnographic studies suggest that the least schooled peasant Old Believers held a mixture of beliefs that blended Christian doctrine with magic and even traces of shamanism. We may legitimately ask how many people shared the belief systems and practices described by Juha Pentikäinen. It can be difficult, moreover, to identify the specifically Old Believer features of the belief systems of these individuals and groups.[36]

In spite of their strenuous efforts to distance themselves from the sinful world around them, Old Believers have rarely lived in complete isolation. Some of the complexity and variety of Old Believer high cultures stems from their continued interaction with intellectual and cultural currents in society as a whole.[37] In contrast with the traditional view of the Old Believers' cultural isolationism, derived in part from their own self-perception, recent studies have shown that the movement's intellectuals knew the main developments in "secular" scholarship and prided themselves on that fact. The great writers of the Vyg school, for example, knew well the theory and practice of Baroque rhetoric in its Ukrainian variant and put their knowledge into practice in their own works.[38] Andrei Borisov, the most important leader in the same community in the late eighteenth century, took pride in his understanding of the basic principles of modern science and occasionally alluded to scientific discoveries in his sermons.[39] We should not, of course, jump from one extreme to its opposite: the intellectual openness of the most sophisticated Old Believers should not be exaggerated, nor should we credit them with a profound understanding of disciplines or concepts that did not help them achieve their primary purpose—the cultural and institutional defense of traditional Russian Orthodoxy. The image that Old Believer high culture was hermetically sealed from the outside world and thus the uncontaminated remnant of earlier Russian religious belief and practice, however, can no longer be maintained.

Likewise, in spite of their often expressed ideal of a life in but not of the world, Old Believers have, in fact, maintained social and economic relations with outsiders.[40] All but the most remote communities had regular contact with the marketplace, the imperial administration, and non–Old Believer neighbors. The organizational focal points of the movement, such as Vyg and the Moscow and St. Petersburg centers, had regular, ambiguous, and complex relationships with the rulers of the empire and their local representatives. Even the *stranniki*, or fugitives—the most militant in their rejection of the government, the established Orthodox Church, and all their works, like the "perfect" in other religious communities—could not live without the help of less rigorous sympathizers through whom they maintained minimal contact with the outside world.[41] The tension between the desire to isolate themselves from a corrupt world and the practical necessity of contact with unbelievers is a never-ending theme in the history of Old Belief in Russia and in the diaspora and is a recurrent motif of their sacred texts.

Thus, the complexity of Old Believer cultural systems across space and time defies simple characterization. In particular, the concept of "popular" or "folk" religion should be used with extreme care when discussing the history and culture of the movement. As we have seen, Old Belief was a complex combination of groups, institutions, and tendencies that changed continually under a rubric of changelessness. Some of the phenomena mentioned above clearly fall into any reasonable definition of popular religious culture; many others do not. And we know too little about some dimensions of the movement to offer any responsible characterization at all.

Moreover, as we have seen, historians of popular Christianity in Western Europe define the object of their inquiry in several different ways. Some of their definitions may help us understand Old Believer cultures; some clearly do not. Old Belief was not a movement of the laity as distinct from the clergy. It was, moreover, clearly not a religion of the illiterate: as a textual community, the Old Believers emphasized the importance of literacy in order to understand and transmit the movement's sacred writings. Therefore, there is probably much truth to the widespread assumption that, until well into the present century, literacy rates among the Old Believers were considerably higher than among adherents of official Orthodoxy.[42] At the same time, however, this reasonable hypothesis remains to be verified. Moreover, we do not know the level of literacy of Old Believers in particular places and times, or the implications of their command of reading and writing. To mention but one concrete example, we do not know how well the copyists who reproduced the polemical and devotional classics of the movement understood the words they copied.

Three of the insights of historians of popular Christianity in Western Europe are unquestionably helpful in approaching the study of Old Belief. First, without doubt, Old Belief drew most of its support from marginalized or disenfranchised social groups. It probably recruited the majority of its adherents from the peasantry. At the same time, Old Belief attracted support among many social groups, and at various stages of its history, clergy (particularly monastics) and wealthy merchants provided intellectual leadership and vital financial support. In addition, Old Believer polemical and historical writings suggest that the movement's intellectuals viewed themselves as spokesmen of a counter-society, a fully developed social order that stood in opposition to the officially sanctioned society of imperial Russia.[43] Second, church and state in Russia attempted to "Christianize" society, to discipline and channel popular religiosity, just as they did somewhat earlier in Western Europe. Gregory Freeze's studies analyze the campaigns of the official Orthodox hierarchy and clergy in the late eighteenth and nineteenth centuries to bring decency and good order to parish life.[44] The Old Believers played a complex role in this process. From the beginning, Old Believer intellectuals attempted to preach and enforce the rigorous practice of unadulterated Orthodoxy. Several of them, like Avvakum, emerged from the so-called Zealots of Piety and, as young priests, clashed with their parishioners when they attempted to enforce the moral teachings of the church and to suppress survivals of pre-Christian folk tradition.[45] Ironically, then, their conflict with Nikon and his supporters involved two competing visions of how best to purify the Russian church and discipline its unruly flock. Once Old Belief had built its own institutional structures, its leaders struggled unceasingly to enforce the most rigorous standards of Orthodox worship and moral discipline among their followers. The third insight of historians that applies to many features of Old Belief is that elite and popular religious cultures spontaneously influence each other. Beginning with Avvakum's autobiography, for example, many Old Believer hagiographical works, edifying tales, and poems blend ideas, images, and rhetorical strategies from both.[46] Moreover, further exploration of Russian archives will probably uncover more individuals like Pokrovskii's "Altai peasant" who, in their oral and written confessions, reveal highly individual mixtures of ideas and symbolic statements from many sources, elite and popular.

Old Belief presents a particularly significant example of the conceptual difficulty of building an analysis of religious and cultural movements around the theoretical distinction between "high" and "popular" cultural worlds, even if we accept the now dominant view that the two influenced one another. The movement offers comparative perspectives on the very complex interconnections between high and popular religious cultures, and between the cultures of the literate, semiliterate, and illiterate, and illustrates in particularly dramatic form the many ways in which self-conscious traditionalists adjust to life as faithful Christians in a changing world. In other words, if we can break away from the assumption that Old Belief is a uniquely Russian phenomenon that has few similarities or parallels with other movements of religious protest or reform in Christendom, we will discover that informed study of the movement can make a significant contribution to the continuing discussions of "popular religion" within Christendom and beyond.

At the same time, given the conceptual ambiguities of the label "popular religion," scholars would be well advised to give their highest priority to elucidating particular religious traditions or communities and to exploring the parallels or connections between them. In the specific case of Old Belief, the recent revival of scholarly interest in the movement, especially in Russia itself, provides not only encouragement but also sobering reminders of the tasks that face us. Without doubt, large parts of the movement's social, political, and regional history remain unexplored. Old Believer cultures need our attention even more desperately. If Old Belief is a textual community, we need a far better understanding of its central texts, to say nothing of modern scholarly editions and studies of their transmission. Russian scholars have made a promising start in this area. We also need a far better understanding of Old Believer theology, liturgics, and moral teaching as variants of Eastern Orthodoxy and, more broadly, universal Christian doctrine and practice.[47] Insights from symbolic anthropology will help us analyze the interconnected cultural systems of Old Belief and explain their attractiveness to many generations of Russian Christians.[48] In short, the better historians of Russian religion and culture understand Old Belief, the more fruitful will be their contribution to debate on the typology of religious movements and the social and cultural significance of religious belief and practice in the development of human societies.

SEVENTEENTH-CENTURY ORIGINS

Three

Ecclesiastical Elites and Popular Belief and Practice in Seventeenth-Century Russia

THE RUSSIAN CHURCH SCHISM of the seventeenth century is the focal point of this brief examination of popular belief and practice and the struggles of ecclesiastical elites to shape control and change them. In the chapter I will review and reflect on the most important phases of the interaction between the leaders of Russian Orthodoxy and ordinary parishioners between the late 1630s and the beginning of the eighteenth century in the light of recent studies of Christian communities elsewhere in early modern Europe. It contains no new archival discoveries: most of the documents and monographs on which it draws have long been familiar to historians of Russia. These sources, moreover, reflect the perceptions of government officials or ecclesiastical polemicists. Thus, as Eve Levin cautions, when describing popular religious beliefs and practices, the sources are likely to focus on "the most heterodox elements," those that diverge most dramatically from established norms.[1]

In spite of the country's enormous territory, the discussion will consider Russia as a single unit for two reasons. First, even a glance at scholarship on Western and Central Europe shows how limited and scattered are the surviving sources on Russian parish life and popular religious practice.[2] For one thing, historians of Russia must live without systematic parish records. Second, in spite of the Muscovite monarchy's vast size, movements of popular religious protest spread quickly, in large measure through the efforts of itinerant agitators and exiles.

What then is the purpose of this reexamination of familiar territory? First, in recent years, scholars—Vera Rumiantseva[3] and Georg Michels,[4] in particular—have uncovered new sources, primarily reports of governmental investigations, on religious movements in the seventeenth century. Their publications have added significantly to our knowledge of popular movements of religious dissent and the enforcement of the Nikonian liturgical reforms and resistance to them. Second, recent writing on the development of religious communities elsewhere in Europe provides a stimulating conceptual vehicle on which to revisit the Russian scene. As we shall see, in Russia, as elsewhere on the continent in the early modern period, the government and the ecclesiastical leadership collaborated in maintaining confessional uniformity and enforcing "decency and good order" in worship and public morals.[5] Indeed, the concept "confessionalization" and its implications have long been axiomatic to historians of Russian religion and society.

In undertaking comparative analysis, we must of course keep in mind that Russian Orthodoxy is, above all, a religion of the sign, not of the word. Believers communicate with God primarily through their participation in the church's rites. In Orthodoxy, liturgy, belief, and practice are ultimately inseparable. Thus, in spite of minor differences in theology, major divergences in church organization and discipline, and a long history of animosity, Orthodoxy has far more in common with Roman Catholicism— and to some degree Anglicanism—than any branch of Protestantism.[6] Moreover, in seventeenth-century Russia, religious struggles took place in a large, long-established, comparatively centralized monarchy, which, in spite of many obvious differences, bore much closer resemblance to England, France, or Spain than to the small city-states and principalities of Central Europe.[7]

The title of this chapter contains two terms that require further explanation. "Ecclesiastical elites" refers to two groups of people. First are the patriarch, bishops, and parish priests of the Eastern Orthodox Church. Second, during and after the church schism of the mid-seventeenth century, the conservative opposition to the Nikonian reforms, later known as the Old Belief, began to bring forth its own leaders and create its own unofficial organizational structures. Over the latter half of the seventeenth century and into the eighteenth, its leaders formed a second "ecclesiastical elite"—to be sure, canonically self-appointed, internally divided, and often fugitive from the power of official church and state.[8] "Popular religion" refers to the beliefs and practices of ordinary parishioners or those of comparatively uneducated or marginal individuals and groups in defiance of established authority.[9]

The following discussion will focus on six important points of contact between ecclesiastical leaders and ordinary parishioners. These are the reform movement of the so-called Zealots of Piety and the popular beliefs and practices they attempted to change; the Nikonian liturgical reforms and their initial enforcement; the popular movements of religious renewal or protest uncovered by governmental and ecclesiastical investigators in the middle decades of the seventeenth century; the campaign of the royal government and the hierarchy to root out opposition to Nikon's reforms; the explosion of violent resistance to changes in church and state, particularly self-immolation; and the initial efforts of the leaders of the conservative movement of resistance, the Old Believers, to channel and discipline the beliefs and practices of their followers.

Ecclesiastical reform became a burning issue in seventeenth-century Russia on the accession of Tsar Aleksei Mikhailovich (1645–1676).[10] A small, informal group of would-be reformers, known to later generations as the Zealots of Piety, gathered around the young monarch who was already establishing a reputation for sincere piety and intense interest in ecclesiastical matters.[11] Among its prominent members were the tsar himself; his friend F. M. Rtishchev; his confessor, Stefan Vonifat'ev; the prominent parish priest Ivan Neronov; his younger protégée, the priest Avvakum; and the rising star of the ecclesiastical firmament, Metropolitan Nikon of Novgorod. As they looked at life in the parish, the Zealots (some of them experienced parish priests) saw two fundamental problems: confusion and disorder in worship and the survivals of pre-Christian rites that still captivated and entertained many villagers. In attacking these problems, the Zealots implicitly confronted an even deeper problem. In comparison with much of Western Europe, the parish was loosely organized and, in practice, only tenuously connected to the higher ecclesiastical authorities. As individual reformers were already discovering, a parish priest, usually a descendant of priests, could minister to his people most easily by abiding by village tradition and not pressing them too hard to fulfill their ritual and moral obligations as Orthodox Christians.[12] In a crisis, he might well find that his bishop was far away indeed. Paradoxically, as we shall see, the government and ecclesiastical hierarchy acted as though they could exercise effective control over parish life and the behavior of ordinary believers.

The Zealots' aspirations closely resembled those of ecclesiastical reformers in Western and Central Europe, especially Roman Catholics. They envisioned a vibrant Christian community in which, under the supervision of the hierarchy, priests celebrated the Eucharist and other offices with dignity and order and maintained high moral standards among their flocks. Popular devotional life was to be purified by removing extraneous elements and dubious forms of devotion.[13] A revival of preaching was one step toward their lofty goals. In Russia, achieving liturgical uniformity and good order was a daunting challenge. Full Orthodox worship requires a variety of service books; over centuries of hand copying, significant inconsistencies had crept into these texts. From about 1500, the more enlightened Russian hierarchs had realized the importance of establishing standard, authoritative texts. In the early seventeenth century, the problem remained unsolved and, with the aid of that dangerous foreign innovation the printing press, the leaders of the Russian church began once again to address the problem. The Zealots fully supported the effort.

Initially, however, the Zealots gave special attention to two issues, neither of which was new. Ivan Neronov and his fellow parish priests in Nizhnii-Novgorod sent a petition to Patriarch Ioasaf in 1636, asking for his support in restoring order and dignity to services of worship. The petitioners recited a litany of apparently long-standing abuses—*mnogoglasie* (the practice of chanting up to "five or six" different parts of the service simultaneously); other liturgical shortcuts (for example, omitting the hours before the Divine Liturgy); and singing vespers in the morning. They also complained at length about rowdy behavior during services. Priests' children played noisily in the altar area while, in the congregation, men and women came and went, talked loudly, and acted the fool. False monks, fake fools-in-Christ, and other panhandlers harassed worshippers. In a particularly ingenious scam, beggars, giving false names and addresses, asked the faithful for money to redeem them from bond-slavery.[14]

From the patriarch's point of view, many of these complaints were clearly justified and the remedies obvious. In 1646, Ioasaf issued a general decree that all priests, deacons, and "all Orthodox Christians fast, live in purity with all discipline (*vozderzhanie*) and distance themselves from drunkenness, injustice and all kinds of sin." The clergy should see to it that their parishioners "should stand in God's church with fear and trembling and love, silently without any whispering," and focus their minds on God and pray "over their sins with tears, humble sighs and contrite hearts without malice or anger." A tall order indeed! The patriarch ordered parish clergy to put a stop to precisely the forms of irreverent behavior about which the Nizhnii-Novgorodians had complained.[15]

Attacking mnogoglasie was more controversial. Liturgical shortcuts had crept into Russian Orthodoxy for good reason.[16] In Orthodoxy, there is no such thing as a *missa brevis*. Over the centuries, monastic services had become the norm in parishes. The Divine Liturgy and the other services put severe demands on the patience and stamina of even the most devout laypeople.

Thus the willingness of many priests and parishioners to do almost anything to shorten services is, if not admirable, at least quite understandable. When the first attempts to end these traditional practices encountered vigorous opposition, Ioasaf retreated, and in 1649, an ecclesiastical council supported a return to the status quo.[17] The reformers, however, would not give up their demand for an orderly liturgy with no overlapping or shortcuts (*edinoglasie*).

The second of the reformers' agendas—the survival of pre-Christian rites and impious entertainments—had troubled the leaders of the church for centuries. The Nizhnii-Novgorod petition of 1636 took up and expanded on the complaints of the church fathers in the Stoglav council of 1551, and once Tsar Alexis ascended the throne, royal decrees echoed the cry.[18] The list of sinful behavior is lengthy and remarkably—indeed suspiciously—consistent throughout the documents. In midwinter and late spring, instead of coming to church, ordinary people went out to drink, gamble, tell fortunes, and enjoy the performances of the traditional folk entertainers (*skomorokhi*) with their irreverent and obscene patter and songs, their musical instruments, their trained bears, and their dancing dogs. Women and girls swung on swings. For their health, villagers bathed in the nearest river or lake at the new moon or the sound of thunder or washed themselves with silver coins. They also allowed folk healers into their houses to practice their arts.

The documents describe the observance of the annual rituals of Rusalii and Koliada.[19] Between the feasts of the Ascension and John the Baptist, villagers in the Nizhnii-Novgorod area gathered four times in different villages: women and girls brought food offerings and danced around a birch tree. Beginning on Christmas Eve, revelers celebrated Koliada, the winter solstice, with drinking, musical instruments, pagan songs, and all kinds of fortune-telling. Masked mummers entertained them, including several young men representing a mare (*kobylka*).

Even in Lent, the devilish entertainments went on. The skomorokhi went the rounds of houses and streets, and swings appeared in the central square. Entertainers even parodied the Resurrection.[20]

As we would expect, these graphic descriptions come exclusively from prominent Orthodox priests and the government. How literally can we take the details of these accounts? In general, the picture they present harmonizes with earlier written sources and later ethnographic observation. Moreover, it seems improbable that conscientious parish priests would not know roughly what their parishioners were up to, no matter how much they disapproved of their conduct. At the same time, a pinch of skepticism seems justified. For one thing, the government's decrees describe "pagan" practices in remarkably consistent, stereotypical phrases. In addition, the documents assume that folk practices were essentially the same all across Russia, from Nizhnii-Novgorod to Dmitrov, near Moscow; Belgorod, in the south; and Verkhotur'e in western Siberia.

What did these rituals and entertainments mean to the participants? On this we can only speculate. They were certainly carnivalesque with a vengeance.[21] They allowed the participants to shed their inhibitions (on occasion, their clothes), drink, sing and dance, and in the process mock the respectable world and its powers. But what did participants think they were doing? Were they practicing a pre-Christian nature religion or just having a riotous good time?[22] While any answer must be hypothetical, the most likely explanation lies somewhere in between. In the lives of seventeenth-century peasants, these survivals of ancient systems of belief were part of a complex syncretism of Christian and pre-Christian elements, of faith and magic expressed in annual cycles of rituals governed by two complementary calendars.

The ecclesiastical reformers' view of these popular practices was unequivocal. They were determined to abolish them for reasons that would make good sense to confessional leaders elsewhere in Europe.[23] In origin they were clearly pagan, and the skomorokhi who led the revels may once have functioned as priests or shamans; they distracted parishioners from their Christian duties during some of the great festivals of the church year; the disorderly and licentious behavior they encouraged undercut Christian morality and decency; and they had bad practical consequences, not least the deaths and injuries in the ritual brawls and the usual consequences of illicit sexual encounters.

In Russia as elsewhere Lent appeared to defeat Carnival. At the prodding of the reformers, Tsar Alexis, already known for his personal antipathy toward folk entertainment, issued a series of decrees, beginning in December 1648, ordering local governors to ban skomorokhi and suppress the rituals associated with them. The tsar ordered governors to proclaim his decree in every village and hamlet in their jurisdiction and authorized them to flog or, for repeated offenses, exile those who persisted in the old ways.[24]

Issuing decrees was much easier than changing deep-rooted patterns of behavior, however. Scattered evidence suggests that the skomorokhi, driven underground or into the remote countryside, continued to practice their ancient trade into the eighteenth century. Many of the agrarian rites and folk entertainments survived long enough for modern ethnographers to record them.[25] And, in subtler ways, ordinary Russians continued—indeed continue—to incorporate ancient folkways such as charms, incantations, and folk healing into a Christian or post-Christian way of life.

Not surprisingly, the implementation of the Zealots' program of reform aroused violent opposition among the laity. The prominent Zealot Avvakum's hagiographic autobiography, written roughly twenty years after the events, describes his clashes with a prominent aristocrat, V. P. Sheremetev, local notables, and ordinary parishioners while he was parish priest of Lopatitsy. To be sure, Avvakum's methods of enforcing order and decency were hardly subtle. He describes his encounter with folk entertainers: "and again the devil raised up a storm against me. There came to my village dancing bears with tambourines and domras, and I, sinner that I am, being zealous in Christ I drove them out; one against many I smashed their masks and tambourines in a field and took away two great bears. One of them I clubbed, and he came to life again; the other I set loose in the fields."[26] In return, Avvakum survived berating, beatings, a severely bitten hand (by a parishioner), and an assassination attempt in which the weapon misfired.[27] Twice, in 1648 and 1652, in fear for his life, he fled his parish for the safety of Moscow. The second time, he received a major promotion to become dean of the cathedral in Iurevets on the Volga. The assignment lasted only eight weeks until

> The devil instructed the priests and peasants and their women; they came to the patriarchal chancellery where I was busy with church business, and in a crowd they dragged me out of the chancellery (there were maybe fifteen hundred of them). And in the middle of the street they beat me with clubs and stomped me, and the woman had at me with stove hooks. Because of my sins, they almost beat me to death and they cast me down near the corner of a house. The Commandant rushed up with his artillerymen, and seizing me they raced away on their horses to my poor yard. But people came up to the yard and the town was in tumult.[28]

Unfortunately, in only a few instances does Avvakum's "Life" give the specific reasons for these clashes. In Sheremetev's case, he refused to bless the boyar's son, because contrary to time-honored custom, the young man was clean-shaven. One of the clashes with local officials occurred when he intervened to rescue a young woman toward whom the grandee had dishonorable intentions. Similarly, he explained the riot in Iurevets by the fact that he had rebuked the priests and their women for "fornication" (*bludnia*). It is, of course, entirely possible that the disorders had causes other than Avvakum's rigor. Between 1648 and 1652, many urban centers in Russia exploded in uprisings against rising taxes and a depersonalized and more intrusive bureaucratic administration.[29]

Other reformist priests suffered through similar tribulations. As foot soldiers in a campaign to reform parish worship and morals from above, they took the brunt of parishioners' anger at the demand that they abruptly and radically change their traditional way of life. One after another, they found parish ministry untenable, trapped as they were between the aspirations of the reformers in Moscow and the recalcitrance of their flocks.

The reform campaign took a sharp turn when Nikon succeeded Ioasaf as patriarch in 1652. As metropolitan of Novgorod, Nikon had proved to be an energetic reformer, a capable and courageous administrator, and an ardent advocate of the church's leadership in society. In the stormy seven years of his active tenure as patriarch, however, the reforming coalition and ultimately the Russian Orthodox Church as a whole were fatally divided.

What took place must be examined in its international context. Religious reform from above—"confessionalization," if you like—began in Russia roughly a century later than in Catholic and Protestant Europe.[30] And, by the mid-seventeenth century, Russian political and ecclesiastical leaders, although cautious, were becoming aware of some of the implications of developments elsewhere. Some of the Zealots—the tsar, Rtishchev, and Nikon, among others—responded enthusiastically to international currents in ecclesiastical learning and culture, especially when transmitted through other Orthodox churches with which they desired closer contact.

The messages they received were often ambivalent. From the Orthodox in Ukraine, battleground against revitalized and aggressive Catholicism, the Muscovite church received a body of apocalyptic literature summarizing biblical and later Eastern Christian teachings on the End Time. These works achieved considerable influence not only among the defenders of Orthodoxy in Ukraine but also in Muscovy.[31] At the same time, Ukraine provided Russia with new styles of Orthodox scholarship, education, and art all taken from Counter-Reformation Catholicism and recruited for the defense of the Eastern church. The more analytical, rationalistic approaches of the Ukrainian scholars who began to enter Russian service made all but the most sophisticated and tolerant Muscovites uneasy.[32] Frank Sysyn has made clear why these learned clergymen, whose erudition suited the needs of their homeland so well, had such a divisive impact on the Muscovite church and Russian cultural life.[33]

Nikon's elevation to the patriarchal throne brought another source of inspiration to the fore. The tsar, the new patriarch, and some of their collaborators turned toward ecumenical Eastern Orthodoxy as represented by the Greek Church in order to revitalize Russian Orthodoxy. For his part, Nikon also hoped that closer ties with the rest of the Orthodox world would help him recapture for the church the legal autonomy and moral hegemony that, in his view, it had lost in a series of defeats and compromises, culminating in the Law Code of 1649. Although the Russian church had never lost touch with its Greek sister and had, in recent decades, received a steady stream of needy Greek prelates, to say nothing of charlatans, the admiration of tsar and patriarch for the practices of the Greek Orthodoxy and their increasing dependence on Greek émigré advisers shocked their contemporaries. After all, it was the Greeks' apostasy at the Council of Florence that had thrust Orthodox Russia into the center of world history. Here, too, ironies abound. For the center of Greek Orthodox scholarship and publishing was Roman Catholic Venice. Moreover, in his defense of the dignity of the church and its personification, Patriarch Nikon began to adopt the arguments and language of the popes of the High Middle Ages.[34]

The link between these developments and life in the parish lay in the continued republication of services books. For, as all of the reformers had long understood, consistent and dignified worship was impossible without consistent liturgical texts. Nikon quickly gave this campaign a new twist. His Greek advisers had convinced him that, in cases where the two Orthodox traditions diverged, the Greek Church had preserved the authentic practices of the early church while Russians, in their ignorance, had introduced local eccentricities into the liturgy. Accordingly, the new Psalter of 1653 omitted the customary instructions on the sign of the cross. Nikon soon issued new ones instructing the faithful to cross themselves with three fingers extended in the Greek manner rather than two as Russian tradition decreed.[35] Thereafter new editions and changes in liturgical practice followed one another in rapid succession.[36]

The Nikonian editions of liturgical texts deliberately attacked customary Russian practice. In addition to the sign of the cross, the more dramatic changes included the four-pointed instead of the eight-pointed cross on the sacred wafer and on church buildings; the triple rather than double alleluia after the Psalms and the Cherubic hymn; the number of prostrations and bows in Lent; a new transliteration of "Jesus" into Slavonic (*Iisus* instead of *Isus*); and small but significant alterations in the wording of the Nicene Creed.[37] For ordinary parishioners, these changes would probably have seemed less jarring than the enforcement of edinoglasie or the suppression of agrarian festivals and carnivalesque entertainment. They were significant enough, however, involving as they did some of the most frequently repeated words, gestures, and visual symbols in the liturgy. Nikon did not help matters by insisting, against the advice of the patriarch of Constantinople and his royal protector that only reformed usage was acceptable. In 1656, Nikon repeatedly branded the two-finger sign of the cross and other traditional Russian practices as heretical.[38]

The reforms and the patriarch's intransigence in enforcing them split the reform coalition in two. In a series of increasingly agitated letters written in late 1653 and early 1654 to the tsar and Vonifat'ev, Ivan Neronov severely criticized Nikon's abandonment of Russia's heritage and the arrogance with which he was treating his former friends. The three-finger sign of the cross and the altered number of deep bows (*poklony*) in services were specific examples of these destructive policies.[39] In one letter to Vonifat'ev, Neronov told of hearing a voice from an icon urging him to resist Nikon's reforms.[40] In his later autobiography, Avvakum told the same story and claimed that both he and Neronov had immediately realized that Nikon had destroyed Russian Orthodoxy, the last bastion of true Christian faith.[41] The two priests quickly fell afoul of their ecclesiastical superiors. The authorities imprisoned Neronov in a remote northern monastery; Avvakum was exiled to Siberia. According to tradition, the one bishop who in 1654 openly questioned the reforms, Paul of Kolomna, lost his see and perhaps his life for his stand.[42]

Prominent clergymen were not the only vocal opponents of the reforms. In 1657, the ecclesiastical and governmental authorities arrested the Rostov weaver Sila Bogdanov and two companions for publicly condemning the new service books. Under intense interrogation, Bogdanov flaunted his convictions and, for his pains, was imprisoned in the same monastery to which Neronov had been sent earlier.[43]

Thus, even though the first protests against the Nikonian reforms were isolated and easily suppressed, they began the process of division within Russia's ecclesiastical elite. From these small beginnings, there emerged two competing elites with two competing visions of reform from above, one consistent with contemporary international standards in the Orthodox world and beyond, however poorly understood, and the other faithful to local Russian tradition.

The first version of reform triumphed. Supported by Tsar Alexis's government, the Orthodox hierarchy under Nikon's authoritarian leadership rigorously enforced the new canons, and even after the patriarch withdrew from office in 1659 and was deposed for dereliction of duty in 1666, the process of "confessionalization" continued unabated. Using the records of the Patriarchal Printing Office, Georg Michels has shown that in Moscow the new books sold well and that, over time, their use spread downward from the ecclesiastical hierarchy throughout the church.[44]

What does the hierarchy's apparent success in enforcing the new canons suggest? That most Russians, clergy and laypeople alike, had little interest in the minutiae of liturgical change, as Michels argues? The willingness of a priest to accept the new service books does not, of course, tell us whether his parishioners followed their instructions in practice or continued to cross themselves in the old way. Or, as Duffy argues in the case of England, did the coercive power of the royal administration and the church overpower potential opposition before it had a chance to form? The speed and vigor with which the authorities pursued individuals as diverse as Neronov and Bogdanov surely set an intimidating example for their contemporaries. One example illustrates the interpretative dilemma. In his study of the first Old Believers in Ukraine, Michels points out that the priest Koz'ma, traditionally viewed as the first missionary of the Old Faith in Starodub, had perforce used the reformed liturgy in his parish in Moscow before leaving the capital. Therefore, the author argues, Koz'ma must have left Moscow for reasons unconnected with the Nikonian reforms and come out in opposition to them in Ukraine only because, given local political conditions, it was expedient for him to do so.[45] But may his move to a more congenial setting not have allowed him to give public expression to deep-seated doubts and convictions that, if openly revealed in Moscow, would have brought extremely unpleasant consequences? Either explanation is, in the end, a matter of speculation.

Faced with such pressure, opposition to the Nikonian reforms coalesced very slowly. From within the ecclesiastical elite, individual opponents of Nikon's reforms wrote treatises attacking both the general philosophy and the specific details of the changes in the liturgy. Spiridon Potemkin, the learned archimandrite of the Pokrovskii Monastery, composed the first tract of this type, probably in 1658. Between 1665 and the late 1670s, his successors produced a "canon" of anti-Nikonian polemical and devotional texts—Nikita Dobrynin "Pustosviat"'s lengthy petition; the "scrolls" of the priest Lazar'; Deacon Fedor's "Response of the Faithful" and letters; Avraamii's "Secure Shield of Faith" and petition; and the autobiographies of Avvakum and his cellmate Epifanii.[46] To this list Michels rightfully adds Bishop Aleksandr of Viatka who, although he did not write a major anti-Nikonian tract, collected a library of raw materials for such a task and organized a loose network of opponents of the reformed church.[47] This remarkable body of Old Believer polemical literature, whose authors wrote at great risk or from prison, met several pressing needs. It responded to the official publications defending the reforms, the *Skrizhal'* (1656)[48] and the *Zhezl pravlenie* (1668) of Simeon Polotskii, the most prominent representative of Ukrainian scholarship at the tsar's court. In a broader sense, these writings expressed the growing frustration of Nikon's opponents within the clergy: these men may well have hoped that the obvious truth of their position would convince the tsar and the hierarchy to abolish the new liturgical usages or, at the very least, allow the continued practice of the old. In this they were profoundly disappointed.

The ecclesiastical council of 1667 destroyed all hope of restoring Russian ecclesiastical tradition. Led by visiting Greek prelates, the fathers of the church required the exclusive use of the Nikonian practices, declared heretical such traditional Russian practices as the two-finger sign of the cross and the double alleluia, and anathematized all those who refused to give up their opposition to the new order.[49] The categorical nature of the council's protocols destroyed any hope of future reconciliation. The anathemas were to remain in force until the 1970s.

The council's intransigence put the defenders of tradition in an impossible position. Their ranks divided. Through threats and appeals to preserve the unity of the Body of Christ, the leaders of the church convinced some prominent opponents—Neronov, Bishop Aleksandr, and Nikita Dobrynin—to recant.[50] Avvakum, Fedor, Lazar', and Epifanii chose the path of resistance and martyrdom.

Thus, in the late 1660s and early 1670s, a conservative intelligentsia emerged within the ecclesiastical elite and constructed the intellectual and polemical foundations of Old Belief. Prominent parish priests for the most part, they wrote their most ambitious works for men like themselves who knew the Bible and the Orthodox liturgical and devotional texts that circulated in Muscovy before the mid-seventeenth century. Over the following decades, later sympathizers copied many of these works—some of them remarkably abstruse—and circulated them among their followers.[51] The core messages of the canon of Old Believer sacred texts were clear and dramatic. First, the Nikonian reforms were wrong for clear canonical and historical reasons. Second, they violated the Orthodox traditions of Russia. As conservative polemicists repeatedly pointed out, if only the Nikonian usages were correct and all others heretical, all earlier Russian saints, princes, and laypeople must literally be damned. Third, the Nikonian reforms marked the beginning of the End Time. This conclusion came naturally to those who accepted the symbolic statements of earlier Muscovite ecclesiastical writings that the Russian church was the last—and last possible—refuge of true Christian faith and took seriously the apocalyptic prophesies imported from Ukraine.

It is not difficult to understand the appeal of these general messages to ordinary laypeople, men and women who could not possibly have read the great petitions of Nikita Dobrynin or Avraamii. How these convictions spread downward from the elite to significant numbers of ordinary people is a complex and open question.

Some clues can be found in the official investigations of the so-called Kapiton movement of reform and protest in the middle decades of the century.[52] Most of what we know about Elder Kapiton himself comes from later official Orthodox and Old Believer sources. Probably a self-appointed prophet of humble origins, Kapiton led a succession of small informal monastic communities in various corners of Northern and Central Russia between the 1620s and about 1660. Insofar as it can be reconstructed, his teaching had several central features. He advocated an asceticism far more extreme than the most rigorous teachings of Eastern Orthodoxy. One manifestation was continuous, severe fasting, even in the church's feasting seasons. He and his followers also rejected the authority of the Orthodoxy clergy on grounds of moral corruption. Although the sources are less clear on this point, his moral and ascetic rigor seem to have sprung from the conviction that the Apocalypse was at hand.

Much more precise evidence about some of Kapiton's followers in Viazniki survives in records of their interrogation in 1665. These itinerant or self-proclaimed monks and ordinary laypeople lived in informal monastic settlements. By their own admission, they fasted rigorously throughout the year. One of their accusers, Archbishop Ilarion of Riazan', charged them with going even farther and preaching ritual suicide through starvation in anticipation of the Apocalypse.[53] When investigators arrested the monks Vavila and Leonid and some of their followers, others burned themselves to death rather than surrender.[54] Under torture, the leading suspects remained defiant. They admitted that they would, on principle, have nothing to do with official Orthodoxy and its clergy. Several, moreover, specifically referred to the Nikonian reforms—a "schism of the books" (*knizhnoi raskol*)—as one of the reasons for which they rejected the church's authority.[55] In 1666, the investigation uncovered more of Kapiton's followers in the Vologda and Nizhnii-Novgorod areas. One of those arrested, Stepanida L'vova, defiantly described her austere way of life and her angry rejection of the clergy.[56]

Thus, at this early date, the disciples of Kapiton displayed several of the defining characteristics of later Old Belief: the creation of self-generating monastic communities, radical opposition to the authority of the royal administration and the clergy, a belief in the imminence of the Apocalypse, and in extremis, the practice of group suicide. The available evidence suggests that in the 1660s such groups were small, scattered, and eccentric. Moreover, the radicals' statements under interrogation suggest that Nikon's reforms were not the primary reason for their hostility to church and state.

The world of the radicals in Viazniki and Vologda could not have been farther removed from the patriarch's court or the Moscow mansion in which Boiarynia Morozova, leading patroness of the anti-Nikonians, hid Avraamii and a number of women devoted to the old ways. The radicals surely were a "popular" religious movement, however we define that elusive term. Nevertheless, the two groups shared a deep antipathy to the reformed church and an increasing willingness to defy its leaders and their royal protector, whatever the cost.

Miracle cults were a far more widespread form of popular devotion in mid-seventeenth century Russia than the "*Kapitonovshchina.*" Devotion to wonder-working icons and saints—well-known, obscure, or in some cases, imaginary—appears to have proliferated among the clergy and all classes of the laity in the sixteenth and early seventeenth centuries, to the increasing consternation of the hierarchy.[57] Suppressing even the most dubious of popular cults raised the specter of serious opposition to church and state. Allowing miracle cults to flourish without the scrutiny and sanction of the hierarchy also presented dangers, however, not least the very real possibility that the Old Believers would use them to support their attack on the Nikonian reforms.[58]

Thus, in spite of the risks, the ecclesiastical hierarchy, beginning with Patriarch Nikon himself, strove with the government's backing to regulate the cults and, in the latter half of the seventeenth century, suppressed public manifestations of a number of the more dubious or threatening of them.[59] In the best-known example, Patriarch Ioakim convened church councils in 1677 and 1679 to reexamine the case of Anna of Kashin, a fourteenth-century princess whose popular cult had led, by about 1650, to officially sanctioned local veneration and preparations for her formal canonization. After a review of the evidence, including a detailed analysis of the historical inaccuracies in Anna's "life" and the miracles attributed to her remains, the councils concluded that, while a lady of undoubted piety, Anna did not merit recognition as a saint.[60] Eve Levin's recent article analyzes popular miracle cults and their regulation in the eighteenth century.[61]

From the very beginning of the Nikonian reforms and the opposition to them, the royal government and the Orthodox hierarchy worked together to suppress any overt manifestations of religious dissent or schism (*raskol*). The urgency of this task largely distracted them from the struggle against pagan rites and entertainments.

Two of the cases we have described illustrate this collaborative campaign. Metropolitan Iona of Rostov first brought Sila Bogdanov and his disciples to Patriarch Nikon's attention. After the metropolitan had questioned the suspects, Tsar Alexis ordered the boyar, Prince A. N. Trubetskoi, and the powerful chancery official Almaz Ivanov to take over the investigation. These two prominent statesmen carried the investigation to its conclusion. Meanwhile, the metropolitan interrogated the two priests who were the suspects' confessors and sent them on to Moscow for further questioning. Moreover, the tsar's government asked the metropolitan to report in greater detail on the "subversive words" (*neistovye slova*)[62] that Bogdanov had uttered in his presence. The accused, it turned out, had said that "he did not fear the tsar or his courts and that the reign of the Antichrist had begun." He called Nikon the "precursor of the Antichrist."[63] Similarly, in 1665 the parish priest, Vasilii Fedorov, and some months later, Archbishop Ilarion of Riazan' informed the ecclesiastical authorities and the tsar respectively of the existence of the Viazniki radicals. In response, the government dispatched a detachment of musketeers (*strel'tsy*) to round them up and an investigative commission, led by the boyar Prince I. S. Prozorovskii, to conduct the interrogations. At the end of the process, some of the lesser defendants who escaped execution were imprisoned in several monasteries where, predictably, they proved difficult to control.[64]

Thus from the time of the Nikonian reforms, the royal government and Orthodox hierarchy collaborated in suppressing opposition, which, as they understood, was directed indiscriminately against both.[65] The decrees of the council of 1667 made effective collaboration an even more urgent necessity. Responsibility for enforcing the Nikonian rites and suppressing dissent and raskol fell to the clergy.[66] Parish priests bore the primary responsibility for enforcing the reformed canons. As a check on the loyalty of their flocks, they were to make sure that their parishioners fulfilled their minimal obligations as Orthodox Christians—annual confession and communion—and report those who failed to do so. They were also to inform higher authorities of any individuals who openly held to the old rites or engaged in other forms of suspicious conduct.[67]

Clearly, then, this design for the imposition of the new order was part of the larger process of giving the Orthodox hierarchy more effective control over the beliefs and practices of ordinary parishioners. As Michels carefully demonstrates, the leaders of the church gradually succeeded in disseminating the new liturgical order downward through the provincial dioceses and large monasteries to the parish level. This process was part of a broader campaign of the hierarchy to exert tighter control over parishes and monastic communities, especially the small unsupervised ones. The dissemination of the new liturgical texts, however, was not complete in the remotest corners of the realm until the 1680s or 1690s. Moreover, as this process went on, some of the reform's most vociferous opponents were the itinerant monks and nuns whose entire way of life made them opponents of tighter discipline in the church.[68]

The responses of the angry and dispossessed of Russian society mirrored the policies of state and church. Increasingly, in the last decades of the seventeenth century, opposition to the Nikonian liturgical reforms became inextricably entangled with defense of corporate rights, local autonomy, or traditional practices against the incursions of the increasingly intrusive central bureaucratic structures of state and church. In 1668, the Solovetskii monastery revolted and, for eight years, held off besieging government forces. A variety of motives drove the rebels. Successive abbots and their monks defended the monastery's traditional freedom from the control of the hierarchy and the secular authorities. Rejection of the Nikonian reforms, however, was their chief rallying cry.[69] As the siege continued, the monks and their allies became ever more militant and the government more frightened and desperate. When the great fortress finally fell, government forces killed all of its surviving defenders.[70] In similar fashion, defense of the traditional rites became entangled with the struggle to preserve Cossack freedoms in both northern Ukraine and the lower Don valley.[71] Most frightening of all, in 1682 the rebellious garrison of Moscow, in alliance with Old Believers led by Nikita Dobrynin, took control of the capital and brought the government to its knees.[72]

In response to this dramatic demonstration of its vulnerability, the regency government of Princess Sophia made a more determined effort than ever to suppress religious dissent and subversion in the name of faith. Calling the government's police agencies and parish priests to arms, the decree of December 1684 ordered them to hunt down and interrogate any parishioners who had been lax in their religious duties. Those who rejected the new rites had a radical choice: submission to the reformed church or death. The death penalty was automatic for any missionaries of the Old Belief or anyone who, after submission, reverted to the old ways. Even impeccably loyal church members who gave shelter to Old Believers were to be severely punished.[73]

Savage persecution begot desperate opposition. In the late 1680s and early 1690s, the government confronted an epidemic of mass suicide by fire. The most spectacular episodes took place in Karelia. Twice, in 1687 and 1688, a sizable number of rebels captured the Paleostrovskii Monastery and, when surrounded by government troops, burned themselves to death rather than submit to interrogation and execution or, perhaps even worse, apostasy. Similar cases of self-immolation occurred in an informal monastic community at Berezov "na Voloku" in 1687 and around the village of Pudozh in 1684 and 1693.[74]

Contemporaries knew that the leading figures in these shocking episodes were a motley lot. Some were itinerant monks; others were local peasants. Their motives and actions were equally mixed. In the best tradition of "social banditry," many had weapons and did not hesitate to use them. Emel'ian Ivanov Vtorogo, a prominent local peasant, chose to escape from the first siege with the monastery treasure, instead of dying for the Old Faith, and lived to raid Paleostrov again. Moreover, as the contemporary Old Believer Evfrosin charged, some of the rebels forced others to die by fire unwillingly.[75]

For all that, self-immolation was an extreme and shocking expression of religious convictions. When they lived in informal monastic communities or conducted armed assaults on villages and monasteries, the rebels claimed that they acted in defense of the old rites. In the Pudozh case of 1693, for example, the rebels turned the churches "upside down." They took out all of the liturgical books, icons, crosses, altar cloths, and liturgical vessels and washed them down, leaving only "local" icons and crosses. With these they blessed the waters of the local lake, bathed themselves, and rebaptized all of the onlookers.[76] In a word, they reconsecrated these churches and their people into the Old Belief.

Mass suicide was a direct extension of their campaign. To be sure, all branches of Christianity regard suicide as a grave sin. Nevertheless, the leaders of frightened and emotionally overwrought communities of men, women, and children saw it as the best response to an unbearable dilemma. Several strands fed into this response. First, the leaders of the Kapiton movement allegedly regarded suicide as the ultimate expression of Christian asceticism. Second, the first Old Believers were extremely angry men and women, even by the standards of an angry and violent age, for they were convinced that the rulers of church and state had destroyed true Orthodoxy, damned millions of their fellows, and put their own souls in mortal peril. Future martyrs like Avvakum and the Boiarynia Morozova took every opportunity to express their rage and contempt at the new order in church and state.[77] In their minds, the End Time had come. The government's increasingly relentless pursuit of religious dissenters strengthened the conviction that, in some sense, the Antichrist reigned.

All of these convictions and emotions fed into the wave of self-immolations in the 1680s and 1690s. In 1684, for example, the monks Andronnik and Iosif "preached that the world had come to an end and that the only way . . . to be saved was by committing suicide."[78] Moreover, if the Antichrist's power was reaching even the remotest corners of the northern forest, the faithful remnant of true Christians had to make a stand. Impatience for a confrontation with the forces of evil may well have reinforced less edifying motives for capturing nearby monasteries, churches, and administrative centers. Once government troops came in pursuit, the preachers of self-immolation followed a scenario that, in their eyes, transformed suicide into martyrdom. Imprisonment was to be avoided at all costs, for with it came torture and the risk of apostasy and damnation. Instead, when government troops approached, the Old Believers barricaded themselves into their stockades, often prepared in advance to be ignited quickly,[79] and fought back as long as possible. Once capture was imminent, they set the buildings alight and died.

To such incidents, the government and Orthodox hierarchy reacted with shock, outrage, and disbelief. The regency government, for example, ordered both Metropolitan Kornilii of Novgorod and the governor of Olonets to take energetic action to preserve order and uniformity within their jurisdictions. In the wake of the first occupation of Paleostrov, the metropolitan received orders to clean up the ravaged monastery and resettle it with reliably Orthodox monks, while the *voevoda* and his troops were to capture the surviving rebels and dissenters.[80] Self-immolation presented the authorities with a particularly painful dilemma. The government gave its local representatives guidelines that, in practice, were impossible to implement: to round up all opponents of the regime as quickly as possible without, at the same time, doing anything that would set off mass suicide.[81]

Prominent Old Believers were equally ambivalent. From his Arctic dungeon, Avvakum expressed his admiration of the early martyrs by suicide and gave the appearance of encouraging the practice.[82] Other Old Believers strongly opposed self-immolation. Writing in 1691, Evfrosin attacked the practice as contrary to traditional Christian teaching and charged that its advocates were fanatics who resorted to deceit, drugs, and violence to control their gullible and frightened followers.[83] In the end, Evfrosin won the argument. In later generations, the leaders of the main Old Believer communities revered the earlier victims as saints and martyrs but did everything they could to avoid further incidents in their own day.[84] It was an ongoing struggle, for the memory of the earlier martyrs continued to tempt the most militant Old Believers when they faced persecution.

In the 1690s, a new generation of Old Believer leaders emerged from the movement's burgeoning network of informal monastic communities. In the best-known example, Daniil Vikulich and the brothers Andrei and Semen Denisov founded the Vyg community in 1694 in a remote corner of Karelia. At about the same time, other centers appeared at Vetka along the Polish frontier, in Starodub in northern Ukraine, in Kerzhenets east of Nizhnii-Novgorod, and in the Pskov area.

At the beginning of the eighteenth century, the leaders of these communities made up the Old Believer "ecclesiastical elite." Like the founders of their movement, they aspired to direct their followers into an austere and disciplined Christian life, centered on pre-Nikonian liturgical practices and cultural forms. They faced a formidable task. As the years passed, priests consecrated before Nikon died out. And without validly consecrated priests, there could be no sacraments except for those such as baptism, which laypeople themselves could celebrate in extreme circumstances. Thus, early Old Believer communities faced a difficult choice. Some attempted to maintain a full sacramental life by receiving and anointing renegade priests from the official church. Others, like Vyg, became priestless out of necessity and canonical principle, not by choice. Adapting traditional Orthodox worship to fit these new circumstances was an undertaking of the most pressing urgency. Moreover, the new generation of Old Believer leaders had to maintain their authority over the ordinary believers who followed them without the support of the state or a hierarchical ecclesiastical structure. Indeed, the state was the enemy; all the new communities played cat-and-mouse with the imperial government, and in the end, several were devoured.

In these challenging circumstances, the new leaders of the Old Belief adapted several techniques to establish and maintain their authority. Like Avvakum and other early leaders—and, indeed, like their Orthodox counterparts—they could be spiritual directors to their followers.[85] Following the giants of the 1660s and 1670s and, later, Evfrosin, they wrote polemics defending their position and refuting their enemies. Within a generation or two, they had created a history and martyrology of their movement. Works like Ivan Filippov's *History* and Semen Denisov's *Vinograd rossiiskii*[86] both sanctified and sanitized the Old Believer tradition: they glorified the memory of past martyrs while, at the same time, telling their followers how to live in the present. How these long and elaborate works reached and influenced ordinary believers, especially those outside the main monastic communities, is a complex issue. The later history of the Old Belief provides several partial answers. First, since Old Belief is a "textual community," its leaders valued literacy and saw that boys learned to read in the best medieval Orthodox manner. Second, the men and especially the women of the Old Believer communities made innumerable copies of manuscript books of pre-Nikonian texts and the classics of their own movement. To this day, such books turn up regularly in peasant houses in the remotest corners of Russia, where, if not avidly read, they are at least deeply revered as holy objects. Finally, Old Belief developed its own elaborate oral culture, which, through stories and spiritual verses (*dukhovnye stikhi*), spread the principal messages of the Old Faith even among the illiterate.[87]

Ultimately, the key to the survival of Old Belief and its leaders was the structure of the monastic communities themselves. In order to provide stable refuges and centers of inspiration and learning in a threatening world, the Denisovs and their contemporaries required the residents of their settlements to live by a strict rule that, over the years, became ever more elaborate. Vyg and the companion Leksa convent adopted clear hierarchical structures of authority; their leaders enjoyed a measure of power that would have made a traditional abbot jealous. The first rule, adopted in 1702, makes the priorities of the leaders clear: austerity and rigor in worship and in daily life. Frivolousness, wavering, or any hint of sexual impropriety was the enemy.[88] Oddly enough, although leading peasant followers in a remote area the Denisovs showed no concern at all about the pagan survivals that had irritated their precursors among the Zealots of Piety. Had the church succeeded in suppressing the more flamboyant of these practices in the intervening years? Or did avoiding these temptations simply have lower priority for the Denisovs than the task of creating a godly community? Both suggestions may have some merit.

At the beginning of the eighteenth century, the official Orthodox Church stood on the brink of radical reorganization. The decisions of Peter I to leave the office of patriarch vacant and then, in 1721, to create the Holy Synod to govern the church had momentous consequences for the ruler, the members of the hierarchy, and the laity.[89] If anything, the changes served only to increase the responsibility of bishops and priests for the political loyalty and orderly behavior of their flocks. To mention the most extreme case, the notorious decree of 1722 required confessors to report any conspiracies or evil thoughts against the emperor to his security organs. Refusal to violate the sanctity of confession brought savage penalties.[90] At the same time, as the works of Gregory Freeze show, the synodal church continued to struggle through the eighteenth and much of the nineteenth century to create effective parishes by nurturing an educated clergy and making ordinary parishioners both fulfill their liturgical duties with real understanding and conform to the moral teachings of the church.[91]

For most Old Believers, Peter's reign was equally disastrous, for it meant paying double taxes, wearing discriminatory markers, and for those overheard calling Peter the Antichrist, serving a life sentence at hard labor. There were, however, some encouraging signs. Although we have no statistics, the Old Believers probably gathered many new adherents among the millions of ordinary Russians both battered by Peter's skyrocketing taxes, military conscription, and forced labor and repelled by the forced Europeanization of the ruling elite.[92] Moreover, when it suited him, Peter adopted a policy of de facto toleration: in the best-known case, the emperor agreed to leave the Vyg community alone in return for services rendered.[93]

Like their counterparts among the Orthodox clergy, the leaders of the growing Old Believer denominations ("accords") continued to struggle to keep discipline and order among their followers. In addition to insisting on dignity and austerity in worship and a strictly moral life, the leaders of Vyg and the other main communities also worked hard to rein in the extremists among them who advocated confrontation with the rulers of the world of the Antichrist or who preached self-immolation. The absence of clearly defined hierarchical structures of authority within the Old Belief made the task extremely difficult.

Finally, two features of Russian popular religious life remained essentially unchanged. Throughout the eighteenth and nineteenth centuries, prophets and prophetesses appeared in Russian villages and, no matter how eccentric or extreme their teaching in Orthodox eyes, attracted a following, to the consternation of the state, the official church, and the leaders of Old Belief. And, even though Lent seems to have triumphed and the more dramatic manifestations of carnival disappeared, the change took place very slowly, and magic charms and incantations remained an integral part of the lives of peasants whatever their formal confessional affiliation.[94] In that sense, as Hsia puts it, "For the vast majority of the populace, confessionalism represented a veneer that preserved traditional practices and beliefs."[95]

Religious Radicalism in Seventeenth-Century Russia

Reexamining the Kapiton Movement

IN RECENT YEARS, historians of Western Europe and the New World have made the worldview and religious convictions of ordinary men and women in past centuries the subject of many meticulous and subtle works of scholarship. The impact of their research has spread far beyond the graduate seminar to best-seller lists and movie houses. For a variety of reasons, among them a paucity of appropriate sources and a lack of imagination, scholars of the Russian past—with a few brilliant exceptions—have not made systematic attempts to reconstruct the cosmology and religious convictions and practices of ordinary believers in premodern times.[1]

The Kapiton movement of radical religious protest provides one window through which to observe the beliefs and observances of Russian peasants and townspeople in the middle decades of the seventeenth century. The *Kapitonovshchina* has long fascinated and puzzled historians of the seventeenth-century church and society. Any serious historian of the church schism of mid-century and the origins of the Old Believer movement must come to grips with the fact that groups of monks and peasants engaged in radical criticism of the Russian Orthodox Church decades before the liturgical reforms of Patriarch Nikon in the 1650s.[2] Doing so is no easy task, for the historian must study Kapiton and his followers through the screen of texts written by their enemies within the official church and the governmental apparatus. Nothing that Kapiton or his sympathizers wrote—if indeed they could write—has come down to us.

The subject poses more general questions as well. Most obvious is the relationship of the most radical currents in Russian religious life to the complex movements of protest against the Nikonian reforms. Once these currents had coalesced into the Old Believer movement with its own institutional and ideological structures, its chief apologists claimed Kapiton and his disciples as martyrs for the Old Faith.[3] Most later historians treat the relationship between the radicals and the most prominent leaders of the anti-Nikonian protests such as Avvakum as a far more complex and elusive matter. And some recent Soviet scholars, most prominently A. I. Klibanov, take precisely the opposite position, arguing that the Kapitonovshchina had little or nothing to do with the more conservative Old Believer movement. Instead, by rejecting the authority of the church and offering a searching critique of its moral lassitude and oppressive practices, Kapiton and his followers formed a link in the long chain of radical religious dissent in Russia stretching from the *strigol'niki* and Judaizer heretics of medieval Novgorod and Pskov to the rationalistic and socially radical sectarians of the eighteenth and nineteenth centuries.[4]

Finally, study of popular religious culture in premodern societies raises significant conceptual problems. Going to the heart of the matter, the legitimacy of the terms "popular" and "culture" in the analysis of religious movements in premodern Europe is a matter of debate. Carlo Ginsburg and others question the usefulness of the world "popular" since it implies a clear distinction between "high" or literate and "popular" cultures, which the documentary evidence does not support. "Culture" likewise is misleading, in that it implies a single system of beliefs and values. More, it has been argued, can be gained by viewing the religious convictions and practices of ordinary people of premodern times as a series of interrelated cultures that varied according to their region of origin and the national identity and gender of their bearers.[5]

In the face of these theoretical and practical problems, why take up the well-worn and difficult topic of the Kapitonovshchina once again? V. S. Rumiantseva's book, *Narodnoe antitserkovnoe dvizhenie v Rossii v XVII veke*, and the collection of documents she published under the same name give us two reasons to return to familiar ground. First, she has brought to light interesting new archival documents on radical currents of religious protest. Second, the essays making up her monograph attempt to place her findings in a new conceptual framework, which examines the interconnections of the many strands of religious protest with contemporary social and institutional realities, without indulging in a simple mechanical decoding of their convictions as statements of popular social protest cast in the rhetoric of a religious worldview.[6] In this respect, Rumiantseva's work is representative of a welcome tendency among a younger generation of Soviet historians to study statements of religious belief and moral conviction in their own terms and context and to accept the fact that, within any complex religious system such as Eastern Orthodox Christianity, the acceptance of a particular theological proposition or moral imperative leads believers to logical conclusions in their thinking or behavior. At the same time, it seems to me, her work—unlike, for example, that of N. N. Pokrovskii and his colleagues in Novosibirsk—does not pursue this approach consistently.[7] Instead, at critical points, her interpretation falls back into a mechanical—and in a Soviet context, conventional—reading of religious protest as the expression of the political and social agendas of particular classes or groups in society.[8]

Any attempt to reconstruct the worldview of Kapiton and his followers immediately encounters two inescapable problems. One lies in the nature of the surviving evidence. All we know about Kapiton and other seventeenth-century religious radicals comes either from bureaucratic documents such as administrative orders and police reports or from religious texts of a later time. Both types of sources have obvious pitfalls. Even when the police records contain the direct testimony of men and women accused of active opposition to church or state, they record statements made under extreme duress. Those who answered their accusers' questions usually did so as briefly and uninformatively as possible, on occasion claiming ignorance of matters with which they were surely familiar.[9] The most militant made clear that they preferred to die rather than say anything at all.[10] As we shall see, the polemical and devotional texts of the spokesmen of official Orthodoxy or Old Belief present a much more detailed picture. At the same time, their testimony suffers not only from being recorded decades after the events described but also from the authors' clear ideological bias. Metropolitans Ignatii of Siberia and Dmitrii of Rostov and Evfrosin, the opponent of self-immolation within the Old Believer camp, all saw in Kapiton and his later followers the epitome of what they opposed.[11] At the other extreme, Semen Denisov shaped his hagiographical account to make Kapiton fit the mold of a respectable martyr for Old Belief.[12]

The second involves classifications. Who can be considered an adherent of the "Kapiton movement"? Official ecclesiastical sources of the seventeenth century tended to use the name "Kapiton" and the nouns and verbs derived from it as a semantic bogeyman. At the same time, these words were not entirely devoid of meaning. Government reports, in particular, made more precise use of the terminology. The more respectable protesters against the

Nikonian reforms such as Avvakum were not called *kapitony,* and at the other end of the spectrum, the official documents describing the investigation of Elder Varlaam and the other religious radicals in Novgorod in the early 1680s, for example, label them as *raskol'shiki* (schismatics) and "heretics," never as Kapiton's followers.[13] For all of its imprecision, then, the label "kapitony" was normally attached to simple men and women who rejected the authority of the church and shared some of the convictions and practices imputed to Kapiton himself.

The Kapitonovshchina appeared in a society in rapid transition. In struggling to overcome the chaos of the Time of Troubles and striving to establish its rightful place in an international order dominated by new forms of military and bureaucratic organization and new technologies, the Muscovite government adopted a number of radical measures, among them rapidly increasing the size and pretensions of the tsars' bureaucratic administration and enserfing the manorial peasantry. Many of its subjects reciprocated by abandoning accepted intellectual positions and habits of obedience. Reflecting on the Time of Troubles, bookmen asked why, if the Muscovite monarchy was the last defender of authentic Christianity on earth, God had allowed its people to suffer the horrors of famine, civil war, and foreign occupation? Humbler men and women who had grown accustomed to fending for themselves and defending their own interests asked themselves why they should accept the claims of the new Romanov dynasty and accede to the demands of its bureaucrats.

The Muscovite church enjoyed no immunity from the problems of secular society. Like any landlords, its monasteries and cathedral chapters had to round up their fugitive peasants and reestablish orderly estate management. Far more significant, as Patriarch Nikon saw clearly, some of the steps that the government took to mobilize the resources of society had the effect of further compromising the legal autonomy and freedom of action of the church and its leaders. Moreover, as those leaders knew all too well, their authority over their flock was shaky at best. Caught between the demands of tradition and the hierarchy and the impatience of their parishioners, parish priests often took shortcuts in celebrating the liturgy such as the notorious *mnogoglasie* (reading or chanting several parts of the service simultaneously) and ignored the obvious moral failings of the villagers. For their part, significant numbers of ordinary believers displayed indifference to the liturgy and to church discipline, in extreme cases making manifest their contempt for the Eucharist. Village customs and entertainments gave ample evidence of the survival of pre-Christian traditions in spite of centuries of struggle to eradicate them.[14] Given the paucity of evidence about parish life in earlier centuries, it is difficult to determine which, if any, of these problems were unique responses to the social and cultural tensions of the early seventeenth century and which were age-old features of popular life.[15]

Kapiton appeared on the scene as the latest in a long line of monastic reformers, albeit a self-appointed and decidedly eccentric one. The state of the sources permits only a fragmentary reconstruction of his life and teachings. He was a peasant from the village of Danilovskoe in the Kostroma area on the upper Volga.[16] By the 1620s he had assumed the leadership of a hermitage on the Vetluga River. His formal qualifications for leadership are hard to determine. The recently published vita of the Old Believer elder Kornilii describes him as a priest, but less sympathetic commentators label him only a "self-tonsured" monk.[17] As to the level of his education, Metropolitan Ignatii, a hostile witness, insists he was "ignorant of the Holy Scriptures and did not know how to read a single word in books."[18] When, in later times, he opposed Nikon's reforms, he based his arguments on "readings which he had heard."[19] While it suits Ignatii's polemical purpose to emphasize Kapiton's lack of education and consequent failure to understand and accept the policies of the ecclesiastical hierarchy, his statements make sense given the social milieu from which Kapiton came and the probability that he had no formal rank within the church.

From the beginning of his ministry, Kapiton's most powerful appeal was his extreme asceticism. According to his "Life" by Kornilii, who lived for a time in his hermitage, Kapiton "burdened himself with the most severe fasting, eating only very little dry bread and raw herbs every second day, wearied himself with bowing in prayer (*poklony*), wore heavy chains and slept very little."[20] In engaging in these rigorous ascetic exercises, he followed the example and, by implication, shared in the spiritual authority of the "desert fathers" of the early Church, the main source of inspiration for all later Eastern Orthodox hermits.

Going so far beyond the usual norms of Christian self-discipline had several meanings and purposes. In many religious traditions, fasting serves as a way of disciplining the body and freeing the spirit for communion with the divine. It also gives believers a means of imitating in their own bodies the sufferings of Christ.[21] Often in Christian history, the most intensely devout of believers have concluded that the more severely they mortified the flesh, the more intense would be their experience of God.

Severe fasting and other extreme forms of self-discipline help their devotees deal with the surrounding world and the powers that dominate it. A wide variety of commentators point out that eccentric patterns of eating are one of the few ways in which dependent or powerless individuals can gain control over their own bodies and destinies and disassociate themselves from the prevailing norms of their families and communities. In addition, such rigorous physical self-denial trains believers to face future suffering or martyrdom. Thus, while the surviving evidence on Kapiton's early years makes no explicit claim that he lived in expectation that the Apocalypse would come soon, his conduct certainly prepared him for that eventuality.

Initially, Kapiton's rigorous self-discipline posed no problems for the leaders of the church or the government. After leading other hermitages, he received in 1634 a patent from Tsar Mikhail Romanov to found a Monastery of the Holy Trinity near his native village.[22] All went well for five years. In 1639, however, the tsar's government instructed the *voevoda* of Iaroslavl' to arrest Kapiton and confine him in the Spasskii Monastery under strict monastic discipline isolated from visitors. The monks of his monastery and the nuns of the associated Morozova convent fled into hiding rather than reject the teachings of their leader.[23]

Although the governmental decrees do not state how Kapiton attracted the ire of church and state, the essence of his crime is clear enough—rejection of their authority over him and his followers. The polemics of Evfrosin and Metropolitan Ignatii offer several examples of his rebellious attitude. First, as his enemies pointed out, he appears to have undertaken his mission and taken on a monastic vocation on his own initiative. Second, Evfrosin suggests, Kapiton's justifiable sense of his own righteousness led him to arrogance (*samosmyshlenie*) and contempt toward those less rigorous than himself.[24] In particular, Ignatii charged, Kapiton's excessive rigor led him to reject the authority of many of the clergy. Whenever he saw a priest eating or drinking a little too much, he refused ever again to receive his blessing.[25] Third, his rigorous self-discipline took him well beyond the limits of normal Orthodox practice. According to one account, he slept standing, supported by hooks hanging from the ceiling.[26] In addition, Ignatii testifies that he insisted that his followers continue to eat fasting foods even on Saturdays and the church's great feast days. Going even further, he adds, Kapiton refused to give his followers Easter eggs and, in their place, distributed dyed onion bulbs.[27] This practice is a logical application of his insistence on continuous fasting. At the same time, it shocked outsiders like Ignatii because it contradicted the deep significance of eggs as symbols of fertility, rebirth, and the Resurrection.[28] Finally, Ignatii claims that Kapiton objected to certain icons—Our Lady in royal robes and a crown, for example—and refused to show respect for them. Like some of his more famous contemporaries such as Nikon and Avvakum, he rejected all icons painted in new artistic styles favored by the royal court and much of the ecclesiastical hierarchy in the mid- and late seventeenth century.[29] Of unorthodox views on central Christian doctrines, however, the extant sources show virtually no traces.[30]

In short, in spite of his extremism and eccentricity, Kapiton appears to occupy a place in the long line of Orthodox reformers who rebelled against the organized church's compromises of its ascetic ideals and aspired to create a purer, more rigorous form of monasticism. At the same time, his insistence on setting his own standards of Christian conduct and his rejection of clergy or of icons that did not conform to his own strict standards amounted to a rejection of the authority of the Orthodox Church and its leaders. The latter were entirely justified in seeing him as a threat.

After 1639, Kapiton continued his ministry as a fugitive. Tsar Aleksei Mikhailovich's warrant for his arrest in 1651 described him as living on the Shacha River in the Kostroma area in a hermitage made up of "monastics [startsev] and laypeople, youths [robiat]."[31] Once again, apparently, he and his followers disappeared before the authorities could take them prisoner. Before long he moved to the Shuia area, where just as before his austere life and teachings won him a significant following.

Meanwhile, in 1653, the new patriarch Nikon began his campaign to bring uniformity to the liturgical practices of the Russian church and make them conform to contemporary Greek usage, which he mistakenly assumed to be more ancient and authentic than the local tradition. The substance of Nikon's reforms and the arrogance with which he introduced them set off an explosion of protest. According to the most varied witnesses, Kapiton was one of the adamant opponents of the reforms, a stand that probably further increased his following.[32] Certainly, from that time on, those who claimed to be his disciples made rejection of the Nikonian reforms both the focal point and the ideological justification for their opposition to the ecclesiastical hierarchy and the state that supported it.

Although he lived in an age of confrontation and violence and made no attempt to avoid controversy, Kapiton apparently died peacefully among his followers. By the end of the 1650s he had settled near Viazniki. In the mid-1660s the police authorities who interrogated his disciples were told that he had died some years earlier.[33]

For many years after his death, the memory of Kapiton's teaching continued to inspire groups of disciples and to disturb government officials and the Orthodox hierarchy. Whenever the leaders of church and state discovered a nest of Kapiton's followers, they took decisive steps to root out the contagion. Year after year the authorities investigated centers of the Kapitonovshchina such as the Viazniki region with the aim of restoring the church's control over local believers and, when that proved impossible, isolating and destroying those who adamantly refused to accept its authority.

In one unusually well-documented case in 1665, two separate denunciations of radical religious communities on crown lands near Viazniki prompted the tsar's private chancery, the *Prikaz Tainykh Del*, to launch an investigation. The first was the work of the priest, Vasilii Fedorov, who for his pains was murdered on his way home from Moscow. Fedorov testified that in the forests near Viazniki there were communities of priests, monks, nuns, and laypeople who rejected the authority of the church. They never attended the liturgy in parish churches, confessed to priests, accepted the guidance of their official spiritual directors, nor received the Sacrament. Instead, they celebrated the liturgy themselves from service books that antedated Nikon's reforms. When one of them died, Fedorov continued, he or she was buried without a formal funeral service. If Orthodox priests attempted to visit them with the cross and the Gospels (*s sviatyneiu*), they did not let them in but instead ran away.[34]

The second accuser, Bishop Ilarion of Riazan', put heavy emphasis on the apocalyptic and political dimensions of the Viazniki radicals' convictions. Their leaders, the monks Vavila and Leonid, had gathered about two hundred followers including monks, nuns, and young women and taught them to reject the authority of the government and to expect the imminent end of the world. As Ilarion put it, "they utter such insults against Your blessed rule [*derzhava*] that it is impossible even to express them in writing." Since the Christian polity had lost its legitimacy, all that remained was to wait for the end of the world, an event that the radical preachers expected within a year.

As persecution intensified and expectations of the End of the World intensified, fasting took on a radical new meaning. In anticipation of the Apocalypse, Ilarion claimed, the men and women of the Viazniki communities extended their rigorous asceticism to its ultimate end—they stopped eating altogether. Any residents of the communities who would not willingly starve themselves to death, he went on, were imprisoned in "graves," in pits, and under huts so that they could neither eat nor escape.[35]

This sensational testimony had the anticipated effect. Already convinced that Kapiton's followers posed a threat to good order in church and state, the government sent A. N. Lopukhin and later Prince I. S. Prozorovskii, supported by troops, to conduct yet another investigation. The list of questions the officials were to ask suspects under arrest reveals the government's principal preoccupations—the rejection of its authority was symbolized, for example, by the doctrine that the Antichrist now ruled and by the rejection of the authority of the ecclesiastical hierarchy.[36]

The government's fears of militant opposition were quickly confirmed. Moving resolutely, Lopukhin's troops seized Vavila and Leonid in a settlement on Iukhra Lake and, within a month, had rounded up roughly one hundred suspects. Most prisoners reacted to arrest with frightened militancy, displaying hostility to all representatives and symbols of the Nikonian church and refusing to give even the most basic information about themselves. Some went even further. On December 27, 1665, when Lopukhin's troops surrounded a small group of buildings on Kshara Lake, the inhabitants refused to let them in and, after a confrontation in which a soldier was allegedly wounded, burned themselves to death.[37] This early example of self-immolation conformed to the same pattern as the later incidents, which claimed many more victims. The desire for martyrdom for Christ and panic at the prospect of arrest, which certainly meant torture and perhaps, even worse, apostasy, combined to make men and women willing to kill themselves rather than fall into the hands of the agents of the Antichrist.[38]

Under questioning, those arrested confirmed many of the government's suspicions. A number testified that the reforms of Nikon had led them to reject the official church. For example, Elder Efrem said he had left the Egorovskii Monastery because "there was a division [*raskol*] of Christians in the world; some worshipped according to the old books and some according to the new. And now the sign of the cross is not the same as before."[39] Another prisoner referred to the "schism of the books" (*knizhnoi raskol*) in the church.[40] In a more reasonable tone, Elder Iona and his followers testified that "for two or three years or more they had not made their communion because they began to have doubts [*dlia togo chto stalo im sumnitel'no*] because in the church they had begun to celebrate according to the new books and in the services everything was changed."[41] None of them left any doubt that they had rejected the ministry of the reformed church and had chosen, on their own authority, to preserve the old ways. To do so, they had created communities based on the Eastern Christian ideals of monastic asceticism in which they supported themselves by the work of their own hands.[42]

Under the interrogators' spotlight, the leaders of the Viazniki radicals made significant additions to their followers' depositions. Vavila admitted that he had carried on Kapiton's teachings, advising his followers not to attend the liturgy in Orthodox churches and to continue to fast during feasting seasons. He also confessed that he buried the dead without funeral services (*bes peniia*), but he denied encouraging anyone to starve themselves to death, let along forcing anyone to do so.[43] When the investigators accused him of teaching that the Antichrist reigned and that the church had been corrupted,

Vavila stated that "today the church and its bishops [*sviatiteli*] are no bishops." As if to underline the point, he spat at the cross that Prozorovskii held out to him, presumably to tame the evil spirits that were prompting such outbursts.[44] For his blasphemous and subversive teachings, Vavila was burnt at the stake.[45]

Leonid and his compatriot, another Vavila nicknamed "the Young,"[46] made equally damning admissions. In his testimony, Leonid described in detail how Vavila had encouraged a number of followers, including several of Leonid's own relatives, to starve themselves in order to save their souls. When confronted with this accusation, Vavila conceded that it was true, but denied that the practice was part of Kapiton's legacy. Their testimony led Leonid and Vavila the Young directly to the stake.[47]

As refracted through the reports of their inquisitors, the Viazniki radicals appear as simple men and women who sought salvation in an exceptionally austere monastic style of life. Socially most were of peasant origin, including a number who were obviously fugitives from serfdom. A few came from the urban areas. Undoubtedly, such men and women had grievances against the established social and political order. At the same time, it is understandably difficult to find expressions of explicit political or social dissent in their testimony. The central motive to which they would admit was the desire to save their souls through self-discipline and to avoid the contamination of the Nikonian church. Informal and unregulated religious communities served as magnets for people with such aspirations, not least because the Law Code [*Ulozhenie*] of 1649 forbade monasteries to admit fugitive peasants.[48]

The investigation of Kapiton's followers in Viazniki also yielded interesting evidence on their cultural life and aspirations. Early in the investigation, Lopukhin's men seized a number of books, mostly printed liturgical texts. The listed confiscated materials also include popular works of apocalyptic significance such as sermons of St. Ephraem Syrus; the life of St. Sergius, one of the greatest leaders of Russian monasticism; and "various notebooks." The Viazniki settlers treasured these works even though, according to the testimony of the boy Stepka, elder Leonid was illiterate and Vavila could read only a little. Stepka helped Leonid by reading to him aloud.

Leonid's attempt to educate himself in book culture is symptomatic of the Viazniki settlers' determination to justify their convictions through appeal to the traditional canon of ecclesiastical texts. Evidently they collected any books or manuscripts that came to hand. Moreover, among the materials confiscated were two published "teaching Psalters," suggesting that community members intended to teach one another to read and, perhaps, to copy manuscripts of vitally important texts.[49] While the evidence from Viazniki is slight, it indicates that these early radicals felt the same need to master the resources of bookish culture as did the leaders of larger and more stable Old Believer communities in later times.

Within a matter of weeks, the investigation of the Viazniki disciples of Kapiton ended with the execution of the leaders and the imprisonment of a number of their followers. Destroying the radical settlements, however, did little to quell the spirit of resistance to the new order in the church. As the inquisitors were concluding their work, the peasants of Pirovo, on the estates of the Holy Trinity Monastery, refused to let the clergy celebrate the liturgy in their parish church from the new service books. Although they had no apparent connection with Kapiton's followers, they were no less determined. They blockaded the church and forced the visiting clergy to leave the village. Then, when the authorities arrested the village priest and locked him in a room, his wife escaped, and her shouts drew the villagers who attempted to free him. As a consequence, in effect, short of sending in troops the monastic and governmental authorities had to abandon their attempts to impose the new order on the village.[50]

The search for Kapiton's disciples turned attention to two other regions—Vologda and Nizhnii-Novgorod. In the spring of 1666, the government sent Prozorovskii to the Vologda area to look into charges that a certain Foma Artem'ev, a peasant on the estates of I. D. Miloslavskii, was "kapitoning, not going to church or consulting his spiritual director" and that four members of his family had died without the last rites.[51]

As in Viazniki, the investigation quickly revealed the peasants' hostility to state and church. In three separate incidents, families immolated themselves as government troops approached. Those whom the soldiers succeeded in arresting gave their interrogators equally little doubt of their radical rejection of the established order.

The men and women arrested in the Vologda probe—approximately seventy in all—differed considerably from the Viazniki suspects. For one thing, they were peasants who lived in normal family units, not informal monastic communities, and made no claim to a distinct religious vocation. At the same time, they looked to the Viazniki elders for leadership: one woman testified that her husband had taken their daughters away to Viazniki to live in a hermitage (*pustyn'*).[52]

The Vologda suspects, moreover, were remarkably blunt in revealing their convictions to the interrogators. Betrayed to the authorities by her husband, Stepanida L'vova epitomized the attitude. "For three years she did not go to church or partake of the sacraments. In feasting seasons [*miasoed*], since she did not go to church, she did not eat feasting [*skoromnyi*] food and prayed at home in her hut and did not sleep with her husband because of the fast. For three years, she has not approached a priest for his blessing and has no intention of doing so now. She said that she has hands of her own that can make the sign of the cross without a priest. And she does not go to church because now they celebrate by the new service books."[53]

In the testimony of those arrested, the same themes recur repeatedly— rejection of the new liturgy and the authority of the church and rigorous asceticism including fasting, even at traditionally inappropriate times, and sexual abstinence. Dietary practices apparently varied: in addition to abstaining from meat, dairy products, and eggs, some refused to eat fish as well. A badly preserved passage in the archival record of the investigation reveals a final peculiarity in the practices of Kapiton's Vologda followers. They apparently refused to venerate some icons (*ikony*) and showed a particular reverence for images (*obrazy*) of St. Damian. Their affection for Ss. Kosmas and Damian makes good sense since Christian tradition regarded the pair as exemplars of generosity and incorruptibility. Unlike the hierarchs and priests whose authority they rejected, Kosmas and Damian never accepted fees or took bribes.[54]

The official records of the investigation of Kapiton's followers in the Nizhnii-Novgorod area are extremely fragmentary. Official inquiries began before the Razin revolt swept through the area and resumed in its aftermath. Interestingly enough, the surviving documentation contains no explicit evidence that any of Kapiton's followers joined the revolt. Doing so would have required a radical change in their strategy of struggle against church, state, and society. For, like the representatives of other radical religious currents, Kapiton's disciples usually chose not to fight the powers of a corrupt, oppressive, and doomed world but, rather, to flee from their power into the "desert," and when they could flee no longer, to accept martyrdom at their persecutors' hands or their own.[55] Some followers of Kapiton may have joined the revolt of the Solovetskii monastery as the commander of the besieging troops, I. Meshcherinov, charged in 1674.[56] His testimony loses some of its weight, however, because it includes the statement that many followers of Kapiton fought with Razin. Moreover, the kapitony headed a substantial list of undesirable types from runaway peasants and bondsmen to Swedes and Tatars who, he claimed, had infiltrated the monastery, thus making his task that much more difficult. The central thrust of his report was to underline the increasingly radical antigovernmental attitude of the monastery's defenders.

The testimony of the Nizhnii-Novgorod kapitony reveals that they rejected the authority of the reformed church and the government as militantly as their compatriots elsewhere. Among them too the sources reveal a culture that blended folk attitudes with book learning. In January 1672, the beekeepers of the court village of Varmaleia persisted in refusing to recognize the authority of the tsar or the church. When the governor, V. F. Postrikov, sent musketeers, sixty-seven of its inhabitants burned themselves to death. The victims left two records of their convictions. One was quoted almost verbatim in a miscellany published in Moscow in 1647.[57]

The other, which expresses their anguished militancy in their own words, encapsulates the ideas and emotions of Kapiton's disciples. Addressing Postrikov, they asked, "Why are you torturing Orthodox Christians? . . . We do not go to church because they do not call Our Lord Jesus Christ our pastor. They sing the Antichrist's chant . . . and now you are bringing us to the new faith which the wily Nikon and the patriarchs, those dogs' muzzles [*sobach'i ryly*], changed. . . . Who crucified Christ? Tsars, patriarchs, and priests. And now they are betraying the world. And now you are forcing us to cross ourselves [in the new way] . . . and you will answer for it at the Last Judgment. . . . Indeed we do not fear the tsar, we fear . . . Our [Lord] Jesus Christ . . . and we will die for the faith of Christ and for the true saving cross."[58]

The letter of the people of Varmelia serves as a fitting epitaph for the Kapiton movement as a distinct current within the radical opposition to the Orthodox Church and state in seventeenth-century Russia. By the end of the 1670s, governmental persecution and the incidents of self-immolation had taken their toll. In another sense, however, the Kapitonovshchina was far from dead. As the continuing anti-Kapiton polemics of Orthodox churchmen and conservative Old Believers and Old Believer hagiography both attest, the memory of Kapiton's example and teachings lived on. Later Old Believers who shared his sense of moral urgency and the intense apocalyptic expectations of his followers took some of the same radical measures, not only against the government and the established Orthodox Church but also against more moderate defenders of the old ways, such as the leaders of the Vyg community.

Reexamining the Kapiton movement raises many important questions and suggests several conclusions. To begin with, the Kapitonovshchina is one measure of the multiplicity of oppositional currents within the Russian church and society in the mid-seventeenth century. Among the relatively small number of its demonstrated adherents, there was considerable variety of conviction and practice. At the same time, in addition to obedience to

Kapiton's leadership or respect for his memory, several features united them—their extreme ascetic practices, their increasingly firm conviction that the Apocalypse was at hand, and their rejection of the spiritual authority of the Russian Orthodox Church structure, a stance that emerged with particular clarity after the Nikonian reforms. Moreover, as Rumiantseva's study makes clear, the kapitony competed for the government's attention with many other individuals and groups with whom they shared a profound hostility toward the reformed order in church and state.

The cultural horizons of the groups' adherents were also varied; most of them were apparently illiterate, but written texts clearly shaped the thinking and provided authoritative support for the convictions of a number of them. In other words, Rumiantseva's findings present new and suggestive evidence on the relationship between bookish literate culture and oral traditions in popular religious movements. In practice, her evidence destroys any neat compartmentalization of the two by making clear, for one thing, that oral reading of "high" ecclesiastical texts helped semiliterate or illiterate men and women to reach their own understanding of their faith and use it to interpret the events of their own day.[59] These helpful insights pose a whole series of questions deserving further investigation. To what extent, for example, did memory serve in the transmission of liturgical, scriptural, and patristic texts among uneducated believers? What meaning did sacred books have for the illiterate? These and many other issues require further investigation.

Second, the weight of the evidence, including Rumiantseva's new findings, supports the traditional position that after the imposition of the Nikonian reforms the Kapiton movement, which had begun decades earlier, joined with the other currents of opposition to the new order. In other words, Kapiton and his followers can legitimately be viewed as Old Believers. Throughout their existence they remained one of its most radical elements within the coalition of opposition to church and state. In particular, Kapiton's extreme asceticism and militancy and the apocalyptic expectations of his later followers shaped the doctrinal stance and emotional state of the men and women who first chose self-immolation as the appropriate path for true Christians when confronted by the power of the state.[60]

Finally, the Kapiton movement reveals the depth of popular antipathy toward the established church in seventeenth-century Russia. The ecclesiastical leadership faced bitter resentment of its institutionalized power and encountered grave suspicion of its doctrinal orthodoxy and moral probity. Saying so raises a host of questions. To what extent did popular resistance to clerical control represent anything new? Or did ancient resentments express themselves in new ways? Our limited knowledge of the religious life of ordinary believers in earlier times makes these issues very difficult to address.

Did Kapiton's followers rebel against the authority of the church because its leaders were too strict or because they were perceived as being too lax? The evidence we have examined suggests that both answers are true in part. In Christian history, movements of extreme asceticism have often sprung up in opposition to church leaders who appear to have lost the fire of their faith or the sharp edge of their moral integrity. Then, having established devotional practices or patterns of self-discipline that they believe to be more rigorously and authentically Christian, rigorists such as Kapiton and his followers rebel against the authority of ecclesiastical leaders who, instead of leaving them in peace, attempt to force them along a more moderate path.

What particular features of seventeenth-century Russian society, politics, and ecclesiastical life reinforced these ancient patterns? Were there, for example, any peculiar features of local society in the regions that nurtured the Kapiton movement? Over the course of their brief history, the kapitony appeared at scattered points in a wide arc of territory north and east of Moscow, ranging from Vologda in the north to Viazniki on the Kliaz'ma River in the south. In her study, Rumiantseva diligently looked for socioeconomic explanations for the phenomena she encountered. The archives yielded few clues. The fact that a number of the episodes recorded in the surviving documents took place on lands owned by the Romanov family as the ruling dynasty or as private landlords explains little, since the best source of evidence—the papers of the *Prikaz Tainykh Del*—is in effect the private archive of Tsar Aleksei Mikhailovich and provides documentation only on the royal estates. The materials at our disposal nevertheless permit a few general statements. The landscape of the upper Volga valley and the surrounding territories provided Kapiton and his followers with refuges in the forest, where at least for a time they could hide from the temptations of the world and the pressure of the authorities. Moreover, once opposition to church and state took root in the region, it became an integral part of the local tradition. Much of the area remained a hotbed of Old Belief for centuries.

The impact of high politics on the emergence of the Kapiton movement is an equally complex issue. It is a truism to mention the enserfment of the peasantry and the growth of the royal bureaucracy as causes of social and religious unrest in seventeenth-century Russia. The problem, of course, is not that these traditional explanations are incorrect but, rather, that by explaining so much, they explain very little. At the same time, we should bear in mind the possibility that the regions and social groups that most vigorously opposed social, political, and religious change may have been precisely those in which the growing pretensions and increasing effectiveness of the royal administration attacked local traditions most destructively. Similarly, the practical impact of the efforts of ecclesiastical reformers such as the Zealots of Piety and Nikon himself on the lives of ordinary Russians is hard to gauge.

In a word, there is still much to learn. The ordinary men and women who gave their testimony to the investigators of the *Prikaz Tainykh Del* remind historians of a later century that they have barely begun to understand the cultural worlds of ordinary Muscovites of the seventeenth century.

The Origins of the Old Believer Cultural Systems

The Works of Avraamii

> Then a second portent appeared in heaven: a great red
>
> dragon with seven heads and horns; on his heads were
>
> seven diadems, and with his tail he swept down a third of
>
> the stars in the sky and flung them to the earth.
>
> —Rev. 12:3–4

THE PURPOSE OF THIS CHAPTER is to examine the formation of the Old Believer "cultural system" in the 1660s and early 1670s. The concept of "cultural system" has received its most extensive analysis in the work of Clifford Geertz. In his essay "Religion as a Cultural System," Geertz defines culture as "an historically transmitted pattern of meanings embodied in symbols, a system of inherited conceptions expressed in symbolic forms by means of which men communicate, perpetuate, and develop their knowledge about and attitudes toward life."[1] Cultural systems, it follows, are clusters of symbolic expressions, including religious rituals, that help men and women explain and give meaning to their lives.[2] The following discussion attempts to show that the culture and style of life of the Old Believers of Russia formed just such a cultural system—or, more accurately, a closely interrelated set of cultural systems. Our focal point will be the work of a group of learned men in creating—in large measure, consciously and deliberately—the first of these systems from the materials provided by the rituals and teachings of ecumenical Eastern Orthodoxy as refracted through the social formations, cultural norms, and customs of late Muscovite Russia.[3]

Geertz's essay unwittingly offers a remarkably acute summary of much of the historical writing on the Old Believers. As he puts it, "One of the main methodological problems in writing about religion scientifically is to put aside at once the tone of the village atheist and that of the village preacher, as well as their more sophisticated equivalents, so that the social and psychological implications of particular religious beliefs can emerge in a clear and neutral light."[4] These metaphors are remarkably apt descriptions of the proponents of the populist and ecclesiastical historians of Old Belief whose views we have examined in chapter 1.

A second frequently invoked term will also appear regularly in the following discussion. The process of creating Old Believer cultural systems consisted, in substantial measure, of "canon formation," that is, assembling and creating the body of sacred writings that defined the beliefs, ritual practices, and moral standards of the movement's members.[5] In this sense, Old Belief became a textual community, defined, to a substantial degree, by its sacred texts.[6]

Old Belief began as a protest against the liturgical reforms of Patriarch Nikon (1652–1667). The unrest began almost as soon as Nikon assumed office. A small number of priests and monks vociferously objected to his policy of revising the service books of the Russian church to conform to ancient Greek usage, which, as they insistently pointed out, really meant the contemporary practice of Greek Orthodox Christians under the Turks or in exile in the Latin West. Before long, however, a movement of opposition to the Nikonian church and the government that supported it spread across the landscape and deep into Russian society.[7] In particular, after the ecclesiastical Councils of 1666–1667, which deposed Nikon but reaffirmed his reforms and anathematized his most prominent critics, the opposition became increasingly militant and the teachings of its leaders became the rallying cry of protest against social injustice and the increasing centralization and bureaucratization in both church and state. The symbolic language of faith had become a cry of rebellion.[8]

Thus, as many scholars have observed, Old Belief was from the beginning a complex phenomenon that reflected the regional traditions, social origin, and cultural world of the individuals and groups who defended the Old Faith or rebelled in its name.[9] Moreover, three and a half centuries after Patriarch Nikon, Old Belief is still very much alive. In light of the movement's longevity and social and regional complexity, it is reasonable to assume that the Old Believers created a multitude of cultural systems. The literary and ethnographic evidence supports this hypothesis: whatever they may have thought, the Old Believer writers of the mid-seventeenth century, the "Vyg fathers" of the eighteenth, the urban merchants of the late imperial period, and the peasant Old Believers of recent times in Russia and the emigration lived culturally in distinctly different worlds. At the same time, Old Believer cultures unquestionably shared fundamental assumptions supported, in most cases, by shared liturgical practices and a common repertoire of sacred writings. Old Believer cultural systems have overlapped at many points and interconnected with one another over time and across the physical and social landscape of Russia and the world beyond.

In this chapter I examine the writings of the first Old Believer polemicists whose works, in large measure, shaped the future directions of the movement. This first cultural system, as I have called it, took shape in a particular intellectual, social, and vocational milieu. A small group of literate clergymen and monks created it with the support of a few socially prominent lay patrons.[10] Although very different from the leading intellectuals of the tsar's court,[11] these men knew the services and canons of Eastern Orthodoxy intimately and were, to varying degrees, familiar with many of the most important Eastern Christian theological and devotional writings either in full Slavonic translations or as excerpts in anthologies. Together they formed the Old Believer "intelligentsia," and as such they established the borders, defined the content, and articulated the rallying cries of the conservative ecclesiastical culture they gave their lives to defend. Their polemical and devotional writings set forth the ideological component of the Old Believer cultural system.

The relationship between this learned elite and its followers is not easy to elucidate.[12] Except for police records, historians know the Old Believers mainly through the polemical, devotional, and historical writings of these intellectual leaders. There is abundant evidence that ordinary Old Believers revered many of the movement's leaders, most of whom were also martyrs for the faith. If nothing else, they repeatedly copied some of the most important of their writings and maintained a rich oral and written tradition celebrating their lives and holy deaths.[13] At the same time, we have a very limited conception of the ways in which ordinary Old Believers with little or no education received and understood the teachings of these leaders. Local elders played an important role in translating and interpreting the more esoteric liturgical fine points and moral strictures for their followers. Moreover, oral traditions such as the *dukhovnye stikhi* (spiritual verses) instructed as well as inspired the faithful.[14]

Having said this, however, we must admit that scholars of Old Belief still must do a great deal of work to elucidate the theoretical dimensions of this question and to unearth additional concrete evidence to help answer it.[15]

Although Nikon's reforms aroused virulent opposition from the very beginning,[16] a decade passed before his critics began to produce a polemical literature in which they defended Russian ecclesiastical tradition and attacked the changes he had introduced in the church's worship and governance. In those first years, only Spiridon Potemkin, the learned Archimandrite of the Pokrovskii Monastery, attempted a thorough and systematic refutation of Nikon's reforms. His "Book," probably completed in 1658, attacked Nikon's most controversial decisions, such as the adoption of the three-finger sign of the cross and the rewording of the Slavonic text of the Creed, with a battery of citations from the Fathers of the Eastern Church and more recent literature. He also argued in detail that the age in which he lived fitted the biblical and patristic prophesies of the Apocalypse, citing Nikon's reforms as particularly compelling proof.[17]

After 1664, the number of Old Believer "dogmatic-polemical" and "historico-hagiographical" compositions rapidly multiplied.[18] N. Iu. Bubnov argues, in his work on the early Old Believer "book," that the years between 1664 and 1682 marked the "developed" or "book" (*knizhnii*) period of writing and copying. Old Believer spokesmen in three centers—Moscow, the Solovetskii monastery, and Pustozersk—composed an entire library of polemical and devotional works, including "manuscript books," groups of texts that were repeatedly copied together as a single unit.[19] The main reasons for this sustained intense literary and polemical activity are clear. As the years passed, the opponents of the Nikonian reforms realized, to their horror, that they could not convince the tsar and the leaders of the church to reverse the changes they found so objectionable. The ecclesiastical councils of 1666 and 1667 sent an unmistakable message, deposing the controversial patriarch but reaffirming the new liturgical usages and anathematizing all who would not be reconciled to the new order. To reinforce these decisions, the government sent the four most intransigent militants—Avvakum, Epifanii, Fedor, and Lazar'—to prison in Pustozersk on the Arctic coast after subjecting the last three of them to mutilation. Old Believer polemicists responded with a particularly intense burst of creative activity in the late 1660s and early 1670s.

In other words, these years saw the formation of the Old Believer canon and, more broadly, initial cultural system. The movement's learned leaders—its "intellectuals," if you will—foraged through the Eastern Orthodox tradition gathering polemical ammunition for their guerrilla war against the Nikonian church. Even more important, they wrote the polemical and devotional works that became classics of early Old Belief. In chronological order, after Potemkin's work, the first major critique of the Nikonian reforms was the petition of Nikita Dobrynin "Pustosviat" (the Hypocrite), completed in 1665 after years of effort.[20] Shortly thereafter, over the course of 1666 and 1667, the spokesmen of the Solovetskii monastery sent Tsar Aleksei Mikhailovich a series of petitions imploring him to reverse the reforms and restore traditional Russian usage. The fifth, the last and longest of the series, included a very detailed critique of the new liturgical texts.[21] In 1666, the authorities confiscated a series of "scrolls," which attacked the new order in a similar vein. Their author, the priest Lazar' of Romanov-Borisoglebsk, continued his polemical activities with a lengthy petition to the tsar from prison in Pustozersk in 1668.[22] Beginning in 1666 another of the martyrs of Pustozersk, the deacon Fedor, kept up a steady stream of attacks on the new order. Among his many works were a letter to the Council of 1666; the still unpublished "Response of the Orthodox," written in 1668 or 1669; an "Epistle to the Faithful about the Antichrist," dated 1670; and a lengthy epistle to his son, completed in 1678–1679.[23] While Fedor and his fellow prisoners wrote in their remote prison, the monk and former fool-in-Christ Avraamii kept a center of Old Believer polemical activity alive in Moscow until his martyrdom in 1672. His writings will receive more detailed scrutiny later in this chapter.

For many years, the archpriest Avvakum has epitomized Old Belief. Thanks to their literary brilliance and the fascinating personality of their ever present author, his writings have received intensive scholarly attention. His autobiographical saint's life has been published many times in Russian and other languages. Imprisonment transformed an activist priest into a writer. Although his earliest short polemics date from the 1660s, he wrote his "Life," completed his "Book of Discourses," and wrote his "Book of Interpretations" in the 1670s. Avvakum's cellmate Epifanii wrote autobiographical works closely related to his own.[24]

These large compositions along with innumerable shorter homilies, petitions, letters, and tales formed the early Old Believers' contributions to the canon of Christian literature as they defined it. Within that canon, modern scholars and nonspecialists would undoubtedly focus their attention almost exclusively on Avvakum's dramatic life and arresting personality. None of the other authors or works listed above offers much to attract the reader of today. Their own contemporaries and later generations of Old Believers saw matters differently. The best inventories of manuscript collections give us a rough idea of which compositions copyists chose to duplicate most often. V. G. Druzhinin's indispensable catalogue, *Pisaniia russkikh staroobriadtsev*, attempted to list all of the manuscripts of Old Believer compositions in the archival collections of the Russian Empire in 1912. A simple tabulation of Druzhinin's findings presents a startling picture. Judging from the extant copies, the Fifth Solovetskii Petition was the most popular early Old Believer work (thirty-four copies), followed by the various redactions of Avraamii's "Petition" (twenty-eight). With the exception of the "Response of the Orthodox," which was not listed at all, Druzhinin's catalogue indicates considerable interest in all of Deacon Fedor's writings, including his lengthy epistle to his son. Druzhinin knew nine copies of Spiridon Potemkin's book and up to twelve copies of individual chapters, five copies of Lazar's petition to the tsar, and only one of Nikita Pustosviat's great petition. Surprisingly enough, Druzhinin listed only eight manuscripts of Avvakum's "Life"; his most frequently represented work was the *Kniga na krestobornuiu eres'* (Against the cross-denying heresy), with eighteen copies.[25]

Using manuscript inventories, even one as reliable as Druzhinin's, in this manner has obvious risks.[26] Any catalogue reflects the time at which it was compiled. Since Druzhinin wrote, researchers have uncovered a myriad of previously unknown manuscripts of Old Believer provenance: since the end of the Second World War, the major centers of research on Old Russian culture have organized annual expeditions to look for undiscovered copies of old books and manuscripts in the most remote regions of the country. Taken as a whole, their efforts have been remarkably successful. Thanks largely to the late V. I. Malyshev, the number of known manuscripts of Avvakum's "Life" has now risen to more than forty.[27] Additional copies of the Fifth Solovetskii Petition and the works of Deacon Fedor and Avraamii also regularly come to light.[28] To mention yet another example, one or more of Avraamii's compositions appears in 31 of the 133 manuscripts in the Library of the Academy of Sciences in St. Petersburg analyzed in N. Iu. Bubnov's inventory.[29] Manuscript inventories may also reflect the regional, social, or denominational roots of the collections. All of the St. Petersburg collections of Old Believer materials come primarily from the north of European Russia, where the influence of the priestless groups and their primary cultural center in the region, the Vyg community, predominated. Even accepting these caveats, however, the frequency with which manuscript copies have survived provides at least a rough indication of the relative importance copyists attached to the works under their pens.

By this criterion, the works of Avraamii, especially his "Petition" and shorter works, were a very important part of the early Old Believer canon. They did not owe their place of honor to their intellectual originality or literary brilliance. The value of Avraamii's works for contemporary and later

Old Believers lay, instead, in their encyclopedic character: he summarized the most important convictions and arguments of the movement's intellectuals in both learned and popular form.

For this reason, Avraamii and his works provide a convenient entry into the emerging Old Believer cultural system. For a brief time at the turn of the 1660s and 1670s, he occupied a central position in the movement. We know comparatively little about his life. Avraamii was the name in religion of the fool-in-Christ Afanasii. An early critic of Nikon's policies, he probably took part in a secret "council" of opponents of the reforms in 1654. According to Avvakum, his spiritual director, "before he became a monk, he wandered barefoot in only a shirt, winter and summer." Avvakum also praised him for his remarkable gift of tears and his quiet, sorrowful demeanor.[30] His role as a fool-in-Christ (*iurodivyi*) allowed him to preach the defense of tradition, but not to write. When the government arrested most prominent Old Believers in connection with the Councils of 1666 and 1667, Avvakum convinced him to give up the life of a iurodivyi and take the tonsure. The change allowed him to serve as leader and chief editor for the Moscow Old Believers who remained at liberty, including Boiarynia Morozova and her household. He immediately began to collect, edit, and summarize the main Old Believer writings and the earlier sources required as "proof texts" to support their contentions. Before long his activities attracted the attention of the government. On February 6, 1670, he was imprisoned in the Mstislavskii Dvor, which belonged to the patriarch. Like the prisoners of Pustozersk, he cultivated good relations with his guards and, with their help, continued to write and circulate attacks on the new order. He was burned at the stake early in 1672.[31]

In his brief period as editor and polemicist, Avraamii compiled a substantial body of work.[32] The earliest and largest of his twelve known compositions is "The Christian's Secure Shield of Faith" (*Khristianoopasnyi shchit very*), compiled between 1667 and 1669 in response to the decisions of the ecclesiastical councils of 1666 and 1667.[33] This enormous text, which understandably was rarely copied, represents in effect the library or archive of the Moscow Old Believer community. As Bubnov's detailed analysis demonstrates, the work contains compositions of most prominent critics of the Nikonian reforms, such as Ivan Neronov, Epifanii, Deacon Fedor, Avvakum, and spokesmen of the Solovetskii and St. Cyril–Beloozero Monasteries as well as Avraamii's own contributions. Drawing on earlier Orthodox literature, it also includes sermons of St. John Chrysostom and Maksim Grek, selections from compilations of homilies, and the "Tale of Simeon of Suzdal'" denouncing the Council of Florence (1438–1445).[34]

Drawing upon these materials, Avraamii wrote his best-known work, the "Petition to Tsar Aleksei Mikhailovich" in 1670 or the beginning of 1671.[35] A thorough exposition of fundamental Old Believer convictions, the "Petition" quickly became a classic. The rest of his individual works are short and fall into three general categories—letters, notes on apocalyptic themes, and popular pamphlets and tales. Judging from the frequency with which they were copied, the most popular were the "Question and Answer," a popular polemic written in the summer of 1670, and the letters from prison to "a certain lover of God" and to Boiarynia Morozova.[36] Bubnov also argues convincingly that the popular tale of the interrogation of Evdokim and Peter, traditionally attributed to Deacon Fedor, was actually Avraamii's work.[37]

Avraamii's literary activity also included the compiling of "manuscript books," which served as a counterweight to the publications of the reformed church. Bubnov lists four such compilations, assembled between 1669 and late 1671—"Instruction to the Faithful" (*Pouchenie vernym liudem*), "Disputation" (*Prenie*), "Disputation on Faith" (*Prenie o vere*), and "Sermon on the Righteous" (*Slovo o pravednikakh*). All but the last of these combine short popular works of Deacon Fedor and Avraamii. The "Instruction to the Faithful," the longest and most complex of the books, varies from one manuscript to the next. At its fullest it consists of nine works of Avvakum, including the one for which it is named, Fedor and Avraamii; several of the latter's contributions also appear as chapters in "The Christian's Secure Shield of Faith."[38]

The contents, manner of presentation, and length of Avraamii's writings suggest that he intended them for very different readers. The "Christian's Secure Shield of Faith" has the usefulness and charm of an encyclopedia. It was probably intended to be used as such. Although ostensibly a private document, the "Petition to the Tsar" was probably intended for a wider, comparatively well-schooled readership. It is certainly significant that we find the numerous copies of the work in collections of Old Believer polemics, not in the royal archives. The shorter letters are particularly puzzling. Avraamii and other Old Believer writers may have intended the addressee to share them with the faithful. It should be noted, for example, that Avraamii included his letter to Morozova in both the "Instruction to the Faithful" and the "Homily on the Righteous."[39] The simpler expositions of the faith, such as the "Question and Answer" and the manuscript books, probably addressed a wider audience. Although the hagiographic tales may have been intended for oral performance, their simple prose style suggests that Avraamii wrote them for an unsophisticated readership. All of these hypotheses and suggestions require further investigation.

Before we analyze the cultural system that Avraamii's works reveal, we should take note of the polemical methods he and his contemporaries used to argue their case. Like many Christian polemicists in all ages, Avraamii and his allies and enemies presented their convictions as series of direct statements, supported by examples from sacred history or "proof texts" from the accepted canon of sacred writings. The more proof texts and examples the better! In Avraamii's words, polemicists aimed to mobilize "a legion of proofs" (*tmy svidetel'stva*) or point to a "cloud of proofs from the Scriptures" (*oblak ot pisaniia svidetel'stva*) in order to lift the reader out of the "ditch of ignorance" (*rov nevedeniia*).[40]

Avraamii's arsenal of polemical weapons was enormous. He made frequent reference to the Old and New Testaments, especially the Gospels and Revelation, quoted or mentioned virtually all of the best-known Eastern church fathers, and referred regularly to the decisions of the seven ecumenical councils of the early church. Avraamii's Russian repertoire was no less impressive. To support his contentions, he cited a wide variety of service books of the Orthodox church, published[41] or in manuscript, the *Kormchaia kniga*, compositions attributed to Maksim Grek, the *Stoglav*, the *Prosvetitel'* of Joseph of Volokolamsk, and the texts, such as the writings of Philotheus of Pskov and the Tale of the White Cowl, which developed Russian variants on the history of universal Christian empire (the *translatio imperii*). All of these writings provided Avraamii with ideas, quotations, or anecdotes demonstrating the truth of his own convictions. The context from which these fragments came or the polemical thrust of the text in which they occurred concerned him little. The writings of Joseph, Nil, and Maksim, for example, were equally suitable grist for his mill. Avraamii's works also drew on a large store of negative examples: he took pains to tie each of Nikon's controversial reforms to one or more of the notorious heresies of the early church. The strongly anti-Orthodox Pope Formosus (c. 816–896) served as a useful polemical villain. Moreover, Avraamii made no effort to hide his scorn for Nikon himself and for the ecclesiastical intellectuals like Simeon Polotskii who supported his reforms. Not all contemporaries were his enemies: his compositions refer to two works of contemporary critics of the Nikonian reforms—Spiridon Potemkin's "Book" and an unnamed "scroll" of his collaborator, Deacon Fedor.[42]

This method of argumentation, as employed by Avraamii and other Old Believers, rested on three central assumptions. First, true Christian faith is timeless and not subject to change.[43] Consequently variations in statements of belief or practices can only mean that one position is orthodox and all others heretical. To add anything to the faith or to subtract anything from it destroys it. "For, in Holy Writ, we are commanded with the holy fathers' very terrible oaths if anyone changes [*podvignet*] even one word from these traditions [*sic*]."[44] Second, learning and worldly wisdom lead men astray. When, in his "Question and Answer," interrogators point out that Avraamii has studied neither rhetoric, philosophy, nor grammar, he agrees without apology and adds that he reads "books of the law of grace" and a few works of prophesy on the basis of which he continues to defend his views.[45] Finally, in maintaining the purity of that faith, even the smallest details have great significance. Literalism in the defense of the faith is a virtue since, in the words that Avraamii twice quoted from the Great Catechism, "heresy comes in by a single letter of the alphabet," a statement with which the early church fathers would readily agree.[46] None of these assumptions distinguished the early Old Believers from Christians in many other places and times. What set Old Belief apart from other conservative Christian movements of protest or renewal were not the ground rules on which its spokesmen based the defense of their position, but the most important postulates of its cultural system and the rituals and symbols, which were more than anything else its distinguishing characteristics.

What, then, were the central ideological elements in the early Old Believers' cultural system? At its heart lay the conviction that the beliefs and practices of the Russian Orthodox Church were authentic expressions of true Christian faith. In Avraamii's words, "I am not an apostate from the holy conciliar and apostolic church, but I hold the true Orthodox faith, handed down by the holy Apostles, confirmed at the seven ecumenical councils and sealed with the blood of the holy martyrs."[47] As part of the authentic Christian tradition, the Russian land and church had their own sacred history.[48] The Russian church displayed all of the signs of a strong Christian community—true belief and practice, its own saints and church councils, and pious princes who protected the faith.

Following the logic of Christian argument, if Russia guarded the true Christian faith, any other Christian community that differed in belief or practice must have fallen into error. Examples were not hard to find. Avraamii shared the pervasive Eastern Orthodox conviction that the Latin West had fallen into heresy and threatened by warfare, intrigue, or casuistry to drag the Orthodox down to ruin. A pious Muscovite had only to remember the Union of Brest to understand the danger.[49] The Greek Church had also fallen by the wayside. The shameful Council of Florence and the subsequent fall of the Byzantine Empire to the Turks demonstrated clearly the price of apostasy. By extension, the Russian church and the princes who guarded it had inherited the mantle of true ecumenical Christianity. In the best-known symbolic statement, Moscow had become the Third and last Rome.[50]

Against this background, Nikon's decision to reform the liturgical practice of the Russian church according to Greek models struck Avraamii and a number of his contemporaries as incomprehensible. To begin with, his program contradicted the most fundamental assumptions of the Russian Orthodox community; his policies unmistakably implied that Russian Orthodoxy was not fully authentic and that the nation's practice of the faith was flawed. Avraamii and his fellow Old Believers found these presuppositions absurd. As they repeatedly asked, were all of our ancestors, all Russian saints, all Russian rulers heretics? "You put forth [*vozlagaete*] a lie and slander against the conciliar church of Christ and against . . . the earlier . . . Great Princes and the five patriarchs and the metropolitans and Wonder-workers that they did not hold the true and full [*vsesovershenu*] faith."[51]

Nikon's reforms were equally indefensible on more practical grounds. Impoverished and powerless under the Turks, the Greek Church offered not models to be emulated but cautionary tales of heresy, apostasy, and corruption to be avoided at all costs.[52] As Avraamii wrote in one of his gentler passages on this theme, "our fathers knew of the corruption of the faith among the Greeks and did not trust them, and lived in the Orthodox faith without strife and pleased God."[53] Moreover, like other Old Believer polemicists, Avraamii portrayed the leading reformers, especially Nikon's controversial adviser Arsenius, as particularly lurid examples of moral turpitude.[54] Nikon did not escape Avraamii's ire. In several scornful passages, he attacked the former patriarch's hubris in naming his magnificent new monastery the New Jerusalem and renaming the Istra River the Jordan.[55]

Under such leadership, the patriarch's program of liturgical reform was hopelessly flawed in every respect. In theory, Nikon and his advisers based their new service books on ancient Greek models. In practice, as Avraamii pointedly observed, in its misery the Greek Church had preserved very few genuinely ancient books and manuscripts, and as a consequence, the reformers had been forced to rely on newly printed Greek service books from Venice, Rome, and Paris in the Latin West.[56] From such sources no good could be expected. In many details, the reforms contradicted the ancient and authentic practice of Russian Christianity and, by implication, led unsuspecting believers into heresy. More discriminating than the authors of the Fifth Solovetskii Petition, Avraamii concentrated his polemical fire on a few of the most controversial innovations—the three-finger sign of the cross,[57] the use of the four-pointed or Latin cross,[58] the triple alleluia,[59] the transliteration of the name Jesus into Slavonic,[60] and the changes in the wording of the Creed (*rozhdenna, ne sotvorena* [begotten, not created], *ne*

budet kontsa [will have no end], and the omission of *istinnyi* [true] in referring
to the Holy Spirit).[61] In all of these cases, he used a myriad of arguments
and proof texts to demonstrate that the new usages were not only arbitrary
and wrongheaded but also heretical. The ultimate rebuttal of the reformers'
positions was to be found in their own publications: successive editions of
the new service books contradicted each other.[62]

Nikon's assault on traditional Russian Orthodoxy and the heretical
implications of his concrete reforms led Avraamii, like many of his
contemporaries, to conclude that universal history had entered a new phase,
the End Time.[63] Time and again, he reminded his readers of the prophesies
of the Book of Revelation, the apocalyptic scenarios of St. Ephraem Syrus,
the authors whose excerpted writings made up the *Kniga o vere* and the
Kirillova kniga, and Russian speculations on the Third Rome. Again and again,
he alerted them to the imminent advent of the Antichrist and, in the letter
"To a Certain Lover of God," he remarked pointedly that Nikon "very much
resembles" (*zelo podobitsia*) the precursor of the Last Judgment.[64] Repeatedly
in his writings he reminded his reader of the apocalyptic image of the great
dragon who, with his tail, "swept down a third of the stars in the sky and flung
them to the earth."[65] Avraamii had no doubt that the time was ripe. First, in
the year 1000, the Latin West had completed its descent into apostasy; then in
another six hundred years, the Orthodox in the Polish-Lithuanian monarchy
had betrayed the faith by accepting the Union of Brest. Finally, "in 1666,
because in that year Nikon, the destroyer, distributed his heretical Service
Books [*Sluzhebniki*],"[66] the drama was completed and the biblical prophecy
of the number of the Beast (666) fulfilled.[67] Only if the tsar intervened, like
the pious Christian emperors of old, granted the defenders of the Old Faith a
"just trial" against the Nikonians, and reversed the reforms could Russia and
the world be spared the Apocalypse.[68] The whole tenor of Avraamii's works
suggests that he expected no such reprieve.

Such are the basic outlines of the ideological component of the early Old
Believers' cultural system as Avraamii explained it. No one who has read any
of the best general works on Old Belief will find much new or surprising in
his views. The system as Avraamii expounded it, however, is remarkable in
its comprehensiveness and inner consistency. It provided a symbolic pattern
constructed from inherited materials, which explained the historical origin,
nature, and future consequences of the cultural, social, and ecclesiastical
conflicts of mid-seventeenth-century Russia. In other words, the system
gave men and women a worldview by which they could live and for which
they could die.

The cultural system had many obvious theoretical and practical implications. If the End Time had come, the Old Believers represented the remnant whose duty it was to preserve true Christianity at any cost. As Avraamii paraphrased Scripture, "When He comes to judge the living and the dead, He will not find His faith on earth except among the few hiding in the deserts and the mountains."[69] Concretely, this meant preserving the rituals and beliefs of pre-Nikonian Orthodoxy uncorrupted. How best to accomplish this objective has remained a subject of debate among Old Believers to this day.[70]

To sustain them in the last days, the faithful could look to the example of the new martyrs—Avvakum and the other prisoners of Pustozersk.[71] Avraamii also described himself in the rhetoric of martyrdom and admonished his followers with fictional accounts of his sufferings and those of others.[72] In addition to examples of faithful conduct, Avraamii provided his spiritual children with rigorous schedules of prayer and self-discipline.[73] The materials that he collected in the "Christian's Secure Shield of Faith" also contain admonitions to true Christians to avoid eating, drinking, and friendship with unbelievers, and in what appears to be his own editorial comment, he urged them to pray in their own homes rather than taking part in the corrupted services of the Nikonians.[74] In a word, Avraamii's writings hinted at the emergence of a separate community of faithful Christians who would devote their lives to the preservation of true Orthodoxy until the End of Time. The practical work of creating an Old Believer counter-society, however, lay far in the future.

To appreciate the attractive power of the early Old Believers' cultural system and to understand its limitations, we should examine the polemical foundations upon which it rested. In building their case, Avraamii and other early Old Believer polemicists devoted much of their effort to attacking specific details of the Nikonian reforms both for their own sake and as illustrations of the more general arguments about the authenticity of Russian Orthodox tradition. Detailed examination of Avraamii's case against two particular changes—the three-finger sign of the cross and the threefold alleluia—will illustrate his arguments, his polemical methods, the "cloud of witnesses" he cited, and the extent to which his compositions continued the work of his predecessors. In both cases, he attempted to show that the new usage contradicted earlier Orthodox practice, particularly in Russia, and in theological terms was both illogical and heretical. His treatment of the sign of the cross was remarkably consistent throughout his writings: the "Christian's Secure Shield of Faith" and the "Petition" cite exactly the same sources, and he copied a number of sentences directly from the earlier work to the later one.[75]

To prove that earlier Orthodox Christians used the two-finger sign, he cited a remarkably long and indiscriminate list of authorities—Sts. Meletius, Theodoret, and Peter of Damascus, fragments of whose writings had become part of the Russian canon,[76] Maksim Grek, the *Stoglav*, the *Prolog* for February 12, chapters 37 and 49 of the *Kormchaia kniga* of 1518/19, the Kiev *Grammatika* of 1595, the Great and Small Catechisms, chapter 14 of the *Kirillova kniga*, and chapter 9 of the *Kniga o vere*.[77] Iconographic evidence also served him well. An icon of the Virgin attributed to Metropolitan Peter of Moscow, one on the city gates of Kolomna, and other old icons showed Christ blessing the onlooker with the two-finger sign.[78] Presumably on these grounds, he stated several times that Christ himself used the two-finger sign.[79]

The countervailing evidence of the Nikonians he dismissed with scorn. Their main proof text, cited in Nikon's *Skrizhal*, was a work attributed to a recent Greek author identified as the "hypodeacon, Studite, Damaskin."[80] Avraamii scornfully dismissed him as a modern and unknown author. As the compiler of the *Kniga o vere* demonstrated, the earliest proponent of the three-finger sign was the notorious and heretical Pope Formosus. Moreover, he observed, until very recently Greek ecclesiastics who visited Russia had expressed no objection to local usage.[81]

Avraamii's theological case rested on a single assertion. He assumed that, when believers cross themselves, they reenact the Crucifixion. Thus, with their fingers, they should represent Christ in His two natures. If the three-finger sign signifies the Holy Trinity, to cross oneself makes the absurd statement that the Trinity suffered and died on the Cross. Stretching the point further, he argued that the three-finger sign, in effect, denies Christ's true humanity and negates the Incarnation.[82] "For the Trinity did not suffer on the cross, but one [person] of the Trinity, the Son of God, in his flesh, but not his divinity."[83] This final declaration allowed him to liken the Nikonians to all the heretics of the early church who held unorthodox views on Christ's humanity. To give his position greater authority, Avraamii included not only specific proof texts but quotations from Scripture and the fathers proclaiming the Incarnation or warning against the consequences of false belief.

Other summary statements of the early Old Believers' position have many similarities to Avraamii's. Gerasim Firsov's very early attack on Nikon's *Skrizhal*, Deacon Fedor's letter to the Council of 1666, the Fifth Solovetskii Petition, and Nikita Pustosviat's "Petition," all presented the same list of witness testifying that the two-finger sign of the cross is the authentic Christian usage.[84] Nikita Pustosviat made similar use of iconographic evidence. In two respects, Nikita's defense of Russian tradition is subtler than Avraamii's. He carefully refuted Nikon's use of Meletius as a proof text for the three-finger sign by pointing out that the gesture to which the disputed quotation alluded describes not an episcopal blessing of the flock but a graphic attempt to score points in a debate against the Arians on the nature of the Trinity.[85] Nikita also stated the Old Believers' theological position more clearly than Avraamii. In his opinion, in the two-finger sign of the cross, the thumb, fourth finger, and little finger represent the Trinity, the index and middle finger the two natures of Christ, and the downward slant of the middle finger His coming to earth in the Incarnation.[86] With Avraamii, he insisted that the three-finger sign is theologically absurd since the Divinity cannot suffer except in Christ's human nature.[87]

Similarly, Avraamii followed his predecessors very closely in defending the so-called threefold alleluia. In arguing that Nikon's service books erred in adding a third alleluia to the prevailing usage, "Alleluia, alleluia, glory to Thee, O God," Deacon Fedor, Nikita Pustosviat, and the Fifth Solovetskii Petition all relied heavily on the statements of Maksim Grek, the *Stoglav*, and the Life of St. Evfrosin of Pskov.[88] The latter tells how the saint defended true Christian practice against the "defrocked priest and thrice-married Iev," who preached the fourfold alleluia. According to the story, Evfrosin journeyed to Constantinople to seek Patriarch Joseph's advice. With the patriarch's blessing, he returned to Pskov to bring his struggle to a victorious conclusion. Iev's punishment for leading the faithful astray was a lingering, terrible death.[89]

In addition to his own evidence, Nikita also offered a refutation of some Nikonian arguments. He insisted that Revelation 19:1–6 could not serve as proof of the fourfold alleluia because each of the three ranks of celestial beings mentioned in the passage cried "alleluia" only once. He also dismissed any earlier Russian sources for the fourfold usage on the grounds that they were probably forged and planted in monastic libraries by the heretic Iev and his accomplices.[90]

Avraamii's treatment of this theme added relatively little to the work of his predecessors.[91] He cited the same proof texts and used the same refutations of the Nikonian arguments. In two respects, however, the discussion carried Avraamii's polemical fingerprints. As usual, he made a somewhat clumsy attempt to explain the theological significance of his position. Alluding to a passage in which the Mother of God appeared to the writer of the "Life" of Evfrosin in a vision, he argued that the alleluia celebrated the Resurrection. Since Christ rose as both God and Man through the agency of the Holy Spirit, the threefold alleluia appropriately accorded equal honor to each of the three persons of the Trinity. To add an additional "alleluia" meant both to add a fourth person to the Trinity and to dishonor the Holy Spirit by implying that it proceeded from the Father and the Son. To Orthodox Christians, both positions were rank heresies. Moreover, as was his custom, he interpreted each reform he opposed as one more sign of the advent of the Antichrist.[92]

These examples, which could easily be multiplied, illustrate the extent to which the early Old Believer polemicists built their cultural system on a common repertoire of proof texts. Each writer added his own polemical or stylistic touches to the common stock of pronouncements, examples, and arguments. In this company, Avraamii acted primarily as an archivist and compiler, laboriously assembling all of the evidence that might help his cause. In addition to his thoroughness, his work stands out for its rather turgid theologizing and for its recurring emphasis on the Apocalypse.

As Avraamii's work illustrates, the early Old Believer cultural system was a remarkable edifice. As the passages we have discussed illustrate, the most important writings in which Old Believer intellectuals explicated it have an aura of authority, arising from the intensity of the authors' convictions, the density of the exposition, and the sheer number and variety of the evidence they cited. Although the persuasiveness of their arguments and the effectiveness of their proofs varied greatly, their most forceful polemical blows were telling indeed.

The writings that set out the Old Believer cultural system are unabashedly literalistic. Most Christians in most ages would find such an attitude quite comprehensible. When men and women argue the central issues of the faith, the precise wording—the "last letter a"—has enormous significance. Even so, the early Old Believers and their descendants in the faith were remarkably indiscriminate in their literalism. In their eyes, all of their differences with the Nikonians were matters of vital importance: all proof texts that might support their arguments were equally valid. To a potential adherent, however, the rigidity and pedantic consistency of the cultural system of the early Old Believers probably only intensified its attractive power.

In the end, the most important test of any cultural system is not its intellectual sophistication but the power of its symbolic language to give meaning to men's and women's lives. The early Old Believers' system had just such power. The survival of their cause and their writings in spite of persecution is the best measure of their achievement.

The writings of Avraamii, archetypal archivist, compiler, and system-builder, illustrate the speed, rigor, and seriousness of purpose with which the early Old Believers assembled a cultural system in which they and their followers could live and through which they could continue to resist the new order in the Nikonian church and the Russian state and society. Avraamii elaborated his variant of the system between about 1668 and 1671, immediately after the Councils of 1666 and 1667 and before Avvakum and the other Pustozersk fathers had written their major works. As consistent as it was rigid, this system contained all the symbolic elements men and women needed to understand and deal with the world around them. These included a closed ideological system, a sacred history of the faithful remnant of true Russian Orthodox believers, a code of rituals for worship, simple moral principles, and a few practical guidelines for everyday life. The coherence and strength of this system armed the Old Believers for their struggle to survive the persecutions that had already begun when Avraamii wrote and soon claimed him. Its apocalyptic vision, a special emphasis in Avraamii's exposition, gave meaning to their sufferings and reinforced the hope that those who endured to the end would be saved. Although the system was the creation of conservative learned clerics, it provided concepts, images, and rallying cries with which ordinary men and women could comprehend the rapidly changing and threatening world around them and fight back against its demands. In short, the cultural system that Avraamii and his collaborators constructed formed the cornerstone of the Old Believer movement and provides the most important explanation for its remarkable staying power.

The Miracle of Martyrdom
Reflections on Early Old Believer Hagiography

The true Orthodox faith . . .

is sealed with the blood of the martyrs.

—Avraamii

This I consider to be great and truly miraculous [*divno*]

that God would find me worthy to be burned in His name.

—*The Tale of Boiarynia Morozova*

HAGIOGRAPHY FORMS AN INTEGRAL PART of the cultural life of Old Belief. Like other Christians in the East and the West, the Old Believers have treasured the stories of the lives and the martyrdom of defenders of the faith. When they rejected the reforms of Patriarch Nikon and began their struggle to preserve rigorous and authentic Russian Orthodoxy as they understood it, the Old Believers not only continued the cultural traditions of Russian Orthodoxy but also added to them works honoring the memory of the saints and martyrs of their own movement.[1]

The Old Believer variant of Muscovite Russian culture was the creation of a group of conservative clergymen and a few lay supporters in the mid- to late seventeenth century. Judging by their works, the first Old Believer writers struggled to defend the Russian Orthodox culture of their time, which they equated with the timeless ecumenical Orthodox tradition. At the same time, in defending Muscovite Orthodoxy, they had to define and codify it—a process that consisted in part of setting themselves in opposition to the liturgical enactments and theological arguments that Patriarch Nikon and his allies advanced in support of their program of liturgical and administrative reform in the church. Thus their act of negation was simultaneously an act of creation.

The polemical writings of the first generation of Old Believers were part of a larger design. From the beginning, they and their followers aspired to maintain an authentically Christian way of life. Their polemical attacks on the Nikonian reforms directed attention to the liturgical observances that their words defended. For in their view liturgy, not theological conviction, was the center of Christian life. Moreover, by implication (and to some extent explicitly), their polemics told followers how they should live in the apocalyptic circumstances in which they found themselves. Thus, within a generation or two, the Old Believers created their own liturgical cycle, elaborate institutional structures, ideological and polemical statements, a rigorous moral code, and a distinct artistic culture. In short, they built a separate world with its own culture.[2]

In creating a cultural world of their own, the early Old Believers drew heavily on Muscovite ecclesiastical culture of the mid-seventeenth century.[3] As they defined the canon of acceptably Orthodox texts, the early Old Believers included writings of the Eastern church fathers available in Russian translations or miscellanies and many classics of the Russian Orthodox tradition. To this collection of acceptably Christian works, they gradually added defenses of their own position and edifying works for their followers.[4] Similarly, they made the classic tradition of Russian icon painting and the plainchant of the pre-Nikonian church their own.

This remarkable burst of creativity took place in circumstances of deprivation and persecution. The official church and the state gave the first Old Believers ample reason to believe that the apocalyptic expectations common in seventeenth-century Russian Orthodoxy applied to them—that they were martyrs and that their sufferings were the prelude to the End Time. Driven into the "desert" or the catacombs, the first Old Believers adopted ever more rigorous tests of true Orthodox belief and practice, since their very souls depended on holding correct belief and observing precisely the forms of worship that embodied it.

To illustrate these propositions, I propose to examine selected works of the early Old Believer canon, which were not ideological texts or polemics in the strict sense. Like all groups of Christians, the Old Believers defined themselves not only by liturgical observances or theological propositions but also by their stories. The Eastern Orthodox tradition provided them with a large repertoire of biblical and patristic stories and saints' lives.[5] To this canon the first Old Believer writers added their own narratives, usually written in a direct manner in a mixture of exalted and popular language (in contrast to the convoluted complexity of their formal treatises and polemics). Although none of these works follows strictly the usual pattern of the saint's vita, all of them are in some sense works of hagiography for they describe the saintly lives, the sufferings, and the martyrdom of defenders of the Old Faith.

How is a scholar to read texts of this kind? First, we should heed Paul Bushkovitch's advice to read each text in its entirety, and if its primary theme and purpose are religious, to concentrate on elucidating the religious messages rather than mining it for information on political events or social conditions.[6] Second, readers (even those inclined to view cultures as systems) must be sensitive to the inconvenient facts and discordant notes in any text so as not to become prisoners of their own interpretative structures, for all cultures contain their own inconsistencies and paradoxes. Finally, readers must read the text in its political, social, and cultural context, measuring its contents and style against the realities of the day and the textual traditions that may have shaped it.

The Old Believers' urge to write their own hagiography is not difficult to understand. Since they regarded themselves as the faithful remnant, the last bastion of true Orthodox Christianity, they needed to convince themselves and others that they possessed all the important attributes of an authentic Christian community, including edifying stories of suffering and death for the faith. Hagiographic tales served both as proof texts demonstrating the truth of the Old Believers' convictions and as examples of holy behavior for the edification of the faithful.

By far the best-known of the early Old Believer hagiographic works is the "Life of Avvakum," whose title explicitly links it to the genre of saints' lives.[7] This focus of this chapter, however, will be the hagiographic narratives of the Moscow center, in particular the short narrative works of Avraamii and *The Tale of Boiarynia Morozova*.[8] The discussion will focus on the ways in which these texts treat the theme of martyrdom, their authors' use of the miraculous, and the ways in which these two elements intertwine. Implicit in the task are two further questions—the extent to which Old Believer treatment of these central issues of Christian hagiography differed from earlier Russian Orthodox writings and the degree to which these narratives reflect prevailing currents in Orthodox high culture in mid- and late seventeenth-century Muscovy.[9]

Before discussing the works themselves, we need to adopt definitions of the most important terms, "martyrdom" and "miracle." Literally a "witness," the term "martyr" was traditionally reserved for those who were put to death for the Christian faith. "According to the traditional view, a miracle is a sensible fact . . . produced by the special intervention of God for a religious end, transcending the normal order of things." In the history of Christian devotional writing, miracles have taken a wide variety of forms and played many different roles in edifying literature and popular devotional practice.[10]

Any discussion of premodern literary, polemical, or devotional writings raises important but vexing questions about the date of their composition, the readership they reached, the speed with which they reached it, and the ways the readers "received" and understood their contents. The dating of the texts we will examine poses no significant problems: serious textological studies date all of them to the years between 1669 and 1675. The time and pattern of their spread throughout the scattered Old Believer communities of the empire is much more complicated. Unlike the vitae of Avvakum and Epifanii, which have come down to us in the authors' own hands, the works of Avraamii and *The Tale of Boiarynia Morozova* survive in later copies, the earliest of which date from the end of the seventeenth and beginning of the eighteenth centuries.[11] The vast majority of extant manuscripts date from the latter half of the eighteenth century and the nineteenth. Any suggestions about the identity of the readers or hearers of these compositions are at best highly speculative.

For a brief period as the 1660s became the 1670s, the monk Avraamii was one of the most prominent spokesmen of the Old Belief in Moscow. Avraamii was the name in religion of the fool-in-Christ Afanasii. After the arrest of several other leaders of the ecclesiastical opposition in 1666 and 1667, Avvakum, who greatly admired Avraamii's rigorous asceticism, convinced him to take the tonsure.[12] Avraamii's new status allowed him to serve as leader of the Moscow Old Believers (including Boiarynia Morozova and her household) and to collect an arsenal of devotional and polemical writings with which he and his allies could fight the Nikonians. Avraamii also wrote his own compositions, which became treasured contributions to the emerging Old Believer canon of sacred texts.[13] Such a prominent opposition leader could not for long work openly in Moscow. He was imprisoned on February 6, 1670, and was burnt at the stake in April 1672.

Two of Avraamii's compositions and a third sometimes attributed to him can be considered hagiographic. The first of the three, the fictional tale of the torture of the elders Petr and Evdokim, was probably written between February 17, 1669, and February 13, 1670.[14] Scholars have offered different

hypotheses about its author: N. Subbotin published the text as a work of
Deacon Fedor, but more recently N. Iu. Bubnov has convincingly attributed
it to Avraamii.[15] While imprisoned in the Mstislavskii Dvor in Moscow in the
summer of 1670, Avraamii wrote the longest of the three, the "Question
and Answer" (*Vopros i otvet*).[16] The very short and as yet unpublished
"Tale of the Dispute of Kondratii with the Ecclesiastical Authorities" was
probably written in prison in 1671.[17] Unlike the tale of Petr and Evdokim,
the "Question and Answer" and the tale of Kondratii are at their core
autobiographical. At the beginning of the "Question and Answer," Avraamii
explicitly identifies himself as the central figure in the story. The fact that the
hero of the tale of Kondratii is also a prisoner in the Mstislavskii Dvor and
undergoes interrogation by representatives of the church hierarchy suggests
that he is Avraamii in disguise.[18]

In all three cases, Avraamii uses the narrative to present central propositions
of early Old Believer ideology in a comparatively simple and popular manner.
In each, the story centers on the interrogation of the hero by representatives
of the ecclesiastical hierarchy, sometimes joined by powerful lay officials. As
he responds to the inquisitors' questions, the central character makes many of
the same polemical points Avraamii did in his longer, more complex polemical
works, the "Petition" and the "Christian's Secure Shield of Faith."[19] At the center
of the debate lies the contrast between the authentic Orthodox faith of the
Russian church before the Nikonian reforms and the heretical changes in belief
and practice through which Nikon and his ally Arsenius the Greek destroyed
that faith and set off the Apocalypse. To illustrate this central conviction, the
heroes of the stories offer concrete evidence. Petr and Evdokim insist, for
example, that Nikon brought heresy into the Russian church by introducing
the three-finger sign of the cross: this usage, they argue, is the sign of Satan,
since it implies an unspeakable heresy, namely, that Christ has three natures.
In the "Question and Answer," Avraamii defends the traditional eight-point
cross as distinct from Nikon's four-point variant and attacks Nikon's decision
to change the stamp of the cross on communion wafers. Petr and Evdokim
and Avraamii also criticize the deletion of the epithet "true" (*istinnyi*) from a
passage referring to the Holy Spirit.[20]

Aggressive defense of the true faith invariably leads to suffering and
martyrdom. Angered by Petr and Evdokim's attacks on Nikon's reforms and
their proclamation that the reign of the Antichrist has begun, the tsar orders
them boiled in a huge kettle. Like the young men in the fiery furnace,[21] the
heroes accept their fate confidently, praying that they might share in Christ's
resurrection and that, through their sacrifice, their tormentors might be

confounded and brought to the true faith. After several minutes in the boiling water, a miracle saves them: with great noise, fire descends from heaven and smashes the kettle so that the martyrs emerge unscathed. So shaken is the tsar that he lets Petr and Evdokim go free.[22]

The autobiographical central figures in the "Question and Answer" and the tale of Kondratii find no such escape. When Avraamii stubbornly insists on defending the Old Faith, the Metropolitan of Krutitsa pulls him around by the beard, slaps his face, and in the process knocks off his cloak, cowl, and skull cap. As physical abuse and persuasion fail to convince Avraamii to submit, his frustrated interrogators threaten him with strangling, a suitable fate for an intransigent heretic. Kondratii is similarly beaten and put in chains. In the end, the ecclesiastical authorities defrock Avraamii and prepare to hand him over to the civil authorities. Later readers would have had no difficulty remembering or imagining the unwritten final chapter of the story—Avraamii's death at the stake.[23] Other than the example of the heroes' remarkable strength of character, the only reference to the miraculous in these stories is ironic: Avraamii's inquisitors chide him for stirring up the people with tales about men who survive boiling in a kettle or who have had their tongues cut out, yet speak.[24] Avraamii himself experienced no miraculous rescue.

What, then, were the central messages of these stories and to whom did they speak? Although questions of authorial intention and probable readership or audience are risky, the simple language and narrative structure suggest that Avraamii composed these works for a comparatively large and varied public— the women and men, for example, who made up Morozova's large household. In telling the stories, he drew on the store of familiar Jewish and Christian images that he and his readers shared. The heroes resemble the Old Testament prophets and Christ in standing courageously before the mighty of this world and speaking the truth. Like these illustrious precursors, Petr and Evdokim are wanderers who have no earthly home. Like Christ before his interrogators, Petr and Evdokim and Avraamii bear physical abuse and humiliation silently. At the same time, they carry out the biblical injunction to preach the Gospel, contradicting the heretical statements of their adversaries.[25] As the fate of their predecessors makes clear, their unbending devotion to the faith leads inevitably to martyrdom.

The central image of the stories, then, is martyrdom. In a moment when the soul of Russia and indeed the fate of the whole world hung in the balance, God called faithful Christians to stand firm in the true faith, confront the powers of heresy resolutely, and relive the sacrifice of the prophets, the martyrs, and Christ himself. While Christ might use miraculous means to spare them suffering, the true miracle was their strength to remain faithful until the end.

Old Believer hagiography flourished in the mid-1670s. Avvakum and Epifanii wrote their autobiographical saints' lives in prison in Pustozersk and, in Moscow, *The Tale of Boiarynia Morozova* carried on the tradition of Avraamii. In his thorough study of the *Tale*, A. I. Mazunin argues that Andrei, the steward of Morozova's household, composed the first version of the work between the end of 1675 and the middle of 1677.[26] Mazunin divides the extant manuscripts into three redactions—the Extended, the Abridged, and the Short. He argues that the Extended Redaction is the oldest and represents a condensation of the lost original text made in Moscow in the late seventeenth century and preserved in the manuscript tradition of the Russian north. This version of the *Tale* has close connections to Avraamii's work: several manuscripts of the Extended Redaction also contain Avraamii's writings. Moreover, Mazunin has noted a number of passages that the author appears to have borrowed from the "Question and Answer." The Abridged Redaction, Mazunin argues, was composed in the Old Believer settlements in Kerzhenets at the very beginning of the eighteenth century. According to his analysis, Semen Denisov, the leader of the Vyg community, used the Extended Redaction to create the Short Redaction in the 1720s as a chapter for his martyrology, the *Vinograd rossiiskii*, and later to recast it as a separate composition.[27] Thus, if Mazunin's conclusions are correct, the evolution of the *Tale* from one redaction to the next provides an interesting type case of changing perceptions of holiness and examples of evolving literary taste among the Old Believers in the seventeenth and eighteenth centuries.

Like other Old Believer narrative and devotional writings, *The Tale of Boiarynia Morozova* is not easy to classify. In the manuscript tradition, copyists usually labeled the text a "story" (*skazanie*). Among a variety of other labels, the choice of the modern editor—"tale" (*povest'*)—occurs only once, as does the term "saint's life" (*zhitie*). Nevertheless, the three redactions all bear a resemblance to the ideal type of Byzantine or Old Russian saint's life.[28] The Extended Redaction has a heading that begins with the date of the saint's feast and gives her name, accompanied by epithets attesting to her sanctity.[29] The Abridged Redaction, but not the other two, opens with a lengthy preface by the author. All three versions then provide a brief biographical sketch of the heroine's family background and her life up to the moment when her latent saintly qualities became fully manifest. As was customary, the author or editor devoted most attention to the events that fully revealed the heroine's sanctity and ended the composition with an account of her martyrdom and a description of the miracles she performed. Although the Extended Redaction ends abruptly, the two later versions of the text both conclude with a traditional paean of praise to the martyrs Morozova and her companions.[30]

In outline, the events narrated in the *Tale* are well known.[31] Boiarynia Morozova, widow of the boyar Gleb Ivanovich Morozov, made her household in Moscow a center of opposition to the Nikonian reforms. Up until that time, the events of her life did not distinguish her from other prominent noblewomen of the tsar's court. She had married, borne one son, Ivan, and lost her husband. When Nikon began his reforms, she and her sister Evdokiia, by marriage Princess Urusova, followed the teachings of Avvakum. Their stand attracted the attention of the ecclesiastical and secular authorities; eventually, even the tsar and the Boyar Council debated what to do with her. A succession of distinguished visitors unsuccessfully attempted to persuade her to accept the three-finger sign of the cross. When she remained intransigent, the authorities increased their pressure; after a period of house arrest, she and her sister and a third woman named Mariia were imprisoned in a succession of convents in Moscow. Repeated interrogations, torture, and threats of execution failed to intimidate them. The martyrs attracted a great deal of sympathetic attention and, in a manner dramatized in Surikov's painting, used every opportunity to bear public witness for the Old Belief. To put an end to the embarrassment, the authorities confined the three women in an underground prison in Borovsk and starved them to death.

At the center of the story is a series of confrontations between Morozova and her companions and the authorities. Again and again, gently or harshly, the representatives of the Nikonian church and the state demand that Morozova submit to the new order: each time she firmly refuses. When forced to attend a liturgy celebrated according to the reformed canons, she refuses to cooperate and upbraids the nuns around her. When the patriarch attempts to anoint her to heal her presumed psychiatric illness, she defends herself like a wrestler and pushes his arm away. Even while hanging on the *triaska* (strappado), she upbraids her torturers, conduct that serves only to lengthen her time in agony. As her end nears, she resolutely prepares herself and her companions for death, attempting only to win a few favors from sympathetic jailers in order to relieve her sufferings a little.

In short, the story once again is a tale of martyrdom. The author repeatedly emphasizes Morozova's sacrifice in giving up her wealth and social standing, her stubborn determination to defend the Old Belief, her deliberate choice of a martyr's fate (as illustrated, for example, by her repeated expressions of joy at being kept in chains like St. Paul), and her determination to die for her convictions. The most moving passages are those in which a starving Morozova begs a frightened guard for a few scraps of food and asks him to wash her shift in the river so that she will have clean clothes to meet Christ, her bridegroom.

The *Tale* poses a second problem of classification. To what extent, if any, can it be read as a source on female spirituality, since, like the early seventeenth-century tale of Uliianiia Lazarevskaia (or Osor'ina), it is probably the work of a man who knew the heroine well?[32] A number of themes or emphases in the text differ from Avraamii's hagiographic tales or the "lives" of Avvakum and Epifanii. First, in her confrontations with the authorities Morozova, unlike her male counterparts, makes little attempt to discuss the theological and liturgical issues that separate the Nikonians and Old Believers.[33] Perhaps then, as among Old Believers today, theologizing was men's work. Second, among the issues that she and her interrogators do debate is her duty as a mother. Although she makes no attempt to hide her love for her son, Ivan, whose marriage she had hoped to celebrate, she makes it clear that her only ultimate love is Christ. If necessary, she would watch her son being torn apart by dogs at the place of execution and still not recant. Third, unlike their male counterparts, Morozova and her companions use passive resistance in the most literal sense. Morozova pretends to be ill in order to avoid attending the second marriage of Tsar Aleksei Mikhailovich. Later, she and Urusova take this tactic to extremes: pretending to be disabled, they force their persecutors to carry them everywhere on stretchers and bast mats or drag them on sleds. Only when Nikonian clergy attempt to minister to them against their will do they abandon the pretense, stand up, and defend themselves vigorously.[34]

Morozova's most important worldly loyalties are to the community of women who assist her in serving Christ—first, the holy women who gather in her house, then her confessor, Melaniia, and her companions in martyrdom. In spite of many obvious inconveniences, she begs Melaniia to agree that she be tonsured a nun and regularly consults her about the best ways of fulfilling her monastic vows in the horrible circumstances in which she finds herself. When the authorities separate Morozova, Urusova, and Mariia, the three women and their supporters take extraordinary risks to visit and comfort one another. If anything, the need for mutual support is even greater than that experienced by the male martyrs in the other works of early Old Believer hagiography. Nevertheless, the heroines' boldness and determination equal that of men. In the pun that occurs repeatedly in Old Believer hagiography, the women stood up for Christ courageously (*muzhestvenno*).

As in Avraamii's stories, the miraculous plays a comparatively minor role in the *Tale*. Indeed, the relative absence of miraculous episodes is surprising, since in the Western and Eastern hagiographic traditions, miracles provide one of the reliable proofs of sanctity. In the Extended Redaction, there are only three miracles, two of which occur in the afterword.[35] In the first, at the moment of Morozova's death, Melaniia sees a vision of her in shining monastic garments (the *skhima* and *kukol*), with radiant face, kissing an icon of Our Lady and with a cross sewn on her robes. The other two miraculous episodes seem to refer to Morozova's active life. When the priest Dorofei gives the three martyrs Holy Communion, they are transfigured and their faces glow like those of angels. As with Christ, transfiguration prefigures suffering and death. On another occasion, the prayers and tears of the three martyrs cure Melaniia of a grave illness.

The Abridged Redaction of the text places greater emphasis on the miraculous. In place of the stories of transfiguration and healing, its creator substituted Deacon Fedor's vivid account of a flood in his underground cell in Pustozersk. Each year, when spring reaches the Arctic, the prisoners' cells fill with water. On this occasion, however, Avvakum—who has quarreled with Fedor over questions of doctrine—convinces the guards to build a ditch so that all of the water pours into Fedor's cell. Standing on his knees in the flood, the latter prays for the intercession of Morozova, who has only recently died, and within a quarter of an hour the water has disappeared.[36]

In contrast, although the Short Redaction follows the literary conventions of the saint's life particularly closely, Semen Denisov incorporated few miraculous elements into his version of the story. In addition to the description of an unburied body (in this case, Morozova's), which remains white and does not decay, Denisov added one new story. When the jailers take away Morozova's cross and prayer beads, she has a vision of an angel carrying an icon of the Crucifixion and, from that moment, regards herself a nun.[37]

As the writer of the *Tale* makes clear, however, the most important miracle of all is the heroines' resolution in defending the faith. As Morozova responds to the tsar's message asking her to submit, the luxury and power of a noblewoman's life no longer appeal to her. "This I consider great and it truly is miraculous [*poistinne divno*] that God would allow me to be burned in His name at the stake that has been prepared for me at the place of execution [*na Bolote*]."[38]

In contrast, miracles and the supernatural loom much larger in the hagiographic autobiographies of Avvakum and Epifanii. Epifanii's "Life" consists largely of a succession of encounters with devils, over whom he is ultimately victorious.[39] In Avvakum's work, some of the miracles are extraordinary occurrences that can ultimately be explained in human terms.[40] At the same time, many events in Avvakum's story are miraculous by any standard. The "Life" describes many miracles of healing. The best-known, about which Avraamii's interrogators complained, is the healing of Fedor, Lazar', and Epifanii, who rediscover how to speak after the executioner has cut out their tongues. Moreover, Epifanii's severed fingers heal remarkably quickly. On a number of occasions, Avvakum himself heals the sick and demon-possessed through prayer and anointing.[41] These miracles—particularly those retold together toward the end of the text— demonstrate Avvakum's sanctity and the rightness of his cause; unlike the lists of miracles at the end of other saints' lives, however, God works these wonders through a living saint, not a dead one.

Supernatural forces intervene in other ways as well. God communicates with men through dreams and visions. Avvakum's call to his mission takes the form of a vision of three golden ships, two for Avvakum's spiritual children and the third for him and his family, as a sign that he should continue his pastoral work. Like Epifanii, Avvakum fights against devils; the stories of these struggles play a far less prominent role in Avvakum's "Life" than in his cellmate's, however.[42]

The contrast between *The Tale of Boiarynia Morozova* and the lives of Avvakum and Epifanii, all written in the mid-1670s, illustrates once again the richness and variety of early Old Believer culture. In its emphasis on the earthly activities of the heroine rather than on the miraculous, Morozova's life more closely resembles the early seventeenth-century life of Uliianiia Lazarevskaia than the vitae of Avvakum and Epifanii. That saints' lives of women differed from those of men is no accident. Since the Russian hagiographic tradition provided far more models for the lives of male saints than of their female counterparts, the male author of the original text of Morozova's life probably felt fewer constraints of tradition in telling a story whose central figures were all women.[43] Moreover, as Carolyn Walker Bynum has argued in her analysis of Western European materials, the lives of female saints reflect the social relations and customs of the societies from which they emerged: as described in their lives, female saints lived more respectable and predictable lives, without dramatic breaks, conversions, or outbursts of inspired eccentricity, because their position in society simply did not allow them to engage in the more radical conduct of some saintly men.[44]

The vita of Morozova and Avraamii's writings also support, in their own ways, Paul Bushkovitch's interpretation of the elite religious culture of seventeenth-century Muscovy as being less centered on the miraculous than on the moral dimension of Christian teaching.[45] The author's emphasis on the personality of the heroine and the details of her daily life reflects another feature of seventeenth-century Russian writing—the stress on human individuality, exemplified above all by the life of Avvakum.[46] Taken together, these observations suggest that early Old Believer hagiographic writings reflect many of the characteristics of high ecclesiastical culture of the middle and late seventeenth century. These compositions serve as one illustration of the extent to which early Old Believer culture encapsulated the attitudes, values, and literary conventions of the time and society in which it took shape.

To conclude, the first Old Believer hagiographic narratives stressed the resolute defense of pre-Nikonian Russian Orthodoxy. Except for stereotypical situations dictated by the requirements of the hagiographic tradition, the miraculous plays a relatively small role in Avraamii's hagiographic tales and *The Tale of Boiarynia Morozova*. In their autobiographical works, Avvakum and Epifanii place greater emphasis on the miraculous; and Avvakum in particular, like Christians in many other places and times, tended to see God's hand in fortuitous events that could be explained in natural or human terms. Yet, for the writers of all these compositions, the greatest miracle of all was the strength to endure martyrdom for the Old Faith.

The first Old Believer writers had every reason to carry on the tradition of Christian hagiography. Since the blood of the martyrs demonstrates the truth of the faith, the Old Believer communities needed their own prophets and martyrs to show that they—and they alone—still carried on the authentic Christian tradition. Moreover, unlike their more narrowly ideological treatises, hagiographic compositions provided compelling examples of saintly conduct for the faithful to emulate.

In the late 1660s and 1670s, Old Belief produced its first martyrs and established its own tradition of martyrology. From that time forward, the lives of the martyrs became an enduring feature of Old Believer cultures. Life and literature reinforced each other. The struggle for survival of a persecuted minority produced many genuine martyrs in imperial and Soviet times. Moreover, the hagiographic tradition provided the martyrs with an interpretative lens through which they could understand their sufferings. In many instances, miracles in the usual sense played a minor role in their hagiographic writings. Like all conservative Christians, Old Believers did and do believe that God intervenes in the natural order on behalf of the faithful. At the same time, the central emphasis of much Old Believer hagiography, including the earliest examples, lies in the lesson and examples (*exempla*) of martyrdom, the requirement that the faithful remain resolute, vigilant, and willing to suffer death in defense of the faith.

EIGHTEENTH- *and* NINETEENTH-CENTURY COMMUNITIES

Old Believer Communities
Ideals and Structures

THE FOLLOWING ANALYSIS AND ARGUMENTS rest on the fundamental assumption that the Old Believers, both priestly and priestless, are best understood as Eastern Orthodox Christians. As they built their communities they saw themselves primarily as the guardians of a more authentic variant of Russian Orthodoxy than that of the official church. Comparison with other forms of Christian belief and practice, particularly Protestantism, can be enlightening but, if taken too far, distorts our understanding of Old Belief.

If our assumption is valid, the experience of the diverse branches of Old Belief in organizing their common life and worship offers us a window into the range of possibilities within the Russian Orthodox tradition. For, given the extremely difficult circumstances in which the Old Believers lived for most of their history, they developed a wide variety of structures to provide themselves with spiritual comfort and mutual support. These reflected the political, economic, and regional circumstances different communities had to deal with. In times of persecution, for example, smaller, more flexible structures were better suited for the struggle to preserve the faith, while in relatively peaceful times larger and more elaborate organizations provided the faithful with a richer liturgical and communal life. The structure of the Old Believers' communities also gave expression to their widely divergent understandings of how true Orthodox Christians could and should live in the End Time—a source of many of the divisions within the movement.

As we shall see, Old Believer communities combined elements of the cenobitic monastery or convent, the idiorrhythmic monastic community, the *skit* (an isolated monastic community), the lay parish, the charitable institution, and the peasant village. Which of these elements predominated varied with the intentions of their leaders and the changing social and institutional structures of the larger society within which the Old Believers were living. Thus, the predominant modes of organization changed over time. Until the late eighteenth century, the most prominent model was the cenobitic monastery. Throughout the nineteenth century, the recognized centers of Old Belief were parishes with charitable institutions in the main cities of the empire. But until recently the most durable form of organization has been the skit. Strictly speaking, a skit is a small, remote monastic community. In Old Believer usage, however, the word has sometimes meant any small, remote settlement of the faithful or even, in some instances, communities of considerable size.[1] This flexible use of the term precisely reflects the "mutual penetration of the skit and the lay peasant settlement" that historians and ethnographers have encountered everywhere among rural Old Believers from the beginning of the movement.[2] Of course, in practice, none of these ideal organizational types existed in pure form. In many instances, Old Believer organizations are very difficult to characterize neatly, for their greatest strength has been their adaptability.

Moreover, the following discussion may not truly reflect the day-to-day reality of Old Believer life. It rests on selected statements of the Old Believers' ideals and intentions and on normative documents such as monastic rules and communal regulations. Both types of sources show how the Old Believers aspired to organize their communities and create authentically Christian ways of life. By definition, they leave out the messier problems and less desirable forms of behavior that occur when any human institution inevitably falls short of its ideals.[3] Some historians argue that, if a normative document repeatedly condemned a certain kind of behavior, it was probably a real problem for the community in question. This assumption seems to me risky, however: repeated prohibitions may just as well reflect the literary prototypes on which the rule is based or the values—or obsessions—of the rule's author. In the present state of our knowledge, there is really no escape from this dilemma. The published reports of government investigators tend to view Old Believer practices and morals in a very negative light. Nineteenth-century officials' repeated accusations of widespread sexual promiscuity among Old Believers, for example, seem to arise largely from the fact that most of them refused to marry in the official Orthodox Church and the priestless accords had only informal substitutes for the Sacrament of marriage, or none at all. Thus even in traditional and outwardly respectable family relationships, almost all Old Believers canonically "lived in sin." Other than their leaders' own statements and official reports, we have little reliable information about the inner life of Old Believer communities; many potential sources in state archives and the unpublished records of the communities themselves, where they survive, remain to be explored.

Through most of the movement's history, Old Believer communities had no officially recognized status. As "unofficial" religious institutions, they governed their own affairs independent of any hierarchical structure or national organization.[4] As is well-known, the priestless branch of Old Belief—those who rejected the possibility of maintaining an authentically Orthodox clergy after the death of the last priests consecrated before the Nikonian reforms— lacked a central locus of authority and experienced an unending succession of schisms over such vital issues as the possibility of Christian marriage and relations with the Russian state, the domain of the Antichrist. From these divisions emerged the largest priestless groups, the Fedoseevtsy and Pomortsy, who assumed a distinct identity at the beginning of the eighteenth century, and the Filippovtsy, who split with the Pomortsy several decades later. Although the decision of all priestless accords to live as Orthodox Christians without clergy hardened into a tradition, their stance should be understood as a tactical response to the ultimate emergency—the End Time—and not as the adoption of a new understanding of the relationship between the believer and God and his fellow Christians. Again and again, most recently in the last two decades, priestless Old Believers have displayed a yearning for the restoration of a full sacramental life, if only a truly Orthodox clergy could be found.

The determination of the priestly accords to continue celebrating all the sacraments led them to retain or, if necessary, re-create traditional structures of authority. Until the mid-nineteenth century, priestly Old Believers maintained a clergy by receiving fugitive priests from the official Orthodox Church. Since these *beglopopovtsy* did not have bishops, however, their organizational structures resembled those of the priestless groups and responded primarily to local concerns. Moreover, because fugitive priests were difficult to recruit and their credentials often appeared dubious in Old Believer eyes, the priestly communities continually searched for a way to reestablish the episcopate. Finally, in 1846, a deposed Bosnian bishop, Amvrosii, agreed to join the Old Belief and lead a diocese from Belaia Krinitsa in Bukovina, then part of the Austrian Empire. Amvrosii soon consecrated other bishops and priests. Many Old Believer groups had deep suspicions about the canonicity and Orthodoxy of the new primate, centering on his non-Russian origins and complicated background and the fact that, contrary to canon law, he consecrated other bishops alone. In spite of these doubts, however, the Belaia Krinitsa hierarchy attracted widespread support, because its creation restored both a full sacramental life and the traditional hierarchical structures of Orthodoxy.[5] Nevertheless, even among the Belokrinitsy, bishops had to deal with a well-established tradition of parish autonomy. Old Believer polemicists of the "Silver Age" contrasted the autonomous, active Old Believer parish, which they saw as the direct successor of the pre-Nikonian Russian parish, with the relatively powerless and passive official Orthodox parish of the day.[6]

One important branch of Old Belief lived on the frontier between the priestly and priestless traditions. The *chasovennye* became the predominant accord in the Urals and Siberia. They began as an offshoot of the Kerzhenets communities near Nizhnii-Novgorod, which had flourished in the early eighteenth century and, like them, accepted fugitive priests. Over time, as candidates for the Old Believer priesthood became harder to find and many of the faithful had increasing doubts about their sincerity and morals, more and more of the chasovennye came to believe that the surest way to preserve true Russian Orthodoxy was to live without priests. In the end, their position carried the day. By the mid-nineteenth century, the chasovennye retained features of the *beglopopovshchina,* in theory, but functioned as priestless in practice; and in recent times, its adherents' attitudes and practices have closely resembled those of the more radical priestless traditions.[7]

Apart from the Belokrinitsy, Old Believer communities, lacking hierarchical structures of authority, allied themselves with one another voluntarily and settled issues through consultation, negotiation, and debate. Following Orthodox tradition, most of the accords or branches of the movement relied upon local councils to set standards for worship and Christian conduct and to settle disputes among the faithful. These councils were made up, of course, not of bishops but of the monastic or lay leaders of local communities. In other instances throughout their history, Old Believers used less formal negotiations or exchanges of polemical writings to address issues in dispute. Even within highly structured communities with forceful leaders such as Vyg, the traditional center of the Pomortsy, major decisions required discussion with and approval by the members of the community.[8]

Two examples illustrate this tradition of consultation. The first is the long debate among and within the priestless accords over the possibility that true Christians could legitimately marry in the absence of clergy. An Old Believer council formally debated the issue in Novgorod in 1694. Then

Feodosii Vasil'ev and Ivan Alekseev, who both sought a way for Old Believers to marry, visited Vyg to debate the question in 1703 and 1728 respectively. Finally, toward the end of the eighteenth century, the spokesmen of Vyg and the leaders of the new Moscow center of the Pomortsy reopened the debate. These discussions took place in several forums such as face-to-face meetings at Vyg, exchanges of letters, and a series of councils, and they ultimately ended with the parties' agreement to disagree.[9] In the second case, N. N. Pokrovskii has charted the history of the councils of the chasovennye, scattered in small communities across Siberia, from 1723 to 1994. Their protocols record debates of the utmost seriousness about issues ranging from central questions of ecclesiastical organization to minute details of the daily life of a true Christian.[10] In many instances such as these, councils and negotiations served only to reveal the irreconcilable differences among the participants and, in that sense, contributed to the frequent schisms for which Old Belief has been notorious.

Clearly, then, no individual or community could claim to speak for all Old Believers or impose common doctrines, liturgical practices, or forms of organization on the movement as a whole. Even the most important early centers of Old Belief, such as Vyg and the Moscow communities, achieved that position primarily through moral and cultural influence and the material prosperity that allowed them to aid their fellow believers.

Until the late eighteenth century, the most important Old Believer communities modeled themselves on the great cenobitic monasteries of Muscovy. In the clearest example, in their writings, the leaders of the Vyg community often referred to it as a *kinoviia* or *monastyr'* and claimed that it was the direct successor of the Solovetskii monastery. Moreover, in constructing its buildings and creating its liturgy and devotional literature, they followed the precedent of the most renowned monasteries of pre-Nikonian Russia as far as circumstances permitted.[11] Its organizational structure also followed the model very closely. Although the head of the community was called the *nastoiatel'* or *bol'shak*, he was chosen by the community as was the tradition in Solovki, and his role was very similar to that of the abbot in earlier cenobitic communities. There is, however, one significant distinction between the abbot (*igumen*) of a traditional monastery and the nastoiatel' of Vyg; the former was also the primary priest of the community, whereas the leader of a priestless community could not, by definition, fill that role.[12] The titles and functions of the other chief officials—cellarer, treasurer, *nariadnik*, who had responsibility for the economic ventures of the community and the workers in them, and *stroiteli*, who represented the community's interests in the main cities of the empire—copied earlier practice precisely.[13] To the traditional list of officers, Vyg added a *gorodnichii* to take care of visitors, supervise the residents' relations with the outside world, and watch over their conduct.[14]

Both the ideal type and the formal rule of cenobitic monasteries emphasize that all residents must work and worship together as equals. Ideally, all property belongs to the community, whose members are fed and clothed from common resources, according to need. It would be a mistake to take ideal types and normative statements absolutely literally. Institutional reality was somewhat more flexible. In spite of strict prohibitions on private property, including food and clothing, Solovki allowed its monks to keep their own books, icons, and money during their lifetime. Indeed, the cloister's devotional practices encouraged monks to keep suitable books in their cells for significant periods of time.[15] The rule for the Vyg monastery and the associated Leksa convent was, if anything, even stricter than those of earlier monasteries. It made absolutely clear that monks and nuns were not to have their own food, clothing, or money. At the same time, if the cellarer approved, individuals might keep gifts of clothing from their families. Icons that new postulants brought with them to Vyg might, at the cellarer's discretion, be placed in one of the chapels (or, by implication, might remain in the individuals' cells). While the Vyg rule does not explicitly address the question of books, it is reasonable to assume that, as in Solovki, the devotional requirements and cultural activities of Vyg would require some individuals to keep books—the community's or their own—in their cells.

Moreover, studies of Solovki and Vyg suggest that, after an initial period of extreme rigor, both communities enforced their rule less strictly and, in particular, that exceptions were made for affluent postulants and visitors. Indeed, L. K. Kuandykov has made the interesting suggestion that, from its beginnings in peasant egalitarianism, Vyg's increasing size and prosperity made it more and more similar to the great monasteries of the Russian North, with their elaborate hierarchical structures and economic enterprises. Neither the exceptions to the letter of the rule nor the evidence of greater laxity and inequality over time, in my view, contradicts the fundamental aspiration of these communities' founders and their successors to build and maintain a disciplined monastic way of life or their overall success in doing so.

In the last two decades, among the large volume of new Russian publications on Old Belief, a few scholars have attempted to resurrect the argument of nineteenth-century populists that communities like Vyg followed not the model of the cenobitic monastery but that of the northern peasant village. M. L. Sokolovskaia's work is a particularly clear example.[16] Although his articles take a more complex approach, Kuandykov nevertheless concludes his analysis of the Vyg rule in the first third of the eighteenth century by suggesting that "under the pressure of the peasant masses . . . there emerged a type of community more acceptable to peasants—a synthesis of an economic *artel* and a charitable institution [*bogadel'nia*]."[17] Even if we accept his assumption that the repeated condemnations of illicit eating, private property, and social contact between the sexes in the evolving rule indicates that these were persistent problems within the community, it is not clear what evidence he based this conclusion on. Unfortunately, to my knowledge, he did not publish the subsequent study in which he promised to spell out his argument.

The "neopopulist" scholars also emphasize the fact that, after the first generation, none of the leaders of Vyg or Leksa was formally consecrated a monk or nun even when that was possible.[18] In my view, this unquestionably valid observation in no way contradicts the aspirations of the Denisov brothers and their colleagues to create a cenobitic monastic community governed by a precise and elaborate rule.[19] Moreover, it ignores the tradition in many priestless groups of having prayer leaders, monks, and nuns consecrate others to follow in their footsteps. While not within the apostolic succession in a strict Orthodox or Roman Catholic sense, this practice amounted to "succession of a personal-spiritual [*pneumatischer*], but not an institutional-legal kind."[20]

Regardless of their historiographical underpinnings, recent publications have made significant new contributions to our understanding of the structure of the Vyg community and the ways in which it functioned. First, N. S. Demkova's edition of the full text of the interrogation of Tereshka Artem'ev in 1695 sheds additional light on the structure of the first Old Believer settlements in the Vyg valley and the attitudes of their inhabitants before a cenobitic community took shape. According to Artem'ev's testimony under interrogation, large numbers of Old Believers had moved from the surrounding area into the Vyg valley, a situation of which the authorities were already uneasily aware.[21] Artem'ev described two centers some distance apart. One was a loosely organized idiorrhythmic monastic community, in which men and women lived separately. Its leader, the fugitive monk Kornilii, directed the spiritual lives of the inhabitants and allegedly provided a form of the Eucharist, although he was not a priest. The second reflected the mixture of religious militancy and social banditry epitomized by the earlier raids on the Paleostrovskii Monastery and subsequent mass suicides in the name of the Old Belief in 1687 and 1688.[22] Old Believer laypeople, led by Daniil Vikulich (a disciple of the fugitive monk Ignatii, a leader of the first raid), lived in a heavily armed and fortified settlement, prepared for a siege and for self-immolation if resistance failed. According to Artem'ev, their militancy extended to raids on neighboring villages to spread the Old Faith, by force if necessary.[23] Even Ivan Filippov's history of Vyg, which presents the community's origins in a most respectable light, links Vikulich with the leaders of the raids on Paleostrov and tells how he organized a posse, followed a captured Old Believer, and rescued him from the guards who were taking him to prison.[24] It is a tribute to Andrei Denisov's extraordinary leadership that he was able to combine these two currents of Old Belief into a single highly organized community. At the same time, the history of Vyg is marked by a never-ending tension between the desire to build a stable refuge for the true faith and the impulse to confront the forces of the Antichrist whatever the cost.

Second, Elena Iukhimenko's exhaustive study of the literary culture of Vyg and Leksa and Kuandykov's articles on the evolution of their monastic rule provide us with a more nuanced understanding of these communities' growth and its consequences, and of the ways in which they adapted to their changing economic and political circumstances. As Kuandykov pointed out, when monastic communities achieve material prosperity and respectability (which, in Vyg's case, included de facto toleration), they tend to lose their founders' rigor and fire.[25] Iukhimenko's book demonstrates the increasing extent to which, in the last century of their existence, Vyg and Leksa came to depend on wealthy lay patrons elsewhere in Russia, particularly in St. Petersburg and Romanov. She attributes this need for outside support to the changing demographic structure of the communities. As they prospered, their populations rose, but the number of women and the elderly grew disproportionately. As a result, their leaders needed money to pay hired laborers as well as to meet the government's demands for double taxes and payment in place of recruits for the army. Thus, communities that were once largely self-sufficient had to rely heavily on charitable donations of wealthy supporters.[26]

Third, recent scholarship has underlined the remarkable complexity of the network of Old Believer settlements surrounding the main monastery and convent. These included a number of skity and *poseleniia* (villages) whose residents accepted the leadership of the "Vyg fathers." Some of the more remote skity were small monastic communities in their own right. Other skity combined features of a normal northern peasant village and a monastic community. According to the Vyg rule, a skit had a chapel and one or two monks who were responsible for conducting priestless services and seeing to it that the inhabitants observed all parts of the monastic rule except celibacy. Economically, some of the largest skity such as the Sheltoporozhskii concentrated on agriculture. Others were more specialized: the people of the Berezovskii Skit, for example, painted icons and fished but did not farm at all. The poseleniia were essentially peasant villages of Old Believers that owed allegiance to Vyg and were expected to contribute to meeting its financial responsibilities toward the government. With data from the first three eighteenth-century censuses (*revizii*), Sokolovskaia argues that about 99 percent of the peasants in the settlements around Vyg and Leksa originally came from the surrounding districts.[27] Moreover, once in Vyg's orbit, they moved, if at all, mainly from settlement to settlement within it.[28]

The capacity of the skit to combine elements of the monastic community and the village in many variations made it a particularly durable form of organization for rural Old Believers. As their later history demonstrated all too well, communities as large as Vyg and Leksa had both the advantages and disadvantages of their size. In times of peace and relative toleration, they had the skilled population and the economic resources to serve as vital organizational centers and cultural resources for fellow Old Believers all across Russia. In times of persecution, however, these characteristics made them easy targets. The government of Nicholas I succeeded in destroying Vyg, but the life of the skity went on.

In the present state of scholarship, we know far less about the internal structure of the other major concentrations of Old Believers in the eighteenth and early nineteenth centuries such as Kerzhenets; Vetka and Starodub in Belarus; and Irgiz in the lower Volga valley. For one thing, the brevity and lack of precision of the sources at our disposal sometimes make it difficult to tell whether Old Believer settlements in these areas were monasteries like Vyg or skity.

In Vetka and Irgiz, some monastic communities grew to considerable size. One Vetka monastery, the Lavrent'ev, reportedly had more than one thousand monks in the mid-eighteenth century and a nearby convent had a hundred nuns.[29] The Lavrent'ev maintained a very strict rule with one exception that distinguished it from Vyg—its wealthiest members kept their private property.[30] Others had more than two hundred monks, while in each of the women's settlements lived about thirty nuns and numerous laywomen.

Scattered throughout the frontier areas of Vetka and Starodub were many smaller settlements of various types. Some of them resembled Vyg in its very first years in that they brought together Old Believer monks or nuns and fugitive laypeople. Moreover, small skity of monks and nuns and settlements of Old Believer peasants and their families existed side by side. Indeed, in some instances, very small communities of nuns or monks lived inside lay villages.[31]

The priestly Irgiz monasteries, settled initially by refugees from Vetka, bore a closer resemblance to Vyg at its zenith. At their height in 1828 the three main monasteries, the Upper, Middle, and Lower, and two convents, the Uspenskii and Pokrovskii, had a total of about three thousand monks and nuns. The men's communities were cenobite monasteries led by elected abbots and councils of elders. Two other officers worked with the abbot—a treasurer and an *ustavshchik*, who supervised the internal life of the community and enforced the monastic rule. Early in their history, the leaders of the Irgiz monasteries strictly prohibited private property and maintained common worship and a common table. As these communities grew in size and prosperity, however, they too relaxed their initial rigor. From their foundation, the Pokrovskii and Uspenskii convents had a looser, idiorrhythmic structure and, unlike Leksa, had no formal ties to the men's communities other than the exchange of the products of their farming and handicraft work. Prominent laymen from outside had a stronger influence over the decisions of the leaders of the Irgiz communities than was the case in Vyg, except perhaps in the final decades of the latter's existence. Although we have too little detailed information on the monasteries in Vetka and Irgiz to make a definitive judgment, it would seem that Vyg, at its height, most closely followed the pre-Nikonian model of a cenobitic monastery.[32]

All the large monastic communities of the eighteenth and early nineteenth centuries share two important characteristics. First, whenever possible, they provided books, icons, vestments, and in the case of Irgiz, priests for their followers throughout Russia, and they provided the children of the faithful with traditional Orthodox schooling.[33] Second, because of their size and visibility and their role in spreading the Old Belief, the imperial government eventually destroyed them in one way or another. The authorities closed the Vetka communities by force in 1735 and again in 1764, although the Lavrent'ev Monastery survived. The gendarmes of Nicholas I closed Vyg and the Upper and Middle Monasteries of Irgiz and forced the Lower Monastery to join the *edinoverie*, a uniate church created in 1800 by the secular arm in the hope of bringing priestly Old Believers into communion with the official Orthodox Church.[34] Understandably, after the mid-nineteenth century, the Old Believers built no more cenobitic monasteries as large and complex as Vyg.

Nevertheless, throughout the history of Old Belief, the ideal of the classic cenobitic monastery retained its power. Even in twentieth-century Siberia, the chasovennye would still have preferred to build large monastic communities like Vyg if circumstances had permitted.[35] In some instances, later Old Believer communities retained some of the features of the great monasteries of the past, albeit on a smaller scale. For example, migrants from Irgiz created a number of monastic skity in the Cheremshan area near the lower Volga. Some of them reached a significant size: at its largest, the Uspenskii Skit had 130 monks.[36] The Kurenevskie monastery and convents in Podolia, although small, took very traditional forms. The men's community, in which 128 monks, novices, and laymen lived at the beginning of the twentieth century, followed strictly cenobitic patterns. Its organization had many traditional features, including an abbot, treasurer, and council. The first of the two convents, which had as many as 42 nuns and novices, followed more idiorrhythmic practices, under which the sisters did not keep a common table and owned personal property. The second convent, founded in 1908 by the energetic Abbess Faina, appears to have been more tightly organized. In spite of their differences in structure, both convents customarily deferred to the decisions of the monastery on the most important issues, and all three of the Kurenevsk settlements owed ultimate allegiance to the national center of the Belokrinitsy in Moscow. The last remnants of monastic communities in Sheremshan and Kurenevsk survived into the late 1920s and early 1930s, respectively. The end of the Kurenevsk monastery was particularly brutal: in the horrible conditions of 1933, local "activists" took its books and icons for firewood or lumber for a pig barn and the few remaining monks starved to death.[37]

The emergence of the Preobrazhenskoe and Rogozhskoe Kladbishcha and the Moninskaia Molennaia in Moscow in the reign of Catherine II radically changed the balance of power within Old Belief in several ways.[38] First, they were located in the second city of the empire, the historic capital of Orthodox Russia. Second, they were in essence parishes consisting largely of laypeople, not monastic communities. Third, because of their central location and their founders' energy and wealth, they quickly assumed leadership within the movement. On controversial issues such as the canonicity of marriage, older communities like Vyg found themselves on the defensive, responding to initiatives from Moscow.

For a variety of reasons, the Moscow centers combined many elements in complex patterns. First of all, they belonged to different branches of Old Belief. The priestly Old Believers of the Rogozhskoe community strove to follow the traditional Orthodox structure of bishops and priests and to retain all of the sacraments of Eastern Orthodoxy. Until the middle of the nineteenth century, like all of the priestly, they had no hierarchy of their own and depended entirely on fugitive clergy. As an escape from this dilemma, the leaders of Rogozhsk welcomed the establishment of the Belokrinitskaia hierarchy; the community eventually became the residence of the Old Believer archbishop of Moscow. The Preobrazhensk and Moninsk communities belonged to the Fedoseevtsy and Pomortsy priestless accords, respectively. Lay leaders conducted the prayer services of these parishes (in Western terms, an elaborate form of the Ministry of the Word without the Eucharist) and administered such sacraments as their accords had saved from the ruins of authentic Orthodoxy—baptism and in the case of Moninsk, marriage. Preobrazhensk had a reputation for the extreme rigor and precision of its services as well as for its militancy in rejecting all possibility of Christian marriage and prayers for the imperial family.[39]

Second, these communities registered themselves legally as cemeteries (*kladbishcha*) and almshouses (*bogadelennye doma*), not parishes, whence their official titles and popular names. For one thing, Old Believer parishes and monastic communities, even those that enjoyed de facto toleration in the late eighteenth and early nineteenth centuries, were illegal. Moreover, the circumstances in which the Moscow communities emerged from underground underscored their role as charitable foundations. In 1771, at the height of the terrible epidemic of cholera in Moscow, both Il'ia Kovylin, the formidable founder of Preobrazhensk, and the leaders of Rogozhsk received permission to set up quarantine blockades on the outskirts of Moscow, hospitals to care for the sick, and cemeteries to bury the dead. In dealing with officialdom in the comparatively tolerant times of Catherine II and Alexander I, they operated within the legal guidelines for all charitable institutions and carefully created the impression that they ministered only to fellow Old Believers. The leaders of the synodal church, however, suspected with considerable justification that service to the sick and needy often led to conversion to Old Belief.

The circumstances of their founding dictated that the Moscow communities would be complex institutions composed of many elements. Throughout their history, they maintained almshouses, hospitals, and cemeteries. Somewhat less conspicuously, their chapels and prayer houses functioned as parish churches that served the needs of the priestly and priestless Old Believers of the city. Moreover, the visibility that their legal status gave these communities made them the most important centers of their respective accords in all of Russia.

Throughout their checkered history, the status of charitable institution saved the Moscow communities from extinction in difficult times. The history of their relations with the imperial government followed exactly the same patterns as those of the other Old Believer centers. After the years of de facto toleration under Catherine II and Alexander I, the imperial regime began to attack on several fronts. In Alexander's last years and the reign of Nicholas I, the government prosecuted Old Believer priests, closed the churches and chapels or gave them to the *edinovertsy*, arrested and exiled their leaders and prominent lay supporters, and put the charitable institutions under its direct control. Like Vyg, Moninsk did not survive the assaults of Nicholas's gendarmes. Preobrazhensk and Rogozhsk bowed before the storm, but lived on, reemerged into the open as charities beginning in the reign of Alexander III, and enjoyed a "golden age" of freedom of worship and social ministry between 1905 and 1917.

Third, prominent merchants and other laymen established and ran the Moscow communities. Lay leadership was a central feature throughout Old Belief in the late eighteenth and nineteenth centuries. As we have noted, even in monastic communities such as Vyg and the Irgiz settlements, wealthy lay supporters exercised more and more influence as the years passed. In Preobrazhensk and even in priestly Rogozhsk, the ultimate authorities were the lay overseers, not the clergy.

What were the aspirations of the founders of the Moscow communities? In spite of the Old Believers' reputation for dealing with the government in a devious manner, Il'ia Kovylin was remarkably honest in a petition to Alexander I in 1808. In the plan for Preobrazhensk that accompanied his request to renew the community's legal status as a charitable institution and his appeal for freedom from outside interference, he claimed that its central mission consisted of serving ill, elderly, and orphaned Old Believers' physical and spiritual needs. "The times and circumstances demand that we build almshouses and hospitals for the care and tranquility of elderly and sick Old Believers and orphan children and a chapel in order to offer prayers to Almighty God according to the stipulations of the old printed books [*staropechatnye knigi*]."[40] In another passage, he described the community's objectives as "to conduct services unhindered according to the ancient regulations and rule of the Holy Fathers laid out in the old books and to provide a safe refuge for the needy among our brethren."[41] He also made clear that the community provided housing for craftsmen such as carpenters, stonemasons, and plasterers temporarily in Moscow without their families. If Kovylin's statements misled the government, it was only in deemphasizing the importance of Old Believer worship and ignoring the possibility that service to the needy could be a form of missionary activity—understandable tactical choices under the circumstances.

In spite of their prominence, there has been until recently relatively little detailed information about the inner structure and workings of the Moscow communities. Historians and polemicists have paid much more attention to the merchant dynasties that supported them and the polemical battles among them. Fortunately, we have many physical descriptions of the communities' buildings and sketches of their organizational structure at various times in their history. For example, Kovylin's plan describes a community of about eight hundred residents in two sets of buildings separated by inner walls. In one lived elderly and ill men and the out-of-town craftsmen who lodged there; in the other were the women and the orphans. The community committed itself to educating the children in reading, writing, industriousness, and a useful trade through which they could support themselves. The orphans were to remain in the community up to the age of seventeen when they were expected to move out. Each section had its own chapel or prayer rooms. A group of guardians (*popechiteli*)—all successful businessmen and honorable citizens, Kovylin insisted—administered the community. One of their most important functions was to manage the bequests to the community by investing them wisely or lending them to reliable borrowers.[42] Although Kovylin's plan mentioned these activities in the form of a request for official approval, acceptance of bequests and making loans were probably already well-established practices in Preobrazhensk. For one thing, those Fedoseevtsy who took seriously Kovylin's teachings on the impossibility of canonical marriage either remained celibate or lived in informal unions and therefore could not have legitimate heirs. For many, the logical heir was Preobrazhensk.

T. D. Goriacheva's and E. M. Iukhimenko's new studies give us detailed analyses of the Rogozhskoe community in the nineteenth and early twentieth centuries. Although they describe a priestly community, their findings are remarkably similar to Kovylin's and P. G. Ryndziunskii's less detailed descriptions of Preobrazhensk and to Goriacheva's comparative data on the Chubykinskii almshouse in St. Petersburg. According to Goriacheva, the number of residents of the community ranged from more than 1,000 in the 1830s to 444 at the beginning of 1918. Iukhimenko states that the Rogozhsk almshouse had 558 residents in 1872 and 730 in 1877, with a heavy predominance of women.[43] In the mid-nineteenth century, Preobrazhensk was slightly larger: it had 508 male and 1,119 female residents. According to the documents defining the legal status of Rogozhsk, all residents had to be Old Believers by family tradition, legal residents of Moscow, and poor or ill. In both Rogozhsk and Preobrazhensk, the number of parishioners who lived outside the walls of the community ran into the thousands. According to one rough estimate, Preobrazhensk had up to 10,000 parishioners in 1819.[44] In 1841, according to official records, the priests of Rogozhsk served as confessors for 3,028 parishioners. The real number was clearly much higher. According to Iukhimenko, Rogozhsk had about 20,000 parishioners at the beginning of the nineteenth century, and the figure rose to between 35,000 and 68,000 in the 1820s.[45]

The structure of governance of the Moscow communities reflected their legal status as charitable institutions. Even in priestly Rogozhsk, all of the recognized officers were laymen.[46] There all the parishioners who owned property in Moscow had the right to choose electors (*vybornye*) of whom there were thirty in 1869. The electors in turn selected two popechitili, normally wealthy businessmen, for three-year terms to manage the community's finances and the care of the residents. The electors were to see to it that these guardians carried out these duties responsibly and had the right to replace them if they did not. Under the *Ustav* (Regulation) of 1883, the council of electors also chose three priests and two deacons to celebrate the sacraments. The number of clergy rose steadily to six priests and three deacons in 1906, and in the fall of 1917 the community adopted plans to add still more.[47] Real executive power, however, clearly lay with the guardians, whose responsibilities included everything from the community's investment portfolio to the selection of singers for the choir. Their authority even over spiritual matters deeply troubled some Old Believers: in a newspaper article published in 1906 under the pseudonym *Staroverets* (Old Believer), a writer complained bitterly about the "oligarchic" guardians' power over the clergy at Rogozhsk.[48]

Even though the vast majority of the residents of Preobrazhensk did not follow a monastic rule, the guardians attempted to maintain strict order through a myriad of regulations enforced by officers whom they appointed. In this regard, their rigor—pedantry perhaps—resembles that of the Vyg fathers. Under their direction, an *ekonom* received and registered the bequests on which the treasury depended, and a *kontorshchik* kept the financial records and conducted official correspondence. A host of lesser officers made sure that residents and visitors to the community behaved appropriately. The *dvorovyi starosta* screened visitors and made sure that their paperwork was in order. They, the *storozha, nadzirateli,* and *nadziratel'nitsy* made sure that the residents attended services daily, returned to the community at an appropriate hour each evening, and observed proper decorum. They were to keep beggars outside the gates and away from the cemetery. To this structure the community in 1897 added the office of female guardians, who served for three years and had responsibility for the female residents as well as for the community's food and kitchens. In the same year, Rogozhsk also set up a board of female guardians.

Although our information is less detailed, the other urban communities apparently had very similar systems of governance. In the relatively small Chubykinsk community of St. Petersburg, the parishioners chose forty electors, who selected three guardians for five-year terms. In this instance, however, the guardians had authority only over the community's finances.

Parallel to the guardians was a governing committee of five members plus a chair, who handled relations with the outside world. In the St. Petersburg case, the distinction between the prerogatives of the guardians and the committee was not entirely clear.

In Preobrazhensk, the administrative structure had grown in complexity from Kovylin's time to the mid-nineteenth century. By then, the governing body of the community was a council of twenty-six men from whom were chosen the five guardians who, as in Rogozhsk, managed day-to-day administration. The wealthiest benefactors of Preobrazhensk normally became guardians, and even among them, one leader enjoyed overwhelming influence just as Kovylin had. In the mid-nineteenth century, that man was F. A. Guchkov, scion of the wealthiest Moscow business family.

Although the main Moscow communities and those in St. Petersburg were governed by laymen to serve lay parishioners and residents, we should not forget their monastic component. They usually contained the "cells" of at least a few *startsy* or *staritsy* (monks and nuns, literally "male and female elders"), especially the latter. In 1845, for example, 167 nuns and novices lived in five separate communities within Rogozhsk.[49] Later in the century, the Fedoseevtsy maintained an idiorrhythmic convent—labeled a "charitable institution" for the benefit of officialdom—on the outskirts of St. Petersburg.[50]

For the most part, the complex mixture of elements in the Old Believers' urban communities served them well. As their leaders hoped, for much of their history they provided thousands of parishioners with the full repertoire of worship services and carried out their charitable mission. Their imposing buildings provided an Old Believer counterpoise to the great cathedrals of the synodal church.[51] Like Vyg before them, they provided their followers throughout Russia with books and icons. And, as historians of the Russian economy have so often stressed, the Moscow communities, especially Preobrazhensk, provided credit for aspiring Old Believer entrepreneurs and sheltered peasant migrants to the city, who often became workers in the wealthy Old Believers' enterprises. In short, the Moscow communities' position as the predominant centers of Old Belief legitimized lay leadership and made the combination of parish and charitable institution the primary organizational model, particularly in urban areas. In the brief "golden age" of the early twentieth century when they were free to function with limited outside interference, the urban parishes of all of the main Old Believer groups enjoyed a similar degree of autonomy and initiative.[52]

To be sure, the experience of Preobrazhensk, Rogozhsk, and the other urban communities under Nicholas I and Stalin also demonstrates the vulnerability to attack of such centrally located, visible, and prosperous religious centers. Nevertheless, they have endured, and they remain to this day national centers of the priestless and priestly Old Believers.

After the October Revolution, priestly and priestless parishes continued to function. After a brief period of respite in which the new regime concentrated its antireligious fervor on the mainstream Orthodox Church, they faced the same trials and tribulations as all of the other major Christian denominations—arrests of leaders and active parishioners, confiscation of many church buildings, and pressure to follow the dictates of the Soviet regime. At the same time, if they met the state's requirements, they were at least able to continue public worship in some of their church buildings and maintain their traditional form of governance under the watchful eye of the Ministry of Religious Affairs. As compared with their Russian Orthodox counterparts, the Old Believers had the advantage of their long experience in adapting to hostile governments.

Roy Robson's study of the Grebenshchikovskaia Obshchina in Riga between 1945 and 1955 addresses several of the central issues that almost certainly affected Old Believer parishes throughout the Soviet Union. Founded in 1760, the Riga community closely resembled its model, Preobrazhensk in Moscow. Named in honor of a wealthy benefactor, it consisted of an almshouse and a large parish church known for the authenticity and rigor of its services and for its schools.[53] After 1917, of course, the history of the Riga Old Believers and their circumstances in Latvia differed significantly from those of their brethren in Russia. As Robson notes, the Grebenshchikovskaia Obshchina suffered severe persecution immediately after Latvia's annexation by the Soviet Union and during the German occupation. After the end of World War II, however, the community regained ownership of its main buildings, including the church and the attached living quarters, and reestablished its traditional structure of governance. All the same, relations with the Soviet authorities were a mixed blessing and the source of high tension within the community. During Stalin's last years, the leading Old Believer intellectual from Riga, I. N. Zavoloko, remained in the Gulag, and other arrests took place from time to time. Within the Obshchina, two factions struggled for power. The self-styled "progressives" under the community's rector, I. U. Vakon'ia, made good relations with the Ministry of Religious Affairs their highest priority and were not above sending the authorities regular reports on the internal affairs of the Obshchina. The conservatives, led by P. F. Fadeev and A. V. Volkov, strove for a more independent stance in order to preserve the priestless Old Believer tradition in all its purity. The clash of personalities as well as of programs led on occasion to stormy meetings, shouting matches, and competing liturgical observances. Not surprisingly, in the years Robson investigated, the progressive group maintained its leadership of the community.[54] As far as I know, the history of other urban Old Believer parishes in the Soviet period, including the main centers in Moscow and St. Petersburg, has yet to be written.

In rural areas Old Believer life revolved around skity, just as it had in earlier periods of persecution. Both ideological and practical considerations led to the persistence of this pattern of organization. In many cases, the founders and inhabitants of the skity consciously followed the urging of the hermits of the early Eastern Church to flee from a sinful word to the "desert" and a life of prayer and self-denial. N. N. Pokrovskii and N. D. Zol'nikova have pointed out that Siberian Old Believers received these teachings directly in translations of St. Efrem the Syrian (several of his sermons, particularly Sermon 105 on the Apocalypse, and "On admonition and repentance") and indirectly through the Old Believer literary and oral tradition. The more militant the Old Believers, the greater the lure of the pustyn'! Life in small isolated communities strongly appealed to the Filippovtsy and the more radical of the chasovennye.[55] And, for the *beguny* or *stranniki*, the most radical groups of all, flight from the world and all of its institutions was the only truly Christian way of life.[56] The skit also had practical advantages. Since it was a structure smaller, less visible, and more flexible than the monastery or the parish, it was especially suited to times of severe persecution and to branches of the Old Belief whose militancy made them special targets of the government. In Soviet times, rural Old Believers had little choice but to rely on it.

By the twentieth century, the Old Believer skit had an ancient and honorable history. Between the late seventeenth and mid-nineteenth centuries, government inspectors, attempting to control the movement's spread, had unearthed evidence of innumerable small settlements of Old Believers in remote corners throughout the Russian empire—in the European North, Belarus, the Cossack country, the Urals, and Siberia. They ranged from miniature monasteries in which the residents took vows of celibacy and followed a rule of life, under the direction of a monk or nun, to communities of devout laypeople led by a monk. As we have seen, some functioned as satellites of large monastic communities like Vyg and the Irgiz monasteries or were parts of a closely knit network of Old Believer settlements, while the founders of others opted for complete isolation in the most remote locations imaginable. In spite of this remarkable variety, all shared one characteristic—close relations with the local peasant population from which many of their inhabitants had come.[57]

Our best study of skity in the Soviet period appears in Pokrovskii and Zol'nikova's new book on the history and polemical literature of the chasovennye in the Urals and Siberia. As before, they were shaped both by the desire of their founders for a rigorous Christian life in the "desert" and by the policies of the government. Siberian skity were very small, most frequently of one to fifteen residents, and followed a cenobitic way of life with common worship, property, work, and meals. An individual hermit sometimes lived alone within a short distance of a small convent or lay village and served as its spiritual director. The largest, the Sungul'skii Skit in the Urals, which flourished in the 1920s and early 1930s, had up to forty residents. The number of residents of course varied with the circumstances: from the beginning of Orthodox monasticism in Russia, the charisma of the founder of a hermitage often attracted new disciples, thus gradually transforming an isolated settlement into a monastery.

In the Soviet period, residents of the Siberian skity often responded to persecution by migrating long distances to safer areas under extremely risky and arduous conditions. In the early years of collectivization, the migrations of devout Old Believers formed part of a larger pattern of resistance to the new order in the countryside. Given the mixture of pressures driving the migrations, the resulting settlements sometimes combined features of a monastic community and a peasant village. In one example of such a *kvasi-skit* (in Pokrovskii and Zol'nikova's phrase), a group of devout women lived together without formally becoming nuns. When it became clear that, as women living alone in a harsh environment, they could not support themselves, they moved in with their relatives' families in lay peasant settlements but continued to follow a disciplined celibate life. In other instances, women's communities depended entirely on the support of neighboring men's skity or on the nearby lay population, to which they provided spiritual direction.[58] In the most difficult times, the extreme flexibility of these arrangements was invaluable.

In addition, especially among the priestless groups, Old Believer villagers often lived normal lay lives in their commune or collective farm under the spiritual leadership of a lay *nastavnik,* whose authority they accepted—or on occasion rejected—as the spirit moved them. The community in the Pechora region described by V. I. Malyshev from documents of the mid-nineteenth century, for example, consisted entirely of laypeople who elected a *starosta* and nastavnik from among themselves to provide administrative and spiritual leadership.[59] This pattern has proved remarkably durable: participants in scholarly research expeditions have encountered it in recent years. In this situation, Old Believer villagers make special efforts to distinguish their faith and way of life from that of nonbelievers and adherents of competing

Old Believer factions. In the Upper Kama valley, for example, the priestless distinguished between the most rigorous believers, the *sobornye* (the elect), and rank-and-file Old Believers, the *mirskie* (the worldly). Under the leadership of *dukhovniki* and *ustavshchiki*, the sobornye held prayer services in private homes and set and enforced the strict system of taboos that mark off the faithful from the others.[60] How long these arrangements will continue to survive is difficult to say. According to I. V. Pozdeeva, Old Believer life in the Upper Kama villages has changed radically in the last few years.

Each of the fundamental forms of Old Believer organization has contributed to the survival of the movement. The remote monastic communities served as refuges and centers of organization in difficult times and provided the cultural resources—liturgical books, polemical defenses of the Old Faith, icons—to their scattered brothers and sisters throughout the empire. In the late nineteenth and early twentieth centuries, the leading lay parishes made the Old Believers a significant force in national life. And, in Soviet times, the remote skity and villages, along with the more traditional parishes (for all of their vulnerability) kept the faith alive in the face of unrelenting persecution.

In facing the challenges of life in the twenty-first century, contemporary Old Believers hark back to their earlier experiences, particularly in the "Silver Age" of the early twentieth century, in order to identify the patterns of organization and behavior that will best serve their needs. The much-discussed decision of many priestless communities in Russia and abroad to accept priests of one jurisdiction or another and to restore full sacramental life places the parish and the ecclesiastical hierarchy to which it owes allegiance at the center of Old Believer life once again. This may suggest that, in the best of times (few and far between in the Old Believers' historical experience), the parish with its associated institutions provides the fullest liturgical ministry and pastoral support for members of both priestly and priestless traditions. Whatever the future may bring, we may reasonably assume that the Old Believers will continue to adjust creatively to the world around them and draw useful lessons from their rich institutional history.

The Spirituality of the Vyg Fathers

THE OLD BELIEVERS—those Russian Orthodox Christians who rejected the liturgical reforms of Patriarch Nikon and the authority of the government, which supported and enforced them—have constituted a significant and often undervalued current within Russian religious life since the mid-seventeenth century. Founded in 1694 in a remote corner of northern Russia, the Vyg community quickly became the acknowledged center of the "priestless" branch of the movement.[1] Even more significantly, under the leadership of the brothers Andrei and Semen Denisov, Vyg took the lead in the creation of an entire cultural system for the scattered Old Believer population of the Russian empire. The Denisovs and other Vyg writers and artists produced polemical, devotional, and liturgical texts that drew upon the traditions of the Christian East and pre-Nikonian Russian Orthodoxy, early seventeenth-century Ukrainian apocalyptic compilations, and a growing corpus of original Old Believer compositions, beginning with the works of the earliest opponents of the Nikonian reforms, Avvakum, Deacon Fedor, Avraamii, and others.[2]

The goal of this chapter is to present a close reading of some of the most important writings of the "Vyg fathers" of the first half of the eighteenth century in order to identify the spiritual aspirations and devotional and moral practices that, in their view, should make up the central core of the life of the true Christian believer. In other words, the investigation centers on their "spirituality." Many writers who use this admittedly vague concept agree on its more important dimensions. The editor of a recent collection uses the word "spirituality" to refer not to theology as an intellectualized system of belief but to the believer's communion with God through prayer and "the outer life which supports and flows from this devotion." In a similar vein, G. P. Fedotov describes "spirituality" as "the religious life in its innermost and deepest strata, the life with God and all spiritual experiences arising from this source. Prayer is the center . . . of spirituality."[3]

The texts that form the foundation of this discussion include the *Pomorskie otvety*, Semen Denisov's *Vinograd rossiiskii* and "*Istoriia o ottsekh i stradal'tsakh Solovetskikh*," Ivan Filippov's history of the Vyg community, the vita of Elder Kornilii, a selection of the monastic rules governing the life of the Vyg community's central monastery and convent and the outlying settlements and work camps, and some of the Denisov brothers' sermons and panegyrics, including those quoted or summarized in the articles of E. V. Barsov and P. S. Smirnov.[4] With the partial exception of the *Pomorskie otvety*, which Andrei Denisov and his collaborators composed as a polemical response to spokesmen of the official Orthodox Church, all of these texts served primarily to inspire the pious reflections of the faithful.[5] The historical compositions, like the historical books of the Old Testament, served not to reconstruct events but to reveal God's relationship with his people, the community of faith. Moreover, all were couched in an exalted diction with elaborate rhetorical devices and complex rhythmic patterns, in order to inspire their readers and hearers and impress them with the seriousness of their messages.[6] The following discussion centers on the messages themselves and the probable intentions of the authors rather than on the ways in which the texts were received and understood.

Before searching the writings of the Vyg fathers for comments on the spiritual life, we should examine the historical and polemical framework they created to give meaning to the daily life and worship of the community. Russia alone, they argued, preserved the pure Orthodox Christian faith when other branches of Christendom fell into apostasy. Patriarch Nikon's reform of the Russian liturgy destroyed true faith in the last remaining Christian community, precipitated the Apocalypse, and forced the remnant of true Christians to take extreme measures to preserve the faith until the End Time. Some gave themselves up to torture and execution, like the first Christian martyrs before them. Others fled to the wilderness to create havens of true faith. When confronted by the authority of the imperial Russian state (the Antichrist), the monks of the Solovetskii monastery fought back to the death, while the advocates of self-immolation took their own lives in purifying fire rather than submit to its power.[7]

This simple historical scheme, central to the mythology of all Old Believers, revolves around a number of binary polarities. The struggle of Nikon and his followers against the defenders of the authentic Orthodox tradition and the contrast between ancient Christian piety (*drevletserkovnoe blagochestie*) and the newfangled liturgy and faith of the Nikonians are obvious examples.

Some of these polar opposites receive particularly elaborate treatment in the writings of the Vyg fathers and played a central part in shaping their understanding of the world and their place in it. One is the contrast of the "world" with its temptations to sin and apostasy and the way of the *pustyn'* (desert, wilderness, hermitage). The Denisovs repeatedly invoked the men and women of the early church—who preserved the true faith by flight from the world—as norms to be emulated.[8] Moreover, they were fond of recalling the image of the woman fleeing to the desert in Revelation 12:13–17 as a metaphor of their own situation.[9]

It is not difficult to understand the appeal of these images. In polemical terms, the example of the saints in the desert allowed Andrei Denisov to argue that his followers were true to the Eastern Christian tradition even though they lacked many of the external signs of a corporate religious life, a clergy, a hierarchy, and most of the sacraments.[10] Moreover, the woman in flight and the desert fathers and mothers of Christianity provided an alternative ideal to the Orthodoxy of bishops, parishes, and monastic communities built on the principles of this world, which Nikon had so easily and fatally corrupted.

Invoking the precedent of the desert fathers and mothers was no comforting exercise in self-congratulation. Believers in the desert, Andrei Denisov conceded, are still prey to temptation, and God is angrier with their sins than with those of the faithful who live in the world.[11]

A second polarity lies in a military metaphor, that of the soldiers of Christ in combat against the forces of the Antichrist. Semen Denisov's recently discovered tale of the Tara revolt of 1722 describes how the defenders of the true faith confronted the troops of the emperor, first with spiritual weapons and then with physical resistance, which led in the end to the deaths of some of them by their own hand. In this they followed the examples of the most militant defenders of the purity of Israel in the Old Testament and the Apocrypha, such as Phinehas in Numbers 25:7–13 and the Maccabees. Denisov saluted the rebels with an extraordinary mixture of epithets—"fiery enthusiasts for righteousness, fighters for Orthodoxy, brave warriors of Christ, true passion-sufferers, holy martyrs." Men who died in armed combat against the Antichrist were martyrs no less than those who suffered torture and execution.[12]

If a single image dominates the narrative texts of Vyg, it is that of martyrdom. The Old Believer communities derived their legitimacy from the early Christian martyrs and from their recent successors, the first victims of the struggle to defend the Old Faith whose memory they lovingly cherished. These men and women memorably displayed the qualities all Christians should ideally possess—the ability to distinguish true faith from falsehood and the courage to denounce evil and, if need be, to die the most agonizing of deaths in witness to that faith.[13] So profound was the reverence for the martyrs of the past that moderate Old Believer leaders such as the Vyg fathers had to struggle to restrain some of their followers whose yearning for martyrdom led them to actions that threatened the continued existence of the entire community.[14]

As the examples of the heroes and heroines of the *Vinograd rossiiskii* illustrate, the image and rhetoric of martyrdom contain within them yet another contrast of opposites. Consistent with the language of Christian hagiography, Vyg writings repeatedly describe the martyrs for the true faith as victims, nobly accepting a fate they have not chosen. Yet, at the same time, the texts emphasize the activism of the defenders of the faith. In the histories and martyrologies of Vyg, the Old Believers take energetic measures to proselytize and defend their cause—teaching, preaching, writing, and organizing. Even the victims of torture and execution fought back by attempting to escape and, when there was no way out, by using their interrogations and executions as a pulpit to preach resistance to the new order. In this respect, they were not so very different from those who took up arms in defense of the faith, such as the Solovetskii and Tara rebels or the peasants who seized control of the Paleostrovskii Monastery.[15] In the view of the Vyg fathers, the Old Believers took the initiative in the struggle for the soul of Russia. That the reality was often the reverse—that, as I have argued elsewhere, the Russian state often acted first and the Old Believers reacted to its initiatives—does not negate the power of the myth.

Militant activism, spiritual and physical warfare, the ideals of martyrdom— these, then, are some of the central themes of the Vyg texts. Reflecting on them helps us to understand the militancy, apparent fanaticism, and remarkable practical resilience of later generations of Old Believers, whose worldview they helped to shape.

Within this framework, the Vyg fathers set forth their ideals of Christian spirituality. By and large, their teachings reflected the aspirations of the Eastern Orthodox tradition as a whole. Indeed, many of their admonitions to a life of prayer, self-discipline, and good works would be suitable advice to Christians of any time or denomination.[16] More concretely, they drew upon many earlier Russian teachings on ecclesiastical structure and devotional practice. In their compositions, for example, one hears echoes of Nil Sorskii and Joseph of

Volokolamsk and their disciples. Although the two "schools" of Muscovite monasticism had more in common than some scholars and popular writers have recognized, their founders' writings on the spiritual life emphasize quite different things. Nil's "rule" and pastoral letters stress the cultivation of individual spirituality within a communal setting, whereas Joseph's concern centered on the spiritual well-being of the individual through participation in an orderly Christian community. As we shall see, the Vyg fathers inclined toward the latter position. They commended the practice of the "Jesus prayer," a pillar of Nil's devotional teachings, but did so within a vision of the spiritual life centered on the community rather than on the individual believer.[17]

For priestless Old Believers, like other Eastern Orthodox Christians, the life of the believer centered on rigorous observance of the liturgy. After the Nikonian reforms, Christian commitment meant, above all, preserving the authentic, pre-Nikonian traditions at all costs. As Semen Denisov put it in his hymn of praise to the defenders of the Solovetskii monastery, "Holiness is . . . the guarding of uncorrupted and full faith . . . These blessed ones observed the fullness of the faith, uncorrupted piety, unharmed Orthodoxy to the end."[18] In this context, the concepts "faith" and "liturgy" are virtually interchangeable.

For the priestless branch of Old Belief, however, preserving the true faith was easier said than done; for the painful admission that there were no validly consecrated Orthodox priests left in the world and no possibility of consecrating new ones left the bespopovtsy with only those parts of the traditional liturgical system that could be celebrated by the laity. Perhaps the Denisovs' greatest contribution to Old Belief was their creative adaptation of the Orthodox liturgy to the constricting presuppositions within which they worked. Reasoning that the destruction of true Orthodox Christianity within the official church of Russia and the advent of the Antichrist constituted the direst emergency imaginable, they retained the sacraments of baptism and confession by making use of the canons that allowed a layperson to perform these rites in extremis when no priest was available.[19] In spite of their ingenuity, however, the Vyg fathers lived with the painful awareness that the central core of Christian liturgy, the Eucharist, was closed to them.

Having preserved as much of the pre-Nikonian liturgy as their circumstances permitted, the leaders of Vyg saw it as the mainstay of an orderly and strictly moral way of life and of a Godly community. The corporate worship of Vyg was complex and time-consuming. The normal cycle of services consisted of morning prayer, hours, evening prayer, compline, and other short services (*molebny*). All-night vigils and other special services marked the great feasts of the church year.[20] Moreover, the leaders of the community continually admonished their followers to celebrate the liturgy correctly in an orderly and dignified manner "according to the canons."[21] In the tradition of earlier reformers within the Russian church, they took severe measures to guard against frivolity, disrespect, and carelessness during the community's frequent and lengthy services.[22]

The admonitions of the leaders of Vyg in times of crisis underline the centrality of corporate worship and prayer in the spiritual life of the community. For example, Semen Denisov described the defender's response at a critical moment in the government's siege of the Solovetskii monastery—to celebrate the liturgy correctly and with tears.[23] Similarly, in Vyg's own history, when faced with a bad harvest, the arrest of a member, or a confrontation with the government or the official church, its leaders called the residents together for special prayers.[24]

As among other Eastern Orthodox, private prayer, above all the Jesus prayer, occupied an important place in the Christian life.[25] In Semen Denisov's account, some of the captured Solovetskii monks suffered martyrdom with the Jesus prayer on their lips.[26]

Beyond this, Vyg texts give us little sense of the content of private devotions. In one striking exception, the vita of Kornilii gives a detailed account of his spiritual exercises while living as a hermit. At the appropriate hours of the day, Kornilii chanted particular psalms, sang hymns, and performed a fitting number of deep bows (*poklony*).[27] In other words, the passage describes private liturgical observances rather than spontaneous prayer or meditation. The rule of the Vyg community seems, in places, to suggest that private devotions, such as Kornilii's, were a less desirable substitute for corporate prayer. Rules for nuns who were at work away from the Leksa convent included the admonition that they pray together, not each by herself (*tako zhe da moliatsia vkupe, a ne sami sebe kozhdo*). Only if a sister could not join the others for worship was she to follow a stipulated regimen of prayers and bows alone.[28]

As their writings repeatedly emphasized, the Vyg fathers believed strongly in the efficacy of prayer.[29] Again and again, when describing the founders of the community or the early martyrs for the Old Faith, the Vyg fathers used epithets such as *velii molitvennik* (great in prayer).[30] Moreover, they urged their followers to maintain a prayerful attitude. One stipulation of the rule, for example, urges nuns to remain continually in prayer at meals, just as in church (*i iako v tserkvi tako sestry iadushchii prisno molitvu vo ume da derzhat'*).[31]

The Vyg fathers' writings and sermons, however, rarely explore the nature and process of prayer or instruct their disciples how to pray. Andrei Denisov's homilies on prayer are elaborate rhetorical compositions, in which, through cascades of images and numerous examples from scripture and the Fathers, he exhorts his hearers. They remind his followers of the efficacy of prayer, enumerate its rewards, and warn of the dangers of neglecting to pray. While their dignified verbal music may have inspired their hearers to more intense efforts, these sermons gave them few suggestions on how to pray, and for what. Indeed, it is unclear whether Denisov referred to corporate or private prayer or both.[32] The rest of the writings of the Vyg fathers and the actions of the community in moments of crisis strongly suggest that he spoke of communal worship and assumed that the liturgy itself would instruct his followers in the art of prayer.

The Vyg fathers also encouraged their followers to read the scriptures and other sacred texts. In his eulogy to his cousin Petr Prokopiev, Andrei Denisov mentioned among his virtues the reading, copying, and cataloguing of sacred writings.[33] The rule of the community enjoined literate brothers and sisters to read edifying books in times of quiet.[34] To make best use of time and to instruct illiterate brothers and sisters, the rules of the community often prescribed the reading aloud of edifying texts.[35] Which texts were read is not easy to specify. Clearly the Psalter was a favorite.[36] As scholars have long been aware, the leaders of Vyg collected a remarkably comprehensive library, which they used in composing their polemical and devotional works.[37] How many of these books and manuscripts they felt suitable to be read aloud is difficult to determine; it may well be that their own devotional writings were intended, among other purposes, for oral performance. The elaborate rhetorical constructions of their major narrative and polemical works resemble the style of their sermons, which evidently played a central part in the public life and worship of the community.

Consonant with the Eastern Orthodox tradition, the Vyg fathers placed heavy emphasis on the necessity of disciplining bodily urges through rigorous fasting and other forms of self-denial. Their writings frequently describe the martyrs of the faith as great "fasters" and recommended especially rigorous fasting as an appropriate response to crises that threatened the life of the community.[38] By way of contrast, Semen Denisov listed eating apart (*osoboiadenie*), indulging in pastry (*pirogoshchenie*), drunkenness, and smoking (*tabakopitie*) among the vices devoutly to be avoided.[39] In praising fasting, the Vyg fathers by implication admonished their followers to follow rigorously the normal Eastern Orthodox rules on diet. Exceptionally severe dietary practices, such as those observed earlier by the followers of Elder Kapiton, elicited their admiration but not their support. In praising the precursors of Vyg, for example, Semen Denisov admiringly described

Evfimii's extraordinarily severe ascetic regimen, including the refusal to eat meat, fish, and dairy products at any time in the church calendar.[40] He did not recommend such extremes to his own flock.

Among the lists of Christian virtues, *tselomudrie* (chastity) and purity also figure prominently.[41] The need to discipline the flesh, recognized in various guises in all branches of Orthodox Christendom, intersected with canonical problems. In the understanding of the Vyg fathers, most sacraments could no longer be celebrated since no validly consecrated priests existed. This meant that pious men and women could no longer enter into holy matrimony. In practice, then, chastity meant celibacy (*devstvo*), a condition of life the Denisovs often praised as the ideal for all of their followers.[42] The celibate life attracted the Vyg fathers not only as a solution to immediate problems of canon law but also—and probably more profoundly—because they aspired to create a holy community that would carry on the traditions of Eastern Orthodox monasticism. Understandably some of their followers found such counsels of perfection beyond their strength—as the Denisovs' polemical opponents within Old Belief pointed out in shocked tones. As far as we know, the leaders of the community and the brothers and sisters of the central monastery and convent practiced what they preached. Their attitudes are reflected in an intensely personal way in the confession of Ivan Filippov, one of the Denisovs' immediate successors as head of the community. In preparing for death, Filippov lamented among his many sins the fact that he had been married and had children before his conversion to the Old Faith. The violent language of his self-condemnation implicitly likens married life to the most sinful and disgusting of sexual practices.[43] Celibacy alone was appropriate for the true follower of Christ.

Finally, like earlier monastic writers, the Vyg fathers praised hard physical labor and sweat as signs of a pious Christian life.[44] Their emphasis on the virtue of hard work has tempted some scholars to see the Old Believers as Russian Calvinists.[45] This theme in their teaching grows from a very different root, however, not a doctrine of "election" but the ancient Christian ideal of disciplining the appetites and passions reinforced by the practical necessity of building and supporting a community of believers in a remote and hostile environment.

As though the day-to-day demands of the true Orthodox faith were not enough, each Old Believer faced the Last Judgment in an intensely personal way. Every year, before Lent, Vyg leaders read Andrei Denisov's sermon reminding their hearers that God would judge them for any failure to live up to the rigorous ideals of their community.[46] Even the most austere life of prayer and self-discipline, however, gave no guarantee of eternal salvation. The deathbed confessions of Ivan Filippov, Petr Prokopiev, Semen Denisov, and

Petr Onufriev, a resident of one of the outlying settlements of Vyg, betray a profound anxiety that all their prayers, fasting, and hard work may not have atoned sufficiently for their many grievous sins. Each felt the need to list his sins once more and ask forgiveness from his fellow believers.[47]

The narrative and prescriptive writings of the Vyg fathers give considerable attention to the role of women in the defense of the Old Faith. But did these male authors have a vision of a distinctive female spirituality? By and large, I would argue, they did not. Semen Denisov's sermon at the grave of his sister Solomoniia, abbess of the Leksa convent, used traditional female epithets to praise her character—"mother of orphans, joy of widows, refuge of the homeless, sweet consolation of the sorrowing." Turning to her practical activity, however, he lauded her for virtues that would equally become men, such as manly courage (*muzhestvo*), generosity, administrative tact, hard work, and rigor in her religious observances.[48] Likewise, his praise of the female martyrs to the Old Faith contrasted their frail female bodies, subjected to unspeakable tortures, with their bravery (again *muzhestvo*) and militancy in confronting their interrogators and steadfastly facing a cruel death.[49] Whether the women themselves saw the world and the realm of the spirit in different concepts and images we cannot tell. Having said this, it is only just to give the Vyg fathers credit for recognizing that "[n]ot only men, but the weaker part, women and girls, [defended] the ancestral faith most courageously and bore the cruelest of tortures."[50] Moreover, women such as Morozova, Urusova, and later, Solomoniia Denisova played a much more significant symbolic and practical part in the development of Old Belief than women within official Orthodoxy with its hierarchical male-dominated authority structure. Indeed, the prominent role of women in unofficial movements of religious protest and renewal in Russia is only now receiving the scholarly attention it warrants.[51]

There is, of course, much that the Vyg texts do not tell us about the spiritual life of the community's peasant followers. Ethnographic studies have repeatedly shown that the belief system of the faithful—both Old Believers and adherents of the official church—consisted not only of observance of the liturgical practices and moral strictures of the Orthodox tradition, often with local variations but also of a complex tapestry of folk beliefs, taboos, charms, incantations, and rituals.[52]

Apart from their understandable silence on such matters, the writings of the Vyg fathers are remarkable for their failure to probe the implications of the spiritual life or develop a distinct Old Believer spirituality. The latter is perhaps not surprising since the Old Believers regarded themselves as the last true defenders of the Eastern Orthodox tradition, a role that required fidelity and vigilance, not originality. Moreover, the apparent lack of interest in the spiritual life of the individual may also reflect the attitudes and concerns of all of Russian Orthodoxy in the seventeenth and early eighteenth centuries. Jesuit curricula and "Jesuit" architecture entered Muscovite Russia from Ukraine, the intense self-examination and dramatic spirituality of the early Jesuits did not.[53]

Nevertheless, it is striking how rarely the Vyg texts mention devotional practices except in stock phrases or in passing. The "rule" of the community is particularly interesting in this regard. The precise and laconic stipulations of the documents governing its day-to-day life stress the structure of the monastery and convent and the surrounding lay communities and describe the relations among them. Drawing up the "rule" was no mean accomplishment, for in so doing, the Vyg fathers combined traditional structures and practices of Eastern Orthodox monasticism into a unique mix, in effect creating a monastic community of a new type.[54] At the same time, the rule gave little explicit attention to cultivation of the members' spiritual lives. Instead, in devotional matters, the Vyg fathers took a decidedly practical tack, issuing detailed instructions on proper behavior during public worship and in private devotions and setting out the punishments for breaches of liturgical propriety.[55] In an equally matter-of-fact vein, many of its provisions dealt with such down-to-earth problems as how to preserve chastity by keeping the "fire" away from the "straw" at all times, or how to keep the members of the community's work parties in a properly pious frame of mind while away from home.[56]

The strengths and limitations of the rule and of Vyg spirituality stem primarily from its leaders' main goal—building a holy community to preserve uncorrupted Orthodoxy. The Vyg fathers put on the mantle of the saints of the desert, a claim reflected in the name they often gave their community (the *Vygovskaia pustyn'*). The mantle fitted imperfectly, however. Like their supposed precursors, the residents of Vyg lived in a remote and inhospitable place on the fringes of organized society. Like them, they frequently suffered persecution for defending the true faith. Yet the central image of the saints of the desert is an individual one, that of a hermit choosing a life of exceptional austerity in order better to contemplate and serve God. The spiritual life of Vyg was communal, expressed above all in the liturgy. In their writings, the Vyg fathers readily praised individuals of exemplary piety, yet their most insistent message emphasized loyalty to the true Orthodox tradition and to the community, which, in defending it, worked and prayed together.[57]

The Historical Framework of
the Vyg Fathers

ANY COMMUNITY THAT LIVES within the Judeo-Christian
tradition must have a historical understanding of human experience.
Christians and Jews share the conviction that God has acted and acts through
the ongoing events of human life. Moreover, the traditional Christian
understanding of history ultimately positions all significant events on a
continuum stretching from Creation through the climax of history—the life,
death, and resurrection of Jesus Christ—to the End of the World. The Old
Believers were no exception. In fact, they had at least two particularly urgent
reasons for seeking to define their place in the universal scheme of Christian
history. First, their movement arose in reaction to specific historical events
as well as broader institutional, social, and cultural changes in the fabric of
Russian life in the seventeenth century. Second, in their struggle to survive
and establish the legitimacy of their cause, they competed with several other
visions of historical development. Among these were the works of the second
half of the sixteenth and early seventeenth centuries containing what might
be called the Muscovite imperial vision of history, the historical assumptions
through which Patriarch Nikon justified his reforms, and the new historical
and cultural mythologies of the regime of Peter I. In short, the Old Believers
urgently needed a coherent understanding of history, a usable past.

As the intellectual leaders of Old Belief in the first half of the eighteenth
century, the Vyg fathers responded to the challenge with a series of
compositions, placing their community and its followers in the stream of

universal Christian history.[1] The purpose of this chapter is to analyze the broad historical framework in which the writers of Vyg set their concrete narratives of their community's development and their devotional reflections on the meaning of these stories.[2]

The Vyg fathers' view of history appears in its simplest form in the introduction to Semen Denisov's *Vinograd rossiiskii*.[3] From the moment of conversion under St. Vladimir until the middle of the seventeenth century, the Orthodox faith in the Russian lands was perfect and uncorrupted. In a word, Russia was "worthy to be called the second heaven." As Orthodox hierarchs from other lands and even Roman Catholic writers testified, Russian Christians did not esteem false wisdom but guarded a "sound faith and simple piety."[4] Monasteries flourished, and the country produced many saints, whose uncorrupted remains proved their sanctity.

Then God allowed Patriarch Nikon to corrupt Russia's faith. Driven by the promptings of Satan and his own demonic ambition, Nikon introduced novelties in worship and belief that destroyed true faith in the Russian church. Some of the faithful were not deceived. Beginning with Bishop Paul of Kolomna and Archpriest Avvakum and his friends, defenders of the true faith spoke out against Nikon and suffered martyrdom. Their acts of resistance inspired others, like the monks of the Solovetskii monastery, to fight against the new order in the church, and soon the whole country was engulfed in a chaotic struggle for the soul of Russia. It was to remind his readers or hearers of the sufferings of those early martyrs for the true faith and to draw inspiration from their heroic example that Denisov composed the individual reflections that made up his martyrology.

The framework in which Ivan Filippov placed his history of the Vyg community is very similar. Once again, the author begins with the assumption that Russian Orthodoxy remained pure for roughly seven hundred years, from the conversion until the Nikonian reforms. The activities of the Stoglav council of 1551 and the creation of the Patriarchate of Moscow in 1589 prove that the leaders of the Russian church guarded the true faith and that foreign witnesses recognized their achievement. Then the rest of the chapter comprises a detailed description of how Nikon's reforms destroyed the true faith and inspired its defenders to fight against the new order.

After a very brief reprise of these same themes, the second introductory chapter of Filippov's history emphasizes the central message of the entire work— the emergence of the Vyg community as a citadel of true Christianity in a corrupt and hostile world.[5] The founders of Vyg drew inspiration from the example and teachings of the early martyrs to the Old Faith. In particular, Filippov stressed that the new community was the direct successor of the Solovetskii monastery whose residents resisted the Nikonian reforms to the death.

Concentrating on this theme, Semen Denisov's "Istoriia o ottsekh i stradal'tsakh solovetskikh" serves both as a memorial to the martyrs of the Solovetskii monastery and a demonstration that Vyg was its true successor. The author presented his story in simple terms. From its founding, Solovki followed the principles of cenobitic monasticism with full rigor. The monks guarded the true faith uncorrupted, as demonstrated by the appearance among them of prophets, scholars, and martyrs. Like an earthquake, Nikon's reforms destroyed the true faith. In Denisov's account, the leaders of the monastery consistently refused, from the beginning, to use the new service books. At the same time, they sent representatives to Moscow in an attempt to convince the tsar and leaders of the church to let them retain pre-Nikonian practices. The tsar's government responded by sending troops to force the monks to submit. Rather than betray the true faith, the monks fought on and died as martyrs. The author described their sufferings in agonizing detail. Moreover, they urged the population of the surrounding areas not to accept the Nikonian reforms. Fugitives from the monastery spread the message of resistance directly, by preaching, fighting against government troops, or establishing their own hermitages as islands of true Orthodoxy. From their efforts emerged the Vyg community, the true successor to Solovki.[6]

Like all these texts, the story of the martyrs of Solovki relies on clear and simple dichotomies—true faith against the Nikonian liturgical reforms and the holiness of the defenders of Orthodox tradition in contrast to the corruption of their opponents. In Denisov's account, the motives of the heroes and martyrs of the Old Faith are above reproach. He repeatedly insisted, for example, that the defenders of Solovki did not oppose the tsar or the state as such.[7] Moreover, the defenders of the monastery accepted their fate with pious resignation in contrast to the greed and brutality of the besieging troops.

Denisov and Filippov's scheme of historical interpretation draws on the ancient Judeo-Christian tradition of "sacred history" (*Heilgeschichte*). Like their precursors, beginning with the authors of the historical books of the Old Testament, the Vyg fathers traced God's relationship with his chosen people through an examination of concrete historical events. The authors' primary purpose, however, was to give the reader an understanding not of the events themselves but of their theological meaning.[8]

Like other learned Christians, Russian bookmen had long been familiar with the models of the Old Testament and early Christian writers. The historical compilations and polemical works of the sixteenth and early seventeenth centuries drew heavily on the Old Testament and other classics of sacred history and interpreted the historical experience of the Russian lands as part of the cosmic scheme of human history ordained by Divine Providence.[9] In these interpretations, God achieved His purpose through the actions of the Muscovite church, the tsars and their advisers, and in the tales on the Time of Troubles, the Russian people as a whole.

In several respects, the Vyg fathers trod on new ground when they adapted the patterns of sacred history to the new conditions in which they found themselves. From the familiar materials of the Orthodox tradition and Muscovite Russian national history, they constructed a scheme of historical interpretation that legitimized the opponents of the Nikonian reforms and justified their continuing resistance to the established order in church and state. In that sense, the Vyg authors created their own tradition.[10]

Their view of history differed in very important ways from the writings of their Muscovite predecessors in the previous two centuries. Since the leader of the Russian church, Patriarch Nikon, had destroyed true Christianity and the tsar's government had supported his efforts, God could no longer shape the course of human history through the actions of the leaders of the state and the ecclesiastical hierarchy. Under the radically new conditions that followed the Nikonian reforms, the only real historical actors and actresses were the faithful guardians of true Christianity.[11] History continued to unfold only for the Old Believers.

At the same time, there is a profound irony here. For ultimately, the destruction of the Orthodox faith in Russia, the last bastion of authentic Christianity in the world, had brought history to an end and begun the first stage of the Apocalypse, the reign of Antichrist.[12] Strictly speaking, one could no longer write history at all.

Yet the writers of the Vyg school clearly felt the need to record the central events in the life of their community, to set them in a broader historical context, and to reflect on their meaning in the cosmic scheme of things. Writing a sacred history of their tradition and community forced them to struggle with the potential dichotomy between the banal and often unedifying realities of human experience and the exalted messages they wished to convey.

How well did they resolve this conflict? Since the ultimate purpose of sacred history is to reveal and illustrate theological truths, the factual accuracy of the narrative is, at best, of secondary importance. At the same time, sacred history purports to reveal God's action through the unfolding of real human events. In order to convince their readers or hearers of the truth of their message, the authors of sacred history cannot stray too far from the real historical experience of their community or accepted assumptions about human behavior. As we might expect, then, the Vyg fathers constructed their historical framework from facts, most of which later scholars accept as accurate. At the same time, their polemical purpose led them to ignore inconvenient facts contradicting their central arguments and to add the occasional hagiographical story that cannot be verified in the surviving sources. Moreover, the Denisovs' preference for an elaborate and exalted literary style led them to rewrite materials from earlier sources and their own compositions in a more and more abstract and complex language.[13]

Semen Denisov's story of the revolt of Solovki provides a convenient test of these hypotheses. The first feature of the work that strikes the modern reader is the abstract style in which Denisov tells his story. Much of the comparatively small quantity of factual material from which he constructs the narrative also appears in the works of modern historians of the revolt of Solovki.[14] In a recent article, E. M. Iukhimenko has gone far beyond her predecessors in showing the extent to which Denisov used written documents as well as oral testimony in his work. She has also found archival materials that confirm the veracity of previously unverified episodes in the work, such as the interrogation and martyrdom of the monastery scribe, Ivan Zakhar'ev.[15]

At the same time, Denisov carefully avoids all ambiguity. He portrays Abbot Varfolomei as a consistent opponent of Nikon's reforms, even though he appears, in reality, to have yielded to governmental pressure to accept the changes.[16] Denisov likewise ignores Nikanor's submission to the authority of the ecclesiastical council of 1667.[17] It goes without saying that Denisov's work makes no attempt to discuss the independent traditions of the Solovetskii monastery, its economic interests, or its history of stormy relations with the ecclesiastical authorities in Moscow and Novgorod. Finally, the stories that complete the work belong to the genre of hagiography rather than history.

In the *Vinograd rossiiskii*, the hagiographical elements occupy an even more prominent place. Denisov's primary purpose was clearly not to give his readers an accurate record of the lives of the first martyrs of the Old Faith but to inspire appropriate meditations about their lives and deaths as examples of Christian fortitude. It is all the more significant, then, that in Denisov's use of historical facts, this work is very similar to his history of the revolt of Solovki. In his meditation on Avvakum, for example, he mentions several of the most important episodes or events in the archpriest's stormy life but provides few concrete details (those chosen illustrate his spiritual qualities of fervor and steadfastness). The text contains two quotations of Avvakum's words. One—his rebuke to the ecclesiastical council of 1667—contains some of the same ideas as the parallel oration in Avvakum's "Life" but, in detail, differs substantially from the earlier text. The second speech does not occur in the "Life" at all.[18]

In the final analysis, the factual accuracy of the historical framework of the Vyg fathers was probably not of decisive importance to either the authors themselves or their readers. Far more significant were the simple polemical messages that the facts were selected to illustrate.

As far as we can tell, the Vyg fathers had no intention of writing "scientific" history in the modern sense. How can we in the late twentieth century assess their achievement as historical writers? Without question, the writers of the Vyg school provided their followers and later historians with invaluable material on the history, structure, and convictions of their own community. As examples of sacred history, however, the histories of Vyg have quite different textures. The works of Ivan Filippov and other Vyg writers of the mid-eighteenth century tell the community's story and present its teaching simply and directly.[19] By way of contrast, because of his fondness for rhetorical elaboration, Semen Denisov's compositions lack the clarity and forcefulness of the best examples of sacred history such as the historical books of the Old Testament.

Moreover, the sacred history of the Vyg school appears archaic beside other Muscovite Russian and Ukrainian historical works of the seventeenth and early eighteenth centuries.[20] Although they do not completely dispense with supernatural causation, works as different as Fedor Griboedov's history and Andrei Lyzlov's *Skifskaia istoriia* describe the events of human history primarily as the product of dynastic concerns or the political traditions and social customs of nations and communities.[21] It is also significant that, unlike more "secular" historical writings of the time, the historical compositions of the Vyg fathers contain comparatively few references to other historical works, ancient or modern. Instead, the authors usually resort either to standard Baroque allusions (such as, for example, to Homer) or to theological works on historical themes such as St. Gregory the Theologian's sermon on the Maccabees, a hymn to martyrdom.[22]

The strength of the historical framework of the Vyg fathers (and especially the works of Semen Denisov), then, lies not so much in the acuity of their historical analysis as in the religious messages their historical works conveyed, the rhetorical power with which they presented them, and the depth of conviction with which they held them.

In formulating the historical framework in which to view the development of their movement and communities, the early leaders of Old Belief provided their followers with a rudimentary but powerful ideological weapon. The attractiveness of this historiographical scheme cannot be denied. It captivated many generations of Old Believers and exercised a powerful influence over scholars who studied the tradition from outside.[23]

The structure of the frame also contained fundamental weaknesses. It had no room for inconvenient facts or subtleties of interpretation. In broader terms, moreover, it rested on a curiously ahistorical presupposition, namely, that the historical development of Russia had in effect stopped with the reforms of Patriarch Nikon, and the End of the World had begun. Thus the scheme allowed Old Believer historians to describe the further development of the faithful remnant of true Christians—their own people and communities— but provided no tools for dealing with developments in the wider world except insofar as they impinged directly on the life of the faithful. In other words, the historical framework of the Vyg fathers was not only a powerful polemical weapon but a cage that trapped their followers and contributed to their isolation from the wider world.

The Cultural Worlds of Andrei Borisov

IN RECENT YEARS, SCHOLARS have increasingly questioned the stereotypical view that Old Believer cultures were and are self-sustaining islands of traditionalism, isolated from the changing intellectual and cultural currents of Russian educated society.[1] Like most truisms, the perception that the cultural world of the Old Believers has resisted change and remained closed to the outside world has some merit. Since the origin of the movement in the church schism of the seventeenth century, most Old Believers themselves have been convinced that they preserve pre-Nikonian Orthodoxy and its way of life, uncorrupted in all essential details. Moreover, wherever they live, the rituals, customs, and taboos of the Old Believers continually emphasize their distinctness from the surrounding society. Scholars seeking authentic survivals of medieval Russian culture often take the Old Believers' self-perception at face value.

A great deal of evidence suggests, however, that while striving to preserve pre-Nikonian Orthodox worship and associated practices such as fasting, Old Believers have cautiously adjusted to the new ideas, technologies, and habits of the world around them. The endless debates and frequent schisms within Old Belief testify to this process of adjustment as well as to the liturgical and canonical difficulties of preserving historical Eastern Orthodoxy without an indisputably legitimate episcopate and priesthood. Both the spiritual and the intellectual leaders of the movement and their followers participated in this process of cautious adjustment to the outside world.

Interaction with the rest of society took at least two forms. In everyday life, Old Believers who did not live as hermits had to find ways of dealing with non–Old Believer neighbors and governmental institutions. Individuals and communities have solved this problem in a bewildering variety of ways. The second form of adjustment is much rarer and even more challenging. From time to time, individuals or groups within Old Belief have attempted to bridge the intellectual and cultural gap between their tradition and the educated society of their day by using its vocabulary and concepts to defend the Old Faith.

This study examines a figure who, in my view, made such an attempt— Andrei Borisov, head of the Vyg community from 1780 to 1791. Borisov lived in two cultural worlds. As the heir to the rich cultural heritage of Vyg, Borisov's primary role was inevitably that of guardian of the legacy of the first generation of Old Believer leaders and writers and the early leaders of Vyg itself. At the same time, in writings and in conversations with outsiders to the community, he attempted to defend the position of Vyg or Old Belief in general with rhetoric and concepts drawn from contemporary philosophical and scientific discourse.

Borisov's own writings are the primary source of evidence about his convictions and rhetorical strategies. V. G. Druzhinin's catalogue of Old Believer literature attributes nine works to him, all of which survive in a number of copies. These include a composition on the split between the Pomortsy and Fedoseevtsy ("O nachale polagaemom v razdelenie"); "In Praise of Chastity"; the Life of Andrei Denisov; the composition on prayer for the ruler sometimes known as "O imenekh prilagatel'nykh"; a sermon on the same subject; three sermons on the dedication of buildings in Vyg or Leksa, rebuilt after the fires of 1787; and a tale (*povest'*) on the same theme.[2] Druzhinin also lists the sermon on Pentecost previously mentioned in Pavel Liubopytnyi's catalogue of Old Believer writings. In other instances, it is difficult to reconcile Druzhinin's list with Liubopytnyi's.[3] Without question, several of the compositions mentioned by Liubopytnyi are not known to contemporary scholars. Finally, nine works of Borisov have come to light that are not listed by either Liubopytnyi or Druzhinin. In 1915 V. Belolikov published a letter to U. S. Potapov.[4] The others are the "Priskorbnoe povedanie";[5] an Easter sermon for the sisters at Leksa ("Chestneishim sviatochestneishiia kinovii postnitsam");[6] an untitled composition on moral philosophy ("Iskusnyi zhe vo uchenie moral'nom mozhet gradusy");[7] two short philosophical dialogues;[8] an untitled work that begins "Bogoliubiveishii ottsy i bratiia, izvestvuiusia vam";[9] and letters to Daniil Matveev and Paraskoviia Feoktistovna.[10] There is every likelihood that still more of Borisov's shorter works will come to light.

Borisov's writings must be read in the context of his life experience, above all his responsibilities as leader of the Vyg community. Yet, even though he was its last well-known leader and major writer, information about his biography is sparse and not entirely consistent.[11] If, as Liubopytnyi states, he was fifty-seven when he died in 1791, then he was born in 1734.[12] The son of a prosperous and pious merchant, he probably grew up in Moscow.[13] He apparently received a good traditional education, although the sources give no details. The orations composed in his memory state that as a young man he helped his father trade in grain and horses and showed such promise that a number of prominent merchants tried to arrange marriages with their daughters.[14] At this turning point in his life, however, Andrei Borisov chose a very different path. He first visited the Vyg community in 1754 and joined it permanently two years later.[15] He was accompanied by his mother, who had agreed with her husband to separate so that they could pursue their religious vocations.[16]

From the beginning, Borisov's education and learning served Vyg well. In a letter of January 23, 1769, Vasilii Danilov wrote to Borisov praising the latter's brilliance (*blistaiushchiia doblesti*) and erudition (*siiaiushchego v naukakh ... solntsa*) and referring to his leadership in the composition of a life of "our father," almost certainly the "Life" of Andrei Denisov, the greatest leader and scholar of Vyg.[17] At the same time, his learning aroused suspicions that his ideas were not entirely orthodox. In a letter of April 17, 1775, to Daniil Matveev, head of the Vyg community, Borisov complained that "slander against me is circulating to no purpose to the effect that I, the unworthy, have a tendency to step out of the traditions of the holy Fathers."[18] Although Borisov's later career indicates that he defended himself successfully against such accusations, one suspects that throughout his life he continued to struggle with the perception that so learned a man could not possibly maintain Old Believer principles and practices without compromise.

In March 1780, the men, women, and "hospital orphans" of the Vyg and Leksa communities selected Andrei Borisov as their leader (*nastoiatel'*). In what may have been a statement of sincere hesitancy or a ritual expression of Christian humility, Borisov at first declined. The members of the flock insisted that they wished to be "under his fatherly care" (*pod vashim otecheskim soderzhaniem i domostroitel'stvom*). The three groups of inhabitants—the residents of Vyg, the women and men of Leksa, and the orphans—signed separate appeals promising that those whom he chose would help him in leading the community, that the others would obey, and that a "general council" would discipline any who opposed his policies or caused any disturbance.[19] On these conditions, Borisov agreed to lead the community. The authority that the people of Vyg vested in him was reflected not only in his undisputed role as the spokesman and personification of the community but also in the elaborate ceremonial deference they accorded him.[20]

For the most part, the years in which Borisov led Vyg (1780–1791) were quiet. He assumed the leadership of a community that had long enjoyed stability, prosperity, and a position of leadership within Old Belief greater than even its size and wealth would suggest. Moreover, the government of Catherine II preached and practiced religious toleration. Persecution of Old Believers and most other religious minorities ended, and one by one the empress's government repealed the edicts of previous rulers that discriminated against them. Prosperity and toleration also posed challenges, however. Security and comfort threatened to undermine rigorous commitment to the defense of the Old Faith. Moreover, with the coming of toleration the Old Believers in the major urban centers, particularly Moscow, openly organized communities that quickly assumed the leadership of the main branches of Old Belief. For the first time, Vyg, in the cold northern forests, was as remote from the centers of Old Believer life politically and culturally as it was geographically.

In outlining the events of these years, the Vyg chronicle concentrates on the local triumphs and tribulations of a relatively serene, isolated community— the installation of a new icon or bell and the fires that regularly destroyed individual buildings in Vyg and Leksa. At the same time, its compilers took note of the governmental policies that affected the lives of its members.[21] On the national level, the news was good. On July 20, 1782, the government of Catherine II abolished the practice of collecting twice the regular capitation tax from openly practicing Old Believers.[22] In the following year, the government prohibited the use of the pejorative term *raskol'nik* in official documents.[23]

Pavel Liubopytnyi gave Andrei Borisov personal credit for these changes in official policy.[24] His claim must be taken seriously for two reasons. First, throughout his career as a leader of Old Belief, Borisov was known for his connections with the powerful of this world and his ease in their company. Funeral orations in his memory refer to regular contacts with powerful individuals in St. Petersburg and Moscow.[25] In his own letter to Daniil Matveev, Borisov described an occasion at the residence of Catherine II's minister and favorite, G. A. Potemkin, at which he defended Old Belief before leaders of the ecclesiastical hierarchy.[26]

Moreover, the Vyg manuscript tradition preserves clear evidence that Borisov met the governor of St. Petersburg Province, Ustin Sergeevich Potapov, corresponded with him, and used the opportunity to lobby for the repeal of laws that discriminated against the Old Believers. Apparently the two men met when Potapov visited Vyg earlier in 1782 in connection with plans to build a new road from the capital to Archangel.[27] The Vyg manuscript tradition preserves copies of three letters connected with the abolition of the double tax—a memo from Catherine II to Potapov, his brief letter to Borisov, and Borisov's lengthy, rhetorically elaborate reply.[28] Addressing Borisov as his friend (*priiatel'*), Potapov congratulated him on the decree of July 20, which he enclosed, as a sign of "my care for your well-being" (*moe popechenie o vashem blagodenstvii*).[29] Potapov's letter did not comment directly on the role he may have played in initiating or formulating the decree. In his reply, dated October 5, 1782, Borisov thanked Potapov for his help, referred flatteringly to Catherine II's motherly care for her subjects, and described her reign as the "present golden age" (*nastoiashchee zolotoe vremia*).[30] Dramatic metaphors abound: in their joy at the good news, the blind walk unaided to the chapel to give thanks, the deaf hear the news, the lame and the sick leap from their beds, and the dumb speak eloquently.[31] Borisov's letter was no mere rhetorical exercise, however. He warned Potapov of the continuing hostility of the Orthodox clergy toward Old Belief, and toward the end, he asked the governor to use his influence to prohibit the use of the word *raskol'nik* in official documents.[32] In justifying this request, Borisov argued that continuing present practice would make a bad impression on foreigners and hinted that failure to achieve this objective would undermine his credibility with his more militant followers. Whether Borisov's words stimulated the change in official policy is, of course, ultimately impossible to prove.[33]

The disasters of 1787 dominated Borisov's last years. On June 13 of that year, a fire spread by a strong wind destroyed most of the buildings in the Vyg monastery. As though that were not enough, on July 5 most of the Leksa convent burned down.[34] Unseasonable rains ruined the crops.[35] Borisov himself suffered a painful accident when he stepped on a large nail while inspecting the ruins of the mills at Leksa.[36] Racing against the northern winter, Borisov led his followers in rebuilding the two complexes as quickly as possible.

Like the Denisovs before him, Andrei Borisov died in the prime of life after a short illness. While on business in Petrozavodsk, Borisov became ill "in the head" on the night of January 31, 1791. On the return journey, he fell into a fever at Pigmatka on the shore of Lake Onega on February 7. Carried back to Vyg, he died twelve days later.[37]

As leader of Vyg, Borisov had to address two of the central theoretical and tactical issues that divided the Old Believer movement. The fires reopened the vexed question of prayers for the ruler. According to nineteenth-century testimony, the leaders of Vyg asked the Filippovtsy of the Topozerskaia Pustyn' for help in rebuilding the community. Predictably, the Filippovtsy insisted that Vyg give up prayers for the reigning monarch—the practice that had divided the two accords in the first place.[38] Their demand required a complete reversal of the long-standing custom of Vyg, which Borisov himself had defended in a theoretical discourse on the issue, the "Sermon on the Naming of Tsars and Prayer for Them" (*Slovo o naimenovanie tsarei i molenii za nikh*). In it he had argued that Christians are commanded to pray for all people, including their rulers, and for the peace and well-being of the realm. More controversially he insisted, citing a variety of proof texts, that rulers who are honorable and distinguished but not true Orthodox Christians may be referred to as "right-believing" (*blagovernyi*) as well as "pious" (*blagochestivyi*).[39] Even on a theoretical level, the latter argument is strained and could hardly have been expected to convince his opponents.

In their desperate situation, Borisov and his compatriots had little choice but to abandon a practice that their predecessors had reluctantly adopted under duress. Evidence of a later time confirms the change in Vyg's position. In the late 1830s the governor of Olonets A. V. Dashkov reported to his superiors that the community mentioned no Russian ruler after Mikhail Romanov by name in its services and referred to the present ruler and his family as *blagochestivyi*, but not *blagovernyi*.[40]

In Borisov's time, the leaders of Old Belief also continued to debate the thorny question of marriage. At its core, the issue was a canonical one with obvious moral implications. If no truly Christian priests remained on the earth, no sacraments, including marriage, could be celebrated. What were ordinary Christians to do? Throughout its history, the leaders of Vyg gave a simple, consistent answer. True Christians had no choice but to live celibate lives. A council of the residents of Vyg reiterated this policy in 1777.[41] In addition to narrowly canonical issues, two other considerations inspired Vyg's policy. One was the notion, widespread in Christian societies, that a monastic style of life is morally superior to the married life of the laity.[42] Moreover, as the protocol of 1777 reiterated, celibacy was the most appropriate style of life for Christians in the End Time.

Since Vyg and Leksa were monastic communities in aspiration, rigorous insistence on celibacy made sense. Yet this stand complicated their relations with their lay patrons and followers on whose generosity they depended more than ever.[43] Ordinary Old Believer men and women "in the world" did not find these counsels of perfection very helpful. Again and again, recognizing that many of their followers would live together whether they approved or not, leaders of other branches of the movement tried to find canonically appropriate substitutes for the Sacrament of marriage. In Borisov's time, even the Pomortsy split on this issue. Vasilii Emel'ianov, the leader of the Moscow branch of the accord, argued that Christians can marry without the sacrament. The essence of Christian marriage, he argued, is the mutual love and commitment of the couple, supported by their parents, that could be recognized and sanctified by a Christian community without priests. The leaders of Vyg adamantly rejected this view.[44] In 1792, under pressure from Borisov's successors, Emel'ianov publicly agreed to accept Vyg's insistence on mandatory celibacy, but in reality he and his followers continued to defend and act on their own understanding of marriage.[45] In effect, the two centers of the Pomortsy had tacitly agreed to disagree. Thus, in spite of its prestige, Vyg as a monastic community was losing touch with the needs of many of its lay followers.

Before analyzing Borisov's writings, we would do well to paint his portrait as leader of Vyg. The only description of his appearance comes from Old Believer tradition of a later time and paints him in flattering stereotypes.[46] More telling are the rhetorical tributes of his followers. These took two forms—a poem lauding him as the new leader of Vyg[47] and several eulogies composed after his death.[48] The following epithets occur frequently in these compositions— shepherd of the flock[49] and protector of the community; father of orphans;[50] warrior for Christ; and throughout his life, a model of Christian charity.[51] The writers of these texts also emphasized his fame[52] and his connections with powerful figures in official society.[53] In addition to recognizing the practical usefulness of friends in high places, this theme in my opinion also reflects the long-standing desire of the leaders of Vyg to convince themselves and others of the legitimacy and respectability of their counter-society and counterculture.

For our purposes, Borisov's achievements and reputation as a scholar and rhetorician are particularly important. One of the eulogies praises his rich knowledge of the "liberal sciences" (*v svobodnykh naukakh*) and of "sacred writings." The writer goes on to remark, "he had not only the knowledge of the rules of grammar, and an abundance of rhetorical embellishment, but also an exceptional knowledge of philosophical wisdom and a wonderful knowledge of that most celestial science, theology."[54] Few scholars of any age could really attain these high standards.

Ultimately the best measures of Borisov's stature as a writer and rhetorician are his works. Through them, we enter his two cultural worlds.

Before discussing individual compositions, we should identify the most important elements in Borisov's cultural world, the main ingredients in his creative kitchen. The first is the liturgical, literary, and polemical heritage of ecumenical Eastern Orthodoxy as preserved and codified in Muscovite Russia. It included the Bible, an extensive selection of writings from the Eastern Church fathers, liturgical texts, and carefully selected works of the Muscovite period such as the *Stoglav* and the writings of Maksim Grek. The first generation of Old Believer polemicists assembled and selected the core of this "canon" for the defense of the Old Faith.[55]

The second is the heritage of Vyg itself. In addition to the adaptation of the materials available to the first fathers of Old Belief, the cultural heritage of Vyg consisted of a remarkable corpus of new compositions, especially the works of the Denisov brothers and Ivan Filippov's history of the community, and the liturgical and cultural practices and forms of organization that the Vyg community developed as its members attempted to lead an authentically Christian life in new and rapidly changing circumstances. Moreover, the early leaders of Vyg had adapted a variety of cultural and artistic styles to meet the needs of the community. In literature and scholarship, the Denisovs and others had adopted the canon and techniques of contemporary ecclesiastical scholarship—"Ukrainian Baroque learning," to use the term loosely—to serve Old Belief.[56] In the religious arts, they adamantly preserved pre-Nikonian Russian traditions. Borisov had a very rich inheritance.

Finally, as we shall see, Borisov's cultural environment also included the ideological and literary currents in the world around him. Whether he liked it or not, Borisov lived in the last decades of the eighteenth century and, as leader of a large community, had no choice but to deal with the wider world.

The vast majority of Borisov's surviving works belong to the first cultural world. Addressed to the faithful, they fit comfortably within the traditions of Eastern Orthodoxy in general and Vyg in particular. Like the Denisovs before him, Borisov consciously used the intellectual resources of these traditions in defending his community and ministering to his flock. At the same time, as a writer and preacher, he made his own contributions to the growing canon of Old Believer literature.

The clearest statement of Borisov's devotion to tradition and traditional learning is the longest work attributed to him, the "Life" of Andrei Denisov. Vasilii Danilov's letter to Borisov of January 16, 1769, indicates that the latter was engaged in writing the life of the father of the community (*o toliko preslavnom predivnago ottsa zhitii . . . povest' pisati*).[57] The letter also suggests that the "Life" was a collaborative effort; Danilov wrote that he was contributing materials to the work. At the same time, the manuscript tradition and Liubopytnyi's testimony as well as Danilov's comments make clear that Borisov was the main author and compiler of the work.[58]

A substantial number of copies have come down to us.[59] Those that contain full versions of the text fall into two groups, consisting of twenty-eight and thirty chapters respectively. The thirty-chapter redaction contains chapters on Denisov's journeys to Moscow and Petrozavodsk (ch. 17) and the writing of the *D'iakonovy otvety* for the Nizhnii-Novgorod Old Believers (ch. 19), which do not appear in the shorter version.[60] This preliminary survey suggests, however, that the longest and most important chapters of the text vary little from one copy to the next.[61]

Much of the material in the "Life" is clearly derivative. As Borisov freely admitted, he borrowed extensively from Ivan Filippov's history of the Vyg community and other earlier Vyg texts.[62] The sections present in both the published edition of Filippov's work and Borisov's "Life" are precisely those that provide the most detailed factual information about the founding and early history of Vyg and its most serious confrontations with the imperial government. That being the case, historians have gone directly to the edition of Filippov's work for information on these matters.[63]

Thus, Borisov's "Life" is most interesting for the light it throws on the religious ideals, ideas, literary aspirations, and cultural values of the Vyg community in the late eighteenth century.[64] In addition to extensive reflective passages on the meaning of the hero's life and accomplishments, Borisov's work describes Denisov's activities as a scholar and cultural leader in much more detail than other works in the Vyg canon. The following discussion will focus on this theme.

Even though the "Life" is admittedly a collage of sorts, the text follows clear organizational principles. It has two central subjects—the life of Andrei Denisov as an example of Christian virtue and the history of the Vyg community in which he was so central a figure. As the title suggests, Borisov closely followed hagiographic conventions. The work begins with the author's self-justification for undertaking the task. As he puts it, the ancients recognized the usefulness of recording the lives of prominent men like Alexander the Great so that they would never be forgotten and their examples would instruct future generations. How much more appropriate is it to record the lives of heroes of the faith such as Andrei Denisov![65] Borisov then tells the story of the hero's life, beginning with his pious childhood and youth, continuing with his adult ministry, and ending with his holy death and a description of the posthumous miracles that prove his sanctity. In this case, supernatural proof of Denisov's saintliness consists almost entirely of visions of him in heaven along with other fathers of Vyg.[66] The "Life" describes only one posthumous healing.[67]

In describing his life and accomplishments, Borisov frequently referred to Andrei Denisov as a Christian scholar and teacher. In the very first sentence of the "Life," he described his hero as "most wise among the lovers of wisdom" (*v liubomudrykh premudrago muzha*) and "most renowned teacher of the old faith" (*preslavneishago drevniago blagochestiia uchitelia*).[68] These themes recur throughout the narrative of Denisov's early life. Andrei Denisov's fatherland was Russia, a country rich in resources but even richer in its possession of the authentic Christian faith. His forebears were honorable and pious men, descendants of the princes Myshetskii, who settled in the area around Lake Onega during the Time of Troubles because they refused to swear allegiance to the foreign rulers who occupied Novgorod.[69] From birth, Andrei Denisov was faithful to this heritage. His pious parents nourished him "not only with milk but with prayers, not only with bread but with urgent prayers."[70] They also gave him "holy books" so that he could learn to read and write. An exceptionally talented and serious boy, Denisov mastered these skills by the age of five.[71] Being "skilled in book learning," he ascended the steps of Christian scholarship—grammar, rhetoric, and philosophy. Scholarly accomplishment, however, never became an end in itself; his studies made him more determined than ever to achieve the moral goals of the faith: courage, truth, chastity, and good works.[72] Before long, his "love of God and zeal for holiness" (*liubov' k Bogu i . . . revnost' po blagochestii*)led him to an isolated hermit's life and, in time, to a communal monastic life in the emerging Vyg community.[73]

As Borisov portrayed him, the mature Andrei Denisov was a learned and resourceful scholar but one whose erudition was always subordinate to his faith. Several chapters of the work address the theme in different ways. In chapter 13, the author summarizes Denisov's qualities as a leader of the community.[74] He praises him for showing an admirable combination of severity, patience, and gentleness in dealing with his flock. In his personal life he set an example of rigorous self-discipline, continence (*vozderzhanie*), and sense of proportion (*mernost'*).

Scholarship was a central part of Denisov's life: he was an avid, thorough, and thoughtful reader and a skilled writer who worked hard to find a style and rhetoric appropriate to the readers to whom he addressed his words. He also saw the need to pass on his rhetorical skills and learning to his disciples and took great care in correcting their compositions. Borisov summarizes the kinds of learning to which he aspired and to which he directed his students, grammar, poetry-writing, rhetoric, dialectic, logic, kabalistic philosophy, and theology, "understanding that these [skills] were necessary, for without knowledge of Holy Writ it is impossible . . . to be ready to answer any and all questions."[75]

Denisov never rested on his laurels. Although he made the best use possible of his natural talent and the instruction of any teachers he could find, he realized that he could not be fully confident of his learning unless he studied with a "good and skillful teacher." He therefore decided to go to Kiev to study at the academy with the most renowned scholar of his time.[76] As Borisov tells it, Denisov made the journey in 1718 with a party of merchants and his pupil Manuil Petrov. As a pious pilgrim, he visited the shrines and sights of the city and, through contacts, made the acquaintance of the unnamed teacher who asked him to prepare a model sermon as a test of his skills.[77] As his text, Denisov chose Proverbs 16:24, "Kind words are like dripping honey, sweetness on the tongue and health for the body." The written sermon was so impressive that the teacher read it to his students who guessed that it must be a translation from Greek or Latin. Thereafter, Denisov studied rhetoric, philosophy, and theology with the master.[78] Borisov hastens to add that he used his learning "to strengthen and spread the old faith" (*ko ukrepleniiu i razprostraneniiu drevniago blagochestiia*).[79]

Can we believe Borisov's story? V. G. Druzhinin argued that Andrei Denisov probably never studied in Kiev but received his rhetorical and theological education in either Moscow or Novgorod.[80] Although we cannot be sure of the essential truth of Borisov's story, we should not dismiss his testimony too quickly. Writing in a tight community with a strong collective memory, Borisov was unlikely simply to invent such a story. Moreover, if Old Believers regarded Ukrainian learning with suspicion, why would he tarnish the memory of his hero by falsely stating that he studied in Kiev? Recent studies indicate that Vyg scholars were more flexible than Druzhinin assumed and used any and all materials that would strengthen their intellectual defenses.[81]

In the end, however, the rhetorical purpose of the story is far more important than its factual accuracy. As Borisov's long panegyric following the story makes clear, his ultimate purpose was to show that Denisov and his pupils met the highest standards of contemporary Christian scholarship. In the "school of Vyg," the Old Believers had scholars, writers, and teachers who were second to none.

Andrei Denisov and his collaborators put their erudition to very practical use in defending Old Belief against the official Orthodox Church. As Borisov tells the story, Denisov questioned the authenticity of the texts of the protocols of a supposed church council of 1157 and the "Theognostov trebnik," both of which Bishop Pitirim of Nizhnii-Novgorod used in his attacks on the local Old Believers. When confronted with Denisov's opinion, Pitirim angrily called him a "sorcerer" (*volkhv*). Denisov's weapon was not magic but a remarkable knowledge of paleography and text study. Realizing the importance of these manuscripts, he sent Manuil Petrov to Moscow to study them in the Pechatnyi Dvor where they were on public display. Petrov's careful inspection revealed that the works were modern forgeries: although written on old parchment, the manuscripts had clearly been restitched and the language and handwriting of the texts were mixtures of ancient and contemporary usage. Like the first dove who returned to Noah in the ark, Petrov brought his findings back to Vyg, and on that basis, Denisov included a devastating critique of the works in the *Pomorskie otvety*. Not only did he destroy Piritim's most telling evidence against Old Belief, but in the process he virtually invented modern paleography in Russia.[82]

In two passages toward the end of the "Life" summarizing Andrei Denisov's achievements as leader of the community, Borisov praised his learning and his activities as a Christian scholar, along with his piety, wisdom, political skill, and hard work.[83] All of these qualities and activities were inseparable and indispensable to a great leader of Old Belief. His virtues included knowledge of sacred writings, philosophy, and rhetoric so profound that he taught the brothers extemporaneously at any opportunity. His eloquence, which could move even stones, inspired his flock to live devout and rigorous lives.[84] Denisov, the second Chrysostom, made Vyg "the house of wisdom and the dwelling of Christian philosophy" (*dom be premudrosti i zhilishche filosofii khristianskiia*).[85] Having educated himself in Christian learning, he trained a whole generation of scholars to write and speak well, and he taught them scripture and dogma so they could strengthen the faith of other members of the community.[86]

Denisov's learning and intelligence served Vyg well in its relations with the outside world. His polemical writings effectively defended Old Belief not only against the spokesmen of the official Orthodox Church, the "*novshevtv liubiteli i zastupniki*" (lovers and defenders of novelties) but also against Jews, Lutherans, and Calvinists.[87] Wise teachers in foreign countries knew and valued his writings.[88] Moreover, his ability to communicate effectively with a wide variety of people allowed him to discuss political issues as well as the faith with the administrators of the factories at Petrozavodsk and other powerful officials. Even after his death, Denisov's reputation opened the doors of the mighty to the representatives of Vyg.[89]

As these passages demonstrate, the image of Andrei Denisov as a Christian scholar is central to the "Life." In his own life and his other writings, Borisov also pursued this ideal and, as leader of Vyg, worked hard to preserve its position as an important center of Christian scholarship. At the same time, the prevailing intellectual currents in the outside world of the late eighteenth century made Borisov's task of reconciling faith and scholarship even more daunting than Denisov's. Living simultaneously in two cultural worlds was a tempting alternative.

The written texts of Borisov's sermons show that he aspired, like Denisov before him, to be both an exemplar of Christian learning and a compassionate pastor.[90] The four sermons that celebrate the dedication of buildings in the Vyg monastery and the Leksa convent follow the established traditions of Christian preaching and the requirements of the sermon as a genre. Except for a few specifically Old Believer notes, they discuss universal Christian themes, drawing on quotations and images from the Bible. As is customary in many Christian traditions, each begins with a verse from scripture around which Borisov skillfully weaves his reflections and admonitions to his hearers.

By far the longest of the sermons celebrates the rebuilding and rededication, on July 16, 1788, of the settlement and chapel at Vyg, destroyed in the previous year's fire.[91] Elaborating on Psalm 94:19, "In the multitude of my thoughts within me thy comforts delight my soul," Borisov reminded his hearers that their recent tribulations are the Father's way of disciplining those he loves.[92] He also urged them not to forget the many instances of God's mercy toward them and their community. He then launched a defense of Old Believer teaching on which the rebuilt community stood. He reassured his flock that Vyg preserved true Orthodox Christianity by reviewing the entire history of Eastern Orthodoxy theology, from Moses to the *Pomorskie otvety*, the Denisov brothers' great polemical defense of Old Belief. Finally, after comparing the consecration of the new chapel to the dedication of the new temple in Jerusalem after the Babylonian captivity, he urged his listeners not to complain about their sufferings but instead to renew themselves and their community (*Da obnovimsia i my veshchestvenno zhe i neveshestvenno vsi vo vsem sami sviatym i blagim obnovleniem*)[93] by being thankful to God, keeping his commandments, and loving one another.[94]

To a twentieth-century reader, the sermon is eloquent, well-constructed, and entirely fitting for the occasion. Other than the passages specifically defending Old Belief, most of the text would be appropriate in almost any Christian community on such an occasion. Borisov effectively touched the appropriate emotional poles—sorrow at suffering and loss, joy at a new beginning. Moreover, he did so in a language that is both suitably exalted and attractive. Borisov, a profoundly serious man speaking on a serious occasion, even indulged in the occasional play on words: in characterizing Vyg as the final outpost of true Christianity, he played on the word "last" (*poslednii*). "We are the last real people in the last days in the last of the regions of Russia, this cold and infertile northern land."[95] In short, the longest sermon on the renewal of the community is a work of fine but predictable homiletic craftsmanship.

Although related to this sermon thematically, the "Priskorbnoe povedanie" has a very different character.[96] It is a reflective autobiographical narrative of the fires and other misfortunes that befell the community. After comparing himself unfavorably to Job, Borisov suggests two ways to deal with the catastrophe. One is to do good works, loathe sin, and constantly praise God (*Eia zhe izbezhati potshchimsia tvoreniem dobrodetelei, i omerzeniem grekha, i neprestannym slovosloviem presushchestvennago bozhiiago sushchestva*).[97] The other is service to the community, since sacred and civil law both stipulate that, if Christians live in society and benefit from it, they are obliged to meet their societal obligations.[98]

Borisov's shorter sermons show many of the same characteristics as the long rededication sermon. They are admirable, tightly constructed compositions that, for the most part, remind their hearers of universal Christian teachings. The extent to which Borisov quoted, paraphrased, or invoked the Bible would please a zealous Protestant. At the same time, the preacher stresses tradition, discipline, and order, and in the case of the nuns of Leksa, purity and submissiveness.

Three of Borisov's shorter homilies also deal with the renewal of the community. The first, for the dedication of a chapel in the men's quarters at Leksa, dates from September 13, 1785, before the great fires.[99] Borisov built it around a comparison of the magnificence of Solomon's temple with the austerity of the new chapel, which reflected the severe life of the Vyg community. Not only did its people face material deprivation in their harsh environment, but they had to live without the ministrations of a clergy and hierarchy.[100] Nevertheless, Borisov concluded, the people of Vyg had a greater treasure than Solomon— the presence of God and the hierarchy of heaven in their midst (*iako imeem my posredi nas i s nami kupno nyne . . . tsaria tsarei . . . i vsia osviashchaiushchago prenebesnago arkhiereia i spasitelia Isusa Khrista*).[101]

The themes of the two other sermons reflect their hearers, the nuns of Leksa. Borisov constructed the homily of November 21, 1788, on the images of the bride's companions in Psalm 45:14–15 who accompany her to the king; the wise virgins in the New Testament wedding parable; and the Mother of God. All three of these images were to serve as models for the women of Leksa.[102] Sisters who aspired to serve the King and be devotees of Our Lady had to observe the following principles—to pray constantly, to be truly chaste, to occupy themselves diligently with handwork, and "otherwise to be kind, meek, judicious, constant, humble, patient, silent, continent, shy, submissive, reasonable, gentle, and wholeheartedly forgiving."[103] The image of the wise virgins allowed the preacher to make two other points. Like them, the sisters of Leksa should never forget that, living in the End Time, they were waiting for the unexpected arrival of their Lord. Until then, they should buy oil for their lamps at the small price of deeds of Christian charity to the ill and needy members of the community.

Borisov built the second Leksa sermon around the single word that the risen Christ spoke to the Holy Myrrh–Bearing Women at the tomb, "Rejoice" (Matthew 28:9).[104] This theme was an old favorite of Borisov's. On April 7, 1778, he had answered the Easter greetings of the Leksa sisters with a charming letter in which he urged them, like the women at the tomb, to hear in times of sorrow Christ's word "Rejoice."[105] Returning to this theme in the sermon, Borisov urged the sisters to win the Lord's favor by praying continually, being unswervingly devoted to God, and living a strictly celibate life.[106]

One more short sermon has come down to us, the Pentecost homily on the text from Psalms 77:13, "Who is so great a God as our God?"[107] In explicating it, Borisov concentrated on the qualities that characterized or demonstrated God's greatness and organized the text around the word "great" (velikii). In some instances, he took the play on words to extremes: "How great is His exceedingly great greatness" (Koliko zhe velika prevelikaia ego velikost').[108] Among God's qualities he mentioned indivisibility, omnipresence, omnipotence, constancy, and control of nature. God is also good and, through Christ, helps the weak overcome the powers of this world. What should Christians do in response to God's greatness and goodness? Borisov answered that they should live in awe and fear of Him and obey His law in complete honesty. He also urged his listeners to subdue their reason to faith (pleniaem nash razum v poslushanie very) and "imprison all of their strength in God's unfailing love" (plenim vsi nashi sily v bezsmertnuiu Bozhiiu liubov').[109]

Considering that the occasion was Pentecost, Borisov's sermon concentrated to a remarkable degree on general and uncontroversial theological statements and on admonitions to obedience and self-discipline. Only once did Borisov refer to the Holy Spirit, expressing the wish that God would inspire the people of Vyg as He had the first disciples at Pentecost.[110] This comparative neglect of the "charismatic" elements in Christianity harmonizes with the spiritual teachings of the earlier Vyg fathers, who emphasized the liturgy, the community, and discipline over individual devotions or the free play of the Spirit.[111] It may also reflect the broader tendency in late seventeenth and eighteenth-century Russian Orthodoxy to emphasize the moral rather than the spiritual dimensions of Christian teaching.[112]

Any discussion of Borisov's homiletic works would be incomplete without reference to his composition in poetry or rhythmic prose, "In Praise of Chastity" (*Pokhvala devstvennikam*),[113] even though it is unclear whether it was intended to be recited and, if so, in what circumstances. Apparently following syllabic principles, the text consists of roughly twenty-four lines (the manuscripts vary slightly), each of which begins, "O celibates" (*O devstvennitsy* or, less frequently, *O devyia*).[114] The gender of the noun makes it clear that the composition addresses women. The celibates are praised in epithets—brides of Christ, imitators of angels, dwellers in the heavenly city, interlocutors with the heavenly powers, the church of God, and so on. As though these images did not adequately convey his message, Borisov concluded the work with a passage in prose in which, citing the authority of St. John Chrysostom, he elaborated the official Vyg policy on marriage, namely, that husbands and wives should abstain from sexual relations and that those who had not married should refrain from doing so, since a married man is more concerned about his wife than about God.[115]

In short, in his "Life" of Andrei Denisov and his sermons, Andrei Borisov appears as a skillful and learned defender of the Vyg tradition, but Borisov also lived in a second cultural world. Some of his most interesting writings and testimony about him show his interest in contemporary intellectual currents or demonstrate his willingness to break out of the established traditions of Vyg to which, for the most part, he was rigorously faithful. These sources, however, are short and fragmentary and thus must be approached with caution.

To begin, we should note that, whereas Borisov created his more traditional works for the people of Vyg, he addressed his less conventional letters and statements to outsiders, including other Old Believers, on whom he was trying to make a good impression. It is therefore difficult to weigh the significance of these concepts and terms in Borisov's worldview as a whole.[116]

Borisov's most perplexing work is his short letter, written in the winter of 1787, to the Moscow Pomorets, Vasilii Emel'ianov, on morality.[117] It centers on two related themes—the levels, or steps, of virtue and the desirability of founding an Old Believer academy at Vyg.

Borisov began by stating that there are many different ways to envision the levels (*gradusy*) of virtue and illustrated his point with a pyramidal diagram, rising in three steps from industriousness, through experience in valor (*muzhestvo*), to valor itself, then declining to impudence (*derzost'*) and destruction. Borisov expressed his preference for a more complex theory he had learned from an unnamed "philosopher" in St. Petersburg. He summarized it in a six-level diagram labeled "The Glorious Throne of Virtue."

In this instance, the "the man of measure and purity" (*mernyi i chistyi muzh*) ascends five steps to reach the sixth and highest, valor. The right side of the pyramid shows the five stages through which he could fall to destruction. In the rest of the discussion, Borisov seemed particularly concerned that the reader understand the danger that the virtuous man might lose his sense of measure and destroy himself through thoughtless arrogance. To illustrate the steps in the decline from virtue, he used a military analogy: assuming that the number of the enemy remains the same, a sense of measure implies mobilizing a force of equal size, while impudence would dictate fighting one thousand men with one hundred, despair with ten, and destruction fighting such a force alone. Using the image of adjusting a telescope Borisov stressed that, to reach the highest level of the moral pyramid and remain there, a man must strive continually to know himself, his strengths and limitations, and to avoid extremes.[118]

Where Borisov found the inspiration for these ideas is difficult to determine. First, in the Eastern Christian tradition, the ladder symbolizes the believer's spiritual ascent toward a full experience of God's glory and love. Borisov surely knew St. John Climacus's *The Ladder of the Divine Ascent*, the classic of spirituality founded on this metaphor. In this work the author leads his followers up thirty steps from commitment, self-denial, and rigorous discipline through humility and stillness to union with God in the experience of divine love.[119] By contrast, the steps and final goal of Borisov's ladder center on wise moral behavior in this world.

Second, statements that a sense of measure is essential to true virtue and that self-knowledge is vital for reaching that goal are reminiscent of neo-Classical literary commonplaces of the seventeenth and early eighteenth centuries. This may be the explanation for the sarcastic comment of Gilbert Romme, the French visitor to Vyg, that Borisov saw himself as head of a society of Stoics.[120]

Finally, the staircase and pyramid are common Masonic symbols of ascent to true virtue. At the same time, a preliminary survey of literature on Freemasonry has not uncovered a replica of Borisov's pyramid.[121] Perhaps the closest equivalent is the seven-step stairway, reminiscent of Jacob's ladder, leading to the door to enlightenment—an image associated particularly with Masons of the Scottish Rite.[122] Moreover, Borisov's pyramid provides two paths—upward to virtue and downward to destruction. Masonic symbolism emphasizes only the positive, upward direction.[123] These issues clearly require further investigation.

The letter's references to plans for an Old Believer academy also raise more questions than they answer. The wording suggests that Borisov was reacting to initiatives from Emel'ianov and other Moscow leaders to improve the quality of Old Believer education and learning. If this is the case, Borisov's response was one more attempt to maintain Vyg's position of leadership among the Pomortsy. Clearly, he welcomed the idea that children from Moscow would come to Vyg to study "various sciences."[124] What kind of "academy" did Borisov envision? The letter's references to children and youth suggest a secondary school rather than a university or theological academy. The document gives even less guidance on the nature of the sciences the academy would teach. Metaphysics would probably be one.[125] Given his admiration for the neo-Classical learning of the Ukrainian Orthodox academies (in spite of their erroneous teachings on theology or liturgical questions), as demonstrated, for example, by his story of Andrei Denisov's visit to the Kiev academy,[126] it is likely that he envisioned an Old Believer variant of the so-called Jesuit curriculum, centered on language study, rhetoric, philosophy, and mathematics, that had exercised a powerful influence throughout Europe in the preceding two centuries.

In his dealings with educated non–Old Believers, Borisov took particular pains to present himself as a learned man. He embellished his letter to Potapov with metaphors from science. For example, like electricity, his words would break through the clouds of gloom surrounding Vyg.[127] In an extended metaphor from astronomy, he argued that, just as only by observing clouds and eclipses can we truly appreciate the unobstructed glory of the sun and the moon, so only through their sufferings can the people of Vyg truly comprehend the magnanimity of Catherine II. We should note two things about these images. They are literary decorations, not discussions of scientific principles. Moreover, they allude to scientific phenomena that support Christian teaching by testifying to the power and glory of God.

Borisov struck Gilbert Romme as a complex figure. With the values and prejudices of the radical Enlightenment, Romme characterized him as a mixture of enthusiasm and vanity—eager to discuss contemporary science and philosophy but, ultimately, misguided and ignorant. As Romme summarized, Andrei Borisov "wants to seem an acute, politic person, but he is simply a hypocrite and a trickster. He wants to be taken for a philosopher and sees himself as head of a society of Stoics. But he is simply an ignoramus. He has read more than Russians usually read, but he does it without reflection. He wants to talk about everything, but expresses more ignorance than knowledge."[128]

As an example, Romme described a conversation about science. Borisov opened with a question about balloons and how they function. Romme showed him two experiments and remarked that Borisov was more interested in the experiments themselves than discussing the principles they illustrated. Borisov also expressed interest in the physics of electricity and heat and in astronomy. In the latter case, to Romme's amazement, he rejected the heliocentric theory of the universe, which even illiterate peasants knew to be true.

According to Romme's account, Borisov and he spent considerably more time discussing philosophy and literature. Borisov knew something of the ideas of Rousseau, Voltaire, Diderot, Fénelon, and Rollin. He produced a copy of Rousseau's treatise "On the Influence of Science on Morals," probably the Russian translation published in 1768.[129] He raised some unspecified objections to Rousseau's theories but expressed admiration for the philosopher's "morals and stoicism."[130]

In two newly discovered short compositions, Borisov alluded directly to Rousseau. The "Dialogue of a Philosopher with a Peasant about Philosophical Wisdom and Peasant Simplicity" ("Dialogismos ili razglagolstvie filosofa s krest'ianinom o filosofskoi premudrosti i krest'ianskoi prostote") centers on the peasant's insistence that the philosopher is a lover of idleness (*prazdnoliubets*) because he does nothing useful. The philosopher attempts to convince his adversary of the importance of his struggle to understand the secrets of nature. In defending his position the peasant relates that he has heard someone read a work of the "French philosopher Rousseau," which states that his simplicity is better and more praiseworthy than philosophical wisdom. The frustrated philosopher responds that he would rather believe the Creator than Rousseau. The latter, he added nastily, only wrote his book, contradicting received wisdom, in order to show how original he was without thinking of the baleful consequences for his readers. Besides, Rousseau's position contradicted itself for he would have to forget his own philosophical wisdom to achieve the simplicity he praised.[131] Since the text breaks off before the debate concludes, the reader can only speculate which side the author favored. Given what we know about Borisov's life and other writings, it is tempting to speculate that he sided with the philosopher against Rousseau.

The second short work, untitled in the manuscript, also contrasts the ways in which philosophers and ordinary people look at the world. For the latter, nature is simple; but the philosopher knows that it is complex. Common-sense views of the world depend on the observer's vantage point. In an extended metaphor, Borisov points out that a person who lives on the hills and a person who lives in the swamp see nature differently and therefore have different values. Ultimately both viewpoints are correct as far as they go. God has made all of creation good and each environment has its advantages, for "we cannot penetrate the entire goodness of nature." Rousseau's work helps us understand this fundamental truth. As Rousseau observed, "if only we knew the quality and strength of the things we step on, we would be less impressed with the stars in heaven."[132] In this instance Rousseau plays a more positive role, since he helps Borisov make his points about the complexity of nature and the difficulty of understanding it comprehensively.

As Romme described it, Borisov's response to Voltaire was much more complicated. On the one hand, he expressed great admiration for Voltaire's writings, showed his guest a copy of the poem on natural religion,[133] and insisted that he collected all of the author's works that appeared in Russian translation.[134] On the other hand, commenting sarcastically on Voltaire's epitaph "His heart is here, but his mind is everywhere," Borisov suggested adding "and his soul is nowhere."[135] To Romme's annoyance, he made a clear distinction between admiration for the brilliance and enthusiasm of Diderot as a thinker and acceptance of his theories at face value. Borisov expressed particular admiration for Charles Rollin, the widely respected classicist and pedagogical theorist, and asked whether he was recognized as a saint. His comment is not difficult to understand: Rollin combined scholarship with Christian faith and, in his educational writings and practice, put primary emphasis on the classical liberal arts.[136]

Finally, Borisov showed Romme two bas-reliefs from Herculaneum that he had received from a General Mordvinov. He saw these pagan works through Christian eyes, interpreting the one as the Ascension of Christ and the other as Christ blessing Mary Magdalene.

What can we conclude from this testimony of a decidedly prejudiced witness and the other evidence? Borisov's knowledge of the writings of the philosophes was undoubtedly fragmentary at best. At the same time, his reactions to the leading figures of the French Enlightenment suggest an intelligent conservative Christian attempting to come to grips with the intellectual currents in educated society in his time. In spite of many radical differences, Rousseau's moralism, his respect for nature, and his religiosity would make his writings somewhat more palatable from the Christian point of view than Voltaire's brilliant skepticism and pragmatism. Rollin's combination of Christian belief and classical humanism attracted Borisov most of all. Is it too much to suggest, then, that he was attempting, however naively, to be a conservative contemporary intellectual, able to defend his version of the Christian faith in the philosophical idiom of his day?[137] Even if we accept this assumption, many questions remain. Was Borisov capable of playing the role of Christian intellectual effectively? And was such a role possible for any Old Believer leader of Borisov's time? His care to limit his discussions of philosophy and science to outsiders to his community and his justifiable sensitivity to accusations of freethinking[138] suggest otherwise.

Nevertheless, Borisov's aspirations to live in two cultural worlds suggest that he was a more accomplished and much more complex figure than earlier scholars of Old Belief have recognized. Without question, he made substantial contributions to the cultural legacy of the Vyg community that he loved so dearly and knew so well. The fact that, by the end of the eighteenth century, the emergence of new centers placed Vyg on the periphery of Old Belief in no way undermines his accomplishments. The second Borisov—the man who attempted to speak the language of educated Europeans of the late eighteenth century—prefigures later Old Believer intellectuals such as Pavel Liubopytnyi and the members of the "Riabushinskii circle,"[139] who strove to explain and defend the Old Faith in new terms and concepts. Far from living in a world of changelessness and isolation, such men lived—however uncomfortably—both within Old Belief and in the wider world around them.

Eleven

Interpreting the Fate of Old Believer Communities in the Eighteenth and Nineteenth Centuries

INTERPRETING THE HISTORY OF OLD BELIEF presents many challenges. Apart from the inherent complexity of the movement (if we can use so neat a label), historians must wrestle with the ideological assumptions and loyalties of earlier generations of scholars and publicists, for their writings in large measure still shape our varied understandings of the Old Believers' aspirations and our explanations of their fate. As we observed in chapter 1, until recently historians of Old Belief have tended to divide into two camps, the ecclesiastical and the populist. Both have their strengths and their limitations in analyzing the structure, history, and fate of Old Believer communities. With their focus on liturgical, theological, and canonical issues, ecclesiastical scholars of the movement paid relatively little attention to Old Believer communities except as centers of opposition to the teachings and practices of the official Orthodox Church.

The populist approach had both strengths and limitations. Since its proponents saw Old Belief as an expression of the latent radicalism of the lower classes of the Russian Empire, they concentrated on its geographical spread and social composition, its organizational structures, and its political impact. These emphases made Old Believer communities a central element in the populists' understanding of the movement's history. At the same time, the populists' priorities distorted their treatment of the communities' history and fate for, in addition to undervaluing the theological, liturgical, and canonical issues that preoccupied the Old Believers themselves, they tended to neglect or dismiss the more conservative elements in the movement. In populists' writings, priestly Old Believers often appear less authentic than the priestless, and those who reluctantly made their peace with the imperial authorities less admirable than their more radical brothers and sisters. Similarly, the populist system of values tended to give greater moral weight to peasant Old Believers than to the merchants and other townspeople who played leading roles in the movement's later history. Taken together, these ideological commitments and emotional attachments produced a misleading pattern of historical evolution.

In recent decades, scholars of Old Belief have strived to draw on the strengths of both traditional schools of interpretation and to avoid their extremes. The history of the most important Old Believer communities offers a helpful vantage point from which to do so. Yet this subject has received relatively little attention, particularly in recent years.[1] The sole exception is the Vyg community, the most important center of priestless Old Belief from the first years of the eighteenth century until the reign of Catherine II and an important cultural and organizational force until the officials and gendarmes of Nicholas I finally destroyed it in the 1850s.[2] In addition, some recent historians of industrial development and urban life in the late eighteenth and nineteenth centuries have discussed the Old Believer centers in Moscow that suddenly became prominent in the reign of Catherine II.[3] Otherwise, prerevolutionary Russian publications—ecclesiastical and populist—still provide the most useful information on the later history of Old Belief and of the communities that served as its lighthouses.

In spite of the paucity of scholarly research on these issues, several general patterns of historical development are clear and familiar. First of all, from the very beginning, Old Belief brought together around a common banner a wide variety of regional, social, and cultural forces.[4] Over time, the movement became ever more divided and diverse.[5] In particular, the priestless groups in which every man and woman was, by default, his or her own priest repeatedly quarreled and broke apart over canonical or liturgical issues. At the same time, all the main groups that made up the movement shared a number of characteristics, among them the urge to establish quasi-monastic communities as sources of leadership and authority for their adherents.

The pattern of continuous fragmentation had an ambiguous impact on the historical fate of the Old Believers. The divisions within the movement prevented—and still prevent—the Old Believers from addressing the outside world with a single voice. At the same time, the lack of a single organizational structure, combined with their tradition of individual and local initiative and their networks of personal contacts, has made them extremely flexible and resilient in the face of persecution.

Second, the most important Old Believer communities were themselves very complex organizational structures that combined features of monastic and lay styles of life.[6] Moreover, given their size and visibility, the principal Old Believer communities developed complex and shifting relationships with the imperial government and the increasingly secular society beyond their walls. Most of them—Vyg and the Moscow and St. Petersburg communities, for example—had little choice but to reach a modus vivendi with the imperial authority and endure the bitter attacks of their more radical brothers and sisters for their accommodation with the powers of the Antichrist.[7] At the same time, these increasingly respectable communities remained highly ambivalent toward the imperial authorities. In their practical dealings with officialdom, their conduct was profoundly manipulative.[8]

As recent archeographers have emphasized, the principal Old Believer communities served as focal points of a complex and sophisticated cultural system, or systems. Vyg not only produced a number of the classic texts defending the Old Faith but, through its scriptoria and workshops, served as a veritable publishing house.[9] The distinctive and elegant manuscripts from Vyg became the treasured possessions of Old Believers throughout the Russian empire.[10] Vyg also produced large numbers of icons and other devotional objects for the scattered Old Believer communities of the empire. In the late eighteenth and early nineteenth centuries, the Moscow centers likewise distributed liturgical books and icons to their adherents throughout Russia.[11]

Finally, as visible centers of a movement of opposition within an absolute monarchy, the main Old Believer communities depended for their survival on the willingness of the state to tolerate their continued existence. From the beginning of the movement's history until the relatively tolerant reigns of Catherine II (1762–1795) and Alexander I (1801–1825), government and official church took the initiative on most important issues and the Old Believers reacted to their policies. The unavoidably but frustratingly passive stance of their leaders toward the powers of this world helps to explain why, in the course of Old Believer history, many individuals and small groups took extraordinary measures to provoke confrontation with the agents of the imperial government.

In the last years of Alexander I's reign and especially under the regime of Nicholas I (1825–55), relations between the Old Believers and the state became considerably more complicated. The Old Believers continued to see themselves as victims of governmental repression. From the perspective of the imperial government and the official Orthodox Church, however, Old Belief was a powerful subversive force, actively proselytizing among the Orthodox population with promises of both spiritual and material reward and building its own religious and social institutions to undermine the established order in church and state.[12]

Since the existence of the most important communities depended on the inefficiency, venality, repression, or tolerance of the government and its agents, we would do well to review the changes of imperial policy toward religious dissent. The general outlines of that policy are well-known. In the last half of the seventeenth century, the Russian state and the official church attempted to destroy the conservative opposition to recent changes in liturgy, church governance, administrative practice, legal and social relations, and high culture. At first haphazard, the crusade against Old Belief became a war of extermination during the regency of Sophia. The decree of December 1684 made plain that any Old Believers who did not submit to the discipline of the official church were to be destroyed.[13] Left with no other means to defend their convictions, thousands of Old Believers fled beyond the borders of the empire or escaped this world altogether through self-immolation.

Peter I's policies toward the Old Believers were far more complex. In the early years of his reign, mobilizing the nation for war with Sweden occupied all of his energies. Under these conditions, he treated the Old Believers pragmatically, tolerating communities like Vyg that could contribute to the war effort.[14]

At the same time, the emperor savagely defended the honor of his office. His secret agents ferreted out all critics of the regime, Old Believers or not, and subjected them to unspeakable tortures.[15] Moreover, as the years passed, Peter increasingly became aware that Old Belief inevitably included a dimension of political opposition and that even the most respectable of individuals and communities could not be trusted entirely. Accordingly, he took steps to isolate its adherents from the rest of the population by decreeing that they register with the government, wear beards, old-fashioned clothes, and an identifying medal and pay double the usual capitation tax for this dubious privilege.[16] His government also supported the missionary campaign of the official church, designed to win ordinary Old Believers back to the fold by exposing their leaders' ignorance in a series of obligatory public debates. Under these conditions, the main concentrations of Old Believers underwent different fates. The Vyg community met the challenges and thrived. At the other extreme, the Kerzhenets settlements in the Nizhnii-Novgorod region succumbed to the pressure of officials and missionaries, and their inhabitants scattered.

Peter's odd combination of tolerance and repression remained the norm through the middle decades of the eighteenth century. If anything, the regime of Empress Anna attempted to apply his legislation more rigorously than he himself had done, adding the requirement that the Old Believers provide military recruits along with the rest of the population.[17] Her government and that of Elizabeth remained sensitive to any evidence that the Old Believers did not recognize the legitimacy of their rule. Accordingly, when an informer revealed that the members of the Vyg community did not pray for the monarch during their worship, the government launched an extensive investigation. With the very existence of their community at stake, the leaders of Vyg capitulated and agreed to pray for the ruler—a decision that infuriated a number of their most militant followers, led by Elder Filipp, who seceded to form their own communities and carry on the struggle against the power of the Antichrist.[18]

The reigns of Peter III and Catherine II were a veritable golden age of Old Belief. Acting on the Enlightenment notion that religious toleration was both morally sound and practically useful, the two monarchs drastically changed official policy toward religious dissenters. In his brief reign, Peter ordered officials to halt the persecution of Old Believers and invited the inhabitants of the refugee communities in Vetka, just across the Polish border, to return to the empire. After seizing the throne, Catherine systematically repealed earlier punitive legislation and allowed Old Believers to live and worship openly as long as they did not directly challenge her power or commonly accepted standards of morality.[19] Accordingly, older Old Believer communities thrived, and large and vital centers of the movement emerged in Moscow and St. Petersburg. Indeed, given their central location, size, wealth, and extensive charitable activities, the Preobrazhenskoe and Rogozhskoe Kladbishcha in Moscow soon became the institutional hubs of the movement throughout the empire.[20]

The reign of Nicholas I brought unmitigated disaster to the Old Believers' quasi-monastic communities. Although the emperor's policy toward other adherents of the movement was inconsistent, he and his officials hounded the main Old Believer centers mercilessly.[21] First to feel the pressure were the Irgiz communities near Saratov, home of the descendants of former residents of Vetka who had returned to Russia. The local governor, Prince A. B. Golitsyn, forced their leaders to accept the authority of the hierarchy of the official church (the so-called edinoverie), then closed the unofficial monasteries and convents and dispersed their inhabitants.[22] In the last, most repressive years of Nicholas's reign, the main Old Believer centers in Moscow and St. Petersburg suffered a parallel fate. Local officials dispersed the monks and nuns who lived in them, took over the management of their charitable activities, and converted the chapels to official Orthodoxy or the edinoverie.[23]

The final agony of Vyg, already in decline, was particularly painful. The local representatives of the imperial bureaucracy, particularly Prince A. V. Dashkov, subjected the community to unremitting pressure through a combination of bureaucratic pedantry and brutal insensitivity. At his most heavy-handed, for example, he ordered a midwife to examine the nuns of the Leksa convent to determine which of them were virgins. One by one, the community lost its rights, its lands, and many of its people, who were repatriated to their native villages to be replaced by poor non–Old Believer peasants from another part of the country. At the height of "Mamai's devastation," officials knocked down all but one of the chapels in the settlements and made it an Orthodox church.[24]

The zeal with which Nicholas and his officials dogged the Old Believer communities appears puzzling at first glance. In hindsight, the centers of the Old Faith appear to have provided useful social services to the community and, at worst, to have threatened no one. Why then were they persecuted with such doggedness? Part of the answer probably lies in the eagerness of ambitious officials to overfulfill their bureaucratic norms in carrying out a policy of which Nicholas I himself clearly approved.

Much more was involved, however. Going to such trouble to destroy the Old Believer communities implies that the government evidently found them subversive. And, in the perfect autocracy of Nicholas I, subversive they were. First of all, as self-established settlements that, in various combinations, included features of monasteries and lay settlements, the Old Believer centers did not fit any bureaucratic pigeonhole, ecclesiastical or secular. Moreover, in a supreme act of defiance, the priestly Old Believers, after many futile attempts, succeeded in 1846 in establishing their own hierarchy at Belaia Krinitsa on Austrian territory.[25] By creating their own institutions, then, the Old Believers challenged the neat administrative categories of the empire.

Second, instead of gradually disappearing with the passing of time, as earlier rulers had hoped, the Old Believers appeared to be growing steadily in numbers in the first decades of the nineteenth century. According to one view, the Old Believer population of the empire reached its highest point before the mid-nineteenth century in the 1820s.[26] The extent to which the apparent increase in numbers reflected the conversion of adherents of official Orthodoxy or simply the more open allegiance of previously secret Old Believers is hard to determine. Without question, agents of the government and official church believed that conversions from Orthodoxy accounted for the phenomenon. In addition, as the secular and ecclesiastical administrations improved their record keeping, officials became more aware of the large number of *poluraskol'niki*, Old Believers who masqueraded as members of the official Orthodox Church in order to avoid the sanctions against open adherents of the old faith.[27]

In other ways as well they threatened the emperor's beloved ideals of Orthodoxy, autocracy, and nationality. The actions and reactions of officials indicate some of the features of Old Believer life that particularly shocked them. Simply by existing, of course, they challenged the monopoly of the official Orthodox Church. Moreover, even the most respectable of Old Believers continued to question the legitimacy of the imperial power. Nearly a century after agreeing to pray for the monarch, the people of Vyg still refused to use the epithet *blagovernyi* (right-believing) of the present ruler because he was obviously not truly Orthodox.[28] Even more startling was the discovery in 1820 that the Preobrazhensk settlement had a portrait of the reigning monarch, Alexander I, as Antichrist with horns, a tail, and the number 666 on his forehead.[29]

This was not all. Remarking on the strength of Old Belief in the northwestern borderlands of the empire near Vyg, Nicholas made the following revealing comments: "the main foundation of their life is willfulness and debauchery. Therefore it is necessary to strengthen local surveillance, build communications, and provide means for the poor class of inhabitants to get sustenance in order to weaken the sectarians' influence over them."[30] Again and again, official documents note the relative prosperity of the Old Believer communities and repeat the conviction that their wealth allowed them to win converts from the official church.[31] That the Old Believers' hard work, frugality, and good business sense might benefit the empire never occurred to Nicholas and his officials.

The persistent accusations of debauchery and sexual license strike a particularly strange chord to anyone familiar with the history or contemporary style of life of the Old Believers. Apart from its capacity to shock the uninformed, the charge reflected the determination of Nicholas's government and the church to regularize family life and make it conform to traditional Christian teaching and contemporary standards of respectability.[32] Since many of the priestless refused to marry in the official church and, lacking priests, had no Sacrament of marriage within their own communities, they founded families without benefit of any clergy. This long-established practice offended the moral and canonical sensibilities of the Orthodox hierarchy and subverted their attempts to enforce their rigid definition of Christian marriage. Indeed, in the opinion of contemporaries, the Old Believers' more practical and flexible attitude toward marriage drew new adherents away from the official church.[33]

No less subversive of propriety and social order was the prominent role of women in Old Belief.[34] In 1852 a government report noted that the Preobrazhenskoe Kladbishche had, as regular residents, 628 women and 110 men.[35] In the central monastery and convent of the Vyg community, the census of 1836 recorded 71 men, many of them old, and 522 women.[36] Although men held the most important positions of leadership, the Old Believer communities increasingly resembled unofficial convents, providing pious women with institutional support and a way of life distinct from society's usual expectations. From this quiet subversion, I would argue, arose the suspicion that the unofficial nuns of Old Belief led hypocritical and debauched lives.

In the unequal struggle with the Old Believer communities, the imperial government inevitably emerged the victor. The great age of the quasi-monastic communities was over, even though the lure of the monastic vocation lived on and still attracts some Old Believers, particularly women.[37] The destruction or crippling of its most visible centers did not destroy the movement, however. With the resilience they had shown so many times before, the guardians of the old faith regrouped and consolidated their ranks in a semi-legal situation that lasted, with a few exceptions, until the movement emerged strong and well-organized to take advantage of the opportunities created by the revolution of 1905.[38]

Our story, of course, has no end. The Old Believers are alive and well, in Russia and abroad. And historians have only begun to re-create and understand the past of which many Old Believers themselves are only dimly aware. One part of the task of re-creation and comprehension is the study of the history of the Old Believer communities—and, more broadly, of the institutional and social development of the movement as a whole. This approach offers many opportunities to study the language of faith and its implications in concrete political and social settings without falling into either extreme of nineteenth-century historiography. Moreover, such study helps us to understand the problems and prospects faced by Old Believers in our own day. For if the history of their communities in the eighteenth and nineteenth centuries teaches us anything, it reminds us that, during the "recovery of religious identity in the Soviet Union," the Old Believers' fate will depend not only on their own faithfulness and ingenuity but also on the policies of the government under whose rule they live.

OLD BELIEVER LIFE *and* SCHOLARSHIP *in* *the* LATE TWENTIETH CENTURY

Twelve

The Novosibirsk School of Old Believer Studies

THE AIM OF THIS CHAPTER IS TO EXPLORE the innovative research agendas and publications of the Novosibirsk school—Nikolai Nikolaevich Pokrovskii and his colleagues and students—on the history of popular religious movements, in particular the Old Belief. This undertaking forces us to examine many interrelated issues. To begin with, Pokrovskii's work provides a fascinating example of the creative possibilities and limitations faced by gifted and open-minded scholars in the last decades of the Soviet period. Moreover, tracking the writings of the Novosibirsk group into the post-Soviet years shows us to what extent its members' scholarly approaches, methods, and vocabulary did—or did not—change after the fall of the Communist regime.

The Novosibirsk experience takes us in several other directions as well. The school was self-consciously regional; its members published work on many aspects of Siberian history. The region was enormous—from the Urals to the Far East and even, for a time, Alaska. Even more important is the fact that the Novosibirsk school required its members to study regional issues in close connection with problems in the rest of Russia and, on that basis, offer an independent analysis of the latter. The school's heavy concentration on the Old Believers, however, makes excellent sense given the dissenters' large numbers and strong influence on local society, politics, and culture. In addition, there is probably much truth in the widely held assumption of the time that, in the last decades of Soviet power, scholars who did their research and published their findings on the periphery of the Soviet Union had greater creative freedom than their colleagues in Moscow and Leningrad. The achievements of the Tartu school of cultural semiotics are an obvious case in point.

The work of the Novosibirsk school raises once again the fundamental interpretative issues in the history of popular religion in Russia—and all premodern societies, for that matter. First, to what extent did religious convictions and modes of thought drive movements of religious dissent? And to what degree were movements of religious protest ultimately expressions of opposition to political oppression or social inequality? Second, are movements of religious opposition such as Old Belief the creation of dissident religious elites? Or do they mainly reflect the convictions of ordinary laypeople or even the marginal and dispossessed members of society? There are no neat solutions to either of these dichotomies. But each historian must continually keep them in mind.

The study of Old Belief has a long history, particularly in Russia itself. Before 1917, the voluminous literature on the Old Believers could be divided roughly into two categories. Scholars and popular writers who examined the history and political potential of the peasantry tended to see Old Belief as a nominally religious form of resistance to the tsars and to view its adherents as potential converts to the revolutionary cause (I will call this the populist approach). From the point of view of the official Orthodox Church, the Old Believers represented the resistance of uneducated believers and their self-appointed leaders to the authority of the hierarchy and clergy, the reformed liturgy, and contemporary currents of Christian learning and practice in Russia and elsewhere. The work of both schools of thought has retained much of its value. The populist approach studied the Old Believers in their economic, social, and institutional context and emphasized their relationship to movements of opposition to the ruling order, including the mass revolts of the seventeenth and eighteenth centuries. For their part, the Orthodox scholars—in some instances, specialists on missionary work among dissenters—took Old Believer liturgical practices, doctrinal statements, and forms of organization seriously, if only to refute them.[1]

For much of the Soviet period, Russian scholars had little or no opportunity to study Old Belief or any other religious traditions on their own terms. For several decades, the only important works on the subject—Pierre Pascal's classic study of Avvakum and his world, and Serge Zenkovsky's monumental history of Old Belief, for example—were published in other countries.[2] In the 1950s and 1960s, study of the movement experienced a renaissance in Russia thanks largely to Vladimir Ivanovich Malyshev (1910–1976), founder of the collection of Old Russian manuscripts (the *Drevlekhranilishche*) in the Institute of Russian Literature (Pushkin House) in St. Petersburg. Beginning in 1949 Malyshev organized for the institute annual field expeditions to the Far North of European Russia. Building on his earlier experience working alone, he concentrated above all on areas with a strong Old Believer tradition where the probability of finding old printed books and manuscripts was high.[3] One of Malyshev's objectives was to convince the often suspicious owners to donate their treasures to academic institutions such as Pushkin House, where they would be carefully preserved and made available to the scholarly community. Among his discoveries were many previously unknown documents and new variants of well-known texts. On this basis, scholars began to publish new editions of Old Believer writings (particularly the works of Avvakum, a figure dear to Malyshev's heart) as masterpieces of Old Russian literature and thus indispensable parts of Russia's cultural patrimony.

From Malyshev's time, archeographic expeditions have been the driving force behind the resurgence of the study of Old Believer history and culture. Year after year, scholars from a number of academic institutions in Russia have sent teams of researchers into the remote countryside and, by so doing, have in effect divided up the territory of European Russia into their own preserves. Scholars from St. Petersburg and Petrozavodsk concentrate on Karelia and the European North; the Moscow University group on the upper Kama region, the lower Volga valley, and Moldova; and scholars from Perm' on the Far Northeast of European Russia. While all of these groups follow the same general principles of field research, the leaders of each strive for their own unique "voice." For example, Irina Vasil'evna Pozdeeva, the longtime leader of the Moscow University researchers, heavily emphasizes the value of "complex" (*kompleksnye*) expeditions in which scholars of various disciplines—historians, literary and manuscript scholars, ethnographers, linguists, and musicologists—study the cultural heritage and contemporary customs of the same communities simultaneously, in order to establish the complete cultural context of the books, works of art, or oral traditions that are the focal point of their individual research.[4]

In my view, the most productive and imaginative of all the teams of Old Believer scholars is that of Pokrovskii and his associates in Novosibirsk and Ekaterinburg. Like their counterparts in the other centers of field research, the Siberian scholars concentrate on the collection and study of historical and polemical manuscripts in their own vast "territory," which includes the

Ural region as well as all of Siberia, Central Asia, and the Far East. Their publications combine their discoveries in the field with unpublished materials from all of the most important repositories of European Russia as well as local Siberian archives.

Pokrovskii has led the Novosibirsk research group almost from the beginning. A brief survey of his life and career will help us understand his scholarly approach and achievements.[5] Pokrovskii was born in 1930 in Rostov-on-Don, the son of a professor of history at the local university. His father's most important work was a history of the Russian conquest of the north Caucasus and the local response—the guerrilla war led by Imam Shamil'. The book was completed on the eve of World War II; its subject was too sensitive to allow publication and was long known mainly to innumerable censors. The authentic version of the work was finally published in 2000 with an introduction in which the younger Pokrovskii pointed out the timeliness of a history of Russo-Chechen interactions in both his father's time and his own.[6]

World War II interrupted Pokrovskii's childhood. As Nazi armies dashed toward Rostov and the north Caucasus, his family fled on foot over the mountains to Abkhazia and subsequently took refuge in Erevan. After the war the family returned to Rostov, where he completed secondary school. From there, he entered the history faculty of Moscow State University, graduating with a diploma in 1952 and a candidate's degree in 1956. In the Soviet academic system, this was a major achievement for a young man of twenty-six. As a graduate student and young researcher, Pokrovskii had already distinguished himself as a talented and technically sound analyst of unpublished medieval Russian documents—a skill central to his work throughout his life as a scholar. Evidently his intelligence, skill, and hard work made a favorable impression on senior faculty members, above all Mikhail Nikolaevich Tikhomirov.

Tikhomirov played a crucial role in Pokrovskii's career and in the development of historical research in Novosibirsk. Educated before 1917, he managed not only to navigate the swirling currents of Soviet academic life but also to publish a large and remarkably varied body of historical scholarship, studies ranging from the earliest Rus' law codes to urban life from the twelfth to the fifteenth centuries and popular revolts in the seventeenth, and to serve as mentor to an entire generation of scholars of medieval and early modern Russian history. He also did extraordinarily important work as an academic organizer, above all in reviving the Archeographic Commission of the Academy of Sciences and revitalizing its journals and source publications. As head of the commission, Tikhomirov organized the first archeographic field expedition of this kind in Siberia in 1959.[7]

The early years of Pokrovskii's academic career coincided with the Thaw in Soviet society after Stalin's death. In this exhilarating time, Pokrovskii and some friends in and around Moscow University met in informal discussions to analyze the shortcomings of the Soviet system and to propose more fundamental reforms than the Khrushchev regime had undertaken. They wrote and circulated several position papers, which argued, among other things, that the Soviet system was an oppressive perversion of authentic Marxism and, for good measure, included scathing criticism of Lenin and Stalin. Perhaps more important than the group's opinions—its members did not fully agree with one another—was the fact that these young men had created their own informal group and circulated their views without the sanction of governmental or university authorities. Pokrovskii and the others were arrested in the fall of 1957, tried for anti-Soviet agitation and propaganda and forming an illegal organization under articles 58-10 and 58-11 of the Soviet Criminal Code, and, early in 1958, sentenced to long terms in the labor camps of Mordovia. Pokrovskii spent six years in prison. In addition to the usual tribulations, he and some fellow prisoners went on a twenty-four-day hunger strike, hoping against hope to force a review of their convictions.[8] Even after he had finished his sentence, his trials were not over. Forbidden to live in Moscow under the terms of his release, he took a job at the Vladimir-Suzdal' Museum-Preserve away from the main centers of Soviet academic life. Although such speculation is risky, it is easy to imagine that Pokrovskii's empathy for the oppressed and persecuted—not least religious believers—so evident in his writings had its roots, in part, in this experience.[9]

Suddenly Pokrovskii's life and career took a dramatic turn. In 1965, Tikhomirov bequeathed his important private collection of manuscripts and rare books to the humanities sector of the recently founded Siberian Branch of the Soviet Academy of Sciences in Novosibirsk. He insisted that Pokrovskii, who had already done extensive work with the collection, be hired as its curator. The Siberian Academy met this condition, and within a very short time, Pokrovskii received appointments as research associate at the Institute of History, Philology, and Philosophy and as lecturer at Novosibirsk University.[10] Since both institutions were new and located far from the traditional centers of political and academic authority, they provided an ideal setting for a young scholar to establish his own research agendas.

Pokrovskii responded energetically to his new opportunity. Almost immediately he took over the field expeditions, which had begun before his arrival. Siberia and the Urals proved to be ideal regions to look for undiscovered manuscripts and old printed books, for their remote corners were traditional refuges of the Old Believers. His book *Puteshestvie za redkimi knigami*, first published in 1984, provides an evocative account of these expeditions, the research methods the participants used, and the people and places they encountered.[11] Work in isolated Old Believer settlements demanded enormous patience, respect for local traditions of dress (modest clothing, head scarves for women, and when possible, beards for men), and an ability to demonstrate detailed knowledge and respect for Russian Orthodox and specifically Old Believer texts and practices. Thus prepared, the Siberian researchers soon achieved remarkable successes. In 1968, Pokrovskii and his team discovered a priceless manuscript—the oldest and by far the longest account of the 1525 and 1531 trials of Maksim Grek, the Italian-educated Greek scholar and translator—in an Old Believer settlement in the Altai. Its publication three years later established the reputation of Novosibirsk as a major center of Russian historical studies and Pokrovskii as a leading scholar of his generation.[12]

From that time, Pokrovskii's scholarly career has been remarkable for the range of periods and subjects he has investigated and the variety of academic roles he has played—as author, editor, teacher, and mentor. He has slowly but surely reached the pinnacle of Russian academia. The culmination was his appointment as Corresponding Member of the Russian Academy of Sciences in 1987 and as full Member (Academician) in 1992. Even more significantly, he has earned the deep respect of his fellow scholars and achieved the status both in Russia and abroad of founding father of his own school.

From the beginning, Pokrovskii's most persistent focus has been on the history of the Old Believers in the Urals and Siberia and their relations with the imperial government. His first major book, published in 1974, *Antifeodal'nyi protest uralo-sibirskikh krest'ian staroobriadtsev v XVIII v.*, covers official policy toward the Old Believers over the course of the eighteenth century and analyzes the main episodes in which they led "the anti-feudal protests" of ordinary Siberians against the state.[13] Pokrovskii's analysis of the relations between officialdom and Old Believers is subtle and complex. Officialdom consisted of the state bureaucracy and the church hierarchy, which at times worked together and at others pursued contradictory objectives. In the mid- and late eighteenth century a self-consciously "enlightened" central administration fought regular skirmishes with Metropolitans Syl'vester and Pavel of Siberia, Ukrainian clerics who insisted on using repressive policies to force the "ignorant" Old Believers back into the official church.

For their part, the Old Believers split into moderate and radical tendencies within each of the main accords. Moderates and radicals alternatively supported or denounced each other depending on conditions in the wider world, especially the changing policies and actions of the government or official church. The moderates aimed, first and foremost, to preserve and strengthen their communities. When the central government offered limited toleration, they attempted to reach a practical accommodation with it. The more radically inclined sought, above all, to preserve the purity of their beliefs and practices in a world ruled by the Antichrist. When the Siberian hierarchy or local secular officials threatened them, the most radical resorted to the ultimate time-honored form of protest—self-immolation. The ambiguous response of officialdom to the threat or reality of mass suicide illustrates the dilemmas posed by such militants. Again and again, local officials received instructions to respond to potential instances of self-immolation by doing everything in their power to prevent such tragedies from occurring, but at the same time, to do nothing that might impel the militants to carry out their plans. In short, such self-contradictory orders put both local police officials and the militant Old Believers in a position from which there could be no good outcome.

As the title of *Antifeodal'nyi protest* indicates, it is a study of many forms of popular social, political, and religious resistance to the secular and church authorities. By definition, therefore, the author situated the ideas and actions of the participants in the concrete institutional and social conditions in the Urals and Siberia in the eighteenth century. His work on Siberian society in the seventeenth century, published some years later, provides helpful background to the conflicts of the eighteenth. In *Tomsk 1648–1649 gg.: Voevodskaia vlast' i zemskie miry* and *Vlast' i obshchestvo: Sibir' v XVII v.*, written with Vadim Aleksandrovich Aleksandrov, Pokrovskii outlined the traditional conceptions of communal rights and institutions that Russian settlers brought into this enormous frontier region. For its part, the central administration of the empire attempted to impose order on its unruly subjects by administrative fiat from Moscow through its appointed governors. Pokrovskii interpreted the interrelation of the central government and its agents with local society as a process of continuous give-and-take. In some cases Moscow succeeded in imposing its will on the Siberians; in others its agents had to back down in the face of local resistance; in still others, such as the Tomsk revolt of 1648–1649, the irreconcilable differences between the two sides produced armed rebellion against the state.[14] The administrative structure worked best when the central government respected local communal institutions and collaborated with or co-opted the leaders of local society.[15] Pokrovskii's approach and conclusions are remarkably similar to those of the most recent work by Western European and North American scholars on the relations of the state and local society in early modern Europe, Russia included.[16]

The later conflicts analyzed in *Antifeodal'nyi protest* took place against this background. Nevertheless, specific actions of the imperial government and the Orthodox hierarchy set off the most dramatic confrontations, such as the Tara revolt of 1722. In Siberia, Peter I's decree that all Old Believers register with the government and pay twice the normal capitation tax epitomized his burdensome demands on ordinary Russians. Moreover, Siberia's many Old Believers deeply resented the attempts of the local church authorities to force them back into the official Orthodox Church. Finally, the decree that all citizens of the empire swear loyalty to Peter's still unnamed heir provided the spark that set off the conflagration.

A central feature of Pokrovskii's studies of the Tara revolt of 1722, beginning with the chapter in *Antifeodal'nyi protest*, is his insistence that the rebels' beliefs and convictions had their own inner logic. He demonstrated clearly, for example, that Old Believer apocalyptic teachings motivated and justified the protests against the oath of allegiance to an unnamed heir.[17] This emphasis set the tone for all of Pokrovskii's work. Throughout his career, in spite of difficulties with the censors ("in those years, 'religious' subject matter was severely frowned upon" [*ochen' ne liubili "religioznuiu" tematiku*]), he has made the ideological convictions and internal development of the Old Believers a central and independent theme in his writings.[18]

Antifeodal'nyi protest embodies the best qualities of Soviet academic publication of the 1970s in a number of ways. In spite of a few mandatory Marxist-Leninist quotations, Pokrovskii situated his work within the traditional polarity of prerevolutionary populist and ecclesiastical interpretations of Old Belief. If he has a direct scholarly ancestor, it is Afanasii Prokof'evich Shchapov (1830–1876), the mid-nineteenth-century founder of the populist school. Born in Siberia and educated in clergy schools, Shchapov wrote several groundbreaking essays on the *raskol* while a teacher at the Kazan' Theological Academy and the local university. His passionate homily at the funeral of the victims of the government's repression of the peasant demonstrations at Bezdna in 1861 cost him his teaching positions. After his three years of freelance writing and political activity in St. Petersburg, the imperial government exiled him to Siberia where he spent the rest of his life.

Today Shchapov is remembered for introducing the then-novel concept that Old Belief movement was not really a movement of religious protest but, rather, a vehicle for popular resistance to social and economic oppression. In his view, Nikon's liturgical reforms, to which he had no objections, could not possibly have set off a massive movement of social-religious protest. Instead, the cause of the raskol was social oppression and the destruction of popular traditions of local initiative in all spheres, including parish affairs. Shchapov did, however, stress that the "democratic" teachings of the more radical Old Believers provided justification for popular opposition to state and church and made the Old Faith a central element in the mass revolts of the late seventeenth and eighteenth centuries.[19]

In some general respects, Pokrovskii and the Novosibirsk school follow Shchapov's lead. Yet the conditions in which they worked were radically different. During the intervening century and more, the volume of accessible sources on the history of Old Belief, and scholarly and popular literature based on them, has grown enormously. Moreover, in spite of their surprisingly impressive learning, Shchapov's writings were general essays addressed to the educated society of his time. Most important, Pokrovskii and his school take seriously both the theological and the social dimensions of Old Belief. Religious ideas could well inspire political and social protest, but they also had an inner logic of their own that shaped the lives of those who espoused them. In this sense, the Novosibirsk scholars are heirs of the best ecclesiastical historians such as P. S. Smirnov as well as of Shchapov.

Technically as well, *Antifeodal'nyi protest* exemplified the best historical scholarship of the late Soviet period. The author made thorough, and critical use of any and all sources of information on his subject—files in the central historical archives of the Soviet Union and Siberian regional archives, and Old Believer polemical and historical texts. Although very different in their style and content and the circumstances of their creation, official reports in the state archives and Old Believer polemical and historical texts were treated as equally important. Each document, of course, had to be studied in its own context and on its own terms, weighing its reliability and significance. Pokrovskii carefully avoided forcing the evidence of these varied sources into any neat pattern or preconceived ideological framework. If their testimony was inconsistent, it was the historian's duty to say so honestly. Finally, he carefully wove his evidence into a clear and compelling narrative. In all these respects, Pokrovskii's first book illustrates the methods, approaches, and qualities of his subsequent scholarly work throughout his career, and that of his students.

Pokrovskii's next book on Old Belief, *Puteshestvie za redkimi knigami,* presents his methods and findings to a broader readership. It is a wonderful combination of adventure story, travelogue, and description of the discovery and study of historical texts. Published under Soviet conditions, the book's first two editions appeared in printings of 55,000 and 50,000 copies respectively, remarkable for a work that deals, in substantial part, with a religious tradition.[20] At the same time, part of its appeal may have been precisely the rural Siberian setting and the evocation of Russian cultural and religious traditions, fashionable themes from the 1960s into the 1980s. Whatever the reason, Pokrovskii's book achieved the goal to which any historian aims in writing a work of this kind—sharing his methods and findings with a wider public and, one might add, advertising the accomplishments of his research team.

Because of Pokrovskii's voice as narrator, *Puteshestvie* reveals a good deal about his attitudes. He made no bones about his devotion to the populist tradition and allied himself with such earlier members of the social and cultural elite as Leo Tolstoy and Shchapov, who reached out to the masses. Within his own generation he has aligned himself with "liberal nationalists" in Soviet academia such as Dmitrii Sergeevich Likhachev and Sigurd Ottovich Shmidt. Paradoxically perhaps, he has also privately expressed his admiration for Aleksandr Isaevich Solzhenitsyn, whose *Gulag Archipelago* he cited on a number of occasions.[21] *Puteshestvie* also underlines Pokrovskii's intense admiration for the radical Old Believers of his own day—both those who live freely in isolated places and work hard to maintain their cultural and religious traditions and the victims of persecution such as the residents of the monastic settlements who were arrested and sentenced to the Gulag in 1951.

Pokrovskii's latest book on Old Belief, *Starovery-chasovennye na vostoke Rossii v XVIII–XX vv.*, coauthored with Natal'ia Dmitrievna Zol'nikova, was published in 2002. The chapters on the eighteenth and nineteenth centuries are Pokrovskii's work. Zol'nikova wrote the latter half of the book, which deals mainly with people and events of the twentieth. The *chasovennye*, the dominant Old Believer accord in the Urals and Siberia, were a loosely organized, complex coalition of groups. At first its adherents saw themselves as the direct successors of the priestly Kerzhenets communities, but over time and in many areas, they gradually became priestless.

The authors began once again with the neopopulist assumption that Old Belief was ultimately a movement of resistance to official institutions and society. Since the book appeared after the fall of the Soviet Union, they were free to concentrate on the beliefs, attitudes, and practices of an oppositional religious movement without having to tie every word or action to the previously mandatory language of "popular protest."

In one sense, then, *Starovery-chasovennye* is the history of a "textual community." The authors focused on the polemical and historical writings from the early eighteenth century to the late twentieth. The introductory chapter lets the reader know that the authors intended to write an intellectual and cultural history, for it surveys the Old Russian literary tradition with particular emphasis on popular, "folk," or oppositional texts, not least the works of the first generations of Old Believer writers. Then in analyzing the writings of the chasovennye (most unearthed by Novosibirsk and Ekaterinburg field researchers), Pokrovskii and Zol'nikova presented them as compositions with their own inner logic and purpose. They gave each of the polemical and narrative texts a meticulously close reading and showed how the writers drew on the heritage of the Eastern Church fathers, the medieval Russian Orthodox tradition, and earlier Old Believer literature.

On another level, Pokrovskii and Zol'nikova assembled a detailed narrative history of the chasovennye, the dominant Old Believer accord in the Urals and Siberia. The authors constructed this narrative from the records of the periodic councils of the accord and many other writings from the local Old Believer communities unearthed by researchers in the field.[22] Their treatment concentrates on the organizational, canonical, and doctrinal issues that continually defined the various factions among the chasovennye.

In *Starovery-chasovennye*, the authors confront head-on the classic dichotomies faced by scholars of popular religion. The line between elite and popular religious cultures virtually disappears. Many of the Siberian Old Believers were peasants, yet they drew selectively from the classics of Orthodox high culture, the works of highly educated bishops and priests. Moreover, the connection between the social rank of the chasovennye writers and their arguments and prophecies was, in Pokrovskii's phrase, "indirect" (*oposredovanno*).[23] At times, social position reinforced polemical stance. As one of the Ekaterinburg scholars, Viktor Ivanovich Baidin, has argued, the Ural merchant-industrialists supported the moderate position among the chasovennye—acceptance of fugitive priests, seeking accommodation with imperial government when possible, and willingness to join the edinoverie, created in 1800 in order to bring priestly Old Believers into communion with the official Orthodox Church. The peasant chasovennye leaned in the more radical direction of priestless practice, radical rejection of state and official church, and an emphasis on apocalyptic prophecy.[24] Nevertheless, the relationship between ideology and social status was never simple, and the inner logic of their arguments often led chasovennye polemicists to surprising conclusions.

Moreover, the authors allow the reader to hear the Old Believers' own voices.[25] Indeed, their role in encouraging and "commissioning" the creative work of contemporary Old Believer writers raises serious questions about the relationship between contemporary academics and the bearers of the Old Believer tradition. To be sure, the Novosibirsk scholars and their Old Believer contacts such as Afanasii Gerasimovich Murachev live in completely different cultural worlds. Murachev, a very independent, self-assured man, writes in a deliberately archaic style and interprets the events of the late twentieth century within the framework of the Old Believer apocalyptic tradition. Nevertheless, one may legitimately ask to what extent his contacts with them may have influenced his most recent writings.[26]

Within Soviet and post-Soviet academia, one of the Novosibirsk school's avowed purposes is to study the local history and culture of Siberia. As its leader, Pokrovskii's responsibilities include overseeing the research and publications of his fellow historians. The other members of the school, unlike Pokrovskii, tend to concentrate on a single broad theme in Siberian history. Three obvious examples come to mind. Before her recent work on Old Belief, Zol'nikova published books on the parish and clergy in the eighteenth century and on the complex relations between the Russian Orthodox Church and the state in Siberia.[27] Aleksandr Khristianovich Elert's study of Gerhard Friedrich Müller's notes on his Siberian explorations in 1733–1734 and 1739–1743 has demonstrated that there were far more settlements in the region than were listed in the imperial government's records. In addition, his painstaking deciphering of Müller's handwritten German notes has provided him with a great deal of new information on the ethnic composition of Siberia's population, including its indigenous ethnic groups.[28] Natal'ia Petrovna Matkhanova has analyzed the administration and administrators of eastern Siberia in the nineteenth century. In addition to official administrative records, she has made extensive use of the diaries of the governors of the region to illustrate their characters and philosophies of government, their interactions with the central administration in St. Petersburg, and their relations with the local population.[29]

Finally, any description of the Novosibirsk group of scholars would be incomplete without mention of Pokrovskii's colleagues in the field of early Russian literature and intellectual history—his longtime colleague Elena Konstantinovna Romodanovskaia (an Academician in her own right), Liubov' Vasil'evna Titova, Tamara Vasil'evna Panich, and Ol'ga Dmitrievna Zhuravel'. All are distinguished scholars. The subjects of their publications, however, fall outside the scope of this article, except for Titova's admirable edition of Deacon Fedor's epistle to his son Maksim, Zhuravel''s articles on Old Believer historical and devotional writings, and Romodanovskaia's book on the origins of Siberian regional literature.[30]

Last, but not least, Pokrovskii took the lead in all the Novosibirsk group's common enterprises. For years, he continued to lead the field expeditions that trained his students "on the job." He also mentored and encouraged a group of scholars at the University of the Urals in Ekaterinburg who adopted the same basic research agendas and methods. Finally, under his and Romodanovskaia's leadership, the Novosibirsk group regularly publishes its findings in two series— *Arkheografiia i istochnikovedenie Sibiri*, volumes of articles and article-length documents that have appeared since 1975, and *Istoriia Sibiri: Pervoistochniki*, collections of documents, the first of which was published in 1993.[31]

As one would expect, the scholarly qualities of Pokrovskii's students' publications on Old Belief and popular religion reflect their teacher. Natal'ia Sergeevna Gur'ianova's, *Krest'ianskii antimonarkhicheskii protest v staroobriadcheskoi eskhatologicheskoi literature perioda pozdnego feodalizma* traces the evolution of Old Believer apocalyptic political ideas or, in Michael Cherniavsky's term, "political theology."[32] These include the conviction that the End Time had come and that the Antichrist ruled the world. For generations Old Believers debated what this presupposition meant. Their teachings divided into the theories of the "perceptible" (*chuvstvennyi*) and "spiritual" (*dukhovnyi*) nature of the Antichrist. The former meant that the Antichrist was embodied in one particular ruler—most commonly Peter I— or, in another variant, in the entire succession of Russian rulers after Aleksei Mikhailovich. Over time some of the less radical Old Believers argued that the spirit of the Antichrist dominated the world, or the official Orthodox Church in particular, but that no individual embodied it. Whichever view they held, Gur'ianova pointed out, the Old Believers did not reject the government or state power as such. Indeed, they looked back with nostalgia to the idealized Christian rulers of the past.

The second part of Gur'ianova's study analyzes the debates within Old Belief over prayers for the rulers. For if the emperor embodied the Antichrist or ruled over a world dominated by his spirit, was it permissible to continue the traditional prayers for the ruler and his family in the liturgy? At first, the various emerging accords agreed that, in the extreme circumstances of the End Time, it was impossible to offer such prayers. Over time some of the moderate Old Believers, such as the leaders of the Vyg community, reached a limited accommodation with the state and, on the government's demand, reintroduced prayers for the emperor. The more radical adamantly rejected such compromises. The Filippovtsy broke with Vyg over this precise issue. Moreover, the moderates were distinctly uncomfortable about praying for the ruler and debated among themselves how they should do so. Was it permissible to pray for the emperor as "well-born" (*blagochestivyi*) but not as "true-believing" (*blagovernyi*)? Or should they pray for the rulers' conversion to the true faith? Clearly neither of these formulas gave legitimacy to the state or reformed church.

Gur'ianova built her work on an exhaustive search of well-known but poorly catalogued manuscript collections in St. Petersburg and Moscow as well as local discoveries in Siberia. As I can testify, she and her Moscow colleague Elena Mikhailovna Iukhimenko slogged through hundreds of large miscellaneous manuscript books most unhelpfully catalogued simply as *sbornik*, thereby unearthing many undiscovered compositions on apocalyptic themes. She wove her findings into coherent groups of arguments, which she connected to the various accords and the specific circumstances in which they lived. While worded in the obligatory rhetoric of late Soviet times, Gur'ianova's conceptual framework—"peasant antimonarchical protest"—is, for the most part, appropriate. Theories equating the emperor or the official order in church and state with the Antichrist certainly advocated opposition to the imperial government, and the people who expounded them were most often peasants. Ultimately, however, the greatest strength of Gur'ianova's book is the diligence with which she unearthed many new examples of Old Believer apocalyptic theory to add to the canon of long-published texts, analyzed their varied arguments, and studied the contexts from which they emerged.

Two other students of Pokrovskii have combined the neopopulist approach with close reading of texts in a similar way. Before 1990, Lev Kabdenovich Kuandykov published a series of articles on the structure and "rule" of the Vyg community. His arguments stressed the community's origins as an informal, radical peasant community that the Denisov brothers transformed into a hierarchical monastic community modeled, at least in theory, on Solovki. Again in this case, the strongest part of the author's work lies in his meticulous analysis of the prescriptive documents (the "rule" and other *ustavy*) of Vyg. Kuandykov showed more clearly than any predecessor—including the present author—the subtle distinctions between earlier and later rules and the evidence they provide of the evolution of Vyg in the direction of a more rigid structure and tighter discipline. In view of its promise, it is unfortunate that his project never reached its logical conclusion in a book.[33]

Ol'ga Valer'evna Chumicheva's reexamination of the revolt of the Solovetskii monastery, *Solovetskoe vosstanie 1667–1676 gg.*, blends social analysis and text study in a less mechanical way.[34] Perhaps because she published her monograph in post-Soviet times, the author was able to concentrate almost entirely on the analysis of her sources. She careful unraveled the published and archival documents on the revolt, many of them familiar, and produced a detailed, intricate narrative of the course of the rebellion. Step by step she traced the ever-shifting factions and alliances within the monastery. She pointed out, for example, that in September 1669, a moderate faction among the rebels temporarily seized control of the monastery from the radicals. The moderates advocated continuing armed resistance in the name of pre-Nikonian Orthodoxy but rejected the radicals' attempts to make revolutionary changes in religious practice. Like the scholars who studied the revolt before her, she was fully aware of the political and social dimensions of the uprising. The most important feature of Chumicheva's approach, however, is her emphasis on the liturgical and political-theological debates among the rebels and their long-term influence on later Old Believers. Like other members of the Novosibirsk school, she focused primarily on the texts themselves, especially the polemical writings of leaders of the monastery during the revolt, above all Gerasim Firsov, the leading intellectual in Solovki.

Her analysis brought her to a number of important conclusions, the first being that Solovki did not rebel because of the ignorance of its residents. The intellectual leaders of the community such as Firsov understood that symbols such as the two-finger or three-finger sign of the cross were ultimately important not for themselves but as signs of underlying theological doctrines. To be sure, the core participants in the revolt were not learned churchmen but laypeople, including some veterans of earlier uprisings in other parts of Russia and a minority of the monks. Most of the monks opposed the revolt, and a significant number either escaped or were expelled from Solovki during the siege. As the rebellion dragged on, the most radical of the defenders began to function without priests and develop justifications for the practice. In that sense the rebels were not only role models for later rebels against state and church in the name of the Old Faith but also direct precursors of the priestless accords of Old Belief that emerged in subsequent decades.

Gur'ianova's publications in post-Soviet times display a similar shift in emphasis within the neopopulist framework. In her more recent books, she concentrated on Old Believer "high" culture. *Istoriia i chelovek v sochineniiakh staroobriadtsev XVIII veka* analyzes the historical writings of the Vyg school in the first half of the century, especially Ivan Filippov's history of the Vyg community, the last testaments of the community's leaders, and the funeral homilies in their honor. Her work in the most important manuscript collections in Moscow and St. Petersburg uncovered previously unknown polemical and historical texts and variants that allowed her, among other things, to undertake the first scholarly analysis of Filippov's well-known but puzzling history. Comparing the extremely varied manuscripts of this work, she concluded that Filippov deliberately chose not to complete a definitive text of his work, thus leaving to his successors the opportunity to make further editorial changes and to continue chronicling the ongoing history of the community.

The main conclusion of *Istoriia i chelovek* is that, in spite of their quaintly elaborate rhetoric—what Malyshev called "Vyg verbosity" (*vygoretskoe mnogoslovie*)—and the authors' obvious ideological convictions, Old Believer historians' writings display the same qualities as more "secular" writers of the early eighteenth century. They understood the need to weigh and balance the testimony of the written and oral sources from which they worked. Citing Iukhimenko's analysis of Semen Denisov's "Istoriia ob ottsekh i stradal'tsakh solovetskikh"[35] as well as her own findings on Filippov's history, Gur'ianova argued that until today scholars have let the religious convictions and deliberately archaic language of the Old Believer histories blind them to their authors' scrupulous concern for the factual accuracy of their work. Moreover, just like contemporaries such as Tatishchev, the Old Believer historians put heavy emphasis on the role of individual personality in shaping the course of events. In these respects, Gur'ianova concluded, the Vyg historians were as sophisticated as their counterparts in the world of official high culture. In my view, Gur'ianova somewhat overstated her case in her understandable desire to undermine the traditional image of the Old Believers' intellectual poverty and cultural isolation. No matter how carefully they worked, the Vyg historians wrote sacred history, in which the religious message ultimately took precedence over scholarly accuracy. Nevertheless, *Istoriia i chelovek* adds a great deal to our understanding of the Vyg historians' achievement and rightly emphasizes that the quality of their work should be judged against that of their own contemporaries rather than by the standards of later generations.[36]

Most recently, in *Staroobriadtsy i tvorcheskoe nasledie Kievskoi mitropolii*, Gur'ianova continued the study of Old Believer elite culture. Once again she stressed the intellectual sophistication of the leading Old Believer writers of the early eighteenth century, especially the leaders of the Vyg community. In this instance, she focused her attention on their polemical skills and their use of "Kievan" learning in their own defense.

As Gur'ianova made clear, this book builds on Tat'iana Anatol'evna Oparina's *Ivan Nasedka i polemicheskoe bogoslovie Kievskoi Metropolii*, a study of the impact of Ukrainian scholarship in Moscow in the first half of the seventeenth century. Oparina, who received her training in Novosibirsk, traced the development of Muscovite theology in the first half of the seventeenth century. Until Nikon's elevation to the patriarchal throne in 1652, the church hierarchy and the scholars who, like Nasedka, worked in the patriarchs' printing house firmly believed that Muscovite Russian Orthodoxy was the only true faith. All other variants of Christianity, including Eastern Orthodoxy outside of Muscovite territory, were fatally flawed. At the same time, the Muscovite

Church did not have the intellectual and polemical resources to defend the its claims effectively against the challenges of Protestants, Roman Catholics, and the Orthodox outside its jurisdiction. The scholars in the Printing House had no choice but to make extensive use of polemical literature from the Orthodox in Ukraine for anti-Catholic and anti-Protestant arguments and, indeed, basic information about the beliefs and practices of these branches of Christendom. Given the complexity of confessional debates in Ukraine, it was no easy task to select appropriate texts and arguments and weave them into the evolving body of Muscovite Church texts without unwittingly undermining the unique purity of Russian Orthodoxy. Nasedka and his colleagues understood the danger. In a series of editions published in the 1630s and 1640s, they made extensive but selective use of polemical and devotional works from Ukraine and Belarus, tailoring them for Russian use. By far the most influential of these were the apocalyptic miscellanies, the *Kirillova kniga* and the *Kniga o vere,* which appeared in Moscow in 1644 and 1648 respectively. These compilations of prophetic writings quickly achieved great—but ambivalent and thus divisive— influence among the cultural elite in Moscow and later became integral to the Old Believer canon of sacred texts.[37]

Gur'ianova took up the story where Oparina left off. When the church schism took form, the first generations of Old Believer polemicists had to defend their understanding of true Orthodoxy against the leaders of the official church. Like their predecessors, the first critics of the Nikonian reforms used any polemical ammunition they could find. From the beginning, they had no compunctions about citing pre-Nikonian books based on "Kievan" (Ukrainian and Belorussian) materials as long as they had been published in Moscow. In the first half of the eighteenth century the need for polemical flexibility had become even more urgent, not least because, in some well-known instances, the imperial government and Orthodox hierarchy forced Old Believers into public debates with defenders of the Nikonian reforms. In building their case, the leaders of the Vyg community, the leading Old Believer scholars of their day, not only made extensive use of pre-Nikonian Moscow editions such as the *Kirillova kniga* and *Kniga o vere* but also had copies of some of the Ukrainian originals on which such books drew. When compiling the *D'iakonovy* and *Pomorskie otvety* for debates with their opponents, they did not hesitate to cite such "Kievan" writings when polemically necessary. Moreover, Vyg scholars used innovative approaches to the study of manuscripts—such as paleography and the analysis of the paper and bindings of manuscript books—to prove that some of their opponents' most important proof texts were forgeries. In this respect, they surpassed their adversaries in official society. Later in the eighteenth century the distinction between pre-Nikonian Muscovite and "Kievan" polemical works disappeared altogether. In other respects, however, Gur'ianova suggested, Old Believer learning had ceased to be a viable alternative to the official elite culture.[38]

In the preface to his monograph *Starovery-stranniki v XVIII–pervoi polovine XIX v.*, Gur'ianova's colleague Aleksandr Ivanovich Mal'tsev provided an admirable summary of the Novosibirsk school's approach in the last two decades. He praised Shchapov and other nineteenth-century progressives for taking seriously the dimension of social and political protest within Old Belief. At the same time, he argued, they presented a badly distorted view of the movement. Their writings tended to equate all of Old Belief with its most radical fringes such as the *stranniki* (fugitives), in part because they relied on the reports of government inspectors whose job was to investigate political subversion. Mal'tsev explicitly rejected the nineteenth-century populists' claim—echoed by scholars of the Soviet period such as K. V. Chistov and A. I. Klibanov—that the teaching of the stranniki amounted to "religious whitewashing" of social and political protest. A truly balanced understanding of their doctrines, he argued, requires a careful analysis of all of the evidence, written, oral, and visual.[39]

With this in mind, Mal'tsev undertook a systematic study of the fundamental teachings of the first prophet of the stranniki, Evfimii, and his followers.[40] Like other members of the Novosibirsk group, he concentrated on the search for unpublished treatises that would allow him to make a more nuanced analysis of the evolution of Evfimii's convictions and ideas. Mal'tsev admirably fulfilled this mission. His archival searches led him to major new discoveries particularly in Iaroslavl', including two treatises in Evfimii's own hand. On this basis, he was able to explain Evfimii's radical "anarchist" teachings as a condemnation of those Old Believers who consorted with the Antichrist by registering with the government as dissenters and paying the double tax or who "hid behind" the local Orthodox priest who would include them in the list of his parishioners. Even his fellow Filippovtsy, until then one of the most radical priestless accords, alienated him by attempting to reach accommodation with more moderate groups within the movement. At first, Mal'tsev argued, Evfimii accepted that true Christians could live rigorously in "the world" following scripture and the example of the first leaders of the Vyg community whose teachings and example, in his view, later generations betrayed. Within a few years, however, he concluded that "flight," or the life of a hermit, was the only path to salvation. Having chosen radical separation from the world of the Antichrist, Evfimii and his later followers had no dealings with the government and its agents, the rest of society, and all religious structures including other Old Believer accords. Indeed, Mal'tsev argued, the stranniki could be considered anarchists, since they also made no attempt to create any organizational structures of their own. But like the Cathars, centuries earlier, the stranniki gradually came to the realization that a life of total "inner emigration" was possible only with the help of sympathizers who still lived in "the world."[41]

Mal'tsev's new book, *Staroobriadcheskie bespopovskie soglasiia v XVIII–nachale XIX v.*, published after his untimely death, traced the complex relations between the priestless accords within Old Belief. Working meticulously, he chose to emphasize not the much-publicized quarrels and schisms among the priestless but, rather, their persistent attempts to reconcile their differences. Following in the tradition of P. S. Smirnov, Mal'tsev analyzed the negotiations between the leaders of the various priestless accords document by document. In the absence of any clearly defined centers of authority, the bespopovtsy accords had great difficulty achieving cooperation and mutual toleration. Disagreements on liturgical and canonical issues, the personal ambition of individual leaders, and the pride of each accord and community in its own heritage further complicated their attempts at collaboration. In 1727 the Pomortsy and Fedoseevtsy reached an agreement recognizing each other's legitimacy thanks largely to the efforts of individual peacemakers on both sides. The well-known willfulness and ambition of Il'ia Kovylin had much to do with a renewed rift between the two groups later in the century.

As always, one of the important underlying sources of dispute within Old Belief was the tradition of resistance to authority in church and state and the best ways to maintain it in a changing world. In the late eighteenth and early nineteenth centuries most of the main priestless accords evolved in a more moderate direction in response to more tolerant governmental policies and the growing influence of wealthy merchants who strove for stability within Old Belief and good relations with the state. That tendency, in turn, aroused the opposition of radicals and traditionalists—usually men of less privileged social rank—who defended the rigor of earlier generations of the faithful.[42]

To summarize, the individual works of Pokrovskii and his colleagues that we have examined demonstrate the central characteristics of the Novosibirsk school as a whole. First, the Novosibirsk scholars insist on the primacy of sources. In their view, the central task of any historian is to hunt down and analyze meticulously all possible sources of information and insight on any subject that they investigate. Scholars sometimes divide the sources on Old Belief into two categories—investigative records in government and church archives and the Old Believers' own polemical, historical, and devotional writings, whether collected during field research or located in long-established manuscript collections. The Novosibirsk scholars make extensive use of both. Even though the discoveries of their field expeditions are their pride and joy, painstaking, their seemingly endless plodding through the main archives and collections in Russia's historic capitals and regional archives in Siberia and elsewhere is an equally critical part of their arsenal. In *Puteshestvie za redkimi knigami*, Pokrovskii related several anecdotes illustrating the frustrations and triumphs of archival research, such as the search for the manifesto (*protivnoe pis'mo*) of the Tara rebels. Archival catalogues (*opisi*) may be missing or hopelessly inadequate. Materials on a single incident may be scattered through several different archives. Centrally important documents, such as the manifesto, may turn up by accident in a completely unexpected context.[43] Some research projects require the interweaving of documents discovered by researchers in the field with governmental records in the archives. Pokrovskii needed sources of both kinds in reconstructing the case of the Old Believer Orenburg Cossacks, who in 1854 were condemned to walk the gauntlet for insubordination.[44]

Pokrovskii's archival research has produced unexpected glimpses of the personal life and thoughts of individual Russians. In the best-known example, he found the confession of the Altai peasant Artemii Sakalov in the Tobol'sk archives. The authorities arrested Sakalov on the assumption—false, in Pokrovskii's view—that he was an Old Believer because he refused to make his confession to a parish priest. Instead, the investigators discovered, he had written a confession for himself and God in which he revealed a remarkable "mixture of Orthodoxy and paganism, prayer, and blasphemy." He admitted that he used magic charms and incantations addressed indiscriminately to God, the Blessed Virgin, the saints, and devils. Some of the sins on the list of this energetic, stubborn man—blasphemous words while in his cups, for example—are hardly surprising. But how many Russian peasants admitted to having long, amicable conversations with a devil? Pokrovskii's discovery has given us a glimpse of the inner life of a man who was both an extraordinary individual and a representative of his time, place, and cultural milieu.[45] To my knowledge, no other documents of such depth and intimacy have come to light. The publications of the Novosibirsk group, however, do contain more fleeting revelations of the thoughts and emotions of ordinary people such as, for example, the poignant letters of leaders of the Tara revolt to their families.[46]

Second, for the Novosibirsk school, the discovery of new sources leads directly to their rigorous analysis and, in many instances, publication. The monographs of Gur'ianova, Mal'tsev, and Chumicheva all end with editions of unpublished documents that the authors discovered in the course of their work. Pokrovskii and Zol'nikova's study of the chasovennye is actually a two-volume work, the monograph *Starovery-chasovennye* itself and *Dukhovnaia literatura staroverov Vostoka Rossii XVIII–XX vv.*, a volume of sources on their history, many of them the writings of the accord's leaders. The commitment to publish historical sources has recently taken a high-tech turn in Pokrovskii's current work with a team of collaborators, most prominently Gail Lehnhoff of UCLA, to publish a new edition of the *Stepennaia kniga tsarskogo rodosloviia*, based in large part on two newly discovered copies, one of which he recently found in Tomsk.[47]

Third, given his personal and family history, it is hard to imagine Pokrovskii avoiding intense involvement with the larger society in his own time. His empathy for the victims of political repression and religious persecution is obvious whether he writes about the Tara rebels of the 1720s, the persecuted Old Believers of the 1950s, or the Russian Orthodox hierarchy and clergy in the 1920s. The last of these issues merits a brief comment. From his investigations in the 1990s in the previously forbidden Archive of the President of the Russian Federation, Pokrovskii drew a heart-rending picture of the inescapable dilemma faced by the leaders of the church under the new Communist government. He demonstrated that, from the beginning of the campaign to confiscate church property in 1922, the top leaders of the Party aimed at nothing less than the division and ultimate destruction of the church as an institution. In this situation, everything that the Russian Orthodox hierarchy and its flock did to make its peace with the new government or to minister to society's needs was turned against them.[48]

Beyond this, however, it is hard to see any contemporary political agendas hiding behind his publications or those of his colleagues. Moreover, Pokrovskii's civic consciousness has led him to communicate his research findings to a wider public. *A Journey for Rare Books* can serve as a model for any author who aspires to combine the highest standards of scholarship with an attractive popular presentation that evokes the natural world and the strength of individual personalities.

To conclude, Pokrovskii and his colleagues have combined the best qualities of the two main traditions of Old Believer scholarship—the populist and the ecclesiastical. A neopopulist approach is the foundation of their scholarship. By definition, this commitment has led them to concentrate on Old Belief as a movement of resistance of peasants, Cossacks, and the urban poor to the imperial government and the official church. At the same time, the flexibility and resourcefulness with which they used this framework in late Soviet times allowed them to stretch their treatment of the liturgical and theological dimensions of Old Belief to the limits of political orthodoxy and beyond. The populist impulse has also made the "Siberians" even more acutely aware than scholars elsewhere of the degree to which the Old Belief was an extremely complex network of accords and groups with distinct systems of belief and practice that varied from one place and time to another. Their studies made abundantly clear that the lines of demarcation between the Old Believers and the rest of the population were amorphous and, at times, invisible.

At the same time Pokrovskii and his colleagues are also heirs of the ecclesiastical scholars of prerevolutionary times. They take their subjects' own statements about their religious and political convictions with the utmost seriousness. At no time do they assume that their struggles to practice the true Eastern Orthodox faith as they understood it were merely a reflection of underlying political, economic, or institutional grievances. Instead, resistance to authority on theological or liturgical grounds reinforced political opposition and the reverse. The Tara revolt is a particularly telling illustration of the inextricable interweaving of resistance to the government's arbitrary policies and Old Believer apocalyptic prophecies.

Moreover, the Novosibirsk school has all but destroyed the distinction between "elite" and "popular" religion, at least in the case of Old Belief. Without question, the writers of many of the most important compositions in the Old Believer canon were educated and well-informed men by the standards of their day. Nevertheless, the manuscripts of their works and the ideas these contained spread across vast distances and shaped the lives and convictions of seemingly uneducated or illiterate men and women. Similar ideas about the Apocalypse or the historical roots of their tradition appear among Old Believers of widely differing levels of formal education and affiliations with one or another accord. And what is one to make of self-educated peasants such as Miron Ivanovich Galanin or Murachev, who did not hesitate to comment on the confessional and social issues of their day? In the works of the Novosibirsk school, then, Old Belief appears as a movement of nearly infinite variety that combines elements of "elite" learning and "popular" culture in virtually endless variations. This insight has implications for the study of religious movements far beyond the enormous expanse of Siberia.

Finally, since the collapse of the Soviet Union, the balance of elements in the works of the Novosibirsk school and the rhetoric of their publications has changed significantly. Since 1990 Pokrovskii and his colleagues have given increased attention to the theological and liturgical issues, including the debates within Old Belief, which could not be addressed head-on under

Soviet conditions. This new emphasis does not mean a rejection of the neopopulist insistence that Old Belief was, in essence, a movement of resistance to the official order in state, church, and high culture. The recent studies of Old Believer ideas such as Gur'ianova's work on political theology, Mal'tsev's analysis of the teachings of the stranniki and Pokrovskii and Zol'nikova's exposition of the convictions of the chasovennye revealed the profoundly subversive nature of these beliefs and teachings. Indeed, even the recondite writings of moderate Old Believer leaders were intended to subvert the doctrines and practices of official Russian Orthodoxy. Moreover, the heavy reliance in recent publications on the Old Believers' own writings by no means constitutes a neglect of the investigative records used extensively in all of Pokrovskii's work. Finally, we would do well to remember the source of many surviving Old Believer writings. For the last century and more, collectors of Old Believer manuscripts, not least contemporary field researchers, have received most of them, directly or indirectly, from peasants or less privileged townspeople.[49]

The publications of the Novosibirsk school are of as high a scholarly quality and significance as those of scholars of popular religion in Roman Catholic and Protestant Europe. If anything, the Novosibirsk scholars paint on a far larger canvas than their colleagues to the West—and not simply because of the enormous territorial expanse of Siberia. It is unfortunate, then, that Russian and non-Russian scholars of popular Christianity have worked in relative isolation from one another. Judging by their personal comments and their publications especially in Soviet times, scholars in Novosibirsk knew the work of their foreign colleagues on Old Belief but apparently not the work of non-Russian scholars of popular religious movements elsewhere in the world. There are several possible reasons for their isolation from international scholarly currents—lack of access to foreign publications, issues of language, and the refusal of official Soviet academia to recognize the value of any work not published within the orthodox Marxist-Leninist framework. For their part, non-Russian scholars of popular religious movements have been equally isolated from their Russian colleagues. The remarkable accomplishments of the Novosibirsk school deserve to more widely known. Scholars of popular religion in other societies would do well to break through the barrier of language to draw on its achievements.

Afterword

WHEN I BEGAN TO STUDY the Old Believers in the early 1960s, I had no inkling that the decades of my life as a working historian would coincide with the remarkable revival of scholarly study of the movement. Looking back, of course, I can see how fortunate I was to have received the advice and encouragement of such leaders in the rebirth of Old Believer studies as Malyshev and N. S. Demkova, to say nothing of the privilege of meeting I. N. Zavoloko, a living bridge between scholars and believers. Still less did I—or anyone else—foresee the radical changes in Russia in the late 1980s and 1990s that created entirely new conditions for both practicing Old Believers and for the scholars of their tradition.

New political conditions offered the promise of active cooperation between academic scholars and active believers, and the possible emergence of a new generation of individuals who would fully participate in both worlds. One harbinger of the future was the international conference in Novosibirsk in September 1990. The organizers brought together scholars of Old Believer history and culture from around the world along with spokesmen of several branches of the moment. It is hard to capture the excitement and sense of limitless possibilities we all felt in that moment. In retrospect, there were also signs that we were nowhere near a utopian land of common interests and shared agendas. As the meeting progressed, scholars debated with scholars and Old Believer leaders aimed their comments at one another. Since that time, scholars and believers have, for the most part, lived in their own spheres. And this, I would suggest, is to be expected in any religious tradition; for scholars strive to analyze and explain the history, culture, and contemporary condition of religious communities, while believers' primary concern is to express and live their faith as best they can.

Since I live in only one of these two worlds, I will limit my reflections to the present state and future prospects of scholarship on Old Belief. As the chapters in this volume show, the community of scholars has been remarkably productive in recent decades. Meticulous searches in archives and discoveries in the field have led to an outpouring of work on previously neglected dimensions of the movement's history and culture and shed new light on individuals and communities that were already well-known.

By now the traditional polarities in the literature on Old Belief have largely disappeared. The best scholars have combined the ecclesiastical historians' focus on the theological, liturgical, and canonical issues that have preoccupied the Old Believers themselves with serious analysis of the administrative and social conditions in which they lived and the political implications of their choices. At the same time, each historian must inevitably establish hierarchies of causes and, in the case of Old Belief, has to choose whether the movement's adherents strove primarily to save their souls or to cry out against oppressive social and political conditions.

In addition, scholars—especially the Novosibirsk school—have demonstrated that, in Russia at least, the imaginary line between elite and popular religious cultures barely exists. The extent to which educated Old Believers influenced their less sophisticated brothers and sisters and vice versa, however, remains a significant and interesting question.

Finally, recent scholarly work has made us more aware than ever that Old Belief was and is an extremely complex and continually changing movement. Over the course of its history, its adherents have split into a bewildering variety of accords, tendencies, and groups as they have struggled to define true Orthodoxy and develop strategies to defend it in a rapidly changing world.

Where do we scholars go from here? As we have seen, well-established modes of scholarly investigation and analysis are still serving us well. For examples one can point to the achievements of the Novosibirsk school discussed in chapter 12 and to E. M. Iukhimenko's monumental two-volume work on the cultural history of the Vyg community.[1] And, if Iukhimenko was able to add so much to our knowledge about this well-known and well-documented center of Old Belief, how much more could we learn about the innumerable centers and currents within the movement about which we know virtually nothing? It would be helpful to know a great deal more, for example, about the varying fates of Old Believer leaders and their flocks in the Soviet period. We also need to give much more attention to urban Old Believers and to the more conservative or accommodationist strands in the movement.[2]

Moreover, as scholars of history and culture in the wider world adopt new ideological points of departure and modes of interpretation, these can profitably be used to shed new light on Old Belief. A number of recent examples come to mind. Georg Michels's work situates the origins of the movement in the often brutal politics of the Muscovite court and church hierarchy in the late seventeenth century. Irina Paert has brought feminist and gender theory to bear on the competing Old Believer doctrines on marriage and the role of women in the Moscow communities in the late eighteenth and early nineteenth centuries. Essays by Boris Uspensky and M. B. Pliukhanova illustrate the ways in which the semiotics of culture can offer new insights on the origins and distinctive features of Old Believers cultures.[3] It is therefore to be regretted that the scholars of the so-called Tartu school did not give more sustained attention to the movement's cultures. In my own more recent work (especially chapter 5, I attempted to use insights from cultural anthropology to help explain the very rapid consolidation of Old Believer apologetic literature and religious practice in the late seventeenth and early eighteenth centuries. All of these approaches have been refreshing departures from the more traditional literature and have stimulated thinking in new directions. At the same time, the allure of new theories and approaches from other disciplines contains its own dangers—a tendency to overuse theoretical insights and to force inconvenient facts into the patterns they suggest.

Finally, we must always bear in mind that Old Belief is a living, changing movement. To mention only one recent example, many Old Believers—to the horror of some scholars—have "voted with their feet" by moving from priestless practice to one of the priestly accords. Some have even sought accommodation with the Russian Orthodox Church. If nothing else, this change is a reminder that, as they have always done, the Old Believers will continue to defend their tradition in their own way and debate among themselves how best to do so. In spite of their customary rhetoric of changelessness, earlier generations did adopt technological and cultural innovations from their surroundings. Their descendants still keep up this dialogue with a rapidly changing world. Moreover, the determination to defend a rigorous understanding of Eastern Orthodox traditions and practices will still inspire believers who remain Old Believers and those who choose to pursue what one might call the "Old Believer imperative" within the Russian Orthodox Church. So, as they have always done, the Old Believers will decide how best to practice authentic Orthodoxy in their own time and circumstances and will use their own criteria for doing so. We scholars of their history and culture may celebrate or mourn the choices they will make.[4] But they will remain a fascinating example of how religious communities define and defend their beliefs and forms of worship, organize their life, and interact with the world around them. Or, in other words, how a "faithful remnant" survives and maintains the essence of its traditions.

$\mathcal{N}otes$

Abbreviations

AAE—*Akty, sobrannye v bibliotekakh i arkhivakh Rossiiskoi imperii Arkheograficheskoiu ekspeditsieiu Imperatorskoi Akademii nauk*. 4 vols. St. Petersburg, 1836–1858.

AI—*Akty istoricheskie, sobrannye i izdannye Arkheograficheskoiu komissieiu*. 5 vols. St. Petersburg, 1841–1843.

BAN—Biblioteka Akademii Nauk. St. Petersburg.

Barsukov, Pamiatniki—Barsukov, Ia. I., ed. *Pamiatniki pervykh let russkago staroobriadchestva. Letopis' zaniatii Arkheograficheskoi Komissii* 24 (1912): 1–424.

GIM—Gosudarstvennyi Istoricheskii Muzei. Moscow.

IRLI—Institut russkoi literatury (Pushkin House/Pushkinskii Dom), Russian Academy of Sciences, St. Petersburg.

LZAK—*Letopis' zaniatii Arkheograficheskoi Komissii*. 35 vols. St. Petersburg, 1861–1927/28.

ChOIDR—*Chteniia v Imperatorskom Obshchestve Istorii i Drevnostei Rossiiskikh pri Moskovskom Universitete*. 264 vols. Moscow, 1846–1918.

PSZ—*Polnoe sobranie zakonov Rossiiskoi Imperii*. Sobranie pervoe, 45 vols. St. Petersburg, 1830–1843.

RGB—Rossiiskaia Gosudarstvennaia Biblioteka. St. Petersburg.

RGADA—Rossiiskii Gosudarstvennyi Arkhiv Drevnikh Aktov. Moscow.

RNB—Rossiiskaia Natsional'naia Biblioteka. Moscow.

Subbotin, Materialy—Subbotin, N. I., ed. *Materialy dlia istorii raskola za pervoe vremia ego sushchestvovaniia*. 9 vols. Moscow, 1874–1890.

TODRL—*Trudy Otdela drevnerusskoi literatury*. Leningrad–St. Petersburg, 1934– .

1—Past and Current Interpretations of Old Belief

1. For a survey of some of this literature and its possible implications for Old Belief, see Robert O. Crummey, "Old Belief as Popular Religion: New Approaches," *Slavic Review* 52 (1993): 700–712. Republished as chapter 2 of this volume.

2. Georg B. Michels, "Myths and Realities of the Russian Schism: The Church and Its Dissenters in Seventeenth-Century Muscovy" (unpublished Ph.D. dissertation, Harvard University, 1991), and his *At War with the Church: Religious Dissent in Seventeenth-Century Russia* (Stanford, 1999).

3. See Juha Pentikäinen, "Oral Repertoire and World View: An Anthropological Study of Marina Takalo's Life History," *FF Communications* 93, no. 219 (1978).

4. The Novosibirsk conference on Old Belief in September 1990 will serve as the chronological limit of my remarks. The papers were published in *Traditsionnaia duk-hovnaia i material'naia kul'tura russkikh staroobriadcheskikh poselenii v stranakh Evropy, Azii i Ameriki: Sbornik nauchnykh trudov* (Novosibirsk, 1992).

5. For a brief review of early Old Believer polemical literature, see Robert O. Crummey, "The Origins of the Old Believers' Cultural Systems: The Works of Avraamii," *Forschungen zur osteuropäischen Geschichte* 50 (1994): 121–38, here 125–27, republished as chapter 5 of this volume. By far the most comprehensive recent studies of the early Old Believer manuscript tradition are N. Iu. Bubnov, "Staroobriadcheskaia kniga v Rossii vo vtoroi polovine XVII v." (unpublished Ph.D. dissertation, Leningrad, 1990), and his *Staroobriadcheskaia kniga v Rossii vo vtoroi polovine XVII v.: Istochniki, tipy i evoliutsiia* (St. Petersburg, 1995).

6. For a brief summary of governmental policy, see Robert O. Crummey, "Interpreting the Fate of Old Believer Communities in the Eighteenth and Nineteenth Centuries," in Stephen K. Batalden, ed., *Seeking God: The Recovery of Religious Identity in Orthodox Russia, Ukraine and Georgia* (DeKalb, IL, 1993), 144–59, here 149–53, republished as chapter 11 of this volume. For comment on the perception that the Old Believers were a source of moral anarchy, see Gregory L. Freeze, "Bringing Order to the Russian Family: Marriage and Divorce in Imperial Russia, 1760–1860," *Journal of Modern History* 62 (1990): 709–46, here 746.

7. See Michael Cherniavsky's provocative discussion of these two currents in "The Old Believers and the New Religion," *Slavic Review* 25 (1966): 1–39, here 1–3.

8. Makarii, *Istoriia russkago raskola izvestnago pod imenem staroobriadchestva* (St. Petersburg, 1855); P. S. Smirnov, *Istoriia russkago raskola staroobriadchestva*, 2nd. ed. (St. Petersburg, 1895).

9. Subbotin's anti–Old Believer animus, arising from a conservative Nikolaevan striving for a Russia unified in ideology and moral values, is particularly clear in his writings on the Belokrinitsa hierarchy, for example, *Istoriia Belokrinitskoi ierarkhii*, vol. 1 (Moscow, 1874).

10. Especially, N. I. Subbotin, ed., *Materialy dlia istorii raskola za pervoe vremia ego sushchestvovaniia*, 9 vols. (Moscow, 1874–1890).

11. N. Iu. Bubnov, *Staroobriadcheskaia kniga v Rossii vo vtoroi polovine XVII v.* (dissertation abstract) (Leningrad, 1990), 9–10.

12. P. S. Smirnov, *Vnutrennye voprosy v raskole v XVII veke* (St. Petersburg, 1898); *Iz istorii raskola pervoi poloviny XVIII veka* (St. Petersburg, 1908); and *Spory i razdeleniia v russkom raskole v pervoi chetverti XVIII veka* (St. Petersburg, 1909).

13. E. E. Golubinskii, *K nashei polemike s staroobriadtsami* (Moscow, 1905). Also published in ChOIDR, 1905, book iii, 1–260.

14. N. F. Kapterev, *Patriarkh Nikon i Tsar' Aleksei Mikhailovich*, 2 vols. (Sergiev Posad, 1909). Subbotin did his best to suppress Kapterev's work and block his professional advancement. Serge Zenkovsky, *Russkoe staroobriadchestvo* (Munich, 1970), 20.

15. A. P. Shchapov, "Russkii raskol staroobriadstva, razsmatrivaemyi v sviazi s vnutrennim sostoianiem russkoi tserkvi i grazhdanstvennosti v XVII veke i v pervoi polovine XVIII," *Sochineniia A. P. Shchapova,* 3 vols. (St. Petersburg, 1906; repr. 1971), 1:173–450.

16. Shchapov, "Zemstvo i raskol," ibid., 1:451–579.

17. Shchapov's early biography is remarkably similar to those of the leading ecclesiastical historians of Old Belief. Like them, he received an exclusively ecclesiastical education and, as a recent graduate, began his teaching career by lecturing on Russian history in a seminary.

18. See, for example, V. V. Andreev, *Raskol i ego znachenie v narodnoi russkoi istorii* (St. Petersburg, 1870), and I. I. Kablitz [pseud. I. Iuzov], *Russkie dissidenty-starovery i dukhovnye khristiane* (St. Petersburg, 1881). The populists saw all forms of religious heterodoxy as points on a single spectrum of popular opposition to the imperial regime.

19. In his writings on Russian sectarians, the early Bolshevik V. D. Bonch-Bruevich showed, in effect, that the populist understanding of popular religious movements was compatible with Marxism. See his *Izbrannye sochineniia v trekh tomakh* (Moscow, 1959), vol. 1.

20. In its original context, this essay was paired with N. N. Pokrovskii's survey of more recent Russian literature on Old Belief.

21. Cherniavsky escapes from a narrowly populist approach by pointing out that the theological or religious language of the Old Believers "like all language, possessed a logic of its own. And, indeed, in the course of their history the Old Believers . . . could be forced into rather radical theological views because theological terms, no matter why used, evoked theological consequences" (5).

22. Pierre Pascal, *Avvakum et les débuts du raskol* (Paris and The Hague, 1963). The first edition appeared in Paris in 1938.

23. Ibid., xvi–xviii.

24. Zenkovsky, *Russkoe staroobriadchestvo,* here 17–40, 486–96.

25. In addition to his book, see Zenkovsky's essay, "The Ideological World of the Denisov Brothers," *Harvard Slavic Studies* 3 (1957): 48–66.

26. Robert O. Crummey, *The Old Believers and the World of Antichrist: The Vyg Community and the Russian State, 1694–1855* (Madison, 1970).

27. For a summary of the earlier literature on this subject, see ibid., ch. 7. Of particular significance for our discussion are P. Kovalevsky, "Le 'Raskol' et son rôle dans le développement industriel de la Russie," *Archives de sociologie des religions* 3 (1957): 37–56; William L. Blackwell, "The Old Believers and the Rise of Private Industrial Enterprise in Early Nineteenth-Century Moscow," *Slavic Review* 24 (1965): 407–24; P. G. Ryndziunskii, "Staroobriadcheskaia organizatsiia v usloviiakh razvitiia promyshlennogo kapitalizma (Na primere istorii Moskovskoi obshchiny fedoseevtsev v 40-kh godakh XIX v.)," *Voprosy istorii religii i ateizma* 1 (1950): 188–248. Manfred Hildermeier and his research group are reexamining these issues. See his "Alter Glaube und neue Welt: Zur Sozialgeschichte des Raskol im 18. und 19. Jahrhundert," *Jahrbücher für Geschichte Osteuropas* 38 (1990): 372–98, 504–25, and "Alter Glaube und Mobilität: Bemerkungen zur Verbreitung und sozialen Struktur des Raskol im früindustriellen Russland (1760–1860)," ibid. 39 (1991): 321–38.

28. James H. Billington, *The Icon and the Axe* (New York, 1970), ch. 3.

29. Georg Michels's dissertation, cited above, and his "The Solovki Uprising: Religion and Revolt in Northern Russia," *Russian Review* 51 (1992): 1–15.

30. N. S. Gur'ianova, *Krest'ianskii antimonarkhicheskii protest v staroobriadcheskoi eskhatologicheskoi literature perioda pozdnego feodalizma* (Novosibirsk, 1988), and her many articles on Old Believer historiography.

31. Roy R. Robson, "An Architecture of Change: Old Believer Liturgical Spaces in Late Imperial Russia," *Seeking God*, 160–87, and his dissertation, "'The Old Believers in a Modern World: Symbol, Ritual and Community, 1905–1914" (Boston College, 1992).

32. See Robert O. Crummey, "Religious Radicalism in Seventeenth-Century Russia: Reexamining the Kapiton Movement," *Forschungen zur osteuropäischen Geschichte* 46 (1992): 171–85. Republished as chapter 4 of this volume.

33. See, for example, N. N. Pokrovskii, *Antifeodal'nyi protest uralo-sibirskikh krest'ian-staroobriadtsev v XVIII v.* (Novosibirsk, 1974), R. G. Pikhoia, *Obshchestvenno-politicheskaia mysl' trudiashchikhsia Urala (konets XVII–XVIII vv.)* (Sverdlovsk, 1987), and the articles of members of their research groups. Over the years, the research group centered in the library of Moscow State University has also focused its attention on Old Belief in regional settings—Vetka, the upper Kama, and to a lesser extent, the lower Volga and Moldova.

34. For a particularly interesting example of this vast literature, see N. N. Pokrovskii, "'Ispoved' altaiskogo krest'ianina," *Pamiatniki kul'tury: Novye otkrytiia, 1978* (Leningrad, 1979), 49–57.

35. In addition to Michels's work, see V. S. Rumiantseva, ed., *Narodnoe antit-serkovnoe dvizhenie v Rossii XVII veka: Dokumenty Prikaza Tainykh Del, 1665–1667 gg.* (Moscow, 1986), and *Dokumenty razriadnogo, posol'skogo, novgorodskogo i tainogo prikazov o raskol'nikakh v gorodakh Rossii, 1654–1684 gg.* (Moscow, 1990); E. M. Iukhimenko, "Kargopol'skie 'gari' 1683–1684 gg.: K probleme samosozhzhenii v russkom staroobriadchestve," *Staroobriadchestvo v Rossii (XVII–XVIII vv.)* (Moscow, 1994), 64–119, and the shorter publications of Iukhimenko and N. S. Demkova in the same volume. In addition, scholars such as Demkova, Iukhimenko, N. V. Ponyrko, and Gur'ianova have recently found important and previously unknown Old Believer texts in the most accessible and commonly used manuscript collections of Moscow and St. Petersburg.

36. Boris A. Uspensky, "'The Schism and Cultural Conflict in the Seventeenth Century," *Seeking God*, 106–13.

37. See, for example, Clifford Geertz, *The Interpretation of Cultures: Selected Essays* (New York, 1973), and Victor W. Turner, *The Ritual Process: Structure and Anti-Structure* (Chicago, 1969).

38. In this instance, I believe that in the history of Old Belief we can find many examples of both phenomena.

2—Old Belief as Popular Religion

1. Excellent critical summaries of this literature include Natalie Zemon Davis, "From 'Popular Religion' to Religious Cultures," *Reformation Europe: A Guide to Research*, ed. Steven Ozment (St. Louis, 1982), 321–42; R. W. Scribner, "Interpreting Religion in Early Modern Europe," *European Studies Review* 13 (1983): 89–105; John Van Engen, "The Christian Middle Ages as an Historiographical Problem," *American Historical Review* 91 (1986): 519–52; Richard van Dülman, "Volksfrömmigkeit und konfessionelles Christentum im 16. und 17. Jahrhundert," *Volksreligiosität in der modernen Sozialgeschichte*, ed. Wolfgang Schieder (Göttingen, 1986), 14–30.

2. There are a few remarkable exceptions to this statement, in particular the works of K. V. Chistov and A. I. Klibanov. See K. V. Chistov. *Russkie narodnye sotsial'noutopicheskie legendy* (Moscow, 1967); A. I. Klibanov, *Narodnaia sotsial'naia utopiia v Rossii* (Moscow, 1977).

3. Pierre Pascal, *The Religion of the Russian People* (London and Oxford, 1976); Dmitri Obolensky, "Popular Religion in Medieval Russia," *Russia and Orthodoxy,* vol. 2, *The Religious World of Russian Culture,* ed. Andrew Blane (The Hague, 1975), 43–54; Moshe Lewin, "Popular Religion in Twentieth-Century Russia," *The Making of the Soviet System: Essays in the Social History of Interwar Russia* (New York, 1985), 57–71. Linda J. Ivanits, in *Russian Folk Belief* (Armonk, NY, 1989), summarizes the extensive Russian literature on "folk beliefs" and folklore. For a helpful and stimulating analysis of the hoary concept of *dvoeverie* (double faith), see Eve Levin, "*Dvoeverie* and Popular Religion," *Seeking God,* 29–52.

4. Mikhail Bakhtin, *Rabelais and His World,* trans. Hélène Iswolsky (Bloomington, 1984).

5. Aron Gurevich, *Medieval Popular Culture: Problems of Belief and Perception,* trans. J. H. Bak and P. A. Hollingsworth (New York, 1988); and his *Categories of Medieval Culture,* trans. G. L. Campbell (Boston, 1985).

6. The extent to which Old Belief can be viewed as a coherent movement with wide popular support is still subject to debate. In his dissertation, "Myths and Realities of the Russian Schism," Georg Michels stresses the fragmentary nature of Old Belief in the seventeenth century and argues that the movement as such emerged only in the early eighteenth century in response to the policies of Peter I. See his *At War with the Church.*

7. See, for example, Crummey, *Old Believers.*

8. In this chapter I will not deal with the so-called sectarians, whose more rationalistic or "charismatic" approaches to Christian belief, worship, and practice took them much farther from the mainstream of historic Eastern Orthodoxy than the Old Believers. The extremely varied groups that are customarily grouped under the broad label *sektantstvo* can legitimately be studied as examples of popular religious attitudes and practices in eighteenth- and nineteenth-century Russia.

9. The most useful introduction and survey of these issues is Peter Burke, *Popular Culture in Early Modern Europe* (New York, 1978). For a stimulating recent discussion on approaches and methodologies for the study of popular culture, see the AHR Forum, *American Historical Review* 97 (1992): 1369–430. For our purposes, the most helpful comments are those of Natalie Zemon Davis, "Toward Mixtures and Margins," 1409–16.

10. Jean-Claude Schmitt, "Religion populaire et culture folklorique," *Annales: Economies, Sociétés, Civilisations* 31 (1976): 941–53, reviewing Etienne Delaruelle, *La piété populaire au moyen âge* (Turin, 1975).

11. Robert Muchembled, *Popular Culture and Elite Culture in France, 1400–1750,* trans. L. Cochrane (Baton Rouge, 1985), 11.

12. Daily oral reading was prescribed by the "rule" of the Vyg community. See L. K. Kuandykov, "Ideologiia obshchezhitel'stva u staroobriadtsev-bespopovtsev vygovskogo soglasiia v XVIII v.," *Istochniki po kul'ture i klassovoi bor'be feodal'nogo perioda* (Novosibirsk, 1982), 94.

13. Raoul Manselli, *La religion populaire au moyen âge: Problèmes de méthode et d'histoire* (Montreal, 1975), 25–26.

14. For a Russian example, see A. Amfiteatrov, *Russkii pop XVII veka* (Belgrade, 1930).

15. Muchembled, *Popular Culture and Elite Culture.*

16. Manselli, *La religion populaire*, 21–24.

17. A variant of this argument underlies Keith Thomas's pathbreaking *Religion and the Decline of Magic* (New York, 1971). See also van Dülmen, "Volksfrömmigkeit," 15–21.

18. In recent years, many scholars have made this point. See, for example, Manselli, *La religion populaire*, 20–41; Roger Chartier, *Cultural History: Between Practices and Representations*, trans. L. Cochrane (Ithaca, 1988), 37–40.

19. On a theoretical plane, new directions emphasize the complexity of the relationship between the scholar as educated outsider and the cultural phenomena he/she seeks to understand. For example, Pierre Bourdieu's theoretical works stress the continual mutual interaction of social formations and mental structures that begin as the internalization of external reality but quickly take on a life of their own and shape that reality (Chartier, *Cultural History*, 44–45). Reflexive ethnography attacks the presumed objectivity of the educated observer and stresses the extreme difficulty—indeed, impossibility—of escaping from one's own worldview into that of the culture under study. See James Clifford, *The Predicament of Culture: Twentieth-Century Ethnography, Literature, and Art* (Cambridge, MA, 1988), especially "On Ethnographic Authority," 21–54.

20. Carlo Ginzburg, *The Cheese and the Worms: The Cosmos of a Sixteenth-Century Miller*, trans. John Tedeschi and Anne Tedeschi (Baltimore, 1980); Pokrovskii, "Ispoved'." These authors' commitment to let the men they studied "speak for themselves" closely parallels the guiding spirit and expository strategies of the "new ethnographers."

21. See Michels, *At War with the Church* and "The Solovki Uprising."

22. Michels, in *At War with the Church*, chs. 4 and 5, stresses the role of itinerant monks and nuns (officially tonsured or self-designated) and renegade priests in spreading resistance to the Nikonian reforms. See also Crummey, *Old Believers*, 31–38. I have argued that the first Old Believer "cultural system," the tapestry of interwoven polemical and devotional texts, was the creation of a conservative "intelligentsia" within the clergy. See ch. 5.

23. Roy R. Robson uses this term in his book, *Old Believers in Modern Russia* (DeKalb, IL, 1995).

24. I. V. Pozdeeva frames her studies of early Russian book culture with this presupposition. See, for example, her "Drevnerusskoe nasledie v istorii traditsionnoi knizhnoi kul'tury staroobriadchestva (pervyi period)," *Istoriia SSSR*, 1988, no. 1, 84–99. This questionable presupposition does not detract from the value of the more concrete findings of Pozdeeva's group of ethnographers and literary scholars.

25. See A. A. Amosov, V. P. Budaragin, V. V. Morozov, and R. G. Pikhoia, "O nekotorykh problemakh polevoi arkheografii (v poriadke obsuzhdeniia)," *Obshchestvenno-politicheskaia mysl' dorevoliutsionnogo Urala* (Sverdlovsk, 1983), 5–19.

26. See Crummey, *Old Believers*; V. G. Druzhinin, *Raskol na Donu v kontse XVII veka* (St. Petersburg, 1889); N. Sokolov, *Raskol v Saratovskom krae* (Saratov, 1888); Pokrovskii, *Antifeodal'nyi protest*; Pikhoia, *Obshchestvenno-politicheskaia mysl'*; A. T. Shashkov, "Izuchenie uralo-sibirskogo staroobriadchestva vtoroi poloviny XVII–nachala XVIII v. v otechestvennoi istoriografii," and V. I. Baidin, "Ural'skoe staroobriadchestvo kontsa XVIII– serediny XIX v. v dorevoliutsionnoi i sovetskoi istoriografii," *Istoriografiia obshchestvennoi mysli dorevoliutsionnogo Urala* (Sverdlovsk, 1988), 31–50. The local history of Old Belief is the subject of an extensive literature, particularly in regional and ecclesiastical periodicals. We badly need new studies of the major centers of Old Belief, especially the communities in St. Petersburg and Moscow.

27. Manfred Hildermeier's articles "Alter Glaube und neue Welt" and "Alter Glaube und Mobilität" do much to fill this gap. For more recent literature on the subject, see Ch. 7.

28. On the "book culture" of the Old Believers, see the work of I. V. Pozdeeva and her collaborators, for example, "Drevnerusskoe nasledie." G. V. Esipov published paraphrases of a number of inquisitorial records from the reign of Peter I in *Raskol'nich'i dela XVIII st.*, 2 vols. (St. Petersburg, 1861, 1863). For a particularly interesting case from a later period, see Pokrovskii, "Ispoved."

29. Davis, "From 'Popular Religion,'" 323.

30. On the Old Believers' sacred history, see R. Crummey, "Istoricheskaia skhema vygoretskikh bol'shakov," *Traditsionnaia dukhovnaia i material'naia kul'tura russkikh staroobriadcheskikh poselenii v stranakh Evropy, Azii i Ameriki* (Novosibirsk, 1992), 90–96. The English translation is chapter 9 of this volume.

31. Brian Stock, *The Implications of Literacy: Written Language and Models of Interpretation in the Eleventh and Twelfth Centuries* (Princeton, 1983), 90–92.

32. Fortunately, Russian scholars are devoting a great deal of attention to this question. See, for example, R. G. Pikhoia, "Knizhno-rukopisnaia traditsiia Urala XVIII–nachala XX v. (k postanovke problemy)," *Istochniki po kul'ture i klassovoi bor'be feodal'nogo perioda*, 101–14; E. I. Dergacheva-Skop and V. N. Alekseev, "Staroobriadcheskie biblioteki v Sibiri (problemy rekonstruktsii)," *Traditsionnaia dukhovnaia i material'naia kul'tura*, 125–30; A. G. Mosin, "Istochniki po istorii knizhnoi kul'tury zhitelei Viatskoi gubernii (1840–1850)," *Kul'tura i byt dorevoliutsionnogo Urala* (Sverdlovsk, 1989), 103–21.

33. For twentieth-century examples, see N. N. Pokrovskii's description of his anonymous informants in *Puteshestvie za redkimi knigami* (Moscow, 1984), 16–22; E. B. Smilianskaia's discussion of the role of K. I. Dontsov in the Old Believer village of Kunicha in Moldova in "Belokrinitskie prikhody v Moldove (knizhnost' i kul'tura s. Kunicha)," *Traditsionnaia dukhovnaia i material'naia kul'tura*, 179–85; and essays on two remarkable contemporaries, E. A. Ageeva, "Sovremennyi staroobriadcheskii pisatel' A. K. Kilin," and N. D. Zol'nikova, "Sovremennyi pisatel'-staroobriadets s Eniseia," ibid., 277–88.

34. See, for example, the essays of S. E. Nikitina and M. B. Chernysheva in *Russkie pis'mennye i ustnye traditsii i dukhovnaia kul'tura* (Moscow, 1982). The literature on the *dukhovnye stikhi* is extensive and includes a number of editions of texts.

35. Although centered on other issues, Robson's *Old Believers* provides much helpful material on this question.

36. See Pentikäinen, "Oral Repertoire." Pentikäinen's work and the testimony of his informants must be treated cautiously for at least two reasons. First, it is unclear to what extent Marina Takalo and the other informants can legitimately be considered Old Believers. Second, since Pentikäinen works with informants of various Ugro-Finnic ethnic groups, it is unclear whether one would find such extraordinary mixtures of Old Believer scruple and folk syncretism among Great Russians.

37. This theme is central to Robson's *Old Believers*.

38. See, for example, N. V. Ponyrko, "Uchebniki ritoriki na Vygu," TODRL 36 (1981): 154–62.

39. "Zhil'ber Romm u vygovskikh raskol'nikov," *Kraeved Karelii* (Petrozavodsk, 1990), 148–59.

40. A. A. Amosov, V. P. Budaragin, V. V. Morozov, and R. G. Pikhoia make this point in "O nekotorykh problemakh polevoi arkheografii," 14.

41. Cherniavsky, "The Old Believers," 23 and n. 99; Klibanov, *Narodnaia sotsial'naia utopiia*, 201–19.

42. Such was the conclusion of P. I. Mel'nikov, based on his studies of the Nizhnii Novgorod region. See his *Otchet o sovremennom sostoianii raskola v Nizhegorodskoi gubernii* (St. Petersburg, 1854), 288.

43. Crummey, *Old Believers*, 101.

44. Gregory L. Freeze, "The Rechristianization of Russia: The Church and Popular Religion, 1750–1850," *Studia Slavica Finlandensia* 7 (1990): 101–36, and "The Wages of Sin: The Decline of Public Penance in Imperial Russia," *Seeking God*, 53–82.

45. The best discussion of this movement within Russian Orthodoxy in the mid-seventeenth century remains Pascal, *Avvakum*, 148–89. See also Wolfgang Heller, *Die Moskauer "Eiferer für die Frömmigkeit" zwischen Staat and Kirche, 1642–1652* (Wiesbaden, 1988). Peter Burke points to the parallel between the program of the Zealots of Piety and the activities of Protestant and Roman Catholic contemporaries elsewhere in mid-seventeenth century Europe (Burke, *Popular Culture*, 214–15).

46. Archpriest Avvakum, *The Life Written by Himself*, trans. Kenneth N. Brostrom (Ann Arbor, 1979). The most useful Russian editions are *Zhitie Protopopa Avvakuma im samim napisannoe i drugie ego sochineniia* (Moscow, 1960), and A. N. Robinson, ed., *Zhitie Avvakuma i drugie ego sochineniia* (Moscow, 1991).

47. See, for example, Robert O. Crummey, "The Spirituality of the Vyg Fathers," *Church, Nation, and State in Russia and Ukraine*, ed. Geoffrey Hosking (New York, 1991), 23–37. Republished as chapter 8 of this volume. See also Pia Pera, "Theoretical and Practical Aspects of the Debate on Marriage among the Priestless Old Believers from the End of the Seventeenth to the Mid-Nineteenth Century" (unpublished Ph.D. dissertation, University of London, 1986).

48. See, for example, Geertz, "Religion as a Cultural System," *Interpretation*, 87–124; Turner, *Ritual Process*.

3—Ecclesiastical Elites and Popular Belief and Practice in Seventeenth-Century Russia

1. Eve Levin, "Supplicatory Prayers as a Source for Popular Religious Culture in Muscovite Russia," *Religion and Culture in Early Modern Russia and Ukraine*, ed. Samuel H. Baron and Nancy Shields Kollmann (DeKalb, 1997), 96–114, here 96.

2. As compared, for example, with England. See Eamon Duffy, *The Stripping of the Altars: Traditional Religion in England c. 1400–c. 1580* (New Haven and London, 1992).

3. V. S. Rumiantseva, *Narodnoe antitserkovnoe dvizhenie v Rossii v XVII veke* (Moscow, 1986), and two collections of archival documents she has edited, *Narodnoe antitserkovnoe dvizhenie: Dokumenty* and *Dokumenty Razriadnogo, Posol'skogo, Novgorodskogo i Tainogo Prikazov.*

4. Michels, *At War with the Church*. Michels's numerous articles include "The Place of Nikita Konstantinovich Dobrynin in the History of Early Old Belief," *Revue des études slaves* 49 (1997): 21–31; "Muscovite Elite Women and Old Belief," *Rhetoric of the Medieval Slavic World: Essays Presented to Edward L. Keenan on His Sixtieth Birthday by His Colleagues and Students, Harvard Ukrainian Studies* 19 (2006): 428–50; "The Violent Old Belief: An Examination of Religious Dissent on the Karelian Frontier," *Russian History* 19

(1992): 203–29; "The First Old Believers in Ukraine: Observations about Their Social Profile and Behavior," *Harvard Ukrainian Studies* 16 (1992): 289–313; "The Solovki Uprising."

5. For treatments of "confessionalization" that are helpful from a Russian perspective, see Duffy, *Stripping*; R. Po-chia Hsia, *Social Discipline in the Reformation: Central Europe, 1550–1750* (London, 1989); R. W. Scribner, *For the Sake of the Simple Folk: Popular Propaganda for the German Reformation* (Cambridge, 1981); Heinz Schilling, "Between the Territorial State and Urban Liberty: Lutheranism and Calvinism in the County of Lippe," *The German People and the Reformation*, ed. R. Po-chia Hsia (Ithaca, 1988), 263–83, and "Die Konfessionalisierung im Reich: Religiöser und Gesellschaftlicher Wandel in Deutschland zwischen 1555 und 1620," *Historische Zeitschrift* 246 (1988): 1–45; Wolfgang Reinhard, "Zwang zur Konfessionalisierung? Prolegomena zu einer Theorie des konfessionellen Zeitalters," *Zeitschrift für Historische Forschung* 10 (1983): 257–77; Jean Delumeau, "Déchristianisation ou nouveau modèle de Christianisme," *Archives de sciences sociales des religions* 40 (1975): 3–20.

6. Some historians have suggested parallels between Old Belief and Protestantism for two reasons (for example, Billington, *The Icon and the Axe*, 193). First, the priestless Old Believers rejected the priesthood and created self-generating communities led by laypeople. In spite of these superficially "Protestant" arrangements, the priestless regard themselves as the faithful remnant of Eastern Orthodoxy and regret the loss of the full sacramental ministry of the church. Time and again, individuals among them have, for this reason, rejoined the priestly Old Belief or uniate affiliates of the "synodal" Orthodox Church when they can overcome their canonical scruples. In the last two decades, all the major Old Believer communities in North America have relived this recurring story. Second, the Old Believers' ascetic way of life and success in business seems to parallel Calvinism. As I have argued elsewhere, the "Weber" thesis seems inappropriate to Old Belief for theological reasons (Crummey, *Old Believers*, ch. 7, here 135–37). I accept Manfred Hildermeier's counterargument that Weber's more general concept of "this-worldly asceticism" fits the Old Believers and, for that matter, many other religious or cultural minorities. See his "Alter Glaube und neue Welt" and "Alter Glaube und Mobilität."

7. Much of the recent literature on the Reformation concentrates on the latter. See, for example, Hsia, *German People*.

8. Crummey, "Origins."

9. The literature on popular religion in Europe is enormous. General overviews include Davis, "From 'Popular Religion'"; Scribner, "Interpreting Religion"; Richard van Dülman, "Volksfrömmigkeit und konfessionelles Christentum im 16. und 17. Jahrhundert," *Volksreligiosität in der modernen Sozialgeschichte*, ed. Wolfgang Schieder (Göttingen, 1986), 14–30, and the works cited in footnote 5. For a recent discussion of the literature on popular religion as applied to Russia, see Crummey, "Old Belief as Popular Religion," republished as chapter 2 of this volume.

10. For a narrative of the events discussed in this paper, see the two best general works on ecclesiastical reform and the church schism: Pascal, *Avvakum*, and Zenkovsky, *Russkoe staroobriadchestvo*.

11. On the Zealots of Piety, Heller, *Die Moskauer "Eiferer für die Frömmigkeit."* Since the Zealots were an informal group of friends and acquaintances, any interpretation of their aims and activities depends in part on assumptions about who can be considered a member.

12. Parishioners' enthusiasm was undoubtedly dampened by the custom of paying priests for their services, including confession and administering the Eucharist. See S. Smirnov, *Drevnerusskii dukhovnik*, ChOIDR, 1914, book ii, 1–283, here 73. See also Amfiteatrov, *Russkii pop*, 109–14. To distract the authorities from their real activities and goals, peasant radicals in Pudozh in 1693 made a formal complaint that they had been deprived of the sacraments because their village priests charged very high fees for their services. Whatever the truth of the charges, the people who made them evidently believed they were plausible enough to be taken seriously. AI 5:383–85, no. 223.

13. Duffy, *Stripping*, ch. 16, characterizes the Counter-Reformation in much these terms. See also Wolfgang Reinhard, "Gegenreformation als Modernisierung? Prolegomena zu einer Theorie des konfessionellen Zeitalters," *Archiv für Reformationsgeschichte* 68 (1977): 226–52, and A. G. Dickens, *The Counter Reformation* (New York, 1969).

14. N. V. Rozhdestvenskii, "K istorii bor'by s tserkovnymi bezporiadkami, otgoloskami iazychestva i porokami v russkom bytu XVII v.," ChOIDR, 1902, book ii, 1–31, here 19–23.

15. AAE 4:481–82, no. 321.

16. For an extensive list of examples, AAE 4:487–89, no. 327.

17. S. A. Belokurov, "Deianie Moskovskago tserkovnogo sobora 1649 goda," ChOIDR, 1894, book iv, 1–52.

18. *Stoglav*, ed. D. E. Kozhanchikov (St. Petersburg, 1863), 135–41; E. V. Emchenko, *Stoglav: issledovaniia i tekst* (Moscow, 2000).

19. On these festivals, see V. Ia. Propp, *Russkie agrarnye prazdniki* (St. Petersburg, 1995), 45–47, 70–75, 122–24, 136–43; Ivanits, *Russian Folk Belief*, 9–10; and Russell Zguta, *Russian Minstrels: A History of the Skomorokhi* (Philadelphia, 1978), 9–12.

20. Rozhdestvenskii, "K istorii bor'by"; AI 4:124–26, no. 35; N. Kharuzin, "K voprosu o bor'be Moskovskago pravitel'stva s narodnymi iazycheskimi obriadami i sueveriiami v polovine XVII v.," *Etnograficheskoe Obozrenie*, 1879, no. 1, 143–51; Pascal, *Avvakum*, 161–64.

21. Peter Burke, *Popular Culture*, 213–15, rightly includes these Russian practices in this category. Relying primarily on ethnographic materials of the nineteenth and twentieth centuries, Propp, *Agrarnye prazdniki*, ch. 7, also classified many of the practices that shocked the Zealots as "games and amusements."

22. Historians of popular religion in England on the eve of the Reformation have a clear answer to this question. In Ronald Hutton's words, "there is absolutely no evidence that the people who kept these customs were anything but Christian or had any notion that by carrying on these activities they were commemorating other deities." (Ronald Hutton, *The Rise and Fall of Merry England* [Oxford, 1994], 72).

23. For the dynamics of the parallel process in England, see Hutton, *Rise and Fall*.

24. Kharuzin, "K voprosu"; P. I. Ivanov, *Opisanie gosudarstvennogo arkhiva starykh del* (Moscow, 1850), 296–99 (unavailable to me); AI 4:124–26.

25. Zguta, *Minstrels*, 63–65. See also M. M. Gromyko, *Mir russkoi derevni* (Moscow, 1991), 325–29, 345–60.

26. *Zhitie Protopopa Avvakuma*, 62; Avvakum, *The Life*, 46. The translation is Brostrom's.

27. *Zhitie*, 61–64; Avvakum, *The Life*, 45–50.

28. Ibid., 48–50; *Zhitie*, 63–64. I have slightly altered Brostrom's translation.

29. For a survey of the vast literature on this subject, see Robert O. Crummey, "Russia and the 'General Crisis of the Seventeenth Century,'" *Journal of Early Modern His-*

tory 2 (1998): 156–80. Valerie A. Kivelson, "The Devil Stole His Mind," *American Historical Review* 98 (1993): 733–56, is an imaginative analysis of the symbolic significance of the Moscow uprising of 1648.

30. Indeed, this was precisely the time when, according to Schilling, the process of confessionalization ended in the German lands ("Konfessionalisierung," 28–30).

31. H. P. Niess, *Kirche in Russland zwischen Tradition und Glaube? Eine Untersuchung der Kirillova kniga und der Kniga o vere aus der 1 hälfte des 17 Jahrhunderts* (Göttingen, 1977).

32. K. V. Kharlampovich, *Malorossiiskoe vliianie na velikorusskuiu tserkovnuiu zhizn'* (Kazan', 1914); Paul Bushkovitch, *Religion and Society in Russia: The Sixteenth and Seventeenth Centuries* (Oxford, 1992), chs. 6 and 7.

33. Frank E. Sysyn, "Orthodoxy and Revolt: The Role of Religion in the Seventeenth-Century Ukrainian Uprising against the Polish-Lithuanian Commonwealth," *Religion and the Early Modern State: Views from China, Russia, and the West*, ed. James D. Tracy and Marguerite Ragnow (Cambridge and New York, 2004), 154–84.

34. *Patriarch Nikon on Church and State: Nikon's "Refutation,"* ed. Valerie Tumins and George Vernadsky (Berlin, 1982). There is an English translation in William Palmer, *The Patriarch and the Tsar,* 6 vols. (London, 1871–1876), vol. 1.

35. The classic study of Nikon's reforms is still Kapterev, *Patriarkh Nikon.* The current state of the literature on many topics discussed in this paper reflects the fact that during the Soviet period scholars were in effect forbidden to publish serious work on explicitly religious subjects. Russian colleagues relate that, even in the late 1980s, censors required them to remove theological language from their studies of popular ideology or religious practices as a precondition for publication.

36. For a systematic analysis of the changes in the liturgy, see Paul Meyendorff, *Russia, Ritual, and Reform: The Liturgical Reforms of Nikon in the Seventeenth Century* (Crestwood, NY, 1991). On the theological implications of the liturgical reform, Karl Christian Felmy, *Die Deutung des Göttlichen Liturgie im Rahmen der russischen Theologie* (Berlin, 1984), 80–111; Bushkovitch, *Religion and Society,* 61.

37. These were the changes on which later Old Believers concentrated their sharpest criticisms (Crummey, "Origins," 132).

38. Kapterev, *Patriarkh Nikon* 1:192–98; Meyendorff, *Russia,* 61–62.

39. Subbotin, *Materialy* 1:51–78.

40. Ibid., 99–100.

41. *Zhitie,* 65; Archpriest Avvakum, *The Life,* 52.

42. Subbotin, *Materialy* 1:100–102; Pascal, *Avvakum,* 248.

43. Rumiantseva, *Dokumenty Razriadnogo, Posol'skogo, Novgorodskogo i Tainogo Prikazov,* 29–58; "Sudnye protsessy XVII–XVIII vv. po delam tserkvi," ed. E. V. Barsov, ChOIDR, 1882, book iii, 1–42, here 3–13. Michels, *At War with the Church,* 33–38, stresses Bogdanov's isolation and argues that his earlier conflict with Metropolitan Iona probably inspired his protest. Bogdanov illustrates the difficulties of drawing neat divisions between "elite" and "popular" religious culture. On one hand, he consistently told his interrogators he was illiterate; on the other, he carried around a notebook hidden in his hat.

44. Michels, *At War with the Church,* 28–30, 143–44.

45. Michels, "Old Believers in Ukraine," 292–93.

46. Crummey, "Origins," 125–26; Bubnov, *Staroobriadcheskaia kniga,* an indispensable guide to Old Believer polemical literature.

47. Michels, *At War with the Church*, 77–102.

48. This work of the Greek hieromonk John Nathaniel had been published in Venice in 1574. Members of Nikon's inner circle translated and edited it to support their patron's program (Meyendorff, *Russia*, 61).

49. *Deianiia Moskovskikh soborov 1666 i 1667 godov* (Moscow, 1893), 2:3v–8, 30v–33v; Subbotin, *Materialy* 2:210–18, 264–79.

50. Dobrynin later broke once again with the reformed church and, in 1682, was the most prominent Old Believer leader in Moscow.

51. Some of the important early Old Believer writings were copied much more frequently than others. The works of men who made their peace with the official church in 1667 survive in comparatively few copies. Far more copies of the works of the intransigents of 1667 have survived.

52. The following discussion summarizes Crummey, "Religious Radicalism," and relies heavily on Rumiantseva, *Antitserkovnoe dvizhenie* and *Antitserkovnoe dvizhenie: Dokumenty*.

53. Ilarion also accused them of forcing unwilling followers to starve themselves to death in "graves" or pits (Barsukov, *Pamiatniki*, 330–31).

54. Rumiantseva, *Antitserkovnoe dvizhenie. Dokumenty*, 57–59.

55. Ibid., 94, 98–99, 111.

56. Ibid., 189. Her statement is quoted verbatim in chapter 4 of the present work.

57. Bushkovitch, *Religion and Society*, 89–127.

58. For example, Old Believer polemicists often used the "Life" of St. Evfrosin of Pskov to defend the two-finger sign of the cross.

59. Michels, *At War with the Church*, 93–96, and "Place," 25–29, draws attention to a complex dispute in 1659 and 1660, one element of which appears to have been an attempt by the autocratic Bishop Stefan to suppress a local Marian devotion. Significantly, Nikita Dobrynin was his most vociferous opponent.

60. Bushkovitch, *Religion and Society*, 92–94; E. E. Golubinskii, "Istoriia kanonizatsii sviatykh v russkoi tserkvi," ChOIDR, 1903, book iv, 159–69; "Moskovskii sobor o zhitii blagoverynia kniagini Anny Kashinskoi," ChOIDR, 1871, book iv, 45–62.

61. Eve Levin, "False Miracles and Unattested Dead Bodies: Investigations into Popular Cults in Early Modern Russia," *Religion and the Early Modern State*, 253–83.

62. Literally, "crazy words."

63. Rumiantseva, *Dokumenty Razriadnogo, Posol'skogo, Novgorodskogo i Tainogo Prikazov*, 29–58 (quotes, 54).

64. Rumiantseva, *Antitserkovnoe dvizhenie: Dokumenty*, 50–137.

65. Schilling describes essentially the same phenomenon in "Konfessionalisierung," 43–44.

66. In official documents, *raskol* and *raskol'niki* (schismatics) are extremely broad, heterogeneous categories and include all real or imagined dissent against the official church and its teachings and practices.

67. Smirnov, *Dukhovnik*, 224–41.

68. Michels, *At War with the Church*, chs. 4 and 5.

69. The monastery's leaders sent Tsar Alexis a series of petitions protesting the Nikonian reforms. The fifth of these is one of most thorough early attacks on the changes in the liturgy (*Materialy* 3:45–46, 160–71, 209–75).

70. Historians continue to debate the relative importance of these causes in inciting and sustaining the revolt. In addition to the monastery's traditional freedom from the con-

trol of the hierarchy, Michels, in *At War with the Church*, 143–45, and "Solovki Uprising," stresses the importance of exiles and other inveterate troublemakers among its leaders. Earlier studies include N. A. Barsukov, *Solovetskoe vosstanie 1668–1676 gg.* (Petrozavodsk, 1954); A. A. Savich, *Solovetskaia votchina v XV–XVII v.* (Perm', 1927); I. Ia. Syrtsov, *Vozmushchenie Solovetskikh monakhov-staroobriadtsev v XVII v.* (Kostroma, 1888).

71. Michels, "Old Believers in Ukraine"; Druzhinin, *Raskol na Donu.*

72. See V. I. Buganov, *Moskovskie vosstaniia kontsa XVII v.* (Moscow, 1969).

73. PSZ 2:647–50, no. 1102, summarized in Crummey, *Old Believers*, 41–42.

74. For contrasting interpretations of the events, see Michels, "Violent Old Belief," and Crummey, *Old Believers*, ch. 3. For a broad chronological survey of self-immolation, D. I. Sapozhnikov, "Samosozhzhenie v russkom raskole," ChOIDR, 1891, book iii, 1–170.

75. Evfrosin, *Otrazitel'noe pisanie o novoizobretennom puti samoubistvennykh smertei. Pamiatniki drevnei pis'mennosti*, 108:37, 56–57.

76. AI 5:378–94, no. 223, here 389, 392. Michels summarizes this evidence in "Violent Old Belief," 211. It is unclear whether the rebels' plunge into the lake represented a form of baptism or harked back to pre-Christian ritual bathing denounced by the Zealots of Piety earlier in the century.

77. On Morozova, *Povest' o boiaryne Morozovoi*, ed. A. I. Mazunin (Leningrad, 1979).

78. Michels, "Violent Old Belief," 220, citing documents in fund 163 of the Russian State Archive of Ancient Acts, Moscow. He stresses that some of those rescued from the conflagration claimed they had been forced to participate in the ritual suicide.

79. For example, AI 5:389.

80. AI 5:252–62, no. 151.

81. For example, AI 5:380.

82. *Zhitie*, 126; Smirnov, *Vnutrennie voprosy*, 61–66.

83. Evfrosin, *Otrazitel'noe pisanie.*

84. See, for example, the treatment in Ivan Filippov, *Istoriia Vygovskoi pustyni* (St. Petersburg, 1863). A leader of the Vyg community, Ivan Filippov wrote his history in the years just before his death in 1744.

85. Smirnov, *Dukhovnik*, 205–24.

86. Semen Denisov, *Vinograd rossiiskii ili opisanie postradavshikh v Rossii za drevletserkovnoe blagochestie* (Moscow, 1906).

87. See the essays of S. E. Nikitina and M. B. Chernysheva in *Russkie pis'mennye i ustnye traditsii.*

88. Crummey, *Old Believers*, 101–34; L. K. Kuandykov, "Razvitie obshchezhitel'nogo ustava v Vygovskoi staroobriadcheskoi obshchine v pervoi treti XVIII v.," *Issledovaniia po istorii obshchestvennogo soznaniia epokhi feodalizma v Rossii* (Novosibirsk, 1984), 51–63. The limited evidence on the organization of the other communities suggests that their structures were more flexible and their leaders had less control over the other members than in Vyg.

89. See James Cracraft, *The Church Reform of Peter the Great* (Stanford, 1971).

90. Ibid., 238–44; PSZ 6:685–89, no. 4012.

91. Gregory L. Freeze, *The Russian Levites: The Parish Clergy in the Eighteenth Century* (Cambridge, MA, 1977); *The Parish Clergy in Nineteenth-Century Russia: Crisis, Reform, and Counter-Reform* (Princeton, 1983); his introduction to I. S. Belliustin, *Description of the Clergy in Rural Russia: The Memoir of a Nineteenth-Century Parish Priest* (Ithaca, 1985); and his many articles on this subject, including "The Rechristianization of Russia."

92. On popular responses to Peter's policies, see Chernavsky's classic article, "Old Believers."

93. Crummey, *Old Believers*, 66–91.

94. The literature on this subject is very large. See for example, Gromyko, *Mir*, ch. 6; W. F. Ryan, *The Bathhouse at Midnight: Magic in Russia* (University Park, PA, 1999), here 416–28; Ivanits, *Folk Belief*, passim. The word "echoes" (*otgoloski*) is Gromyko's (p. 356). Gromyko notes that, in the nineteenth century, the most strictly devout families prohibited their members from taking part in carnivalesque rituals (*Mir*, 328). For a few examples from our own day, Ryan, *Bathhouse*, 427; E. B. Smilianskaia, "'Iskra istinnago blagochestiia': Religioznye vozzreniia staroobriadtsev Verkhokam'ia," *Rodina*, 1995, no. 2, 101–3; F. F. Bolonev, *Mesiatseslov semeiskikh Zabaikal'ia* (Novosibirsk, 1990); and his "Archaic Elements in the Charms of the Russian Population of Siberia," *Russian Traditional Culture: Religion, Gender and Customary Law*, ed. Marjorie Mandelstam Balzer (Armonk, NY, 1992), 71–84. All except the first of these examples come from the culture of rural Old Believers.

95. Hsia, *Social Discipline*, 154.

4—Religious Radicalism in Seventeenth-Century Russia

1. Among the notable exceptions are Chistov, *Russkie narodnye sotsial'no-utopicheskie legendy*, and the works of N. N. Pokrovskii, particularly "Ispoved'."

2. See, for example, Zenkovsky, *Russkoe staroobriadchestvo*, 144–56, 271–72, 341, 466, 472–75, 489–95; Pascal, *Avvakum*, 62–65.

3. See, for example, Denisov, *Vinograd rossiiskii*, chs. 19 and 21.

4. A. I. Klibanov, "K kharakteristike novykh iavelenii v russkoi obshchestvennoi mysli vtoroi poloviny XVII–nachala XVIII vv.," *Istoriia SSSR*, 1963, no. 6, 85–103. The argument runs through his *Istoriia religioznogo sektantstva v Rossii, 60-e gody XIX v.–1917 g.* (Moscow, 1965), here 41–43. A. I. Rogov presents a more nuanced version of this position in his stimulating overview, "Narodnye massy i religioznye dvizheniia v Rossii vtoroi poloviny XVII veka," *Voprosy istorii*, 1973, no. 4, 33–43.

5. For a thoughtful summary of the discussion of these issues, see Davis, "From 'Popular Religion.'" My own work, *Old Believers*, is an obvious example of the application of the "two cultures" model to religious movements in Russia.

6. Rumiantseva, *Narodnoe antitserkovnoe dvizhenie*. Rumiantseva has published some documents in full in the appendix of the monograph (223–45) and has prepared a separate edition of her most important single source, *Narodnoe antitserkovnoe dvizhenie: Dokumenty*. She has quoted other unpublished sources extensively in the text of her monograph.

7. For example, Pokrovskii, *Antifeodal'nyi protest*. See also Pokrovskii's numerous articles and those of his colleagues and students, such as N. S. Gur'ianova and L. K. Kuandykov.

8. For examples of her brief remarks on the relationship between ideology and social class, see Rumiantseva, *Narodnoe antitserkovnoe dvizhenie*, 204–5, 221.

9. Ibid., 148–64.

10. Rumiantseva, *Narodnoe antitserkovnoe dvizhenie: Dokumenty*, 59–61, 96, 104, 107–8.

11. Ignatii, Metropolitan of Siberia, "Tri poslaniia blazhennogo Ignatiia, mitropolita Sibirskogo i Tobol'skogo: Tret'e poslanie," *Pravoslavnyi sobesednik*, 1855, no. 2, 39–172; Dmitrii, Metropolitan of Rostov, *Rozysk o raskol'nicheskoi brynskoi vere* (Moscow, 1847); Evfrosin, *Otrazitel'noe pisanie*.

12. Denisov, *Vinograd rossiiskii*, 46–47.

13. Rumiantseva, *Narodnoe antitserkovnoe dvizhenie*, 227–42.

14. The evidence uncovered by Rumiantseva (ibid., 83–93) adds new details to the picture presented by earlier historians of these issues. See Kapterev, *Patriarkh Nikon*, 1:1–15. Rumiantseva's assumption that pre- or anti-Christian practices and lack of respect for the clergy and the sacraments were in some sense peculiar to the mid-seventeenth century, because they expressed popular social grievances of the time, seems much too simple.

15. *Stoglav*, 135–42. See also Jack E. Kollmann, Jr., "The Moscow Stoglav ('Hundred Chapters') Church Council of 1551" (Ph.D. dissertation, University of Michigan, 1978), 526–43.

16. Ignatii, "Tret'e poslanie," 96. Rumiantseva points out that Danilovskoe was not a court village but part of a family *votchina* of the Romanovs (*Narodnoe antitserkovnoe dvizhenie*, 108n31).

17. D. N. Breshchinskii, "Zhitie Korniliia Vygovskogo Pakhomievskoi redaktsii (Teksty)," *Drevnerusskaia knizhnost': Po materialam Pushkinskogo Doma* (Leningrad, 1985), 62–107, here 69; A. I. Zhuravlev, *Polnoe istoricheskoe izvestie o drevnikh strigol'nikakh i novykh raskol'nikakh, tak nazyvaemykh staroobriadtsakh, sobrannoe iz potaennykh staroobriadcheskikh predanii, zapisok i pisem* (Moscow, 1890), 1:83.

18. Ignatii, "Tret'e poslanie," 96.

19. Ibid., 99. Rumiantseva rejects this testimony as being inherently improbable on the grounds that uneducated peasants were not interested in quarrels over ritual (*Narodnoe antitserkovnoe dvizhenie*, 71). Her own data, I would suggest, demonstrate precisely the opposite. See, for example, *Narodnoe antitserkovnoe dvizhenie: Dokumenty*, 198.

20. Breshchinskii, "Zhitie Korniliia," 69–70.

21. For a particularly subtle and multifaceted analysis of the significance of fasting in the Christian tradition, see Carolyn Walker Bynum, *Holy Fast and Holy Feast: The Religious Significance of Food to Medieval Women* (Berkeley and Los Angeles, 1987), 31–47.

22. *Iaroslavskiia gubernskiia vedomosti* 1852, no. 49, otd. 3, 408. This charter may be the basis of the tradition recorded by Semen Denisov that Tsar Mikhail knew and admired Kapiton (*Vinograd rossiiskii*, 46). Denisov's statement reflects the tendency of Vyg polemicists to emphasize that the Old Believers' counter-society was a complete, authentically Orthodox and Russian counterpart to official society. See Crummey, *Old Believers*, 97–98.

23. *Iaroslavskiia gubernskiia vedomosti* 1890, no. 12, otd. 3, 4.

24. Evfrosin, *Otrazitel'noe pisanie*, 10.

25. Ignatii, "Tret'e poslanie," 98.

26. Evfrosin, *Otrazitel'noe pisanie*, 10.

27. Ignatii, "Tret'e poslanie," 96–97; Dmitrii Rostovskii, *Rozysk*, 570. The latter's discussion of Kapiton appears to be a précis of Ignatii's text.

28. On the significance of eggs in Russian folk culture, see M. M. Gromyko, *Trudovye traditsii russkikh krest'ian Sibiri, XVIII–pervaia polovina XIX vv.* (Novosibirsk, 1975), 88–89; Propp, *Russkie agrarnye prazdniki*, 96–97. In slightly different symbolic language, Ignatii explained that colored Easter eggs represented the entire world covered with the redeeming blood of Christ ("Tret'e poslanie," 97).

29. Ignatii, "Tret'e poslanie," 97–98. This testimony harmonizes nicely with the insistence that, if he were imprisoned, Kapiton's regimen should include showing reverence for icons. (*Iaroslavskiia gubernskiia vedomosti* 1890, no. 12, otd. 3, 4, quoted in Rumiantseva, *Narodnoe antitserkovnoe dvizhenie*, 72).

30. One unpublished source that Rumiantseva quotes but does not describe claims that Kapiton held an unorthodox view of the Trinity (ibid., 76). Another text to which she alludes is summarized in A. E Bychkov, *Opisanie tserkovnoslavianskikh i russkikh rukopisnykh sbornikov Imperatorskoi Publichnoi Biblioteki* (St. Petersburg, 1882), 1:210, and presents him as an orthodox Old Believer.

31. Smirnov, *Vnutrennye voprosy*, xxxiv, n. 45, quoted from I. V. Milovidov, *Soderzhanie rukopisei, khraniashchikhsia v arkhive Ipat'evskogo Monastyria* (Kostroma, 1887), 1:58–59.

32. For examples, see I. K. Shusherin, *Zhitie Sviateishego Patriarkha Nikona* (St. Petersburg, 1784), 89–90, and Denisov, *Vinograd rossiiskii*, 46–46v.

33. Barskov, *Pamiatniki*, 334. The Old Believer *sinodik* compiled in the Vyg community groups Kapiton with the Viazniki martyrs. See *Svodnyi staroobriadcheskii sinodik*, ed. A. N. Pypin; *Pamiatniki drevnei pis'mennosti i iskusstva*, 44:21; also Rumiantseva, *Narodnoe antitserkovnoe dvizhenie*, 78–79.

34. Barskov, *Pamiatniki*, 329; Rumiantseva, *Narodnoe antitserkovnoe dvizhenie: Dokumenty*, 52.

35. Barskov, *Pamiatniki*, 330–31; Rumiantseva, *Narodnoe antitserkovnoe dvizhenie: Dokumenty*, 52. Rumiantseva questions the truth of this testimony even though, under investigation, two of the Viazniki radicals admitted that it was true, at least in part (ibid., 87).

36. Ibid., 64–65.

37. Ibid., 57–59.

38. On self-immolation, see Crummey, *Old Believers*, 44–57, 187–93, and D. Sapozhnikov, "Samosozhzhenie."

39. Rumiantseva, *Narodnoe antitserkovnoe dvizhenie: Dokumenty*, 94.

40. Ibid., 98–99.

41. Ibid., 111.

42. Rumiantseva, *Narodnoe antitserkovnoe dvizhenie*, 154, 167.

43. Ibid., 225; Rumiantseva, *Narodnoe antitserkovnoe dvizhenie: Dokumenty*, 80–81.

44. Ibid., 81.

45. Rumiantseva, *Narodnoe antitserkovnoe dvizhenie*, 226.

46. This may be the Vavila whom Semen Denisov describes as a convert from Lutheranism and a man learned in grammar, rhetoric, logic, philosophy, theology, and the languages of Christian scholarship (*Vinograd rossiiskii*, 47v). The records of the investigation of 1665–1666 reveal that Vavila the Young had some knowledge of ecclesiastical tradition while elder Vavila was barely literate.

47. Rumiantseva, *Narodnoe antitserkovnoe dvizhenie: Dokumenty*, 86–89.

48. Rumiantseva. *Narodnoe antitserkovnoe dvizhenie*, 153, 157.

49. Ibid., 213n126; Rumiantseva, *Narodnoe antitserkovnoe dvizhenie: Dokumenty*, 57, 90–91, 115–16.

50. Ibid., 124–26.

51. Ibid., 158.

52. Ibid., 177–78.

53. Ibid., 189.

54. Ibid., 186–87. On the cult of Cosmas and Damian in Russia, see V. L. Ianin, "Po povodu zametki P. N. Zholtovskogo 'Larets Mastera Samuila,'" *Sovetskaia Arkheologiia*, 1958, no. 4, 213–15. The fact that the Russian heretics of the fourteenth century, the *strigol'niki*, also accorded Cosmas and Damian special veneration does not point to any direct connection between them and the followers of Kapiton. Rather, this shared alle-

giance arose from their common rejection of the authority of the Orthodox hierarchy and clergy, in part because of its corruption.

55. Crummey, *Old Believers*, chs. 2 and 3.

56. E. V. Barsov, "Akty, otnosiashchiesia k istorii Solovetskago bunta," ChOIDR, 1883, book iv, 1–92, here 80.

57. Rumiantseva, *Narodnoe antitserkovnoe dvizhenie*, 186–87, 216n240.

58. Ibid., 187.

59. The sources of the time reveal a number of ordinary Muscovites who combined elements of the so-called high and folk cultures in their thinking and living. Sila Bogdanov, a Rostov Old Believer, claimed to be illiterate but on investigation showed that he knew a good deal about ecclesiastical history and doctrine and had the notebook mentioned above (chapter 3, n. 43). There is no guarantee, of course, that he could actually read its contents. See E. V. Barsov, "Sudnye protsessy XVII–XVIII vekov po delam tserkvi: 2. Delo o rostovskikh raskol'nikakh Silke Bogdanove s uchenikami 1661 g.," ChOIDR, 1883, book iii, 3–13; Rumiantseva, *Narodnoe antitserkovnoe dvizhenie*, 133–36, 223–24.

60. V. S. Shul'gin reaches the same conclusion in his helpful article, "'Kapitonovshchina' i ee mesto v raskole XVII v.," *Istoriia SSSR*, 1969, no. 4, 130–39. Shul'gin adds the suggestion that, in its social implications, the Kapiton movement was reactionary in that it led oppressed peasants away from social activism. To be sure, among the many strands of religious criticism and protest, one finds individuals and small groups whose convictions resemble those of the later sectarians. See, for example, Rumiantseva, *Narodnoe antitserkovnoe dvizhenie*, 200–204.

5—The Origins of the Old Believer Cultural Systems

1. Geertz, "Religion as a Cultural System," 89.

2. Ibid., 17, where Geertz warns against "schematicism," the tendency to exaggerate the inner coherence of cultural systems. I am grateful to my colleague Aram A. Yengoyan for a copy of his unpublished essay "Culture and Ideology in Contemporary Southeast Asian Societies: The Development of Traditions," which inspired the shape and wording of this passage.

3. At this point a social scientist might object that, when learned men create a "system of meanings," the results of their efforts should be called an "ideology." Use of the latter concept in a study of the polemical and devotional writings of the first defenders of Old Belief would have some obvious advantages. These texts certainly advance a series of general propositions about Christian doctrine and practice and incorporate them into a comprehensive explanation of the meaning of human existence. On the other hand, the concept "ideology" underestimates the extent to which adherence to Old Belief meant not just assent to a set of theological and liturgical propositions but a way of life. Moreover, the word "ideology" by implication exaggerates the extent to which Old Belief differs from other expressions of Eastern Orthodox Christianity, and the degree to which the first writers self-consciously created something new. As they described their activities, they intended only to advocate traditional Russian Orthodox Christianity in its pure, unadulterated form. For these reasons, it seems preferable to speak of the "ideological component" of the Old Believer cultural system rather than of the movement's "ideology."

4. Geertz, "Religion as a Cultural System," 123.

5. For a helpful discussion of canon formation in general and in medieval Western Europe in particular, see E. R. Curtius, *European Literature and the Latin Middle Ages* (New York, 1953), 48–54, 256–72.

6. Stock, *The Implications of Literacy*, 90–92.

7. In *At War with the Church*, Georg Michels argues that the opposition to the Nikonian reforms and their implementation by the Russian Orthodox Church and the imperial government did not coalesce into a coherent movement until the eighteenth century. Michels views the church schism (*raskol*) in the second half of the seventeenth century as a series of individual or local protests, many of which had little apparent connection with the new liturgical practices.

8. The best studies of the origins of Old Belief remain Pascal, *Avvakum,* and Zenkovsky, *Russkoe staroobriadchestvo.*

9. The populist scholars and publicists of prerevolutionary Russia made valuable contributions to our understanding of the regional and social dimensions of early Old Belief. In a somewhat similar vein, Georg Michels's work emphasizes the local conditions and grievances that prompted people to declare their commitment to the old faith in the second half of the seventeenth century. See, for example, his "The Solovki Uprising" and *At War with the Church.* Both approaches, in my view, do not take the mobilizing power of the symbolic language of Old Belief seriously enough.

10. In addition to the works listed earlier, the most useful guides to the early Old Believer leaders and their mutual relations are Smirnov, *Vnutrennie voprosy,* and Bubnov's dissertation, "Staroobriadcheskaia kniga," the published abstract, *Staroobriadcheskaia kniga,* and his book of the same name (St. Petersburg, 1995). See also his "Knigotvorchestvo moskovskikh staroobriadtsev XVII veka," *Russkie knigi i biblioteki v XVI–pervoi polovine XIX veka: Sbornik nauchnykh trudov* (Leningrad, 1983), 23–37.

11. See Bushkovitch, *Religion and Society,* chs. 6 and 7; A. N. Robinson, *Bor'ba idei v russkoi literature XVII v.* (Moscow, 1974).

12. Michels's book raises this issue in social and institutional terms but pays relatively little attention to the spread of the writings of the leading Old Believer polemicists of the seventeenth century.

13. V. G. Druzhinin, *Pisaniia russkikh staroobriadtsev* (St. Petersburg, 1912), remains the best single guide to the Old Believer manuscript tradition. Since the Second World War, Russian scholars have collected large numbers of previously unknown manuscripts that they have listed and described in numerous publications and archival inventories.

14. S. E. Nikitina, "Ustnaia traditsiia v narodnoi kul'ture russkogo naseleniia Verkhokam'ia," *Russkie pis'mennye i ustnye traditsii* (Moscow, 1982), 91–126, here 111–23.

15. *The Reader in the Text,* ed. Susan R. Suleiman and Inge Crosman (Princeton, 1980), is a stimulating collection of essays on "audience-oriented" criticism that includes a brief statement of some of the principal propositions of "reception theory."

16. Such is the claim of Avvakum in a famous passage of his autobiography, written many years after the events. *Zhitie protopopa Avvakuma,* 65.

17. A. K. Borozdin, *Protopop Avvakum: Ocherk iz istorii umstvennoi zhizni russkago obshchestva v XVII veke* (St. Petersburg, 1900), 97–104. This important text has never been published; scholars must rely on manuscript copies or Borozdin's summary. See also Zenkovsky, *Russkoe staroobriadchestvo,* 262–64.

18. N. Bubnov uses these terms in *Staroobriadcheskaia kniga* (abstract), 6–7. As he admits, the distinction between the two types of compositions is somewhat arbitrary and, as the corpus of Old Believer literature has grown, increasingly difficult to maintain.

19. Ibid., 7, 16–27.

20. Subbotin, *Materialy* 4:v–xx, 1–178; Ivan Rumiantsev, *Nikita Konstantinov Dobrynin ("Pustosviat")* (Sergiev Posad, 1916), 329–515, 153–326 (second pagination). At the Council of 1666, Dobrynin recanted and changed "from a stubborn goat to a quiet and innocuous sheep" of the official church (Subbotin, *Materialy* 2:83–91). In 1682, however, he reappeared as the militant leader of the Moscow Old Believers who, in alliance with the mutinous garrison, momentarily brought the government to its knees and was executed when the revolt collapsed.

21. Ibid., 3:45–46, 160–71, 209–12, 213–75.

22. Ibid., 4:xxiii–xxviii, 179–266.

23. Ibid., 4:6, 8:354–60; Smirnov, *Vnutrennie voprosy*, lxiii–lxx; Zenkovsky, *Russkoe staroobriadchestvo*, 340–55.

24. The fundamental edition of Avvakum's writings remains Ia. L. Barskov and P. S. Smirnov, ed., "Pamiatniki istorii staroobriadchestva XVII veka," *Russkaia istoricheskaia biblioteka* 39 (1927). *Zhitie protopopa Avvakuma* is an excellent edition for a general readership. See also A. N. Robinson, *Zhizneopisaniia Avvakuma i Epifaniia: Issledovanie i teksty* (Moscow, 1963), and N. S. Demkova, *Zhitie protopopa Avvakuma* (Leningrad, 1974). The specialized literature on Avvakum and his writings is enormous. For many years, study of Avvakum as a great Russian writer and a rebel against the established order allowed scholars in the Soviet Union to discuss Old Belief in print, albeit with circumspection.

25. Druzhinin, *Pisaniia*.

26. Soon after its publication, other scholars noted gaps in Druzhinin's inventory. See V. Belolikov, *Pisaniia russkikh staroobriadtsev V. G. Druzhinina* (Kiev, 1913).

27. *Pustozerskii sbornik: Avtografy sochinenii Avvakuma i Epifaniia* (Leningrad, 1975), xi–xii.

28. See, for example, V. I. Malyshev, *Drevnerusskie rukopisi Pushkinskogo Doma* (Moscow-Leningrad, 1965); Malyshev, *Ust'-tsilemskie rukopisnye sborniki XVI–XX vv.* (Syktyvkar, 1960).

29. N. Iu. Bubnov, *Sochineniia pisatelei-staroobriadtsev XVII veke* (Leningrad, 1984). The holdings of the Library of the Academy of Sciences, including V. G. Druzhinin's own collection, figure prominently in Druzhinin's 1912 inventory.

30. *Zhitie protopopa Avvakuma*, 100, 373.

31. Bubnov, "Staroobriadcheskaia kniga," 127–31. I am most grateful to the author for lending me a copy of his unpublished dissertation. See also Smirnov, *Vnutrennie voprosy*, ix.

32. Bubnov, "Staroobriadcheskaia kniga," 97–101, 127–74; his *Staroobriadcheskaia kniga* (abstract), 17–18; and Smirnov, *Vnutrennie voprosy*, lxxi–lxxiv.

33. Subbotin, *Materialy* 7:1–258.

34. Bubnov, "Staroobriadcheskaia kniga," 357–66.

35. Subbotin, *Materialy* 7:259–385; E. E. Zamyslovskii, ed., "Chelobitnaia startsa Avraamiia," LZAK, 1877, no. 6, 1–129. These editions are based on two different manuscripts.

36. Subbotin, *Materialy* 7:386–426; Smirnov, *Vnutrennie voprosy*, 08–016. N. V. Shukhtina, "Pererabotki 'Voprosa i otveta' i 'Poslanie k nekoemu bogoliubtsu' inoka Avraamiia v rukopisiakh XVIII–XIX vv.," TODRL 44 (1990): 403–8, argues that Avraamii originally wrote the "Question and Answer" and the letter "to a certain lover of God" as a single composition, which he sent to Avvakum's son Ivan, who forwarded it to his father. Avraamii later revised the work as the two separate compositions that have come down to us. The manuscript tradition reflects later editing of both compositions.

37. Bubnov, *Staroobriadcheskaia kniga* (abstract), 18. The text is published in Sub-

botin, *Materialy* 6:302–9. Druzhinin, who considered the work Deacon Fedor's, listed 21 manuscript copies (*Pisaniia*, 276–77). The remaining short works are two sets of notes on the Antichrist (Subbotin, *Materialy* 7:427–33, 8:361–65), an epistle on the End Time (LZAK 24:157–62); a note "on the deviation of Rome," and a letter to "a certain daughter of Christ" (Subbotin, *Materialy* 8:354–60, 365–68); and the unpublished "Tale of Kondratii," a fictionalized account of Avraamii's own interrogation.

38. Bubnov, "Staroobriadcheskaia kniga," 141–74.

39. Ibid., 141–43, 166–71.

40. Subbotin, *Materialy* 7:215, 415, 8:365.

41. On the first printed Slavonic service books, see Makarii, *Istoriia russkago raskola*, 106–30.

42. Subbotin, *Materialy* 7:183, 215. The "scroll" may have been the letter to the Council of 1666.

43. Ibid., 211–16, 287–91, 415. In this connection, Avraamii repeatedly quotes Proverbs 22:28, "Do not move the ancient boundary-stone which your forefathers set up."

44. Ibid., 410. See also 148, 307; LZAK 24:158–59.

45. Subbotin, *Materialy* 7:395. See also 7:228, 400.

46. Ibid., 33, 320.

47. Ibid., 390. See also 7:66–67, 78–81, 86–95, 182, 198, 212–16, 246–48, 291–92; 6:304–5; LZAK, vol. 24.

48. Ibid., 160; Subbotin, *Materialy* 7:86–95, 337–40, 354, 370; Smirnov, *Vnutrennie voprosy*, 10.

49. Ibid., 11–12; Subbotin, *Materialy* 7:89–92, 99–100, 143–45, 366–67, 8:354–60; LZAK 24:160.

50. Subbotin, *Materialy* 7:87.

51. Ibid., 198, 213.

52. Ibid., 70–73, 96–98, 235–41, 306, 324–25, 339–40, 402–3, 428, 6:305–6, 8:358.

53. Ibid., 7:402.

54. Ibid., 98–99, 149–50, 233–34, 308–9, 314, 323, 336–37.

55. Ibid., 34, 89, 100–181, 371–73, 377–83, 421–22, 6:305–6, 8:367; Smirnov, *Vnutrennie voprosy*, 010–11.

56. Subbotin, *Materialy* 7:26–27, 317, 8:358. Spiridon Potemkin made the same observation (Borozdin, *Protopop Avvakum*, 100).

57. Ibid., 7:28–32, 67–69, 82–84, 188, 210, 215, 242–48, 293–314, 333–34, 337–38, 6:307.

58. Ibid., 7:17–23, 352–62, 407–8; LZAK 6:98–101, 103–7, 24:158.

59. Ibid., 6:61, 70–83; Subbotin, *Materialy* 7:188, 209, 244, 310, 323–38.

60. Ibid., 24–25, 215, 268–72, 314–15, 399–400, 429–31, 8:358–59; LZAK 6:28–31, 63–64, 24:158.

61. Subbotin, *Materialy* 7:24–25, 70–74, 79, 215, 233, 272–87, 315–16, 319, 348–51, 362–63, 370–71, 399–401, 431, 433; LZAK 6:31–42, 64–65, 90–98, 100–101.

62. Subbotin, *Materialy* 7:149, 265, 418, 8:365; Smirnov, *Vnutrennie voprosy*, 9.

63. Subbotin, *Materialy* 7:216, 234–41, 274–75, 334–36, 373–77, 382–85, 417–26, 428, 6:307–8; LZAK 6:33, 80–81, 109–11, 115–17, 24:162.

64. Subbotin, *Materialy* 7:234–41, 249–52, 297, 404–5, 419–25 (421), 8:366–68; Smirnov, *Vnutrennie voprosy*, 09–010; LZAK 24:159; M. B. Pliukhanova, "O nekotorykh chertakh lichnostnogo soznaniia v Rossii XVII v.," *Khudozhestvennyi iazyk srednevekov'ia* (Moscow, 1982), 184–200, here 192.

65. Revelation 12:3–4.

66. Subbotin, *Materialy* 7:422.

67. Ibid., 182, 210, 234–42, 265, 297, 309, 331, 334–35, 362, 364, 375, 384, 422–25, 428, 8:354–56, 368; LZAK 6:26, 50, 59, 77–78, 80, 116; Smirnov, *Vnutrennie voprosy,* 012. It was only appropriate that the Antichrist should time his advent according to "human" chronology (Subbotin, *Materialy* 7:423).

68. Ibid., 309; LZAK 6:60. In more menacing passages, Avraamii denounces the tsar as a heretic and scourge of the faithful (Subbotin, *Materialy* 7:213) and declares, "The whole weight of the church hangs on your neck" (ibid., 216).

69. Ibid., 382, 432; LZAK 6:115. Avraamii attributes the saying to Christ, but the passage is in the third person. The language echoes 2 Timothy 4:1 and Hebrews 11:38.

70. The best introduction to these debates is the work of P. S. Smirnov, *Vnutrennie voprosy,* esp. chs. 3 and 4, and *Spory i razdeleniia.*

71. Subbotin, *Materialy* 7:214, 261–63, 389–90, 403–4, 426–27; LZAK 24:161.

72. Subbotin, *Materialy* 6:304–9, 7:386–416, 8:365; RGB, f. 732 (Gor'kovskoe sobranie), no. 47, 30v–31.

73. Subbotin, *Materialy* 7:425–26; Smirnov, *Vnutrennie voprosy,* 012–13.

74. Subbotin, *Materialy* 7:44, 208–9.

75. Ibid., 28–29, 82–84,188, 210, 215, 242–48, 293–314, 333–34, 337–38; LZAK 6:47–63, 79–80, 82–83.

76. Zamyslovskii notes that the text of Meletius appears in several earlier Russian compilations and that the work attributed to Theodoret is actually an anonymous Russian composition of the fifteenth century (LZAK 6:122–23).

77. Subbotin, *Materialy* 7:291, 294, 302–5.

78. Ibid., 311–12.

79. Ibid., 215.

80. P. J. Chrysostomus, *Die "Pomorskie otvety" als Denkmal des russischen Altgläubigen gegen Ende des 1. Viertels des XVIII. Jahrh. Orientalia Christiana Analecta* 148 (Rome, 1957), 90.

81. Subbotin, *Materialy* 7:304–5.

82. Ibid., 296–301, 337–38.

83. Ibid., 338.

84. Ibid., 3:229–30, 4:71–83, 6:4–5; Pascal, *Avvakum,* 296–97, 377; *Pamiatniki drevnei russkoi literatury* 188 (1916): 145–96. Nikita Pustosviat cited Sts. Meletius, Theodoret, and Peter of Damascus, the *Kniga o vere,* the *Grammatika* of 1595, Maksim Grek, the *Kormchaia kniga,* the Stoglav, *Potrebniki,* and unnamed old books in the Spaso-Evfimievskii, Chudov, and Nikol'skii Monasteries. Pope Formosus again serves as the horrible example of the three-finger sign. The passage is found in chapter 31 of *Stoglav,* 103.

85. Subbotin, *Materialy* 4:79–80.

86. Ibid., 71–72.

87. Ibid., 83.

88. Ibid., 3:32–35, 4:114–23, 6:5.

89. Ibid., 4:115–16. The fourfold alleluia is "Alleluia, alleluia, alleluia, Glory to Thee, O God."

90. Ibid., 118–19, 122–23.

91. Ibid., 7:323–31; LZAK 6:70–77.

92. Subbotin, *Materialy* 7:326–29.

6—The Miracle of Martyrdom

1. When Old Belief took shape as a distinct movement is a subject of debate. Most historians have assumed that one can legitimately consider Old Belief in the late 1660s, 1670s, and 1680s to be a mass movement of religious and social protest. In *At War with the Church* and other publications, Georg Michels has argued that Old Belief became a coherent movement only in the first decades of the eighteenth century, largely in response to the policies of Peter I.

2. In chapter 5, I attempted to apply Geertz's definition of "cultural system" as a conceptual approach to the complex phenomenon known as Old Belief. The concept is useful in its comprehensiveness in that, once the movement reached its full development, it gave its adherents a complete way of life—liturgy, beliefs (or, if you prefer, an ideology), a moral code, rules, and taboos to govern day-to-day life. See Geertz, "Religion as a Cultural System," in Robert L. Moore and Frank E. Reynolds, eds., *Anthropology and the Study of Religion* (Chicago, 1984); the volume contains helpful essays on the theories of Geertz and Victor Turner.

3. Following the helpful suggestions of Davis in "From 'Popular Religion,'" 323, I have argued in chapters 2 and 5 that Old Believer culture should be viewed as a multitude of closely interrelated subcultures.

4. For a discussion of the canon on which one early Old Believer polemicist based his own work, see chapter 5, on Avraamii. On the process of establishing a canon of authoritative texts, see Curtius, *European Literature*, 48–54, 256–72.

5. The most useful introduction to Russian hagiography remains V. O. Kliuchevskii, *Drevnerusskie zhitiia sviatykh kak istoricheskii istochnik* (Moscow, 1871; repr. Moscow, 1988).

6. Paul Bushkovitch, "The Life of Filipp: Tsar and Metropolitan in the Late Sixteenth Century," *Medieval Russian Culture*, vol. 2, ed. Michael S. Flier and Daniel Rowland (Berkeley, 1994), 29–46.

7. *Avvakum, The Life.* The most useful of the many Russian editions are *Zhitie Protopopa*, and *Zhitie Avvakuma i drugie ego sochineniia*, ed. A. N. Robinson (Moscow, 1991). See also Priscilla Hunt, "A Penitential Journey: The Life of the Archpriest Avvakum and the Kenotic Tradition," *Canadian-American Slavic Studies* 25 (1991): 201–24.

8. Bubnov, in *Staroobriadcheskaia kniga*, divides early Old Believer writings into three groups based on the location in which they were written—Moscow, Pustozersk, and the Solovetskii Monastery.

9. See Bushkovitch, *Religion and Society.*

10. Definitions are taken from *The Oxford Dictionary of the Christian Church*, ed. F. L. Cross and E. A. Livingstone (London, 1974), 881, 920. The following works on miracles are particularly helpful: Peter Brown, *The Cult of the Saints* (Chicago, 1981); Benedicta Ward, *Miracles and the Medieval Mind* (Philadelphia, 1982); Pierre-André Sigal, *L'Homme et le miracle dans la France médiévale, XIe–XIIe siècle* (Paris, 1985); and, for the Russian context, Bushkovitch, *Religion and Society*, chs. 4 and 5.

11. One of the two extant autograph copies of the vitae of Avvakum and Epifanii is reproduced in *Pustozerskii sbornik*. As far as I am aware, the earliest extant manuscripts of Avraamii's three compositions—"Vopros i Otvet," "Muchenie nekoikh starets ispovednik, Petra i Evdokima," and "Povest' o prenii Kondratiia s dukhovnimi vlastiami"—are in, respectively, GIM, Sobranie Khludova, 148; RGADA, f. 181, opis' 5, 434/893, 291–98; RGB,

f. 732, Gor'kovskoe Sobranie, 47. All date from between the 1670s and the early eighteenth century. See Bubnov, *Staroobriadcheskaia kniga*, 139; V. S. Kuznetsova, "Povest' o muchenii nekoikh starets Petra i Evdokima," *Literatura i klassovaia bor'ba epokhi pozdnego feodalizma v Rossii* (Novosibirsk, 1987), 206–15; Subbotin, *Materialy* 7:xxviii; Mazunin, *Povest'*, 29, 110. The earliest extant manuscripts are RNB, O.I.341, and BAN, Sobranie Nefedova, no. 4, both of which date from the very end of the seventeenth century.

12. Robinson, *Zhitie Avvakuma*, 59, 319.

13. On Avraamii's life and works, see chapter 5.

14. Bubnov, *Staroobriadcheskaia kniga*, 158. In Russian, the concepts "torture" (*muchenie*) and "martyrdom" (*muchenichestvo*) cannot be neatly separated. In this text, the word *muchenie* is used in the title, but in some versions the answers of the two heroes are labeled *otvet muchenicheskoi* (the martyrs' answer). Of the two manuscripts I have used, RGB, Sobranie Viazemskogo, Q.53, repeatedly uses this phrase, but RNB, Sobranie Obshchestva liubitelei drevnei pis'mennosti, 8°, no. 72, does not.

15. Subbotin, *Materialy* 6:302–9; Bubnov, *Staroobriadcheskaia kniga*, 158–59. Bubnov bases his attribution on the style of the work and the convoy in which it is found in the manuscripts. V. S. Kuznetsova leaves the question of authorship open in her recent edition of the earliest manuscript of the text, "Povest' o muchenii," 206–15.

16. For a recent textological study of the "Question and Answer," and its later reworkings in the manuscript tradition, see Shukhtina, "Pererabotki 'Voprosa i otveta.'"

17. Bubnov, *Staroobriadcheskaia kniga*, 169–71.

18. Subbotin, *Materialy* 7:386; RGB, f. 732, Gor'kovskoe sobranie, no. 47, 30v–31.

19. See chapter 5.

20. Subbotin, *Materialy* 6:306–7, 7:396–97, 402–3 (Apocalypse), 6:304–8 (heresy), 7:407–8 (communion wafers), 6:304, 7:399–401 (Holy Spirit).

21. Daniel, ch. 3 (Kuznetsova notes the similarity, in "Povest'," 206–7).

22. Subbotin, *Materialy* 6:307–9.

23. Ibid. 7:391, 404–5, 410, 415; RGB, f. 732, Gor'kovskoe sobranie, no. 47, 30v–31.

24. Subbotin, *Materialy* 7:409. The references are clearly to the tale of Petr and Evdokim and the stories about the Pustozersk martyrs Epifanii, Fedor, and Lazar', which appear in a number of Old Believer compositions. See Bubnov, *Staroobriadcheskaia kniga*, 158.

25. Subbotin, *Materialy* 6:302–4, 7:386–87, 391–92, 405–6, 414. The passage in the "Vopros i otvet" describing Avraamii's arrest closely resembles the Gospel stories of Christ's arrest.

26. Mazunin, *Povest'*, 66–70, 75–77. See also H. W. Dewey, "The Life of Lady Morozova as Literature," *Indiana Slavic Studies* 4 (1967): 74–87.

27. Mazunin, *Povest'*, 29–33, 49–50, 82–84 ("Question and Answer"), 49–51 (Abridged Redaction), 56–58 (Extended Redaction). Mazunin's argument rests in part on the absence of any mention of Avvakum (whose teachings the Kerzhenets Old Believers rejected) and the prominence accorded Deacon Fedor.

28. Ibid., 110–24. L. A. Dmitriev, *Zhitiinye povesti russkogo severa kak pamiatniki literatury XIII–XVI vv.* (Leningrad, 1973), 4.

29. Mazunin, *Povest'*, 127. The other redactions have simpler headings (156, 186).

30. Ibid., 185, 206–7.

31. Except when noted, this summary is based on the Extended Redaction.

32. M. O. Skripil', "Povest' ob Uliianii Osor'inoi: Istoricheskie komentarii i teksty," TODRL 6 (1948): 256–323.

33. The Short Redaction differs somewhat in this respect. On one occasion, Morozova explains to her captors the theological significance of the two-finger sign of the cross and, on another, lists for them a number of the Old Believers' objections to the Nikonian reforms (Mazunin, *Povest'*, 193–95).

34. Unlike the Life of Uliianiia Osor'ina, the life of Morozova pays comparatively little attention to her acts of Christian charity.

35. Stylistic peculiarities suggest that the afterword, which in most extant manuscripts has a separate cinnabar heading, may be a later addition to the core of the text.

36. Mazunin, *Povest'*, 184.

37. Ibid., 204. In simplifying the story, Semen Denisov left out the character of Melaniia and needed another way of explaining how Morozova became a nun.

38. Ibid., 146.

39. *Pustozerskii sbornik*, 80–91, 112–38; Robinson, *Zhizneopisaniia Avvakuma i Epifaniia*, 179–202.

40. Among the examples are two failed attempts at murder because guns fail to fire, escapes from drowning, Avvakum's hen that continues to lay eggs under the most unpromising circumstances, and miraculously large catches of fish for his hungry family (Robinson, *Zhitie Avvakuma*, 33, 40, 46, 49, 53, 75–76).

41. Ibid., 35, 46, 48, 68–73.

42. Ibid., 32–33, 73–75.

43. I am most grateful to Natalie Zemon Davis and other participants in the 1993 summer workshop on Early East Slavic Culture for this insight.

44. Caroline Walker Bynum, "Women's Stories, Women's Symbols: A Critique of Victor Turner's Theory of Liminality," *Anthropology and the Study of Religion*, 105–25, here 110–15.

45. Bushkovitch, *Religion and Society*, esp. chs. 4, 5, and 6.

46. See M. B. Pliukhanova, "O nekotorykh chertakh."

7—Old Believer Communities

1. *Slovar' russkogo iazyka XI–XVII vv.* (Moscow, 1975–), 24:200; *Tolkovyi slovar' russkogo iazyka*, 4 vols. (Moscow, 1935–1940), 4:215; *Staroobriadchestvo: Litsa, sobytiia, predmety i simvoly* (Moscow, 1996), 260–61; E. M Iukhimenko, *Vygovskaia staroobriadcheskaia pustyn': Dukhovnaia zhizn' i literatura*, 2 vols. (Moscow, 2002), 1:30. Old Believer use of the term was not entirely consistent. In the Nizhnii-Novgorod region, the word could refer to large informal communities, and on occasion it might refer to any center of Old Believer life, urban as well as rural.

2. N. N. Pokrovskii and N. D. Zol'nikova, *Starovery-chasovennye na vostoke Rossii v XVIII–XX vv.: Problemy tvorchestva i obshchestvennogo soznaniia* (Moscow, 2002), 37–58, here 51–52.

3. T. D. Goriacheva, "Ustroistvo Rogozhskogo bogadelennogo doma vo vtoroi polovine XIX–nachale XX veka," *Mir staroobriadchestva* 4 (1998): 247–56, here 255.

4. On another type of unofficial monastic community, in this case convents within the official Orthodox church, see Brenda Meehan, *Holy Women of Russia* (San Francisco, 1993), and her "Popular Piety, Local Initiative, and the Founding of Women's Religious Communities in Russia, 1764–1907," *Seeking God*, 83–105.

5. Robson, *Old Believers*, 29–32.

6. This point is stressed in ibid., 25–28, 124–25, and I. V. Pozdeeva, "Russkoe staroobriadchestvo i Moskva v nachale XX v.," *Mir staroobriadchestva* 2 (1995): 6–41, here 15–18.

7. Pokrovskii and Zol'nikova, *Starovery-chasovennye*, 16–59; Robson, *Old Believers*, 32–34.

8. Crummey, *Old Believers*, 108–10.

9. Ibid., 117–22, 203; I. F. Nil'skii, *Semeinaia zhizn' v russkom raskole; istoricheskii ocherk raskol'nicheskogo uchniia o brake*, 2 vols. (St. Petersburg, 1869), 1:20, 95–96, 118–21, 150–80.

10. Pokrovskii and Zol'nikova, *Starovery-chasovennye*, 59–104.

11. Iukhimenko, *Vygovskaia staroobriadcheskaia pustyn'*, 1:11, 58–64; Kuandykov, "Razvitie obshchezhitel'nogo ustava." Kuandykov is mistaken in arguing that Vyg writers avoided the word "monastyr." To mention obvious examples, Filippov's, *Istoriia*, written about 1740, and the documents that made up the rule of Vyg used it regularly. Admittedly "obshchezhitel'stvo," "pustyn'," and "kinoviia" occur more commonly in these texts.

12. In this respect, the role of the Old Believer *nastoiatel'* was closer to that of the abbess of an Orthodox convent. See, for example, David M. Goldfrank, "Sisterhood Just Might Be Powerful: The Testament-Rule of Elena Devochkina," *Russian History/Histoire russe* 34 (2007): 189–206. The Russian text was published in *Akty rossiiskogo gosudarstva: Arkhivy moskovskikh monastyrei i soborov XV–nachalo XVII vv.* (Moscow, 1998), 298–303 (no. 126).

13. Crummey, *Old Believers*, 107–8; E. V. Barsov, "Ulozhenie brat'ev Denisovykh," *Pamiatnaia knizhka Olonetskoi Gubernii za 1868 i 1869 gg.*, 2:85–116, here 85–105; Savich, *Solovetskaia votchina*, 207–11, 247–48.

14. Kuandykov, "Ideologiia obshchezhitel'stva," 98–99.

15. Jennifer B. Spock, "The Solovki Monastery, 1460–1645: Piety and Patronage in the Early Modern Russian North" (Ph.D. dissertation, Yale University, 1999), 198–99, and her "Weaving Orthodoxy: Creating and Recreating Early Modern Tradition through Daily Rules" (paper presented at the national conference of the American Association for the Advancement of Slavic Studies, November 15–18, 2001). I am grateful to the author for making her work available to me. See also Savich, *Solovetskaia votchina*, 206–7.

16. See, for example, M. L. Sokolovskaia, "Severnoe raskol'nicheskoe obshchezhitel'stvo pervoi poloviny XVIII veka i struktura ego zemel'," *Istoriia SSSR*, 1978, no. 1, 157–67.

17. Kuandykov, "Razvitie obshchezhitel'nogo ustava," 63.

18. Ibid., 53; M. L. Sokolovskaia, "Skladyvanie instituta 'uchitel'stva' v Vygo-Leksenskom [*sic*] obshchezhitel'stve," *Mir staroobriadchestva* 1 (1992): 28–45.

19. On the rule of Vyg and Leksa, see Kuandykov's "Razvitie obshchezhitel'nogo ustava"; "Ideologiia obshchezhitel'stva"; "Vygovskie sochineniia ustavnogo kharaktera vtoroi poloviny XVIII v.," *Istochniki po istorii russkogo obshchestvennogo soznaniia perioda feodalizma* (Novosibirsk, 1986), 120–30; and "Rukopis' no. 3 iz Sobraniia I. N. Zavoloko v Drevlekhranilishche Pushkinskogo Doma," *Sibirskoe istochnikovedenie i arkheografiia* (Novosibirsk, 1984), 121–35.

20. Peter Hauptmann. "Das Gemeindeleiteramt bei den priesterlosen Altgläubigen," *Unser ganzes Leben Christus unserm Gott überantworten: Studien zur ostkirchlichen Spiritualität* (Göttingen, 1982), 474–99.

21. E. M. Iukhimenko, "Pervye ofitsial'nye izvestiia o poselenii staroobriadtsev v Vygovskoi pustyni," *Staroobriadchestvo v Rossii (XVII –XVIII vv.)* (Moscow, 1994), 163–75.

22. On the raids on Paleostrov and a similar attack on Pudozh, see Michels, *At War*

with the Church, 184–85, 203–5, 207–8; his "The Violent Old Belief"; and Crummey, *Old Believers*, 45–57.

23. N. S. Demkova, "Vnov' naidennyi podlinnik "Dela ob olonetskom raskol'nike Tereshke Artem'ev 1695 g.," *Staroobriadchestvo v Rossii (XVII–XVIII vv.)*, 176–89, and her "O nachale Vygovskoi pustyni, maloizvestnyi document iz Sobraniia E. V. Barsova," *Pamiatniki literatury i obshchestvennoi mysli epokhi feodalizma* (Novosibirsk, 1985), 237–48.

24. Filippov, *Istoriia*, 95–98.

25. See notes 12 and 18.

26. Iukhimenko, *Vygovskaia staroobriadcheskaia pustyn'*, 1:462–512, here 478.

27. Spock, "The Solovki Monastery," 183–85, makes a similar observation about the origins of the monks of Solovki.

28. M. L. Sokolovskaia, "Krest'ianskii mir kak osnova formirovaniia Vygovskogo obshchezhitel'stva," *Staroobriadchestvo v Rossii (XVII–XX vv.)*, ed. E. M. Iukhimenko (Moscow, 1999), 269–79; her "Skladyvanie"; Kuandykov, "Ideologiia obshchezhitel'stva," 95–96; his "Rukopis'," 135; his "Filippovskie polemicheskie sochineniia XIX v. o skitskoi zhizni," *Drevnerusskaia rukopisnaia kniga i ee bytovanie v Sibiri* (Novosibirsk, 1982), 113–24, here 115–17; and A. M. Pashkov, "Staroobriadcheskie poseleniia severo-zapada Rossii v 1700–1917 godakh," *Istoriia i geografiia russkikh staroobriadcheskikh govorov* (Moscow, 1995), 93–101. As opposed to the other authors, Sokolovskaia insists that the only difference between a *skit* and a *poselenie* was size: both were lay peasant villages ("Krest'ianskii mir," 272).

29. *Staroobriadchestvo: Litsa, sobytiia, predmety i simvoly; Opyt entsiklopedicheskogo slovaria* (Moscow, 1996), 62–63; M. I. Lileev, *Iz istorii raskola na Vetke i v Starodub'e XVII–XVIII vv.* (Kiev, 1895), 1:361.

30. On the Lavrent'ev monastery, P. I. Mel'nikov [Andrei Pecherskii], "Ocherki popovshchiny," *Polnoe sobranie sochinenii* 7 (St. Petersburg, 1909), 3–375, 307–51.

31. Lileev, *Iz istorii raskola*, 1:371–73, 384–92.

32. Crummey, *Old Believers*, 128–31; *Staroobriadchestvo*, 125–28; N. Sokolov, *Raskol v Saratovskom krae* (Saratov, 1888), 238–74.

33. Lileev, *Iz istorii raskola*, 1:216–22; Sokolov, *Raskol*, 270.

34. Ibid., chapters 6 and 7. In the *edinoverie*, priestly Old Believers could preserve the pre-Nikonian liturgy in return for accepting the authority of the official Russian Orthodox hierarchy.

35. Pokrovskii and Zol'nikova, *Starovery-chasovennye*, 434–35.

36. *Staroobriadchestvo*, 306–8.

37. S. V. Taranets, *Kurenevskoe trimonastyr'e: Istoriia russkogo staroobriadcheskogo tsentra v Ukraine* (Kiev, 1999), 46–58, 74–77; his *Staroobriadchestvo Podolii* (Kiev, 2000), 102–12, 121–30; and his "Kurenevskoe trimonastyr'e (istoriia Kurenevskikh staroobriadcheskikh muzhskogo i zhenskogo monastyrei," *Mir staroobriadchestva* 5 (1999): 312–35.

38. On the Moscow communities, Ryndziunskii, "Staroobriadcheskaia organizatsiia"; Goriacheva, "Ustroistvo"; her "Istochniki po istorii Rogozhskoi staroobriadcheskoi obshchiny (vtoraia polovina XIX–nachalo XX v.); opyt istochnikovedcheskoi kharakteristiki," *Mir staroobriadchestva* 5 (1999): 118–52; E. M. Iukhimenko, *Staroobriadcheskii tsentr za Rogozhskoi zastavoiu* (Moscow, 2005); Irina Paert, *Old Believers, Religious Dissent and Gender in Russia, 1760–1850* (Manchester and New York, 2003), 59–108; Mel'nikov, "Ocherki popovshchiny," 204–307; N. Popov, ed., "Materialy dlia istorii bezpopovshchinskikh soglasii v Moskve: 1. Feodosievtsev Preobrazhenskago kladbishcha: 2. Moninskoe soglasie," *ChOIDR*, 1869, book ii, 71–174, and book iii, 13–186; and V. Vasil'ev, "Orga-

nizatsiia i samoupravlenie Feodosievskoi obshchiny na Preobrazhenskom Kladbishche v Moskve," *Khristianskoe chtenie,* 1887, 568–615.

39. *Staroobriadchestvo,* 175, 232–35, 239–42.

40. Popov, "Materialy," 131–32.

41. Ibid., 134.

42. Ibid., 31–39.

43. Iukhimenko, *Staroobriadcheskii tsentr,* 71.

44. Vasil'ev, "Organizatsiia," 586.

45. Iukhimenko, *Staroobriadcheskii tsentr,* 20; V. E. Makarov, *Ocherk istorii Rogozhskogo kladbishcha v Moskve (k 140-letiiu ego sushchestvovaniia: 1771–1911 gg.)* (Moscow, 1994, repr. of an article published in 1911), 28.

46. Goriacheva, "Ustroistvo" and "Istochniki"; Ryndziunskii, "Staroobriadcheskaia organizatsiia," 202–13.

47. Iukhimenko, *Staroobriadcheskii tsentr,* 85–91.

48. Goriacheva, "Ustroistvo," 252.

49. Iukhimenko, *Staroobriadcheskii tsentr,* 21.

50. For example, N. N. Zhivotov, *Tserkovnyi raskol Peterburga* (St. Petersburg, 1891), 54, 66–67; V. N., "Raskol v Peterburge," *Tserkovno-obshchestvennyi vestnik,* 1878, no. 9, 2–4; Makarov, *Ocherk,* 69; and the sources mentioned in note 37.

51. Robson, *Old Believers,* 53–74.

52. For example, in the late nineteenth and early twentieth centuries, the lay guardians of the Rogozhskoe Kladbishche had a great deal of power over the clergy who served the community. See Goriacheva, "Ustroistvo," and "Istochniki," 129ff. and n. 2.

53. *Staroobriadchestvo,* 78.

54. Roy R. Robson, "Old Believers and the Soviet State in Riga, 1945–1955," *Rude & Barbarous Kingdom Revisited: Essays in Russian History and Culture in Honor of Robert O. Crummey,* ed. Chester S. L. Dunning, Russell E. Martin, and Daniel Rowland (Bloomington, 2008), 287–99.

55. N. N. Pokrovskii, "Krest'ianskii pobeg i traditsii pustynnozhitel'stva v Sibiri XVIII v.," *Krest'ianstvo Sibiri XVIII–nachala XX v. Klassovaia bor'ba, obshchestvennoe soznanie i kul'tura* (Novosibirsk, 1975), 19–49; Kuandykov, "Filippovskie polemicheskie sochineniia"; Pokrovskii and Zol'nikova, *Starovery-chasovennye,* 16–19, 96, 111, 435.

56. A. I. Mal'tsev, *Starovery-stranniki v XVIII–pervoi polovine XIX v.* (Novosibirsk, 1996), 31–32, 225–26.

57. *Opisanie dokumentov i del,* no. 1, 185–86, 588, no. 23, 653–54, 971–74; V. I. Malyshev, "Une communauté de vieux-croyants dans la Russie du nord: L'ermitage des Grandes Prairies," *Revue des Etudes Slaves* 43 (1964): 83–89; Pokrovskii, "Krest'ianskii pobeg"; Kuandykov, "Filippovskie polemicheskie sochineniia"; Pokrovskii and Zol'nikova, *Starovery-chasovennye,* 16–19; Pashkov, "Staroobriadcheskie poseleniia"; E. G. Men'shakova, "Pecherskoe staroobriadchestvo," *Staroobriadcheskaia kul'tura Russkogo Severa* (Moscow-Kargopol', 1998), 28–32; N. Snesarev, "Verkhne-Chirskaia stanitsa i staroobriadcheskii raskol v XVIII veke," *Donskie Eparkhial'nyia Vedomosti* 1878, no. 4, 107–15, no. 5, 135–43, no. 6, 169–80, and no. 7, 203–16.

58. Pokrovskii and Zol'nikova, *Starovery-chasovennye,* 29–47, 428–29.

59. Malyshev, "Communauté."

60. *Russkie pis'mennye i ustnye traditsii,* 40–42, 97–99; Andrei N. Vlasov, "On the History of the Old Belief in the Komi Republic," *"Silent as Waters We Live": Old Believers*

in Russia and Abroad; Cultural Encounter with the Finno-Ugrians (Studia Fennica: Folkloristica, vol. 6), ed. Juha Pentikäinen (Helsinki, 1999), 62–74; Starovery-chasovennye, 65–70.
For a lyrical description of researchers' experiences in Old Believer settlements in Siberia,
see Pokrovskii, *Puteshestvie*, 19–37.

8—The Spirituality of the Vyg Fathers

1. For the history of the Vyg community, see Crummey, *Old Believers*, and P. G.
Liubimirov, *Vygovskoe obshchezhitel'stvo* (Moscow and Saratov, 1924).

2. N. N. Pokrovskii, "Arkheograficheskie ekspeditsii i problemy izucheniia narodnogo soznaniia," *Arkheograficheskii ezhegodnik za 1986 god* (Moscow, 1987), 159–63;
Pozdeeva, "Drevnerusskoe nasledie."

3. *The Study of Spirituality*, ed. Cheslyn Jones, Geoffrey Wainwright, and Edward
Yarnold SJ (London, 1986), xxii; G. P. Fedotov, *A Treasury of Russian Spirituality*
(London, 1950). See also Fedotov, *The Russian Religious Mind*, vol. 1, *Kievan Chris-
tianity: The Tenth to the Thirteenth Century* (Cambridge, MA, 1946); his *The Russian
Religious Mind*, vol. 2, *The Middle Ages: The Thirteenth to the Fifteenth Century* (Cam-
bridge, MA, 1966); and *Christian Spirituality: High Middle Ages and Reformation*, ed.
Jill Riatt (New York, 1987).

4. A. Denisov, *Pomorskie otvety* (Moscow, 1906); S. Denisov, *Vinograd rossiiskii*; his
"Istoriia o ottsekh i stradal'tsekh solovetskikh"; Esipov, *Raskol'nich'i dela XVIII st.*, 2:5–55;
Filippov, *Istoriia*; Breshchinskii, "Zhitie Korniliia Vygovskogo"; A. Denisov, "Povest'
ritoricheskaia o srete v Moskve slona persidskago," *Russkaia starina* 29 (1880): 170–72;
his "Slovo nadgrobnoe ottsu Petru Prokopievichu," *Russkaia starina* 26 (1879): 523–37; E.
V. Barsov, "Andrei Denisov Vtorushin kak Vygoretskii propovednik," *Trudy Kievskoi Dukhovnoi Akademii*, 1867, no. 2, 243–62, and no. 4, 81–95; his "Semen Denisov Vtorushin,
predvoditel' russkago raskola XVIII veka," *Trudy Kievskoi Dukhovnoi Akademii*, 1866, no.
2, 174–230, no. 6, 168–230, no. 7, 284–304, no. 12, 570–88; P. S. Smirnov, "Vygovskaia bezpopovshchinskaia pustyn' v pervoe vremia eia sushchestvovaniia," *Khristianskoe Chtenie*,
1910, nos. 5–6, 638–74, and nos. 7–8: 910–34; V. I. Malyshev, ed., "The Confession of Ivan
Filippov, 1744," *Oxford Slavonic Papers* 11 (1964): 17–27; Barsov, "Ulozhenie brat'ev Denisovykh," and various unpublished rules (*ustavy*) of the Vyg monastery, the Leksa convent,
and the surrounding skity.

5. On the *Pomorskie otvety*, see Chrysostomus, *Die "Pomorskie otvety."*

6. For an analysis of the style of the Vyg fathers, see N. V. Ponyrko, *Vygovskaia
literaturnaia shkola v pervoi polovine XVIII stoletiia* (Leningrad, 1979), the abstract of
her candidate's dissertation. On the rhetorical tradition of the Vyg community, see her
"Uchebniki." As a passage from an original Vyg treatise quoted extensively by Ponyrko
(162) makes clear, effective oral performance was one of the main objectives of the art of
rhetoric as practiced by its leaders.

7. For examples, see *Pomorskie otvety*, 2–3; Filippov, *Istoriia*, 2–27, 76–95; A. I.
Mal'tsev, "Neizvestnoe sochnienie S. Denisova o tarskom 'bunte' 1722 g.," *Istochniki po
kul'ture i klassovoi bor'be feodal'nogo perioda* (Novosibirsk, 1982), 224–41.

8. For example, Barsov, "Andrei Denisov," 257–61; *Pomorskie otvety*, 5–6.

9. Barsov, "Andrei Denisov," 87–91; ibid., "Semen Denisov," 178.

10. *Pomorskie otvety*, 5–6.

11. Smirnov, "Vygovskaia bezpopovshchinskaia pustyn'," 643; Barsov, "Andrei Denisov," 90–91.

12. Mal'tsev, "Neizvestnoe sochinenie," 238.

13. There are many examples in the *Vinograd rossiiskii*. A number of short poems that conclude chapters in the work are built on the rhetoric of martyrdom. For a thorough textological analysis of the *Vinograd rossiiskii*, see E. M. Iukhimenko, "'Vinograd rossiiskii' Semena Denisova (tekstologicheskii analiz)," *Drevnerusskaia literatura: Istochnikovedenie; sbornik nauchnykh trudov* (Leningrad, 1984), 249–66. See also J. Sullivan and C. L. Drage, "Poems in an Unpublished Manuscript of the *Vinograd rossiiskii*," *Oxford Slavonic Papers* 1 (1968): 27–48. It should be noted that the stories of martyrdom contain little sentimentality; instead, they emphasize the steadfastness and courage of the victims.

14. See, for example, the story of Elder Markel in Filippov, *Istoriia*, 330–35.

15. These themes occur repeatedly in the "Istoriia o ottsekh," the *Vinograd rossiiskii*, Filippov's history and the tale of the Tara revolt. The conviction that death in battle for the true faith is equivalent to martyrdom also forms an integral part of Islamic teaching on jihad.

16. For example, "Istoriia o ottsekh," 40–41, and Smirnov, "Vygovskaia bezpopovshchinskaia pustyn'," 922, 928, 930.

17. Nil Sorskii, *Predanie i Ustav*, ed. M. S. Borovkova-Maikova, *Pamiatniki drevnei pis'mennosti i iskusstva* 179 (St. Petersburg, 1912). For an English translation, see Fedotov, ed., *Treasury*, 90–133. Fairy von Lilienfeld published a German translation of these texts and Nil's pastoral letters in *Nils Sorskij und seine Schriften* (Berlin, 1963), 195–283. *Poslaniia Iosifa Volotskogo*, ed. A. A. Zimin and Ia. S. Lur'e (Moscow-Leningrad, 1959). For the text of Joseph's "rule," see 298–319.

18. "Istoriia o ottsekh," 40.

19. Barsov, "Semen Denisov," 175; Smirnov, *Vnutrennye voprosy*, 154–69.

20. Barsov, "Semen Denisov," 173. An obvious point is worth emphasizing. The spirituality of Vyg ultimately centered on the liturgy and was expressed primarily through participation in it. Further investigation should turn to the liturgical practices of the bespopovsty and examine the ways in which the Vyg fathers and other early Old Believers adapted and reinterpreted the system of worship of ecumenical Eastern Orthodoxy.

21. For example, A. Denisov, "Slovo nadgrobnoe," 528.

22. Filippov, *Istoriia*, 142; Barsov, "Andrei Denisov," 90–91; his "Semen Denisov," 174–76.

23. "Istoriia o ottsekh," 26.

24. Barsov, "Semen Denisov," 181; Smirnov, "Vygovskaia bezpopovshchinskaia pustyn'," 656, 916.

25. Barsov, "Semen Denisov," 175.

26. "Istoriia o ottsekh," 30.

27. Breshchinskii, "Zhitie," 99–101.

28. BAN, Sobranie Druzhinina, no. 8, 220–20v.

29. For example, Smirnov, "Vygovskaia bezpopovshchinskaia pustyn'," 916.

30. "Slovo nadgrobnoe," 529; "Istoriia o ottsekh," 38; Filippov, *Istoriia*, 89.

31. BAN, Sobranie Druzhinina, no. 8, 221. Cf. *Poslaniia Iosifa Volotskogo*, 305.

32. BAN, Sobranie Druzhinina, no. 501, 10v–28; ibid., no. 22, 364v–75.

33. "Slovo nadgrobnoe," 528–29.

34. IRLI, Sobranie Zavoloko, no. 3, 109, 111, 113v. Cf. *Poslaniia Iosifa Volotskogo*, 310.

35. Filippov, *Istoriia*, 142; BAN, Sobranie Druzhinina, no. 8, 75v–77; Barsov, "Semen Denisov," 175–77.

36. Barsov, "Semen Denisov," 175; Breshchinskii, "Zhitie."

37. See E. V. Barsov, *Opisanie rukopisei i knig, khraniashchikhsia v vygoleksinskoi biblioteke* (St. Petersburg, 1874), and Pozdeeva, "Drevenerusskoe nasledie."

38. "Slovo nadgrobnoe," 529; Smirnov, "Vygovskaia bezpopovshchinskaia pustyn'," 656.

39. "Istoriia o ottsekh," 38.

40. Ibid., 49–50.

41. Ibid., 38; Filippov, *Istoriia*, 91.

42. Smirnov, "Vygovskaia bezpopovshchinskaia pustyn'," 646–50.

43. Malyshev, "Confession," 22.

44. For example, "Slovo nadgrobnoe," 532–33.

45. Billington, *The Icon and the Axe*, 193.

46. Barsov, "Andrei Denisov," 82–84.

47. Malyshev, "Confession"; BAN, Sobranie Druzhinina, no. 8, 205–15, 217v–18; Barsov, "Semen Denisov," 584n. Even though these texts are couched in predictable verbal formulas, they seem to convey the genuine convictions and emotions of the dying or, at the very least, to reflect the sentiments the leaders of the community felt to be appropriate to the occasion. The Old Believers' intense sense of their own sinfulness and their uneasiness in the face of death is remarkably similar to the attitude of the New England Puritans discussed by David E. Stannard, *The Puritan Way of Death* (New York, 1977), 72–95.

48. Barsov, "Semen Denisov," 579–81.

49. Denisov, *Vinograd rossiiskii*, 47–48v, 74–76.

50. Ibid., 74.

51. Brenda Meehan's work on unofficial women's religious communities within official Orthodoxy is an important contribution to the study of these broad and complex issues. See, for example, her "Popular Piety, Local Initiative, and the Founding of Women's Religious Communities in Russia, 1764–1907," Kennan Institute for Advanced Russian Studies, Occasional Paper 215.

52. There is a growing literature on this subject. For two examples, see Pokrovskii, "Ispoved'," and Pentikäinen, *Oral Repertoire*. Neither of the central individuals in these studies was a rigorously consistent adherent of Old Belief. See also I. V. Pozdeeva, "Vereshchaginskoe territorial'noe knizhnoe sobranie i problemy istorii dukhovnoi kul'tury russkogo naseleniia verkhov'ev Kamy," *Russkie pis'mennye i ustnye traditsii*, 40–71, here 67–68.

53. On seventeenth-century Russian Orthodox spirituality, see G. P. Fedotov, *Sviatye drevnei Rusi* (Paris, 1931), 201–4; his *Treasury*, 134–36; and Georges Florovsky, *Ways of Russian Theology*, part 1 (Belmont, MA, 1979), 86–113. Both authors present a bleak picture of the intellectual and spiritual condition of Russian Orthodoxy in the period. Florovsky, however, expresses admiration for the learning and devotion of the Vyg fathers. Interestingly enough, he characterizes Old Belief as a religion centered on works rather than faith (101).

54. Kuandykov, "Razvitie obshchezhitel'nogo ustava."

55. Barsov, "Semen Denisov," 174–76.

56. BAN, Sobranie Druzhinina, no. 5, 74–78. Semen Denisov's eulogy to Petr Onufriev praises his strict observance of the rules on prayer and fasting even while he was away from Vyg on work assignments (Barsov, "Semen Denisov," 584–85).

57. Serge Zenkovsky makes a similar point in "Ideological World." His pioneering essay, in my view, suffers from his ingenious but ultimately misleading attempt to see in the Vyg fathers precursors of the Slavophiles. While both groups of writers emphasized the centrality in Orthodoxy of a holy community, they proceeded from radically different philosophical assumptions and drew very different conclusions from their reflections.

9—The Historical Framework of the Vyg Fathers

1. The central historical texts of the Vyg tradition are Denisov, "Istoriia o ott-sekh," and Filippov, *Istoriia*. The *Vinograd rossiiskii* also rests on a clear set of historical assumptions.

2. In this chapter I will make no attempt to analyze the historical accuracy of the texts' narrative of the development of the Vyg community itself. I will leave the textological analysis of the compositions under discussion in the competent hands of colleagues. See Iukhimenko, "Vinograd rossiiskii"; her "'Istoriia o ottsakh i stradal'tsakh solovetskikh' Semena Denisova—pamiatnik vygovskoi literaturnoi shkoly pervoi poloviny XVIII v.," *Traditsionnaia dukhovnaia i material'naia kul'tura*, 107–13; and N. S. Gur'ianova, "'Istoriia Vygovskoi staroobriadcheskoi pustyni' I. Filippova (k istorii sozdaniia teksta)," *Istochniki po istorii obshchestvennogo soznaniia i literatury perioda feodalizma* (Novosibirsk, 1991), 178–95.

3. Denisov, *Vinograd rossiiskii*, 1v–13.

4. Ibid., 2.

5. Filippov, *Istoriia*, 76–95.

6. Denisov takes pains to discredit the "Nikonian" monks who moved into the Solovetskii monastery after government troops captured it and killed its remaining defenders ("Istoriia o ottsekh," 38–39).

7. Ibid., 27.

8. For a useful discussion of "myth" and "sacred history," see Cornelius Loew, *Myth, Sacred History and Philosophy* (New York, 1967), 103–7. See also Bernard W. Anderson, *Understanding the Old Testament* (Englewood Cliffs, NJ, 1975), 1–14; Brevard S. Childs, *Myth and Reality in the Old Testament* (London, 1960). Any attempt to juxtapose the concepts "myth" and "history" to analyze the historical presuppositions of the Vyg "school" poses several problems. First, the concept "myth" is difficult to define. Moreover, the definitions used by many scholars of religion from an anthropological perspective are clearly unsuitable for our purposes. Second, the distinction between a "mythical" and a "historical" view of the past is artificial and misleading for several reasons. For one thing, any practicing historian realizes the ultimate impossibility of reconstructing a completely "objective" account of events and institutional and social relationships in earlier times. Moreover, myths become an important part of the social and cultural life of the people who believe and act upon them.

9. See, for example, Daniel Rowland, "The Problem of Advice in Muscovite Tales about the Time of Troubles," *Russian History* 6 (1979): 259–83; his "Towards an Understanding of the Political Ideas in Ivan Timofeyev's Vremennik," *Slavonic and East European Review* 62 (1984): 371–99; David B. Miller, "The Velikie minei chetii of Metropolitan Makarii and the Origins of Russian National Consciousness," *Forschungen zur osteuropäischen Geschichte* 26 (1979): 263–382.

10. In recent years, historians and sociologists have devoted considerable attention to the "invention of tradition." This model, however, offers little help in understanding the work of the Vyg authors. In my view, it puts too much emphasis on the extent to which the invention of tradition is a self-conscious—not to say manipulative—activity. Moreover, the model tends to deny the reality of the traditional "texts" from which the new tradition is created. Finally, according to the model, the "invention of tradition" takes place during the rapid economic and social changes of early capitalism, conditions very different from those of early eighteenth-century Russia. See *The Invention of Tradition*, ed. Eric Hobsbawm and Terence Ranger (Cambridge, 1983), 1–13. Discussions with my colleague Aram Yengoyan have helped greatly in clarifying these issues.

11. See Zenkovsky, "Ideological World." At the same time it is misleading, in my view, to interpret the Vyg fathers as precursors of the Slavophiles, since the two groups of writers derived their theories about the central historical role of the Russian people from radically different presuppositions.

12. See Cherniavsky, "Old Believers"; Crummey, *Old Believers*; Gur'ianova, *Krest'ianskii antimonarkhicheskii protest*.

13. Iukhimenko, "Vinograd rossiiskii," 253; Ponyrko, *Vygovskaia literaturnaia shkola*.

14. See Syrtsov, *Vozmushchenie*; Barsukov, *Solovetskoe vosstanie*; Savich, *Solovetskaia votchina*.

15. Iukhimenko, "Istoriia o ottsakh i stradal'tsakh solovetskikh."

16. Syrtsov, *Vozmushchenie*, 83–85; Savich, *Solovetskaia votchina*, 263.

17. Ibid., 265.

18. Denisov, *Vinograd rossiiskii*, 17v–22. Compare *Zhitie Protopopa Avvakuma*, 93–102. The presentation of the sequence of events and certain similarities in vocabulary suggest that Denisov may have followed some variant of Avvakum's work.

19. N. S. Gur'ianova, "Pomorskie istoricheskie sochineniia XVIII v.," *Istochniki po istorii obshchestvennoi mysli i kul'tury epokhi pozdnego feodalizma* (Novosibirsk, 1988), 92–102. Her *Istoriia i chelovek v sochineniiakh staroobriadtsev XVIII veka* (Novosibirsk, 1996) emphasizes the factual precision of the Vyg historians and their focus on the individual human personality. See the discussion in chapter 12.

20. S. L. Peshtich, *Russkaia istoriografiia XVIII veka*, 3 vols. (Leningrad 1961–1971), 1:38–67; N. L. Rubenshtein, *Russkaia istoriografiia* (Moscow, 1941), 37–50; *Istoriografiia istorii SSSR s drevneishikh vremen do velikoi oktiabr'skoi sotsialisticheskoi revoliutsii* (Moscow, 1971), 49–58.

21. F. Griboedov, *Istoriia o tsariakh i velikikh kniaz'iakh zemli russkoi. Pamiatniki drevnei pis'mennosti* 121 (St. Petersburg, 1896); A. Lyzlov, *Skifskaia istoriia* (Moscow, 1787).

22. Esipov, *Raskolnich'i dela* 2:5; Filippov, *Istoriia*, 26. See St. Gregory the Theologian, Logos XV: "Eis tous Makkabaious," *Patrologiae Greca*, ed. J.-P. Migne (Paris, 1885), 35:911–34.

23. Georg Michels emphasizes this point, with particular reference to the "Istoriia o otssekh i stradal'tsekh solovetskikh," in his article "The Solovki Uprising."

10—The Cultural Worlds of Andrei Borisov

1. For example, Robson, *Old Believers*; Pera, "Theoretical and Practical Aspects of the Debate on Marriage," and her *I Vecchi Credenti e l'Antichristo* (Genoa, 1992). See also

the works of N. V. Ponyrko, E. M. Iukhimenko, and others on the literature and culture of the Vyg community.

2. Druzhinin, *Pisaniia*, 62–68.

3. P. Liubopytnyi, "Biblioteka starovercheskoi tserkvi," ChOIDR, 1863, book i, 3–66, here 12–13. Some of the separate works listed by Liubopytnyi may be variants of the same basic text: numbers 1, 8, and 10, for example, appear to be different redactions of the life of Andrei Denisov.

4. V. Belolikov, "Iz istorii pomorskago raskola vo vtoroi polovine XVIII v.," *Trudy Kievskoi Dukhovnoi Akademii* 1915, no. 9, 128–41, here 132–38; RNB, Q.XVII.200, 171–76.

5. Ibid., 73–77v. This may be the fifth of the five sermons on the rebuilding of the community mentioned by Liubopytnyi ("Biblioteka starovercheskoi tserkvi," 12, item 9).

6. IRLI, Ust'-Tsilemskoe sobranie, no. 53, 57–61v.

7. RGB, f. 17, no. 680, 1–2v. E. M. Iukhimenko discovered this composition and the three texts noted in notes 10 and 11.

8. RNB, Q.XVII.200, 147–50, 263–64. E. M. Iukhimenko drew these works to my attention. Although the manuscript gives no indication of authorship, the works' thematic content and style and the manuscript convoy in which they have been preserved make the attribution to Borisov reasonable.

9. RGB, f. 98, no. 1016, 203–5.

10. RGB, f. 17, no. 388, 154–55, and f. 579, no. 17.4, 91, respectively.

11. The main sources of biographical information are Pavel Liubopytnyi, "Istoricheskii slovar' Starovercheskoi tserkvi," ChOIDR, 1863, book i, 123–77; the Vyg chronicle, "Vygoretskii letopisets," *Bratskoe Slovo*, 1888, no. 10, 793–815; RGB, f. 17 (Sobranie Barsova), no. 419, "Kratkaia biograficheskaia spravka ob Andreia Borisovicha" (heading added later by an archivist); funeral orations on Borisov such as BAN, Sobranie Druzhinina, no. 695, and RGB, f. 98 (Sobranie Egorova), no. 1603, 1–22; and incidental references in Borisov's letters and sermons. Liubopytnyi composed his "dictionary" in 1828, and the unpublished biographical note appears to date from the early nineteenth century.

12. Liubopytnyi, "Istoricheskii slovar'," 124.

13. The manuscript sources differ on the place of Borisov's birth; the funeral orations in his honor consistently refer to him as a Muscovite but an unpublished biographical note states that he was born in St. Petersburg and adds that his father (a serf of the Naryshkins, who bought his freedom) prospered in business ventures in Ukraine, became a merchant, and was acquainted with Princes Potemkin and Vorontsov. BAN, Sobranie Druzhinina, no. 252, 3–3v, no. 695, 12; RGB, f. 98, no. 1603, 12v; RGB, f. 17, no. 419, 1. The view that Borisov was born in Moscow is probably correct; it is more prevalent in the sources, including the earliest texts.

14. BAN, Sobranie Druzhinina, no. 695, 12–13; RGB, f. 98, no. 1603, 5.

15. "Vygoretskii letopisets," 799; Liubopytnyi, "Istoricheskii slovar'," 124.

16. "Vygoretskii letopisets," 799; BAN, Sobranie Druzhinina, no. 695, 12.

17. RGB, f. 17, no. 680, 3–4. I am grateful to N. S. Gur'ianova for this reference and her notes on this text. E. M. Iukhimenko has just published the first study of Danilov, "Neizvestnyi vygovskii pisatel' XVIII v. Vasilii Danilov Shaposhnikov i 'Skazanie o prestavlenii Simeona Dionis'evicha,'" TODRL 46 (1993): 441–52. Iukhimenko's analysis and the text she published demonstrate that Danilov was a much more accomplished writer than his overly modest letter to Borisov suggests.

18. RGB, f. 17, no. 388, 154. I am grateful to E. M. Iukhimenko for this reference and for providing a copy of the text.

19. BAN, Sobranie Druzhinina, no. 79, 69–74 (quote from l. 70).

20. The French visitor and future revolutionary, Ch.-Gilbert Romme described the sisters of Leksa bowing to the ground before Borisov, following him around on their knees, and in a chorus, saluting him with flattering phrases ("Zhil'ber Romm," 153).

21. "Vygoretskii letopisets," 800–802.

22. PSZ 21:634 (no. 15473). A subsequent decree of November 8, 1782, confirmed this change in policy (ibid., 745 [no. 15581]).

23. *Sobranie postanovlenii po chasti raskola, sostoiavshikhsia po vedomstvu Sviateishago Pravitel'stvuiushago Sinoda*, 2 vols. (St. Petersburg, 1860), 1:712, cited by Smirnov, *Istoriia russkago raskola*, 196–97. See also N. Varadinov, *Istoriia Ministerstva vnutrennykh del*, 8 vols. (St. Petersburg, 1858–1863), 8:37. It is not clear that the government and its agents followed the new policy consistently.

24. Liubopytnyi, "Istoricheskii slovar'," 124.

25. BAN, Sobranie Druzhinina, no. 695, 14; RGB, f. 98, no. 1603, 5v.

26. RGB, f. 17, no. 388, 154 ("v samom dvortse u Grigor'ia Aleksandrovicha generala Potemkina pred pervymi arkhiereiami uchinit' spravedlivoe i uchtivoe opravdanie o drevnem blagochestii").

27. Belolikov, "Iz istorii," 129.

28. RNB, Q.XVII.200, 170–76. Belolikov used two other copies, the manuscript collection of the Chernigov seminary, no. 144, and the Uvarov collection, no. 2066.

29. RNB, Q.XVII.200, 170v.

30. Ibid., 171–76. The quote is on l. 174.

31. Ibid., 172–72v.

32. Ibid., 173v, 174v–75.

33. Liubomirov, *Vygovskoe obshchezhitel'stvo*, 100–101, takes a cautious approach to this issue.

34. "Vygoretskii letopisets," 801. Borisov's sermon on the dedication of the rebuilt chapel and settlement at Vyg gives a more detailed, poetic description of these disasters. BAN, Sobranie Druzhinina, no. 9, 180–82.

35. BAN, Sobranie Druzhinina, no. 9, 182v.

36. RNB, Q.XVII.200, 75–75v. This text, titled the "Priskorbnoe povedanie," chronicles many of the misfortunes that befell Vyg in Borisov's time and ends with the idea that one must put the welfare of the community above one's own individual needs. Although the largely autobiographical text is difficult to categorize by genre, it is closely related to the first part of Borisov's sermon at the dedication of the reconstructed Vyg settlement and chapel on July 16, 1788 (BAN, Sobranie Druzhinina, no. 9, 179–220v.). In addition to Vyg's other trials and tribulations, Borisov mentions that the government demanded two recruits from the population of Vyg even though a disproportionate number of its residents were old and infirm. BAN, Sobranie Druzhinina, no. 9, 185v; RNB, Q.XVII.200, 74v.

37. "Vygoretskii letopisets," 802.

38. "Svedeniia o nakhodiashchikhsia Olonetskoi Gubernii v Povenetskom Uezde raskol'nich'ikh skitakh, pustyniakh i molennykh, sobrannyia, vo ispolnenie slovesnago prikazaniia Gospodina Olonetskogo Grazhdanskago Gubernatora I. Bakurevichem," ChOIDR, 1862, book iv, 33–45.

39. "Slovo o naimenovanie tsarei i molenii za nikh," RGB, f. 17, no 626, 5–16; BAN, Sobranie Druzhinina, no. 113, 42–54. In advancing the interests of Old Belief, and of Vyg in particular, the community's leaders had no reservations about approaching powerful

officials including the ruler herself. At the same time, they were never entirely comfortable with the decision (Crummey, *Old Believers*, 181). Catherine II would hardly have found Borisov's arguments flattering!

40. I. A. Shafranov, "Vygoretskoe staroobriadcheskoe obshchezhitel'stvo v kontse XVIII i pervoi polovine XIX v.," *Russkoe Bogatstvo* 1893, no. 10, 171–99, and no. 11, 58–98, here 191; Crummey, *Old Believers*, 211.

41. BAN, Sobranie Druzhinina, no. 9, 29–36, and no. 169, 104–18.

42. IRLI, Karel'skoe sobranie, no. 44, 281–84; BAN, Sobranie Druzhinina, no. 469, 1–74; RNB, Q.XVII.200, 58–59. Borisov's encomium, "In Praise of Celibacy" (*Pokhvala devstvennikom*), certainly reflects this conviction. The same theme runs through Borisov's sermons to the sisters of the Leksa convent.

43. In Borisov's time, relations with the Dolgie, a wealthy St. Petersburg merchant family, were particularly important. The Vyg chronicle carefully notes when members of the family visited or joined the community ("Vygoretskii letopisets," 801–2). In addition, the archival collections contain a note in Borisov's hand congratulating Paraskoviia Feoktistovna, a member of the family who had settled in Vyg, on her name day. RGB, f. 579 (Sobranie Bratstva Sviatogo Metropolita Petra), no. 17, 91. I am grateful to E. M. Iukhimenko for this reference.

44. Basing her case on the testimony of Pavel Liubopytnyi, Pia Pera argues that the Vyg resolution of 1777 on marriage represented a moderate position within Old Believer debates, and that under Borisov's leadership, Vyg retained good relations with the Moscow Pomortsy because Borisov agreed with Emel'ianov's position on marriage ("Theoretical and Practical Aspects of the Debate on Marriage," 197). In my view, the manuscript tradition does not support the latter claim.

45. Nil'skii, *Semeinaia zhizn'*, 1:214–30; Crummey, *Old Believers*, 121, 203.

46. Liubopytnyi, "Istoricheskii slovar'," 124. "The first sight of him captivates [*sic*] each person and compels him to recognize him [Borisov] as an important, exceptional and pious man. He was of medium height, with a long pale face. He had a long thick beard flecked with grey and a joyous and pleasant gaze, endued with [literally, *pozlashchennyi*] majesty and a lofty spirit." Oddly enough, Gilbert Romme, the French radical who visited Vyg, described Borisov's intellectual interests and style at considerable length but made no comment on his physical appearance.

47. RGB, f. 579, no. 17, 1–2.

48. BAN, Sobranie Druzhinina, no. 252, 3–10, and no. 695, 12–36; RGB, f. 98, no. 1603, 1–22. The texts of BAN, Sobranie Druzhinina, no. 695, 12–26, and RGB, f. 98, no. 1603, 1–11, are virtually identical.

49. RGB, f. 579, no. 17, 1v. Echoing John 10:11–13, the writer describes Borisov as a true shepherd, not a hireling.

50. RGB, f. 98, no. 1603, 13v.

51. BAN, Sobranie Druzhinina, no. 695, 12–13; RGB. f. 98, no. 1603, 5–5v.

52. RGB, f. 17, no. 415.3, 2v.

53. RGB, f. 98, no. 1603, 19v, and f. 579, no. 17, 1v.

54. "Ne tochiiu bo grammaticheskikh pravil vedenie, no tochiiu ritoricheskikh krasnoglagolanii izobilie, no i filosofisticheskikh vitiistv preizriadnoe vedenie v nem biashche i samoi toi prenebesnoi nauki glagoliu feologii predivnyi vedets iavliashesia." RGB, f. 98, no. 1603, 6; BAN, Sobranie Druzhinina, no. 695, 15–16.

55. Crummey, "Origins," 128–31.

56. See, for example, N. V. Ponyrko, "Vygovskoe sillabicheskoe stikhotvorchestvo," TODRL 29 (1974): 274-90, and her "Uchebniki."

57. RGB, f. 17, no. 680, 3-4.

58. The manuscript that I have chosen as primary, IRLI, Pecherskoe Sobranie, no. 41, has Borisov's monogram "AB" on the last folio of the text (236v). The paper dates from 1781 and 1782. Malyshev, *Ust'-Tsilemskie rukopisnye sborniki*, 96-97.

59. I have not attempted an exhaustive survey of the manuscripts. In addition to the Pechera collection, no. 41, I have consulted BAN, Sobranie Druzhinina, nos. 53, 757, 960, and 971; BAN, Sobranie Kalikina, no. 171; RGB, f. 98, nos. 1009 and 1950; RGB, f. 17, nos. 156, 383, and 975; RNB, Sobranie Titova, no. 2489; IRLI, Ust'-Tsilemskoe Sobranie, no. 177; and GIM, Sobranie A. S. Uvarova, I, no. 524/236.

60. Compare IRLI, Pecherskoe Sobranie, no. 41, and BAN, Sobranie Druzhinina, no. 757, with BAN, Sobranie Druzhinina, no. 53.

61. Borisov's "Life of Andrei Denisov" is the only book-length Vyg text that, to my knowledge, has ever been published. In the mid-nineteenth century, A. N. Popov prepared a modernized edition of the work with an introduction to be published in the third volume of his *Sbornik dlia istorii staroobriadchestva*, 2 vols. (Moscow, 1864, 1866). The third volume never appeared. The manuscript copy of the projected edition is in RGB, f. 238 (Sobranie A. N. Popova), no. 1323.

62. IRLI, Pecherskoe Sobranie, no. 41, 7.

63. Filippov, *Istoriia*. This edition has been subjected to severe criticism on several grounds but has not yet been superseded. Directly contradicting the assumptions of most scholars, V. G. Druzhinin suggested that some of the chapters published by Kozhanchikov may have been taken from Borisov's life of Andrei Denisov and falsely attributed to Filippov ("Slovesnye nauki v Vygovskoi pomorskoi pustyni," *Zhurnal Ministerstva Narodnago Prosveshcheniia*, 1911, no. 6, 225-48, here 225-26).

64. Druzhinin used the work extensively as a source on these issues. See ibid., and his "Pomorskie paleografy nachala XVIII v.," LZAK 32 (1921): 1-66.

65. IRLI, Pecherskoe Sobranie, no. 41, 4-5v.

66. I have noted elsewhere that miracles such as those of healing also play a surprisingly small part in earlier Old Believer hagiography. See chapter 6 of this volume.

67. IRLI, Pecherskoe Sobranie, no. 41, 232-35.

68. Ibid., 4.

69. Ibid., 8v-12v.

70. "[N]e toliko bo mlekom eliko molitvami, ne toliko khlebom, eliko molebnymi proshenii vospitovaem biashe" (ibid., 13).

71. Ibid., 14.

72. Ibid., 14v-15.

73. Ibid., 16.

74. Ibid., 91-106.

75. Ibid., 104: "eliko k grammatiki i stikhotvorstvu, ritorikii krasoty vseobraznuiu, toliko i k dialektikam, logikam, kabalistichnoi filosofii, i vseobozhennoi prevysochaishei bogoslovii, razsuzhdaia sie byti za vesma nuzhnoe delo, ibo bez vedeniia bozhestvennago pisaniia nevozmozhno, po sviatomu apostolu, byti gotovu otveshchati na vsiakoe voproshenie." What Borisov meant by "kabalistic philosophy" is unclear. In the eighteenth and nineteenth centuries, the word "kabalistic" (related to the Kabala) can have the meaning of "mysterious" or "incomprehensible," but the word normally has a negative connotation. See

Slovar' russkogo iazyka XVIII veka, 9:182, and *Slovar' sovremennogo russkogo literaturnogo iazyka* 5:622.

76. IRLI, Pecherskoe Sobranie, no. 41, 105v–106.

77. V. G. Druzhinin attempted unsuccessfully to identify the teacher ("Slovesnye nauki," 235–36), arguing persuasively that it could not have been Feofan Prokopovich.

78. IRLI, Pecherskoe Sobranie, no. 41, 109–109v.: "i s vsem ritorskom filosofskom feologicheskom uchenii, s velikim prilezhaniem voproshashe togo. On zhe bezpotaenno emu o vsem skazovashe, i priiatno pravilam tem uchashche."

79. Ibid., 110v.

80. Druzhinin considers Borisov's story highly improbable for two reasons—Old Believer prejudice against Ukrainian learning and the fact that Denisov did not know Latin, essential for study at the Kiev Academy ("Slovesnyi nauki," 236).

81. See Ponyrko, "Uchebniki."

82. IRLI, Pecherskoe Sobranie, no. 41, 157–66. Druzhinin based much of his argument in "Pomorskie paleografy" on this passage. He argues that Denisov's unmasking of these forgeries was the first work of scholarly paleography in Russia (3).

83. IRLI, Pecherskoe Sobranie, no. 41, 176–80v, 193–98v.

84. Ibid., 193–94.

85. Ibid., 194v.

86. Ibid., 195: "Ta zhe i protchikh uchashe, brata svoego Simeona, i Trifona Petrova, i Manuila Petrova, i ikonnika Daniila, i Nikifora Semenova, i prochikh, i zhe izuchishasia ot nego tomu zh khudozhestvu, kiizhdo po sile svoei chtob pravopisati i dobre glagolati, znati silu sviatago pisaniia i vedati dogmaty tser'kovnya i ukrepliati i prochikh bratiiu v pravoslavnoi khristianskoi vere."

87. Ibid., 177v.

88. Ibid., 197v.: "da ne tochiu rossiistii, no i v nemetskikh stranakh ot rukopisaniia ego i inym mudrym uchitelem znaem i liubim beiashe."

89. Ibid., 196v–198v.

90. For a more detailed discussion of Borisov's sermons, see Robert O. Crummey, "Propovedi Andreia Borisova," A. M. Pashkov, ed., *Vygovskaia pomorskaia pustyn' i ee znachenie v istorii Rossii: Sbornik nauchnykh statei i materialov* (St. Petersburg, 2003), 40–51.

91. BAN, Sobranie Druzhinina, no. 9, 170–220v.

92. Citations to the Bible follow contemporary Western usage. English translations are from the King James version. The Slavonic Bible sometimes numbers chapters and verses differently. This is true, for example, of the Psalms.

93. BAN, Sobranie Druzhinina, no. 9, 219. Borisov refers to St. Paul's admonition in Ephesians 4:22–24.

94. Ibid., 218: "dolzhni zh liubia ego liubit' i sobliudat' vse sviatyia ego zapovedi i nakazaniia . . . i posemu dolzhni vy i drug druga nelitsemerno po vsegda liubiti."

95. Ibid., 205: "my posledniia v chelovetsekh cheloveki, v samoe sie poslednee vremia v sushchei poslednei iz stran rossiiskikh severnostudenoi i neplodnoi sei strane."

96. RNB, Q.XVII.200, 73–77v.

97. Ibid., 76v.

98. Ibid., 77: "ashche tochiiu radia o edinom sebe, ili nimnogikh, no kak my zhivuchi vo obshchestvakh, mnogazhdy trebuem i sami ot obshchestva zhiznenykh spomoshchestvovatel'stv, sledovatelno dolzhni i sami obshchestvom, vozmozhnym nam

s pomoshchesvovaniem platit' dolg. Sie to i budet soglasno z zakonom sviashchennym i grazhdanskim."

99. Ibid., 231–37v.

100. Ibid., 234v.

101. Ibid., 237–37v.

102. Ibid., 222–30v; RNB, Q.I.1083, 1–8v. The two copies are virtually identical.

103. BAN, Sobranie Druzhinina, no. 9, 225v; RNB, Q.I.1083, 4–4v: "1e, ezhe chasto vsegda molitisia, 2e, istinnoe devstvo imeti, 3e, nelenostno v rukodelii uprazhniatisia, prochee zhe byti milostivym, krotkim, blagorazumnym, postoiannym, smirennomudrym, terpelivym, molchalivym, vozderzhnym, stydlivym, blagopokornym, dobrorazsuditel'nym, nezlobivym, i chistoserdechno proshchatel'nym."

104. BAN, Sobranie Druzhinina, no. 9, 239–45v.

105. IRLI, Ust'-Tsilemskoe sobranie, no. 53, 57–61v; Malyshev, *Ust'-tsilemskie rukopisnye sborniki*, 105–6. Andrei Borisov's monogram is on l. 61v.

106. Ibid., 242.

107. RGB, f. 17, no. 440, 128–35v.

108. Ibid., 129.

109. Ibid., 135–35v.

110. Ibid., 134v: "O ashche by on nyne premiloserdyi nash sozdatel' nizposlal nam s vysoty sviatyi svoi dukh, iakozhe i na vozliublennyia svoia ucheniki."

111. See chapter 8.

112. Bushkovitch, *Religion and Society*, ch. 7.

113. IRLI, Karel'skoe sobranie, no. 44, 281–84; BAN, Sobranie Druzhinina, no. 469, 71–74.

114. The genre and style of this work are difficult to characterize. It does not bear much resemblance to the poems published and analyzed by Ponyrko, "Vygovskoe sillabicheskoe stikhotvorchestvo"; Sullivan and Drage, "Poems"; and in Sullivan's "Eighteenth-Century Russian Verse from the Vyg Community of Old Believers," *Slavonic and East European Review* 67 (1989): 517–29.

115. IRLI, Karel'skoe Sobranie, no. 44, 283v–84.

116. Unlike Borisov's more orthodox writings, these works did not become part of the official canon of Vyg texts. As far as we now know, only single copies survive.

117. RGB, f. 17, no. 680, 1–2v. Once again, I must express my thanks to E. M. Iukhimenko for finding and copying this text. It begins "Iskusnyi zhe vo uchenii moral'nom mozhet gradusy 1 do 10 sdelat' i bole . . ." A title "Morality" (*Moral'*) has been crossed out.

118. Ibid., 2–2v: "dolzhno nam berechisia chrezmernostei, ne sootvetstvuiushchei nashei estestvennoi sile i umnym mysliam. Zde paki mnogoucheniia o poznanii sil svoikh kazhdomu i chrez onykh ustroiat' gradusy vysote i nizu."

119. John Climacus, *The Ladder of Divine Ascent*, trans. Colm Liubheid and Norman Russell (Ramsay, NJ, 1982). Many Russian translations have been published; see, for example, Prepodobnago ottsa nashego Ioanna, Igumena Sinaiskoi Gory, *Lestvitsa* (Sergiev Posad, 1908; repr. Jordanville, NY, 1963). In the mid-nineteenth century, the Vyg library contained a seventeenth-century copy of the work (Barsov, *Opisanie rukopisei i knig*, 28).

120. "Zhil'ber Romm," 156.

121. Borisov's statement that "the pagan Alexander of Macedon received this teaching from Aristotle like milk" (RGB, f. 17, no. 680, 1v) suggests that Borisov or his informant may also have drawn on the Russian tradition of pseudo-Aristotelian texts. The most important of

these, the "Secret of Secrets," however, has no passages that resemble Borisov's text. On this tradition, see W. F. Ryan, "Aristotle and Pseudo-Aristotle in Kievan and Muscovite Russia," *Pseudo-Aristotle in the Middle Ages: The Theology and Other Texts* (Warburg Institute Surveys and Texts, XI; London, 1968), 97–109, and the same author's "The *Secretum Secretorum* and the Muscovite Autocracy," *Pseudo-Aristotle: The Secret of Secrets; Sources and Influences* (Warburg Institute Surveys, IX; London, 1982), 114–23. The Russian text was published in M. N. Speranskii, *Iz istorii otrechennykh knig. IV. Aristotelevy vrata ili Tainaia tainykh: Pamiatniki drevnei pis'mennosti i iskusstva* 171 (St. Petersburg, 1908).

122. See, for example, James Stevens Curl, *The Art and Architecture of Freemasonry: An Introductory Study* (London, 1991), plates 24, 25, 37a, 67, 68, 78a; Paul Naudon, *Histoire générale de la Franc-Maçonnerie* (Fribourg, 1981), 11 (fig. 2) and 148 (fig. 132); and *Masonstvo v ego proshlom i nastoiashchem*, ed. S. P. Mel'gunov and N. P. Sidorov, vol. 1 (Moscow, 1914), plate facing 128. Occasionally one can find six-step stairs in Masonic imagery. Such cases are rare and may well be accidents, since Masonic symbolism emphasized uneven numbers, including five and seven. See Christiane Derobert-Ratel, *Les arts et l'amitié et le rayonnement maçonnique dans la société aixoise de 1848 à 1871* (Aix-en-Provence, 1987), 41, and *English Masonic Exposures, 1760–1769*, ed. A. C. F. Jackson (London, 1986), 77–78, 143–44.

123. Robert Amblain, *Symbolique maçonnique des outils* (Paris, 1982).

124. RGB, f. 17, no. 680, 1: "A mne liubo, chto nashi moskovskiia zaseliat mesta zdes', a akademiiu razvedem; lish zavesti, a to naedut, a detei gorodskikh obuchat; stanem raznym naukam."

125. Ibid., 2v: "Mne ochen' milo, chto u vas uchenyia est' iunoshi; kak Aleksei Iakovlich, metafiziku b prouchil."

126. IRLI, Pecherskoe sobranie, no. 41, 105v–114v.

127. RNB, Q.XVII.200, 174.

128. "Zhil'ber Romm," 154–56. The quotation is on 156.

129. Romme almost certainly refers to Rousseau's prize essay of 1750, *Discours sur les sciences et les arts*, published by the Moscow University press in 1768. *Svodnyi katalog russkoi knigi grazhdanskoi pechati XVIII veka, 1725–1800*, 5 vols. (Moscow, 1963–1967), 3:77.

130. "Zhil'ber Romm," 154.

131. RNB, Q.XVII.200, 147–50. The manuscript does not attribute this work to Borisov. The contents, the peculiar mixture of traditional Vyg rhetoric and contemporary terminology, and the manuscript convoy make his authorship probable. Borisov may refer to the passage in the "Discourse on the Sciences and the Arts," which makes precisely this comparison of academic philosophy with peasant simplicity—to the detriment of the former. See Jean-Jacques Rousseau, *The First and Second Discourses*, ed. Roger D. Masters (New York, 1964), 60.

132. RNB, Q.XVII.200, 263–64.

133. Probably "Poème sur la loi naturelle," *Oeuvres complètes de Voltaire*, 52 vols. (Paris, 1877–1885), 9:441–60. The poem dates from 1752.

134. *Svodnyi katalog*, 1:177–86. By the early 1780s, the probable time of Romme's meeting with Borisov, a number of Voltaire's works had been published in Russian translation. These included *Zadig* and *Candide* as well as some plays and collections of philosophical tales.

135. "Zhil'ber Romm," 154–55.

136. Rollin's best known work on pedagogy is *De la manière d'enseigner et d'étudier*

les Belles-Lettres par rapport à l'esprit et au coeur (Paris, 1726–1728). His books on the history of classical antiquity were also extremely popular and influential.

137. Pia Pera has made a similar argument in her work on Pavel Liubopytnyi. See her "Theoretical and Practical Aspects of the Debate on Marriage," ch. 5. 138. RGB, f. 17, no. 388, 154.

139. See James L. West, "The Rjabušinskij Circle: Russian Industrialists in Search of a Bourgeoisie, 1900–1914," *Jahrbücher für Geschichte Osteuropas* 32 (1984): 358–77, and his "The Riabushinsky Circle: *Burzhuaziia* and *Obshchestvennost'* in Late Imperial Russia," in *Between Tsar and People: Educated Society and the Quest for Public Identity in Late Imperial Russia*, ed. Edith W. Clowes, Samuel D. Kassow, and James L. West (Princeton, 1991), 41–56.

11—Interpreting the Fate of Old Believer Communities in the Eighteenth and Nineteenth Centuries

1. Hildermeier, "Alter Glaube und neue Welt" and "Alter Glaube und Mobilität." On the structures of a wide variety of communities, see chapter 7 of this volume.

2. Crummey, *Old Believers*. See also Liubomirov, *Vygoretskoe obshchezhitel'stvo*, and V. Ostrovskii, *Vygovskaia pustyn' i eia znachenie v istorii staroobriadcheskago raskola* (Petrozavodsk, 1914). The role of Vyg as a center of Old Believer polemical writing and copying makes its history unusually accessible to scholars. Historians make particularly extensive use of Filippov's *Istoriia*. As the recent studies of N. V. Ponyrko, N. S. Gur'ianova, and E. M. Iukhimenko make clear, scholars can still find valuable new materials in the manuscript tradition of the community. See, for example, Ponyrko, "Uchebniki"; Ponyrko and V. P. Budaragin, "Avtografy vygovskikyh pisatelei," *Drevnerusskaia knizhnost': Po materialam Pushkinskogo Doma* (Leningrad, 1985), 174–200; Gur'ianova, "Pomorskie istoricheskie sochineniia"; "'Zhitie' Ivana Filippova," *Khristianstvo i tserkov' v Rossii feodal'nogo perioda (materialy)* (Novoskibirsk, 1989), 227–53; "Dopolnenie k 'Istorii Vygovskoi staroobriadcheskoi pustyni' I. Filippova," *Publitsistika i istoricheskie sochineniia perioda feodalizma* (Novosibirsk, 1989), 221–45; "Problema istoricheskogo povestvovaniia v interpretatsii pisatelei vygovskoi literaturnoi shkoly," *Izvestiia SO AN SSSR, Istoriia, filosofiia i filologiia* 3 (1991): 14–18; "Dukhovnye zaveshchaniia vygovskykh bol'shakov," *Traditsionnaia dukhovnaia i material'naia kul'tura*, 96–102; Iukhimenko, "'Vinograd Rossiiskii'; Vnov' naidennye pis'ma Semena Denisova," TODRL 44 (1990): 409–21; "'Istoriia o ottsakh i stradal'tsakh solovetskikh' Semena Denisova."

3. For example, Ryndziunskii, "Staroobriadcheskaia organizatsii"; and his *Gorodskoe grazhdanstvo doreformennoi Rossii* (Moscow, 1958); Manfred Hildermeier, *Bürgertum und Stadt in Russland 1760–1870: rechtliche Lage und soziale Struktur* (Cologne, 1986); and William L. Blackwell, *The Beginnings of Russian Industrialization, 1800–1862* (Princeton, 1962). See also the more recent studies of T. D. Goriacheva, E. M. Iukhimenko, and Irina Paert cited in this volume.

4. Georg Michels's studies make this point with particular force. See his article, "The Solovki Uprising."

5. Were it not for the arbitrary boundaries drawn by the secular and ecclesiastical authorities of imperial Russia, it would be extremely difficult, in many cases, to determine who was an Old Believer and who was not.

6. See Crummey, *Old Believers*; Hildermeier, "Alter Glaube und neue Welt," 383–

86; and the articles of L. K. Kuandykov, especially "Razvitie obshchezhitel'nogo ustava" and "Vygovskie sochineniia ustavnogo kharaktera vtoroi poloviny XVIII v.," *Istochniki po istorii russkogo obshchestvennogo soznaniia perioda feodalizma* (Novosibirsk, 1986), 120–30.

7. In practice, like other Christians who completely reject the powers of this world, the most radical Old Believers discovered that in order to deal with the practicalities of life they needed the help of less militant sympathizers who continued to live more or less normal lives "in the world."

8. The history of Vyg provides many examples. After its reluctant commitment to pray for the ruler, the leaders of Vyg wrote a number of letters to reigning empresses in a tone of extreme humility and gratitude. At roughly the same time, the community's polemicists justified the decision to pray for the ruler with the argument that earlier Christians had also prayed for heretical or pagan monarchs.

9. See, for example, the comments of Bubnov, "Staroobriadcheskaia kniga." The most popular works written in Vyg were the *Pomorskie otvety* (Moscow, 1906, 1911) of Andrei and Semen Denisov and the latter's two martyrologies, the *Vinograd rossiiskii* and the "Istoriia o ottsekh."

10. See, for example, Abby Smith and Vladimir Budaragin, *Living Traditions of Russian Faith: Books and Manuscripts of the Old Believers* (Washington, 1990), here 27–33.

11. Ryndziunskii, "Staroobriadcheskaia organizatsiia," 222–23.

12. See, for example, Mel'nikov, "Ocherki popovshchiny," 204–9. The same attitudes inform Varadinov, *Istoriia*, a valuable compendium of official reports on the activities of Old Believers and sectarians.

13. PSZ 2:647–50 (no. 1102). See also Crummey, *Old Believers*, 39–47; Lindsey Hughes, *Sophia, Regent of Russia, 1657–1704* (New Haven and London, 1990), 121–24.

14. Crummey, *Old Believers*, 167–70.

15. See Cherniavsky, "Old Believers." A number of the cases of lèse-majesté involving Old Believers are described in detail in Esipov, *Raskol'nich'i dela*.

16. Among the most important laws on Old Belief are PSZ 5:166 (no. 2991), 200 (no. 2996), 590 (no. 3232), 6:641–42 (no. 3944), 678–81 (no. 4009). See also A. Sinaiskii, *Otnoshenie russkoi tserkovnoi vlasti k raskolu staroobriadchestva v pervye gody sinodal'nago upravleniia pri Petre Velikom, 1721–1725* (St. Petersburg, 1895).

17. B. V. Titlinov, *Pravitel'stvo Imperatritsy Anny Ioannovny v ego otnosheniiakh k delam pravoslavnoi tserkvi* (Vilnius, 1905), 418–29.

18. Crummey, *Old Believers*, 159–83.

19. Ibid., 194–97.

20. On the Moscow communities, see Ryndziunskii, "Staroobriadcheskaia organizatsiia"; Mel'nikov, "Ocherki popovshchiny"; Popov, ed., "Materialy" and *Sbornik dlia istorii staroobriadchestva*. There is an extensive literature on the Moscow and St. Petersburg communities in prerevolutionary Russian ecclesiastical periodicals, some of it cited in note 3 above.

21. Nicholas's government assiduously collected information on Old Believer activities and interpreted their findings in the most unflattering light. See Varadinov, *Istoriia* 8; and A. A. Titov, ed., "Dnevnye dozornye zapisi o Moskovskikh raskol'nikakh," ChOIDR, 1885, book ii, pt. 5, 1–40; book iii, pt. 5, 41–80; book iv, pt. 5, 81–120; 1886, book i, pt. 5, 123–92; 1892, book i, pt. 1, 1–98; book ii, pt. 1, 99–251.

22. Sokolov, *Raskol v Saratovskom krae*, 275–329, 373–401, 412–21.

23. Vasil'ev, "Organizatsiia," 604–15; "Iz istorii Rogozhskago Kladbishcha," *Bratskoe Slovo*, 1891, pt. 2, 448–66; V. Nil'skii, "Raskol v Peterburge: Molennaia Kostsova v Volkovskoe Fedoseevskoe Kladbishche," *Istina* 55 (1877): 1–68, here 42–56; V. Nil'skii, "Malo-okhtenskoe pomorskoe kladbishche v Peterburge," *Istina* 42 (1875): 61–88, here 84–87.

24. Crummey, *Old Believers*, 203–18. On the later history of Vyg, see Shafranov, "Vygoretskoe staroobriadcheskoe obshchezhitel'stvo." The most important source on the last years of the community is the Vyg chronicle, different versions of which have been published as "Vygoretskii letopisets"; *Staropomorskii letopisets* (Moscow, 1913 [?]); and "Vygo-leksinskii letopisets," ed. E. M. Iukhimenko, *Vygovskaia pomorskaia pustyn'* (St. Petersburg, 2003), 309–22.

25. For a convenient summary of this episode, see Smirnov, *Istoriia russkago raskola*, 145–59.

26. Mel'nikov, "Ocherki popovshchiny," 391. See also Hildermeier, "Alter Glaube und Mobilität," and Gregory L. Freeze, "Rechristianization," 107–8.

27. On this phenomenon, see Freeze, "The Wages of Sin."

28. Shafranov, "Vygoretskoe obshchezhitel'stvo," no. 10, 191.

29. V. I. Kel'siev, *Sbornik pravitel'stvennykh svedenii o raskol'nikakh*, 4 vols. (London, 1860–1862), 1:43. The government had other reasons to suspect the Old Believers of disloyalty. At the height of the Crimean War, its leaders were acutely aware that the Old Believer communities had close ties with their coreligionists in two enemy states, Austria-Hungary and Turkey. Wartime tensions help to explain why Nicholas's government persecuted the dissenters with particular savagery in the early 1850s.

30. Quoted by Shafranov, "Vygoretskoe obshchezhitel'stvo," no. 11, 62–63.

31. In a very similar vein, Hildemeier's "Alter Glaube und Mobilität" argues that the Old Believers won many converts in the first decades of the nineteenth century because their counter-society offered ordinary Russians far better opportunities for economic prosperity and upward social mobility than the rest of society.

32. Freeze, "Bringing Order," 737, 746.

33. As Freeze felicitously puts it, "Old Belief represented not only the old rites but also the old rights—that is, not only old rituals but also the old freedom in making and unmaking familial bonds" (ibid., 746).

34. It is instructive to compare the status and role of women in Old Belief with the position of the leaders and members of the unofficial women's monastic communities within the Orthodox Church. See Brenda Meehan, *Holy Women*. More recently Irina Paert has addressed the same issues within the Old Believer communities in *Old Believers, Religious Dissent, and Gender*.

35. Vasil'ev, "Organizatsiia," 607.

36. Crummey, *Old Believers*, 206.

37. See, for example, the remarkable story of a contemporary Old Believer nun, A. Lebedev, in "Taezhnyi prosvet: Kak ia ezdil k Agaf'e Lykovoi," *Tserkov'*, 1990, no. 0 [*sic*], 26–32 (published as *Rodina*, no. 9), and 1992, no. 1, 34–41.

38. See Peter Waldron, "Religious Reform after 1905: Old Believers and the Orthodox Church," *Oxford Slavonic Papers* 20 (1987): 111–39. The history of Old Belief between 1855 and 1917 is particularly in need of serious study and analysis. Robson, *Old Believers*, is an important first step in this direction.

12—The Novosibirsk School of Old Believer Studies

1. See Nikolai N. Pokrovskii, "Trends in Studying the History of Old Belief among Russian Scholars," and Robert O. Crummey, "Past and Current Interpretations of Old Belief," *Russia's Dissident Old Believers 1650–1950*, ed. Georg B. Michels and Robert L. Nichols (Minneapolis, 2009), 17–39 and 39–52, respectively.

2. Pascal, *Avvakum*; Zenkovsky, *Russkoe staroobriadchestvo.*

3. *Rukopisnoe nasledie drevnei Rusi: Po materialam Pushkinskogo Doma* (Leningrad, 1972), 3–9. For a list of his publications, see ibid., 406–20. On Malyshev's methods and achievements as a scholar and collector of Old Russian manuscripts, see A. M. Panchenko, "V. I. Malyshev kak arkheograf," *Arkheograficheskii ezhegodnik za 1977 god* (Moscow, 1978), 214–18.

4. I. V. Pozdeeva, "Kompleksnye arkheograficheskie ekspeditsii: Tseli, metodika, printsipy, organizatsii," *Istoriia SSSR*, 1978, no. 2, 103–15. See also *Russkie pis'mennye i ustnye traditsii* and *Traditsionnaia kul'tura Permskoi zemli.*

5. For brief outlines of Pokrovskii's life and career, "Slovo o iubiliare," *Problemy istorii, russkoi knizhnosti, kul'tury i obshchestvennogo soznaniia* (Novosibirsk, 2000), 3–8, and "Pozdravliaem Nikolaia Nikolaevicha Pokrovskogo," *Gumanitarnye nauki v Sibiri*, 2005, no. 2, 110–11. I am grateful to N. S. Gur'ianova for her assistance with this chapter, including providing copies of these articles.

6. N. I. Pokrovskii, *Kavkazskie voiny i imamat Shamilia* (Moscow, 2000), 3–7. A second, supplemented edition was published in 2009.

7. On Tikhomirov and his school, E. V. Chistiakova, *Mikhail Nikolaevich Tikhomirov, 1893–1965* (Moscow, 1987), and "Shkola akademika M. N. Tikhomirova," *Obshchestvennoe soznanie, knizhnost', literatura perioda feodalizma* (Novosibirsk, 1990), 352–68. On Tikhomirov's relationship with Pokrovskii and the latter's move to Novosibirsk, see S. O. Shmidt, "K predystorii izdaniia poslednikh knig akademika M. N. Tikhomirova," ibid., 368–76. See also David B. Miller's entry on Tikhomirov in *The Modern Encyclopedia of Russian and Soviet History* 39 (1985): 37–42.

8. "'Delo' molodykh istorikov (1957–1958 gg.)," *Voprosy istorii*, 1994, no. 4, 106–35. One of the group's unpublished drafts, L. N. Krasnopevtsev's "Krisis sotsializma," is appended to the article (126–35).

9. In a private conversation, for example, Pokrovskii spoke highly of his fellow prisoner Cardinal Josyf Slipyj, primate of the Ukrainian Greek Catholic Church, whose willingness to share food sent by his supporters helped him recover from the effects of the hunger strike.

10. Shmidt, "K predistorii," 371–74. For the text of Tikhomirov's letter of recommendation, see ibid., 373–74.

11. Pokrovskii, *Puteshestvie.* The first edition was published in Moscow in 1984. Two additional printings appeared in 1987 (Moscow) and 2005 (Novosibirsk).

12. *Sudnye spiski Maksima Greka i Isaka Sobakina* (Moscow, 1971). For a description of its discovery and contents and the debates about its significance, see *Puteshestvie*, 78–121.

13. Pokrovskii, *Antifeodal'nyi protest.*

14. "Slovo o iubliare," 5.

15. N. N. Pokrovskii, *Tomsk 1648–1649 gg. voevodskaia vlast' i zemskie miry* (Novosibirsk, 1989); N. N. Pokrovskii and V. A. Aleksandrov, *Vlast' i obshchestvo: Sibir' v XVII v.* (Novosibirsk, 1991).

16. To cite only one example, Valerie A. Kivelson, *Autocracy in the Provinces: The*

Muscovite Gentry and Political Culture in the Seventeenth Century (Stanford, 1996).

17. Pokrovskii, *Antifeodal'nyi protest*, 34–66, and related articles such as "Novyi dokument po ideologii Tarskogo protesta," *Istochnikovedenie i arkheografiia Sibiri* (Novosibirsk, 1977), 221–34, and "Knigi Tarskogo bunta 1722 g.," *Istochniki po istorii russkogo obshchestvennogo soznaniia perioda feodalizma* (Novosibirsk, 1986), 155–90.

18. "Slovo o iubiliare," 4.

19. His works are collected in Shchapov, *Sochineniia*. His most important essays on the *raskol* are "Russkii raskol," "Zemstvo i raskol I," and "Zemstvo i raskol II (Beguny)."

20. In spite of the wealth of everyday details in the first two editions, Pokrovskii carefully avoided giving the names and specific locations of his Old Believer informants. Oddly enough, the more elaborate 2005 edition, which includes not only the names but also photos of contemporary Old Believers, appeared in a much smaller printing—five hundred copies.

21. In "Trends," 17, Pokrovskii mentions Solzhenitsyn's evocation of the Old Believers as an example of the Russian state's struggle against "Russian national traditions" since the seventeenth century. See also Pokrovskii's "Za stranitsei *Arkhipelaga GULAG*," *Novyi mir*, 1991, no. 9, 77–90.

22. Pokrovskii and Zol'nikova, *Starovery-chasovennye*.

23. Ibid., 8.

24. See, for example, V. I. Baidin and A. T. Shashkov's introduction to the writings of M. I. Galanin in *Dukhovnaia literatura staroverov vostoka Rossii XVIII–XX vv. (Istoriia Sibiri. Pervoistochniki*, 9) (Novosibirsk, 1999), 607–17.

25. Selections from the Ural-Siberian Paterik and other accounts of the anti–Old Believer campaign of the 1950s have been published in *Dukhovnaia literatura*. For the selections from the Paterik, 97–158.

26. See, for example, *Dukhovnaia literatura*, 688, 696; *Starovery-chasovennye*, 52, 321. For Zol'nikova's summary and analysis of Murachev's writings, see ibid., 295–313.

27. N. D. Zol'nikova, *Soslovnye problemy vo vzaimootnosheniiakh tserkvi i gosudarstva v Sibiri, XVIII v.* (Novosibirsk, 1981), and *Sibirskaia prikhodskaia obshchina v XVIII v.* (Novosibirsk, 1990).

28. A. Kh. Elert, *Ekspeditsionnye materialy G. F. Millera kak istochnik po istorii Sibiri* (Novosibirsk, 1990), and *Narody Sibiri v trudakh G. F. Millera* (Novosibirsk, 1999).

29. N. P. Matkhanova, *General-gubernatory Vostochnoi Sibiri serediny XIX v.: V. Ia. Ruppert, N. N. Murav'ev-Amurskii, M. S. Korsakov* (Novosibirsk, 1998), and *Vysshaia administratsiia Vostochnoi Sibiri v seredine XIX v.* (Novosibirsk, 2002), and her editions of *Graf N. N. Murav'ev-Amurskii v vospominaniiakh sovremennikov* and *Memuary sibiriakov XIX v. (Istoriia Sibiri: Pervoistochniki)*, 8 and 11 (Novosibirsk, 1998 and 2003 respectively). See also Willard Sunderland, "The Empire's Men at the Empire's Edges," *Kritika* 5 (2004): 515–25.

30. E. K. Romodanovskaia, *Russkaia literatura v Sibiri pervoi poloviny XVIIv. (Istoki russkoi sibirskoi literatury)* (Novosibirsk, 1973), *Povesti o gordom tsare v rukopisnoi traditsii XVII–XIX vekov* (Novosibirsk, 1985), and *Russkaia literatura na poroge novogo vremeni: Puti formirovaniia russkoi belletristiki perekhodnogo perioda* (Novosibirsk, 1994); T. V. Panich, *Literaturnoe tvorchestvo Afanasiia Kholmogorskogo: "Estestvennonauchnye" sochineniia* (Novosibirsk, 1996), and *Kniga Shchit very v istoriko-literaturnom kontekste kontsa XVII veka* (Novosibirsk, 2004); L. V. Titova, *Beseda ottsa s synom o zhenskoi zlobe: Issledovanie i publikatsiia tekstov* (Novosibirsk, 1987), and *Poslanie d'iakona Fedora synu Maksimu: Literaturnyi i polemicheskii pamiat-*

nik rannego staroobriadchestva (Novosibirsk, 2003); and the articles of O. D. Zhuravel' such as "'Devstvuiushchaia tserkov' Khristova na Severe' o. Simeona–pamiatnik sovremennoi staroobriadcheskoi literatury," *Obshchestvennoe soznanie i literatura XVI–XX vv.: Sbornik nauchnykh trudov* (Novosibirsk, 2001), 274–91, and "Staroobriadcheskii pisatel' Afanasii Murachev: Novye sochineniia na evangel'skie siuzhety," *Istoricheskie istochniki i literaturnye pamiatniki XVI–XX vv.: Razvitie traditsii* (Novosibirsk, 2004), 286–307.

31. The *sborniki* that make up *Arkheografiia i istochnikovedenie Sibiri* were published as individual volumes, not usually identified as part of a series.Their general titles are confusingly similar.

32. Cherniavsky, "Old Believers."

33. Kuandykov, "Razvitie obshchezhitel'nogo ustava"; "Ideologiia obshchezhitel'stva"; "Vygovskie sochineniia"; and "Rukopis' no. 3 iz Sobraniia I. N. Zavoloko v Drevlekhranilishche Pushkinskogo Doma," *Sibirskoe istochnikovedenie i arkheografiia* (Novosibirsk, 1984), 121–35.

34. O. V. Chumicheva, *Solovetskoe vosstaniie, 1667–1676* (Novosibirsk, 1998).

35. Iukhimenko, *Vygovskaia staroobriadcheskaia pustyn'* 1:192–226.

36. Gur'ianova, *Istoriia i chelovek.*

37. T. A. Oparina, *Ivan Nasedka i polemicheskoe bogoslovie Kievskoi metropolii* (Novosibirsk, 1998).

38. N. S. Gur'ianova, *Staroobriadtsy i tvorcheskoe nasledie Kievskoi Mitropolii* (Novosibirsk, 2007).

39. Mal'tsev, *Starovery-stranniki,* 3–18.

40. Mal'tsev published an edition of Evfimii's works, A. I. Mal'tsev, ed., *Sochineniia inoka Evfimiia: Teksty i kommentarii* (Novosibirsk, 2003).

41. Mal'tsev, *Starovery-stranniki,* 225–28.

42. A I. Mal'tsev, *Staroobriadcheskie bespopovskie soglasiia v XVIII–nachale XIX v.* (Novosibirsk, 2006). See also his "Soiuznoe soglashenie 1780 goda staroobriadtsev filippovskogo i fedoseevskogo soglasii v ottsenke sovremennikov," *Istoricheskie istochniki i literaturnye pamiatniki XVI–XX vv.* (Novosibirsk, 2004), 61–78.

43. *Puteshestvie za redkimi knigami,* 136–38.

44. Ibid., 206–10.

45. Ibid., 186–203; Pokrovskii, "Ispoved'."

46. Ibid., 136–38.

47. See Gail D. Lenhoff and Nikolai N. Pokrovskii, *The Book of Degrees of the Royal Genealogy: A Critical Edition Based on the Oldest Known Manuscripts (Stepennaia kniga tsarskogo rodosloviia po drevneishim spiskam),* 2 vols. (Moscow, 2007–2008).

48. On the relations between the Russian Orthodox hierarchy and the new Communist government in the 1920s, see N. N. Pokrovskii and S. G. Petrov, eds., *Arkhivy Kremlia: Politbiuro i tserkov' 1922–1925 gg.,* 2 vols. (Novosibirsk and Moscow, 1997–1998).

49. See T. V. Berestetskaia, "V. G. Druzhinin, F. A. Kalikin, S. Gavrilov: Kollektsionery staroobriadcheskikh pamiatnikov," *Staroobriadchestvo v Rossii (XVII–XX vv.),* 438–50.

Afterword

1. Iukhimenko, *Vygovskaia staroobriadcheskaia pustyn'.*

2. The recent studies of the Moscow centers by Goriacheva ("Ustroistvo" and

"Istochniki"), Iukhimenko (*Staroobriadcheskii tsentr*), and Paert (*Old Believers, Religious Dissent and Gender*) are a promising sign.

3. Boris A. Uspensky, "The Schism and Cultural Conflict"; Pliukhanova, "O nekotorykh chertakh."

4. At a scholarly meeting at the turn of 1980s and 1990s, Irina Vasil'evna Pozdeeva described the current condition of the Old Believers in the upper Kama valley with the dramatic pronouncement "*Vse proshlo*" (It's all gone). She referred to the recent decision of the priestless Old Believers in her beloved region to adopt priestly practice and affiliate with the Belokrinitskaia hierarchy. This step—in the new circumstances of the time, a reasonable decision—had, in her mind, destroyed the traditional Russian culture of the region to which she devoted her scholarly life.

Selected Bibliography

Ageeva, E. A. "Sovremennyi staroobriadcheskii pisatel' A. K. Kilin." *Traditsionnaia duk-hovnaia i material'naia kul'tura.* Pp. 277–82.

Amblain, Robert. *Symbolique maçonnique des outils.* Paris, 1982.

Amfiteatrov, A. *Russkii pop XVII veka.* Belgrade, 1930.

Amosov, A. A., Budaragin, V. P., Morozov, V. V., and Pikhoia, R. G. "O nekotorykh problemakh polevoi arkheografii (v poriadke obsuzhdeniia)." *Obshchestvenno-politicheskaia mysl' dorevoliutsionnogo Urala.* Sverdlovsk, 1983. Pp. 5–19.

Andreev, V. V. *Raskol i ego znachenie v narodnoi russkoi istorii.* St. Petersburg, 1870.

Anthropology and the Study of Religion. Ed. Robert L. Moore and Frank E. Reynolds. Chicago, 1984.

Avvakum, Archpriest. *The Life Written by Himself.* Trans. Kenneth N. Brostrom. Ann Arbor, 1979.

Barsov, E. V. "Andrei Denisov Vtorushin kak Vygoretskii propovednik." *Trudy Kievskoi Dukhovnoi Akademii,* 1867, no. 2, 243–62, and no. 4, 81–95.

———. *Opisanie rukopisei i knig, khraniashchikhsia v vygoleksinskoi biblioteke.* St. Petersburg, 1874.

———. "Semen Denisov Vtorushin, predvoditel' russkago raskola XVIII veka." *Trudy Kievskoi Dukhovnoi Akademii,* 1866, no. 2, 174–230, no. 6, 168–230, no. 7, 284–304, and no. 12, 570–88.

———. "Ulozhenie brat'ev Denisovykh." *Pamiatnaia knizhka Olonetskoi Gubernii za 1868 i 1869 gg.* 2: 85–116.

Barsukov, N. A. *Solovetskoe vosstanie 1668–1676 gg.* Petrozavodsk, 1954.

Belokurov, S. A. "Deianie Moskovskago tserkovnogo sobora 1649 goda." ChOIDR, 1894, book 4, 1–52.

Belolikov, V. V. "Iz istorii pomorskago raskola vo vtoroi polovine XVIII v." *Trudy Kievskoi Dukhovnoi Akademii,* 1915, no. 9, 128–41.

———. *Pisaniia russkikh staroobriadtsev V. G. Druzhinina.* Kiev, 1913.

Berestetskaia, T. V. "V. G. Druzhinin, F. A. Kalikin, S. Gavrilov: Kollektsionery staroobriadcheskikh pamiatnikov." *Staroobriadchestvo v Rossii (XVII–XX vv.).* Pp. 438–50.

Billington, James H. *The Icon and the Axe.* New York, 1970.

Blackwell, William L. "The Old Believers and the Rise of Private Industrial Enterprise in Early Nineteenth-Century Moscow." *Slavic Review* 24 (1965): 407–24.

Bolonev, F. F. "Archaic Elements in the Charms of the Russian Population of Siberia." *Russian Traditional Culture: Religion, Gender and Customary Law.* Ed. Marjorie Mandelstam Balzer. Armonk NY, 1992. Pp. 71–84.

———. *Mesiatseslov semeiskikh Zabaikal'ia.* Novosibirsk, 1990.

242   Selected Bibliography

——. *Staroobriadtsy Zabaikal'ia v XVIII–XX vv.* Ulan-Ude, 2009.

Bonch-Bruevich, V. D. *Izbrannye sochineniia v trekh tomakh.* Vol. 1. Moscow, 1959.

Borozdin, A. K. *Protopop Avvakum: Ocherk iz istorii umstvennoi zhizni russkago obshchestva v XVII veke.* St. Petersburg, 1900.

Breshchinskii, D. N. "Zhitie Korniliia Vygovskogo Pakhomievskoi redaktsii (Teksty)." *Drevnerusskaia knizhnost': Po materialam Pushkinskogo Doma.* Leningrad, 1985. Pp. 62–107.

Brown, Peter. *The Cult of the Saints.* Chicago, 1981.

Bubnov, N. Iu. "Knigotvorchestvo moskovskikh staroobriadtsev XVII veka." *Russkie knigi i biblioteki v XVI–pervoi polovine XIX veka: Sbornik nauchnykh trudov.* Leningrad, 1983. Pp. 23–37.

——. *Pamiatniki staroobriadcheskoi pis'mennosti.* St. Petersburg, 2006.

——. *Sochineniia pisatelei-staroobriadtsev XVII veke.* Leningrad, 1984.

——. "Staroobriadcheskaia kniga v Rossii vo vtoroi polovine XVII v." Unpublished doctoral dissertation, Leningrad, 1990.

——. *Staroobriadcheskaia kniga v Rossii vo vtoroi polovine XVII v.* Dissertation abstract, Leningrad, 1990.

——. *Staroobriadcheskaia kniga v Rossii vo vtoroi polovine XVII v.: Istochniki, tipy i evolutsiia.* St. Petersburg, 1995.

Budaragin, V. P. "Avtografy vygovskikyh pisatelei." *Drevnerusskaia knizhnost': Po materialam Pushkinskogo Doma.* Leningrad, 1985. Pp. 174–200.

Burke, Peter. *Popular Culture in Early Modern Europe.* New York, 1978.

Bushkovitch, Paul. "The Life of Filipp: Tsar and Metropolitan in the Late Sixteenth Century." *Medieval Russian Culture.* Vol. 2. Ed. Michael S. Flier and Daniel Rowland. Berkeley, 1994. Pp. 29–46.

——. *Religion and Society in Russia: The Sixteenth and Seventeenth Centuries.* Oxford, 1992.

Bynum, Carolyn Walker. *Holy Fast and Holy Feast: The Religious Significance of Food to Medieval Women.* Berkeley, 1987.

——. "Women's Stories, Women's Symbols: A Critique of Victor Turner's Theory of Liminality." *Anthropology and the Study of Religion.* Pp. 105–25.

Chartier, Roger. *Cultural History: Between Practices and Representations.* Trans. L. Cochrane. Ithaca, 1988.

"Chelobitnaia startsa Avraamiia." Ed. E. E. Zamyslovskii. LZAK 6 (1877): 1–129.

Cherniavsky, Michael. "The Old Believers and the New Religion." *Slavic Review* 25 (1966): 1–39.

Chistiakova, E. V. *Mikhail Nikolaevich Tikhomirov, 1893–1965.* Moscow, 1987.

——. "Shkola akademika M. N. Tikhomirova." *Obshchestvennoe soznanie, knizhnost', literatura.* Pp. 352–68.

Chistov, K. V. *Russkie narodnye sotsial'noutopicheskie legendy.* Moscow, 1967.

Christian Spirituality: High Middle Ages and Reformation. Ed. Jill Riatt. New York, 1987.

Chrysostomus, P. J. *Die "Pomorskie otvety" als Denkmal des russischen Altgläubigen gegen Ende des 1. Viertels des XVIII. Jahrh. (Orientalia Christiana Analecta* 148). Rome, 1957.

Chumicheva, O. V. *Solovetskoe vosstaniie 1667–1676.* Novosibirsk, 1998.

Clifford, James. *The Predicament of Culture: Twentieth-Century Ethnography, Literature, and Art.* Cambridge, MA, 1988.

Cracraft, James. *The Church Reform of Peter the Great.* Stanford, 1971.

Crummey, Robert O. "Ecclesiastical Elites and Popular Belief and Practice in Seventeenth-Century Russia." *Religion and the Early Modern State.* Pp. 52–79.

——. "Interpreting the Fate of Old Believer Communities in the Eighteenth and Nineteenth Centuries." *Seeking God.* Pp. 144–59.

——. "Istoricheskaia skhema vygoretskikh bol'shakov." *Traditsionnaia dukhovnaia i material'naia kul'tura.* Pp. 90–96.

——. "The Miracle of Martyrdom. Reflections on Old Believer Hagiography." *Religion and Culture in Early Modern Russia.* Pp. 132–45.

——. "Old Belief as Popular Religion: New Approaches." *Slavic Review* 52 (1993): 700–712.

——. *The Old Believers and the World of Antichrist: The Vyg Community and the Russian State, 1694–1855.* Madison, 1970.

——. "The Origins of the Old Believers' Cultural Systems: The Works of Avraamii." *Forschungen zur osteuropäischen Geschichte* 50 (1994): 121–38.

——. "Propovedi Andreia Borisova." *Vygovskaia pomorskaia pustyn'.* Pp. 40–51.

——. "Religious Radicalism in Seventeenth-Century Russia: Reexamining the Kapiton Movement." *Forschungen zur osteuropäischen Geschichte* 46 (1992): 171–85.

——. "Russia and the 'General Crisis of the Seventeenth Century.'" *Journal of Early Modern History* 2 (1998): 156–80.

——. "The Spirituality of the Vyg Fathers." *Church, Nation, and State in Russia and Ukraine.* Ed. Geoffrey Hosking. New York, 1991. Pp. 23–37.

Curl, James Stevens. *The Art and Architecture of Freemasonry: An Introductory Study.* London, 1991.

Curtius, E. R. *European Literature and the Latin Middle Ages.* New York, 1953.

Davis, Natalie Zemon. "From 'Popular Religion' to Religious Cultures." *Reformation Europe: A Guide to Research.* Ed. Steven Ozment. St. Louis, 1982. Pp. 321–42.

Deianiia Moskovskikh soborov 1666 i 1667 godov. Ed. N. I. Subbotin. Moscow, 1893.

"'Delo' molodykh istorikov (1957–1958 gg.)." *Voprosy istorii,* 1994, no. 4, 106–35.

Delumeau, Jean. "Déchristianisation ou nouveau modèle de Christianisme." *Archives de sciences sociales des religions* 40 (1975): 3–20.

Demkova, N. S. "O nachale Vygovskoi pustyni, maloizvestnyi document iz Sobraniia E. V. Barsova." *Pamiatniki literatury i obshchestvennoi mysli epokhi feodalizma.* Novosibirsk, 1985. Pp. 237–48.

——. *Sochineniia Avvakuma i publitsisticheskaia literatura rannego staroobriadchestva.* St. Petersburg, 1998.

——. "Texts of Old Belief's Founding Fathers: Their Archival Transmission and Preservation." *Russia's Dissident Old Believers 1650–1950.* Pp. 221–32.

——. "Vnov' naidennyi podlinnik 'Dela ob olonetskom raskol'nike Tereshke Artem'ev' 1695 g." *Staroobriadchestvo v Rossii (XVII–XVIII vv.).* Pp. 176–89.

——. *Zhitie protopopa Avvakuma.* Leningrad, 1974.

Denisov, Andrei. *Pomorskie otvety.* Moscow, 1906, 1911.

——. "Povest' ritoricheskaia o srete v Mosk've slona persidskago." *Russkaia starina* 29 (1880): 170–72.

———. "Slovo nadgrobnoe ottsu Petru Prokopievichu." *Russkaia starina* 26 (1879): 523–37.

———. "Slovo nadgrobnoe Petru Prokopievu." Ed. E. M. Iukhimenko. *Vygovskaia pomorskaia pustyn'*. Pp. 263–83.

Denisov, Semen. "Istoriia o ottsekh i stradal'tsekh solovetskikh." Esipov. *Raskol'nich'i dela* 2: 5–55.

———. *Vinograd rossiiskii ili opisanie postradavshikh v Rossii za drevletserkovnoe blagochestie.* Moscow, 1906.

Dergacheva-Skop, E. I., and Alekseev, V. N. "Staroobriadcheskie biblioteki v Sibiri (problemy rekonstruktsii)." *Traditsionnaia dukhovnaia i material'naia kul'tura*. Pp. 125–30.

Derobert-Ratel, Christiane. *Les arts et l'amitié et le rayonnement maçonnique dans la société aixoise de 1848 à 1871.* Aix-en-Provence, 1987.

Dewey, H. W. "The Life of Lady Morozova as Literature." *Indiana Slavic Studies* 4 (1967): 74–87.

Dickens, A. G. *The Counter Reformation*. New York, 1969.

Dmitriev, L. A. *Zhitiinye povesti russkogo severa kak pamiatniki literatury XIII–XVI vv.* Leningrad, 1973.

"Dnevnye dozornye zapisi o Moskovskikh raskol'nikakh." Ed. A. A. Titov. ChOIDR, 1885, book. 2, pt. 5: 1–40; book. 3, pt. 5: 41–80; book. 4, pt. 5: 81–120; 1886, book. 1, pt. 5: 123–92; 1892, book. 1, pt. 1: 1–98; book. 2, pt. 1: 99–251.

Dolia staroobriadstva v XX–na pochatku XXI st.: Istoriia ta suchasnist'. Kiev, Kurenivka, Chechel'nik, 2007.

Dronova, T. I. *Russkie starovery-bespopovtsy Ust'-Tsil'my: konfessional'nye traditsii v obriadakh zhiznennogo tsikla, konets XIX–XX vv.* Syvtyvkar, 2002.

Druzhinin, V. G. *Pisaniia russkikh staroobriadtsev.* St. Petersburg, 1912.

———. "Pomorskie paleography nachala XVIII v." LZAK 32 (1921): 1–66.

———. *Raskol na Donu v kontse XVII veka.* St. Petersburg, 1889.

———. "Slovesnye nauki v Vygovskoi pomorskoi pustyni." *Zhurnal Ministerstva Narodnago Prosveshcheniia*, 1911, no. 6, 225–48.

Duffy, Eamon. *The Stripping of the Altars: Traditional Religion in England, c. 1400–c. 1580.* New Haven, 1992.

Dukhovnaia literatura staroverov vostoka Rossii XVIII–XX vv. (*Istoriia Sibiri: Pervoistochniki, 9*). Novosibirsk, 1999.

Dutchak, E. E. Iz. *"Vavilona" v "Belovod'e": Adaptatsionnye vozmozhnosti taezhnykh obshchin staroverov-strannikov, vtoraia polovina XIX–nachalo XXI v.* Tomsk, 2007.

Elert, A. Kh. *Ekspeditsionnye materialy G. F. Millera kak istochnik po istorii Sibiri.* Novosibirsk, 1990.

———. *Narody Sibiri v trudakh G. F. Millera.* Novosibirsk, 1999.

Emchenko, E. V. *Stoglav: Issledovaniia i tekst.* Moscow, 2000.

English Masonic Exposures, 1760–1769. Ed. A. C. F. Jackson. London, 1986.

Esipov, G. V. *Raskol'nich'i dela XVIII st.* 2 vols. St. Petersburg, 1861, 1863.

Evfrosin. *Otrazitel'noe pisanie o novoizobretennom puti samoubistvennykh smertei.* (*Pamiatniki drevnei pis'mennosti, 108*).

Fedotov, G. P. *The Russian Religious Mind.* Vol. 1. *Kievan Christianity: The Tenth to the Thirteenth Century.* Cambridge, MA, 1946.

——. *The Russian Religious Mind*. Vol. 2. *The Middle Ages: The Thirteenth to the Fifteenth Century*. Cambridge, MA, 1966.

——. *Sviatye drevnei Rusi*. Paris, 1931.

——. *A Treasury of Russian Spirituality*. London, 1950.

Felmy, Karl Christian. *Die Deutung des Göttlichen Liturgie im Rahmen der russischen Theologie*. Berlin and New York, 1984.

Filippov, Ivan. *Istoriia Vygovskoi pustyni*. St. Petersburg, 1863. New ed., Moscow, 2005.

——. "Istoriia Vygovskoi pustyni (otdeln'nye glavy)." Ed. N. S. Gur'ianova. *Vygovskaia pomorskaia pustyn'*. Pp. 284–309.

Fishman, O. M. *Zhizn' po vere: Tikhvinskie karely-staroobriadtsy*. Moscow, 2003.

Florovsky, Georges. *Ways of Russian Theology*. Pt. 1. Belmont, MA, 1979.

Freeze, Gregory L. "Bringing Order to the Russian Family: Marriage and Divorce in Imperial Russia, 1760–1860." *Journal of Modern History* 62 (1990): 709–46.

——. *The Parish Clergy in Nineteenth-Century Russia: Crisis, Reform, and Counter-Reform*. Princeton, 1983.

——. "The Rechristianization of Russia: The Church and Popular Religion, 1750–1850." *Studia Slavica Finlandensia* 7 (1990): 101–36.

——. *The Russian Levites: The Parish Clergy in the Eighteenth Century*. Cambridge, MA, 1977.

——. "The Wages of Sin: The Decline of Public Penance in Imperial Russia." *Seeking God*. Pp. 53–82.

Geertz, Clifford. *The Interpretation of Cultures: Selected Essays*. New York, 1973.

——. "Religion as a Cultural System." *Interpretation of Cultures*. Pp. 87–124.

The German People and the Reformation. Ed. R. Po-chia Hsia. Ithaca, 1988.

Ginzburg, Carlo. *The Cheese and the Worms: The Cosmos of a Sixteenth-Century Miller*. Trans. John and Anne Tedeschi. Baltimore, 1980.

Golubinskii, E. E. "Istoriia kanonizatsii sviatykh v Russkoi tserkvi." *ChOIDR*, 1903, book 4: 159–69.

——. *K nashei polemike s staroobriadtsami*. Moscow, 1905. Also published in *ChOIDR*, 1905, book 3: 1–260.

Goriacheva, T. D. "Istochniki po istorii Rogozhskoi staroobriadcheskoi obshchiny (vtoraia polovina XIX–nachalo XX v.); opyt istochnikovedcheskoi kharakteristiki." *Mir staroobriadchestva* 5 (1999): 118–52.

——. "Ustroistvo Rogozhskogo bogadelennogo doma vo vtoroi polovine XIX–nachale XX veka." *Mir staroobriadchestva* 4 (1998): 247–56.

Griboedov, F. *Istoriia o tsariakh i velikikh kniaz'iakh zemli russkoi*. (*Pamiatniki drevnei pis'mennosti* 121). St. Petersburg, 1896.

Gur'ianova, N. S. "Dopolnenie k 'Istorii Vygovskoi staroobriadcheskoi pustyni' I. Filippova." *Publitsistika i istoricheskie sochineniia perioda feodalizma*. Novosibirsk, 1989. Pp. 221–45.

——. "Dukhovnye zaveshchaniia vygovskikh bol'shakov." *Traditsionnaia dukhovnaia i material'naia kul'tura*. Pp. 96–102.

——. *Istoriia i chelovek v sochineniiakh staroobriadtsev XVIII veka*. Novosibirsk, 1996.

——. "'Istoriia Vygovskoi staroobriadcheskoi pustyni' I. Filippova (k istorii sozdaniia teksta)." *Istochniki po istorii obshchestvennogo soznaniia i literatury perioda feodalizma*. Novosibirsk, 1991. Pp. 178–95.

——. *Krest'ianskii antimonarkhicheskii protest v staroobriadcheskoi eskhatologicheskoi literature perioda pozdnego feodalizma*. Novosibirsk, 1988.

——. "Monarkh i obshchestvo: K voprosu o narodnom variante monarkhizma." *Staroobriadchestvo v Rossii (XVII–XX vv.)*. Pp. 126–48.

——. "Peasant Antimonarchism and Uprisings in Siberia during the Eighteenth Century." *Russia's Dissident Old Believers, 1650–1950*. Pp. 169–82.

——. "Pomorskie istoricheskie sochineniia XVIII v." *Istochniki po istorii obshchestvennoi mysli i kul'tury epokhi pozdnego feodalizma*. Novosibirsk, 1988. Pp. 92–102.

——. "Problema istoricheskogo povestvovaniia v interpretatsii pisatelei vygovskoi literaturnoi shkoly." *Izvestiia SO AN SSSR. Istoriia, filosofiia i filologiia* 3 (1991): 14–18.

——. *Staroobriadtsy i tvorcheskoe nasledie Kievskoi Mitropolii*. Novosibirsk, 2007.

——. "'Zhitie' Ivana Filippova." *Khristianstvo i tserkov' v Rossii feodal'nogo perioda (materialy)*. Novosibirsk, 1989. Pp. 227–53.

Gur'ianova, N. S., and Crummey, R. O. "Istoricheskaia skhema v sochineniiakh pisatelei vygovskoi literaturnoi shkoly." *Staroobriadchestvo v Rossii (XVII–XVIII vv.)*. Pp. 120–38.

Hauptmann, Peter. "Das Gemeindeleiteramt bei den priesterlosen Altgläubigen." *Unser ganzes Leben Christus unserm Gott überantworten. Studien zur ostkirchlichen Spiritualität*. Göttingen, 1982. Pp. 474–99.

Heller, Wolfgang. *Die Moskauer "Eiferer für die Frömmigkeit" zwischen Staat and Kirche, 1642–1652*. Wiesbaden, 1988.

Hildermeier, Manfred. "Alter Glaube und Mobilität: Bemerkungen zur Verbreitung und sozialen Struktur des Raskol im früindustriellen Russland, 1760–1860." *Jahrbücher für Geschichte Osteuropas* 39 (1991): 321–38.

——. "Alter Glaube und neue Welt: Zur Sozialgeschichte des Raskol im 18. und 19. Jahrhundert." *Jahrbücher für Geschichte Osteuropas* 38 (1990): 372–98, 504–25.

——. *Bürgertum und Stadt in Russland, 1760–1870: Rechtliche Lage und soziale Struktur*. Cologne, 1986.

——. "Old Belief and Worldly Performance: Socioeconomic and Sociocultural Aspects of the Raskol in Early Industrial Russia." *Russia's Dissident Old Believers, 1650–1950*. Pp. 121–38.

Hsia, R. Po-chia. *Social Discipline in the Reformation: Central Europe, 1550–1750*. London, 1989.

Hughes, Lindsey. *Sophia, Regent of Russia, 1657–1704*. New Haven and London, 1990.

Hunt, Priscilla. "Avvakum's 'Fifth Petition' to the Tsar and the Ritual Process." *Slavic and East European Journal* 46 (2003): 483–510.

——. "A Penitential Journey: The Life of the Archpriest Avvakum and the Kenotic Tradition." *Canadian-American Slavic Studies* 25 (1991): 201–24.

——. "Samoopravdanie Protopopa Avvakuma." TODRL 33 (1978): 182–97.

The Invention of Tradition. Ed. Eric Hobsbawm and Terence Ranger. Cambridge, 1983.

Iosif Volotskii (Joseph of Volokolamsk). *The Monastic Rule of Iosif Volotsky*. Ed. and trans. David M. Goldfrank. Kalamazoo, 1983.

——. *Poslaniia Iosifa Volotskogo*. Ed. A. A. Zimin and Ia. S. Lur'e. Moscow-Leningrad, 1959.

Istochniki po istorii Kurenevskikh staroobriadcheskikh monastyrei XIX–pervoi poloviny XX veka: Sbornik dokumentov. Ed. S. Taranets. Vol. 1. Kiev-Kurenevsk, 2006.

Iukhimenko, E. M. "'Egda zhe k nam, nedostoinym, prinesesia chestnaia epistoliia tvoia . . .' (Krug pamiatnikov, sviazannykh s novgorodskim zakliucheniem Semena Denisova v 1713–1717 gg.)" TODRL 57 (2006): 806–38.

———. "'Istoriia o ottsakh i stradal'tsakh solovetskikh' Semena Denisova—pamiatnik vygovskoi literaturnoi shkoly pervoi poloviny XVIII v." *Traditsionnaia dukhovnaia i material'naia kul'tura*. Pp. 107–13.

———. "Istoriia Vygovskoi pustyni Ivana Filippova: Nereshennye problemy." TODRL 58 (2007): 940–54.

———. "Kargopol'skie 'gari' 1683–1684 gg.: K probleme samosozhzhenii v russkom staroobriadchestve." *Staroobriadchestvo v Rossii (XVII–XVIII vv.)*. Pp. 64–119.

———. "Neizvestnaia stranitsa polemiki vygovskikh staroobriadtsev s ofitsial'noi tserkov'iu: Preystoriia 'Pomorskikh otvetov.'" TODRL 51 (1999): 404–16.

———. "Neizvestnyi vygovskii pisatel' XVIII v.: Vasilii Danilov Shaposhnikov i 'Skazanie o prestavlenii Simeona Dionis'evicha.'" TODRL 46 (1993): 441–52.

———. "*Nevezhestvo i premudrost'* v interpretatsii vygovskikh pisatelei-staroobriadtsev." TODRL 55 (2004): 508–16.

———. "Novonaidennye sochineniia vygovskikh pisatelei." *TODRL* 53 (2003): 289–417.

———. "Pervye ofitsial'nye izvestiia o poselenii staroobriadtsev v Vygovskoi pustyni." *Staroobriadchestvo v Rossii (XVII–XVIII vv.)*. Pp. 163–75.

———. "Rukopisno-knizhnoe sobranie Vygo-Leksinskogo obshchezhitel'stva." *Staroobriadchestvo v Rossii (XVII–XX vv.)*. Pp. 45–125. Also TODRL 51 (2001): 448–97.

———. "Staroobriadcheskaia knizhnost' i problema rekonstruktsii drevnrusskogo literaturnogo obikhoda." TODRL 54 (2003): 231–37.

———. *Staroobriadcheskii tsentr za Rogozhskoi zastavoiu*. Moscow, 2005.

———. "'Vinograd rossiiskii' Semena Denisova (tekstologicheskii analiz)." *Drevnerusskaia literatura. Istochnikovedenie. Sbornik nauchnykh trudov*. Leningrad, 1984. Pp. 249–66.

———. "Vnov' naidennye pis'ma Semena Denisova." TODRL 44 (1990): 409–421.

———. "Vygo-Leksinskii letopisets: Istoriia teksta i sozdaniia." TODRL 57 (2006): 254–96.

———. *Vygovskaia staroobriadcheskaia pustyn': Dukhovnaia zhizn' i literatura*. 2 vols. Moscow, 2002.

———. "Vygovskoe vozrozhdenie kontsa XVIII–nachala XIX v." *Vygovskaia pomorskaia pustyn'*. Pp. 17–24.

Ivanits, Linda J. *Russian Folk Belief*. Armonk, 1989.

Iwaniec, Eugeniusz. *Old Believers in Poland*. Poznan, 1981. Polish original, Warsaw, 1977.

John Climacus. *The Ladder of Divine Ascent*. Trans. Colm Liubheid and Norman Russell. Ramsay, NJ, 1982.

Kablitz, I. I. [pseud. I. Iuzov]. *Russkie dissidenty-starovery i dukhovnye khristiane*. St. Petersburg, 1881.

Kapterev, N. F. *Patriarkh Nikon i Tsar' Aleksei Mikhailovich*. 2 vols. Sergiev Posad, 1909.

Kel'siev, V. I. *Sbornik pravitel'stvennykh svedenii o raskol'nikakh*. 4 vols. London, 1860–1862.

Kharlampovich, K. V. *Malorossiiskoe vliianie na velikorusskuiu tserkovnuiu zhizn'*. Kazan', 1914.

Kharuzin, N. "K voprosu o bor'be Moskovskago pravitel'stva s narodnymi iazycheskimi obriadami i sueveriiami v polovine XVII v." *Etnograficheskoe Obozrenie*, 1879, no. 1, 143–51.

Kivelson, Valerie A. "The Devil Stole His Mind." *American Historical Review* 98 (1993): 733–56.

Klibanov, A. I. *Narodnaia sotsial'naia utopiia v Rossii.* Moscow, 1977.

Kliuchevskii, V. O. *Drevnerusskie zhitiia sviatykh kak istoricheskii istochnik.* Moscow, 1871. Repr., Moscow, 1988.

Kollmann, Jack E., Jr. "The Moscow Stoglav ('Hundred Chapters') Church Council of 1551." Unpublished Ph.D. dissertation, University of Michigan, 1978.

Kovalevsky, P. "Le 'Raskol' et son rôle dans le développement industriel de la Russie." *Archives de Sociologie des Religions* 3 (1957): 37–56.

Kozlov, V. F. "Moskovskoe staroobriadchestvo v pervoi treti XX v. (khramy, molel'ni, obshchestvennye organizatsii i uchrezhdeniia)." *Staroobriadchestvo v Rossii (XVII–XX vv.).* Pp. 190–239.

Kuandykov, L. K. "Filippovskie polemicheskie sochineniia XIX v. o skitskoi zhizni." *Drevnerusskaia rukopisnaia kniga i ee bytovanie v Sibiri.* Novosibirsk, 1982. Pp. 113–24.

———. "Ideologiia obshchezhitel'stva u staroobriadtsev-bespopovtsev vygovskogo soglasiia v XVIII v." *Istochniki po kul'ture i klassovoi bor'be feodal'nogo perioda.* Novosibirsk, 1982. Pp. 87–100.

———. "Razvitie obshchezhitel'nogo ustava v Vygovskoi staroobriadcheskoi obshchine v pervoi treti XVIII v." *Issledovaniia po istorii obshchestvennogo soznaniia epokhi feodalizma v Rossii.* Novosibirsk, 1984. Pp. 51–63.

———. "Rukopis' no. 3 iz Sobraniia I. N. Zavoloko v Drevlekhranilishche Pushkinskogo Doma." *Sibirskoe istochnikovedenie i arkheografiia.* Novosibirsk, 1984. Pp. 121–35.

———. "Vygovskie sochineniia ustavnogo kharaktera vtoroi poloviny XVIII v." *Istochniki po istorii russkogo obshchestvennogo soznaniia perioda feodalizma.* Novosibirsk, 1986. Pp. 120–30.

Kuznetsova, V. S. "Povest' o muchenii nekoikh starets Petra i Evdokima." *Literatura i klassovaia bor'ba epokhi pozdnego feodalizma v Rossii.* Novosibirsk, 1987. Pp. 206–15.

Lebedev, A. "Taezhnyi prosvet: kak ia ezdil k Agaf'e Lykovoi." *Tserkov',* 1990, no. 0 [*sic*], 26–32 (published as *Rodina*, no. 9); 1992, no. 1, 34–41.

Lenhoff, Gail D., and Pokrovskii, Nikolai N. *The Book of Degrees of the Royal Genealogy: A Critical Edition Based on the Oldest Known Manuscripts (Stepennaia kniga tsarskogo rodosloviia po drevneishim spiskam).* 2 vols. Moscow, 2007–2008.

Levin, Eve. "Dvoeverie and Popular Religion." *Seeking God.* Pp. 29–52.

———. "False Miracles and Unattested Dead Bodies: Investigations into Popular Cults in Early Modern Russia." *Religion and the Early Modern State.* Pp. 253–83.

———. "Supplicatory Prayers as a Source for Popular Religious Culture in Muscovite Russia." *Religion and Culture in Early Modern Russia.* Pp. 96–114.

Lileev, M. I. *Iz istorii raskola na Vetke i v Starodub'e XVII–XVIII vv.* Vol. 1. Kiev, 1895.

Liubomirov, P. G. *Vygovskoe obshchezhitel'stvo.* Moscow and Saratov, 1924.

Liubopytnyi, P. "Biblioteka starovercheskoi tserkvi." ChOIDR, 1863, book 1: 3–66.

———. "Istoricheskii slovar' Starovercheskoi tserkvi." ChOIDR, 1863, book 1: 123–77.

Loew, Cornelius. *Myth, Sacred History, and Philosophy.* New York, 1967.

Lyzlov, A. *Skifskaia istoriia.* Moscow, 1787.

Makarii, Bishop. *Istoriia russkago raskola izvestnago pod imenem staroobriadchestva.* St. Petersburg, 1855.

Mal'tsev, A. I. "Moskovskii filippovskii sobor 1769 g." *Staroobriadchestvo v Rossii (XVII–XX vv.)*. Pp. 280–89.

———. "Neizvestnoe sochnienie S. Denisova o tarskom 'bunte' 1722 g." *Istochniki po kul'ture i klassovoi bor'be feodal'nogo perioda*. Novosibirsk, 1982. Pp. 224–41.

———. *Sochineniia inoka Evfimiia: teksty i kommentarii*. Novosibirsk, 2003.

———. "Soiuznoe soglashenie 1780 goda staroobriadtsev filippovskogo i fedoseevskogo soglasii v ottsenke sovremennikov." *Istoricheskie istochniki i literaturnye pamiatniki XVI–XX vv.* Novosibirsk, 2004. Pp. 61–78.

———. *Staroobriadcheskie bespopovskie soglasiia v XVIII–nachale XIX v.* Novosibirsk, 2006.

———. *Starovery-stranniki v XVIII-pervoi polovine XIX v.* Novosibirsk, 1996.

Malyshev, V. I., ed. "Une communauté de vieux-croyants dans la Russie du nord: l'ermitage des Grandes Prairies." *Revue des études slaves* 43 (1964): 83–89.

———. "The Confession of Ivan Filippov, 1744." *Oxford Slavonic Papers* 11 (1964): 17–27.

———. *Drevnerusskie rukopisi Pushkinskogo Doma*. Moscow-Leningrad, 1965.

———. *Ust'-tsilemskie rukopisnye sborniki XVI–XX vv.* Syktyvkar, 1960.

Manselli, Raoul. *La religion populaire au moyen âge: Problèmes de méthode et d'histoire*. Montreal, 1975.

Markelov, G. V. "Staroobriadcheskaia ispoved' dlia ikonopistsa." TODRL 51 (2001): 745–53.

Markelov, G. V., and Panchenko, F. V. "O gimnograficheskom tvorchestve na Vygu." TODRL 51 (1998): 417–26.

Masonstvo v ego proshlom i nastoiashchem. Ed. S. P. Mel'gunov and N. P. Sidorov. Vol. 1. Moscow, 1914.

"Materialy dlia istorii bezpopovshchinskikh soglasii v Moskve: I. Feodosievtsev Preobra-zhenskago kladbishcha; II. Moninskoe soglasie." Ed. N. Popov. ChOIDR, 1869, book 2: 71–174; book 3: 13–186.

Matkhanova, N. P. *General-gubernatory Vostochnoi Sibiri serediny XIX v.; V. Ia. Ruppert, N. N. Murav'ev-Amurskii, M. S. Korsakov*. Novosibirsk, 1998.

———. *Vysshaia administratsiia Vostochnoi Sibiri v seredine XIX v.* Novosibirsk, 2002.

Meehan, Brenda. *Holy Women of Russia*. San Francisco, 1993.

———. "Popular Piety, Local Initiative, and the Founding of Women's Religious Communi-ties in Russia, 1764–1907." *Seeking God*. Pp. 83–105.

Mel'nikov, P. I. [Andrei Pecherskii]. "Ocherki popovshchiny." *Polnoe sobranie sochinenii*. 7 vols. St. Petersburg, 1909. Vol. 7: 3–375.

———. *Otchet o sovremennom sostoianii raskola v Nizhegorodskoi gubernii*. St. Petersburg, 1854.

Men'shakova, E. G. "Pecherskoe staroobriadchestvo." *Staroobriadcheskaia kul'tura Russk-ogo Severa*. Moscow-Kargopol', 1998. Pp. 28–32.

Meyendorff, Paul. *Russia, Ritual, and Reform. The Liturgical Reforms of Nikon in the Seven-teenth Century*. Crestwood, NY, 1991.

Michels, Georg B. *At War with the Church: Religious Dissent in Seventeenth-Century Russia*. Stanford, 1999.

———. "The First Old Believers in Ukraine: Observations about Their Social Profile and Behavior." *Harvard Ukrainian Studies* 16 (1992): 289–313.

———. "Muscovite Elite Women and Old Belief." *Rhetoric of the Medieval Slavic World: Essays presented to Edward L. Keenan on His Sixtieth Birthday by His Colleagues and Students*. Harvard Ukrainian Studies 19. Pp. 428–50.

——. "Myths and Realities of the Russian Schism: The Church and Its Dissenters in Seventeenth-Century Muscovy." Unpublished Ph. D. dissertation, Harvard University, 1991.

——. "The Place of Nikita Konstantinovich Dobrynin in the History of Early Old Belief." *Revue des études slaves* 69 (1997): 21–31.

——. "The Solovki Uprising: Religion and Revolt in Northern Russia." *Russian Review* 51 (1992): 1–15.

——. "The Violent Old Belief: An Examination of Religious Dissent on the Karelian Frontier." *Russian History* 19 (1992): 203–29.

Miller, David B. "The Velikie minei chetii of Metropolitan Makarii and the Origins of Russian National Consciousness." *Forschungen zur osteuropäischen Geschichte* 26 (1979): 263–382.

Mosin, A. G. "Istochniki po istorii knizhnoi kul'tury zhitelei Viatskoi gubernii (1840–1850)." *Kul'tura i byt dorevoliutsionnogo Urala.* Sverdlovsk, 1989. Pp. 103–21.

"Moskovskii sobor o zhitii blagoverynia kniagini Anny Kashinskoi." ChOIDR, 1871, book 4: 45–62.

Muchembled, Robert. *Popular Culture and Elite Culture in France, 1400–1750.* Trans. L. Cochrane. Baton Rouge, 1985.

Naudon, Paul. *Histoire générale de la Franc-Maçonnerie.* Fribourg, 1981.

Niess, H. P. *Kirche in Russland zwischen Tradition und Glaube? Eine Untersuchung der Kirillova kniga und der Kniga o vere aus der 1 hälfte des 17 Jahrhunderts.* Göttingen, 1977.

Nikitina, S. E. "Ustnaia traditsiia v narodnoi kul'ture russkogo naseleniia Verkhokam'ia." *Russkie pis'mennye i ustnye traditsii.* Pp. 91–126.

Nil Sorskii. Predanie i Ustav. Ed. M. S. Borovkova-Maikova. (*Pamiatniki drevnei pis'mennosti i iskusstva* 179). St. Petersburg, 1912. Pp. 195–283.

Nil'skii, I. F. *Semeinaia zhizn' v russkom raskole; istoricheskii ocherk raskol'nicheskogo uchniia o brake.* 2 vols. St. Petersburg, 1869.

Nil'skii, V. "Malo-okhtenskoe pomorskoe kladbishche v Peterburge." *Istina* 42 (1875): 61–88.

——. "Raskol v Peterburge: Molennaia Kostsova v Volkovskom Fedoseevskoe Kladbishche." *Istina* 55 (1877): 1–68.

Obolensky, Dmitrii. "Popular Religion in Medieval Russia." *Russia and Orthodoxy.* Vol. 2, *The Religious World of Russian Culture.* Ed. Andrew Blane. The Hague, 1975. Pp. 43–54.

Obshchestvennoe soznanie, knizhnost', literatura perioda feodalizma. Novosibirsk, 1990.

Oparina, T. A. *Ivan Nasedka i polemicheskoe bogoslovie Kievskoi metropolii.* Novosibirsk, 1998.

Ostrovskii, V. *Vygovskaia pustyn' i eia znachenie v istorii staroobriadcheskago raskola.* Petrozavodsk, 1914.

Paert, Irina. *Old Believers, Religious Dissent, and Gender in Russia, 1760–1850.* Manchester and New York, 2003.

Palmer, William. *The Patriarch and the Tsar.* 6 vols. London, 1871–1876.

Panich, T. V. *Kniga Shchit very v istoriko-literaturnom kontekste kontsa XVII veka.* Novosibirsk, 2004.

————. *Literaturnoe tvorchestvo Afanasiia Kholmogorskogo: "Estestvennonauchnye" sochine-niia.* Novosibirsk, 1996.

Pascal, Pierre. *Avvakum et les débuts du raskol.* Paris and The Hague, 1963.

————. *The Religion of the Russian People.* London and Oxford, 1976.

Pashkov, A. M. "Staroobriadcheskie poseleniia severo-zapada Rossii v 1700–1917 godakh." *Istoriia i geografiia russkikh staroobriadcheskikh govorov.* Moscow, 1995. Pp. 93–101.

————. "Vygovskaia pomorskaia pustyn' i ee kul'tura." *Vygovskaia pomorskaia pustyn'.* Pp. 8–16.

Patriarch Nikon on Church and State: Nikon's "Refutation." Ed. Valerie Tumins and George Vernadsky. Berlin, New York, and Amsterdam, 1982.

Pentikäinen, Juha. "Oral Repertoire and World View: An Anthropological Study of Marina Takalo's Life History." *FF Communications* 93, no. 219 (1978).

Pera, Pia. "Theoretical and Practical Aspects of the Debate on Marriage among the Priest-less Old Believers from the End of the Seventeenth to the Mid-Nineteenth Century." Unpublished Ph.D. dissertation. University of London, 1986.

Pikhoia, R. G. "Knizhno-rukopisnaia traditsiia Urala XVIII–nachala XX v. (k postanovke problemy)." *Istochniki po kul'ture i klassovoi bor'be feodal'nogo perioda.* Novosibirsk, 1982. Pp. 101–14

————. *Obshchestvenno-politicheskaia mysl' trudiashchikhsia Urala (konets XVII–XVIII vv.)* .Sverdlovsk, 1987.

Pliukhanova, M. B. "O nekotorykh chertakh lichnostnogo soznaniia v Rossii XVII v." *Khu-dozhestvennyi iazyk srednevekov'ia.* Moscow, 1982. Pp. 184–200.

Pokrovskii, N. I. *Kavkazskie voiny i imamat Shamilia.* Moscow, 2000. 2nd edition, 2009.

Pokrovskii, N. N. *Antifeodal'nyi protest uralo-sibirskikh krest'ian-staroobriadtsev v XVIII v.* Novosibirsk, 1974.

————. "Arkheograficheskie ekspeditsii i problemy izucheniia narodnogo soznaniia." *Arkheograficheskii ezhegodnik za 1986 god.* Moscow, 1987. Pp. 159–63.

————. "'Ispoved'" altaiskogo krest'ianina." *Pamiatniki kul'tury. Novye otkrytiia. 1978.* Len-ingrad, 1979. Pp. 49–57.

————. "Knigi Tarskogo bunta 1722 g." *Istochniki po istorii russkogo obshchestvennogo soz-naniia perioda feodalizma.* Novosibirsk, 1986. Pp. 155–90.

————. "Krest'ianskii pobeg i traditsii pustynnozhitel'stva v Sibiri XVIII v." *Krest'ianstvo Sibiri XVIII–nachala XX v.: Klassovaia bor'ba, obshchestvennoe soznanie i kul'tura.* Novosibirsk, 1975. Pp. 19–49.

————. "Novyi dokument po ideologii Tarskogo protesta." *Istochnikovedenie i arkheografiia Sibiri.* Novosibirsk, 1977. Pp. 221–34.

————. *Puteshestvie za redkimi knigami.* Moscow, 1984, 1988; Novosibirsk, 2005.

————. "Trends in Studying the History of Old Belief among Russian Scholars." *Russia's Dissident Old Believers.* Pp. 17–38.

Pokrovskii, N. N., and Petrov, S. G., eds. *Politbiuro i tserkov', 1922–1925 gg.* 2 vols. Novo-sibirsk, 1997–1998.

Pokrovskii, N. N., and Zol'nikova, N. D. *Starovery-chasovennye na vostoke Rossii v XVIII–XX vv.: Problemy tvorchestva i obshchestvennogo soznaniia.* Moscow, 2002.

Ponyrko, N. V. "Uchebniki ritoriki na Vygu." *TODRL* 36 (1981): 154–62.

———. *Vygovskaia literaturnaia shkola v pervoi polovine XVIII stoletiia.* Dissertation abstract. Leningrad, 1979.

Popov, N., ed. *Sbornik dlia istorii staroobriadchestva.* 2 vols. Moscow, 1864, 1866.

Potashenko, G. *Staroverie v Litve: Vtoraia polovina XVII–nachalo XIX vv.; Issledovaniia, dokumenty i materialy.* Vilnius, 2006.

Povest' o boiaryne Morozovoi. Ed. A. I. Mazunin. Leningrad, 1979.

Pozdeeva, I. V. "Drevnerusskoe nasledie v istorii traditsionnoi knizhnoi kul'tury staroobriadchestva (pervyi period)." *Istoriia SSSR*, 1988, no. 1, 84–99.

———. "Kompleksnye arkheograficheskie ekspeditsii: Tseli, metodika, printsipy organizatsii." *Istoriia SSSR*, 1978, no. 2, 103–15.

———. "Vereshchaginskoe territorial'noe knizhnoe sobranie i problemy istorii dukhovnoi kul'tury russkogo naseleniia verkhov'ev Kamy." *Russkie pis'mennye i ustnye traditsii.* Pp. 40–71.

"Pozdravliaem Nikolaia Nikolaevicha Pokrovskogo." *Gumanitarnye nauki v Sibiri*, 2005, no. 2, 110–11.

Propp, V. Ia. *Russkie agrarnye prazdniki.* St. Petersburg, 1995.

Pustozerskii sbornik: Avtografy sochinenii Avvakuma i Epifaniia. Leningrad, 1975.

The Reader in the Text. Ed. Susan R. Suleiman and Inge Crosman. Princeton, 1980.

Reinhard, Wolfgang. "Gegenreformation als Modernisierung? Prolegomena zu einer Theorie des konfessionellen Zeitalters." *Archiv für Reformationsgeschichte* 68 (1977): 226–52.

———. "Zwang zur Konfessionalisierung? Prolegomena zu einer Theorie des konfessionellen Zeitalters." *Zeitschrift für Historische Forschung* 10 (1983): 257–77.

Religion and Culture in Early Modern Russia and Ukraine. Ed. Samuel H. Baron and Nancy Shields Kollmann. DeKalb, 1997.

Religion and the Early Modern State: Views from China, Russia, and the West. Ed. James D. Tracy and Marguerite Ragnow. Cambridge and New York, 2004.

Robinson, A. N. *Bor'ba idei v russkoi literature XVII v.* Moscow, 1974.

———. *Zhizneopisaniia Avvakuma i Epifaniia: Issledovanie i teksty.* Moscow, 1963.

Robson, Roy R. "An Architecture of Change: Old Believer Liturgical Spaces in Late Imperial Russia." *Seeking God.* Pp. 160–87.

———. "Old Believers and the Soviet State in Riga, 1945–55." *Rude & Barbarous Kingdom Revisited. Essays in Russian History and Culture in Honor of Robert O. Crummey.* Ed. Chester S. L. Dunning, Russell E. Martin, and Daniel Rowland. Bloomington, 2008. Pp. 287–99.

———. "The Old Believers in a Modern World: Symbol, Ritual, and Community, 1905–14." Unpublished Ph. D. dissertation, Boston College, 1992.

———. *Old Believers in Modern Russia.* DeKalb, 1995.

Rollin, Charles. *De la manière d'enseigner et d'étudier les Belles-Lettres par rapport à l'esprit et au coeur.* Paris, 1726–1728.

Romodanovskaia, E. K. *Povesti o gordom tsare v rukopisnoi traditsii XVII–XIX vekov.* Novosibirsk, 1985.

———. *Russkaia literatura na poroge novogo vremeni: Puti formirovaniia russkoi belletristiki perekhodnogo perioda.* Novosibirsk, 1994.

———. *Russkaia literatura v Sibiri pervoi poloviny XVII v. (Istoki russkoi sibirskoi literatury).* Novosibirsk, 1973.

Rousseau, Jean-Jacques. *The First and Second Discourses.* Ed. Roger D. Masters. New York, 1964.

Rowland, Daniel. "The Problem of Advice in Muscovite Tales about the Time of Troubles." *Russian History* 6 (1979): 259–83.

———. "Towards an Understanding of the Political Ideas in Ivan Timofeyev's Vremennik." *Slavonic and East European Review* 62 (1984): 371–99.

Rozhdestvenskii, N. V. "K istorii bor'by s tserkovnymi bezporiadkami, otgoloskami iazychestva i porokami v russkom bytu XVII v." ChOIDR, 1902, book 2: 1–31.

Rumiantsev, I. *Nikita Konstantinov Dobrynin ("Pustosviat").* Sergiev Posad, 1916.

Rumiantseva, V. S., ed. *Dokumenty razriadnogo, posol'skogo, novgorodskogo i tainogo prikazov o raskol'nikakh v gorodakh Rossii, 1654–1684 gg.* Moscow, 1990.

———. *Narodnoe antitserkovnoe dvizhenie v Rossii v XVII veke.* Moscow, 1986.

———, ed. *Narodnoe antitserkovnoe dvizhenie v Rossii XVII veka: Dokumenty Prikaza Tainykh Del 1665–1667 gg.* Moscow, 1986.

Russia's Dissident Old Believers, 1650–1950. Ed. Georg B. Michels and Robert L. Nichols (Minnesota Mediterranean and East European Monographs, 19). Minneapolis, 2009.

Russkie pis'mennye i ustnye traditsii i dukhovnaia kul'tura. Moscow, 1982.

Ryan, W. F. "Aristotle and Pseudo-Aristotle in Kievan and Muscovite Russia." *Pseudo-Aristotle in the Middle Ages: The Theology and Other Texts.* (Warburg Institute Surveys and Texts, XI). London, 1968. Pp. 97–109.

———. *The Bathhouse at Midnight: Magic in Russia.* University Park, PA, 1999.

———. "The Secretum Secretorum and the Muscovite Autocracy." *Pseudo-Aristotle: The Secret of Secrets; Sources and Influences.* (Warburg Institute Surveys, IX). London, 1982. Pp. 114–23.

Ryndziunskii, P. G. *Gorodskoe grazhdanstvo doreformennoi Rossii.* Moscow, 1958.

———. "Staroobriadcheskaia organizatsiia v usloviiakh razvitiia promyshlennogo kapitalizma (Na primere istorii Moskovskoi obshchiny fedoseevtsev v 40-kh godakh XIX v.)." *Voprosy istorii religii i ateizma* 1 (1950): 188–248.

Sapozhnikov, D. I. "Samosozhzhenie v russkom raskole." ChOIDR, 1891, book 3: 1–170.

Savich, A. A. *Solovetskaia votchina v XV–XVII v.* Perm', 1927.

Schilling, Heinz. "Between the Territorial State and Urban Liberty: Lutheranism and Calvinism in the County of Lippe." *The German People and the Reformation.* Pp. 263–83.

———. "Die Konfessionalisierung im Reich: Religiöser und Gesellschaftlicher Wandel in Deutschland zwischen 1555 und 1620." *Historische Zeitschrift* 246 (1988): 1–45.

Scribner, R. W. *For the Sake of the Simple Folk: Popular Propaganda for the German Reformation.* Cambridge, 1981.

———. "Interpreting Religion in Early Modern Europe." *European Studies Review* 13 (1983): 89–105.

Seeking God: The Recovery of Religious Identity in Orthodox Russia, Ukraine, and Georgia. Ed. Stephen K. Batalden. DeKalb, 1993.

Shafranov, I. A. "Vygoretskoe staroobriadcheskoe obshchezhitel'stvo v kontse XVIII i pervoi polovine XIX v." *Russkoe Bogatstvo,* 1893, no. 10, 171–99, and no. 11, 58–98.

Shchapov, A. P. "Russkii raskol staroobriadstva, razsmatrivaemyi v sviazi s vnutrennim sostoianiem russkoi tserkvi i grazhdanstvennosti v XVII veke i v pervoi polovine XVIII." *Sochineniia* 1: 173–450.

254   *Selected Bibliography*

———. *Sochineniia.* 3 vols. St. Petersburg, 1906. Repr. 1971.

———. "Zemstvo i raskol." *Sochineniia* 1: 451–579.

Shmidt, S. O. "K predystorii izdaniia poslednikh knig akademika M. N. Tikhomirova." *Obshchestvennoe soznanie, knizhnost', literatura.* Pp. 368–76.

Shukhtina, N. V. "Pererabotki 'Voprosa i otveta' i 'Poslanie k nekoemu bogoliubtsu' inoka Avraamiia v rukopisiakh, XVIII–XIX vv." TODRL 44 (1990): 403–8.

Sigal, Pierre-André. *L'Homme et le miracle dans la France médiévale, XIe–XIIe siècle.* Paris, 1985.

Sinaiskii, A. *Otnoshenie russkoi tserkovnoi vlasti k raskolu staroobriadchestva v pervye gody sinodal'nago upravleniia pri Petre Velikom, 1721–1725.* St. Petersburg, 1895.

Skripil', M. O. "Povest' ob Uliianii Osor'inoi: Istoricheskie komentarii i teksty." TODRL 6 (1948): 256–323.

"Slovo o iubiliare." *Problemy istorii, russkoi knizhnosti, kul'tury i obshchestvennogo soznaniia.* Novosibirsk, 2000. Pp. 3–8.

Smilianskaia, E. V. "Belokrinitskie prikhody v Moldove (knizhnost' i kul'tura s. Kunicha)." *Traditsionnaia dukhovnaia i material'naia kul'tura.* Pp 179–85.

———. "'Iskra istinnago blagochestiia.' Religioznye vozzreniia staroobriadtsev Verkhokam'ia." *Rodina*, 1995, no. 2, 101–3.

Smilianskaia, E. V., and Denisov, N. G. *Staroobriadchestvo Bessarabii: Knizhnost' i pevcheskaia kul'tura.* Moscow, 2007.

Smirnov, P. S. *Iz istorii raskola pervoi poloviny XVIII veka.* St. Petersburg, 1908.

———. *Spory i razdeleniia v russkom raskole v pervoi chetverti XVIII veka.* St. Petersburg, 1909.

———. *Vnutrennye voprosy v raskole v XVII veke.* St. Petersburg, 1898.

———. "Vygovskaia bezpopovshchinskaia pustyn' v pervoe vremia eia sushchestvovaniia." *Khristianskoe Chtenie*, 1910, nos. 5–6, 638–74, and nos. 7–8, 910–34.

Smirnov, S. *Drevnerusskii dukhovnik.* ChOIDR, 1914, book 2: 1–283.

Smith, Abby, and Budaragin, Vladimir. *Living Traditions of Russian Faith: Books and Manuscripts of the Old Believers.* Washington, 1990.

Snesarev, N. "Verkhne-Chirskaia stanitsa i staroobriadcheskii raskol v XVIII veke." *Donskie Eparkhial'nyia Vedomosti* 1878, no. 4, 107–15, no. 5, 135–43, no. 6, 169–80, and no. 7, 203–16.

Sobranie postanovlenii po chasti raskola, sostoiavshikhsia po vedomstvu Sviateishago Pravitel'stvuiushago Sinoda. 2 vols. St. Petersburg, 1860. Vol. 1, 712.

Sokolov, N. *Raskol v Saratovskom krae.* Saratov, 1888.

Sokolovskaia, M. L. "Krest'ianskii mir kak osnova formirovaniia Vygovskogo obshchezhitel'stva." *Staroobriadchestvo v Rossii (XVII–XX vv.).* Pp. 269–79.

———. "Severnoe raskol'nicheskoe obshchezhitel'stvo pervoi poloviny XVIII veka i struktura ego zemel'." *Istoriia SSSR*, 1978, no. 1, 157–67.

———. "Skladyvanie instituta 'uchitel'stva' v Vygo-Leksenskom [*sic*] obshchezhitel'stve." *Mir staroobriadchestva* 1 (1992): 28–45.

Spock, Jennifer B. "The Solovki Monastery, 1460–1645: Piety and Patronage in the Early Modern Russian North." Unpublished Ph. D. dissertation, Yale University, 1999.

Stannard, David E. *The Puritan Way of Death.* New York, 1977.

Staroobriadchestvo: Litsa, predmety, sobytiia i simvoly; Opyt entsikloopedicheskogo slovaria. Ed. S. G. Vurgraft and I. A. Ushakov.

Staroobriadchestvo v Rossii (XVII–XVIII vv.). Ed. E. M. Iukhimenko. Moscow, 1994.

Staroobriadchestvo v Rossii (XVII–XX vv.). Ed. E. M. Iukhimenko. Moscow, 1999.

Stock, Brian. *The Implications of Literacy: Written Language and Models of Interpretation in the Eleventh and Twelfth Centuries.* Princeton, 1983.

Stoglav. Ed. D. E. Kozhanchikov. St. Petersburg, 1863.

The Study of Spirituality. Ed. Cheslyn Jones, Geoffrey Wainwright, and Edward Yarnold SJ. London, 1986.

Subbotin, N. *Istoriia Belokrinitskoi ierarkhii.* Vol. 1. Moscow, 1874.

"Sudnye protsessy XVII–XVIII vv. po delam tserkvi." Ed. E. V. Barsov. ChOIDR, 1882, book 3: 1–42.

Sudnye spiski Maksima Greka i Isaka Sobakina. Moscow, 1971.

Sullivan, J. "Eighteenth-Century Russian Verse from the Vyg Community of Old Believers." *Slavonic and East European Review* 67 (1989): 517–29.

Sullivan, J., and Drage, C. L. "Poems in an Unpublished Manuscript of the *Vinograd rossiiskii.*" *Oxford Slavonic Papers* 1 (1968): 27–48.

"Svedenie o nakhodiashchikhsia Olonetskoi Gubernii v Povenetskom Uezde raskol'nich'ikh skitakh, pustyniakh i molennykh, sobrannyia, vo ispolnenie slovesnago prikazaniia Gospodina Olonetskogo Grazhdanskago Gubernatora I. Bakurevichem." ChOIDR, 1862, book 4: 33–45.

Svodnyi katalog russkoi knigi grazhdanskoi pechati XVIII veka. 5 vols. Moscow, 1963–1967.

Syrtsov, I. Ia. *Vozmushchenie Solovetskikh monakhov-staroobriadtsev v XVII v.* Kostroma, 1888.

Sysyn, Frank E. "Orthodoxy and Revolt: The Role of Religion in the Seventeenth-Century Ukrainian Uprising against the Polish-Lithuanian Commonwealth." *Religion and the Early Modern State.* Pp. 154–84.

Taranets, S. V. *Dzherela z istorii staroobriadstva Pravoberezhnoi Ukraini kintsia XVII–pochatku XX st.* Kiev, 2007.

———. *Kurenevskoe trimonastyr'e: Istoriia russkogo staroobriadcheskogo tsentra v Ukraine.* Kiev, 1999.

———. "Kurenevskoe trimonastyr'e: istoriia Kurenevskikh staroobriadcheskikh muzhskogo i zhenskogo monastyrei." *Mir staroobriadchestva* 5 (1999): 312–35.

———. *Staroobriadchestvo goroda Kieva i Kievskoi Gubernii.* Kiev, 2004.

———. *Staroobriadchestvo Podolii.* Kiev, 2000.

Thomas, Keith. *Religion and the Decline of Magic.* New York, 1971.

Timofeev, V. V. *Russkie staroobriadtsy v XVIII–XX vv.: Opyt predprinimatel'skoi deiatel'nosti i obshchestvennogo sluzheniia v Rossii i za rubezhom.* Moscow-Cheboksary, 2006.

Titlinov, B. V. *Pravitel'stvo Imperatritsy Anny Ioannovny v ego otnosheniiakh k delam pravoslavnoi tserkvi* .Vilnius, 1905.

Titova, L V. *Beseda ottsa s synom o zhenskoi zlobe: Issledovanie i publikatsiia tekstov.* Novosibirsk, 1987.

———. *Poslanie d'iakona Fedora synu Maksimu: Literaturnyi i polemicheskii pamiatnik rannego staroobriadchestva.* Novosibirsk, 2003.

Traditsionnaia dukhovnaia i material'naia kul'tura russkikh staroobriadcheskikh poselenii v stranakh Evropy, Azii i Ameriki: Sbornik nauchnykh trudov. Novosibirsk, 1992.

Traditsionnaia kul'tura Permskoi zemli. K 180–letiiu polevoi arkheografii v Moskovskom universitete, 30–letiiu kompleksnykh issledovanii Verkhokam'ia. (Mir staroobriadchestva 6). Iaroslavl', 2005.

Turner, Victor W. *The Ritual Process: Structure and Anti-Structure.* Chicago, 1969.

Uspensky, Boris A. "The Schism and Cultural Conflict in the Seventeenth Century." *Seeking God.* Pp. 106–43.

van Dulman, Richard. "Volksfrömmigkeit und konfessionelles Christentum im 16. und 17. Jahrhundert." *Volksreligiosität in der modernen Sozialgeschichte.* Ed. Wolfgang Schieder. Göttingen, 1986. Pp. 14–30.

Varadinov, N. *Istoriia Ministerstva vnutrennykh del.* 8 vols. St. Petersburg, 1858–1863.

Vasil'ev, V. "Iz istorii Rogozhskago Kladbishcha." *Bratskoe Slovo,* 1891, no. 2, 448–66.

———. "Organizatsiia i samoupravlenie Feodosievskoi obshchiny na Preobrazhenskom Kladbishche v Moskve." *Khristianskoe chtenie,* 1887, 568–615.

Vlasov, Andrei N. "On the History of the Old Belief in the Komi Republic." *"Silent as Waters We Live," Old Believers in Russia and Abroad: Cultural Encounter with the Finno-Ugrians.* (Studia Fennica: Folkloristica, vol. 6). Ed. Juha Pentikäinen. Helsinki, 1999. Pp. 62–74.

Voloshin, Iu. *Gosudarevy opisnye malorossiiskie raskol'nicheskie slobody (XVIII v.).* Moscow, 2005.

Voltaire. *Oeuvres complètes.* 52 vols. Paris, 1877–1885.

von Lilienfeld, Fairy. *Nils Sorskij und seine Schriften.* Berlin, 1963.

"Vygo-leksinskii letopisets." Ed. E. M. Iukhimenko. *Vygovskaia pomorskaia pustyn'.* Pp. 309–22.

"Vygoretskii letopisets." *Bratskoe Slovo,* 1888, no. 10, 793–815.

Vygovskaia pomorskaia pustyn' i ee znachenie v istorii Rossii. St. Petersburg, 2003.

Waldron, Peter. "Religious Reform after 1905: Old Believers and the Orthodox Church." *Oxford Slavonic Papers* 20 (1987): 111–39.

Ward, Benedicta. *Miracles and the Medieval Mind.* Philadelphia, 1982.

West, James L. "The Riabushinsky Circle: *Burzhuaziia* and *Obshchestvennost'* in Late Imperial Russia." *Between Tsar and People: Educated Society and the Quest for Public Identity in Late Imperial Russia.* Ed. Edith W. Clowes, Samuel D. Kassow, and James L. West. Princeton, 1991. Pp. 41–56.

———. "The Rjabušinskij Circle: Russian Industrialists in Search of a Bourgeoisie, 1900–1914." *Jahrbücher für Geschichte Osteuropas* 32 (1984): 358–77.

Zenkovsky, Serge. "The Ideological World of the Denisov Brothers." *Harvard Slavic Studies* (1957): 48–66.

———. *Russkoe staroobriadchestvo.* Munich, 1970.

———. *Russkoe staroobriadchestvo.* 2 vols. Moscow, 2006. I. *Dukhovnye dvizheniia semnadtsatogo veka;* II. *Dukhovnye dvizheniia XVII–XIX vekov: Stat'i.*

Zguta, Russell. *Russian Minstrels: A History of the Skomorokhi.* Philadelphia, 1978.

Zhenshchina v staroobriadchestve. Petrozavodsk, 2006.

"Zhil'ber Romm u vygovskikh raskolnikov." *Kraeved Karelii.* Petrozavodsk, 1990. Pp. 148–59.

Zhitie Avvakuma i drugie ego sochineniia. Ed. A. N. Robinson. Moscow, 1991.

Zhitie Protopopa Avvakuma im samim napisannoe i drugie ego sochineniia. Moscow, 1960.

Zhivotov, N. N. *Tserkovnyi raskol Peterburga.* St. Petersburg, 1891.

Zhuravel', O. D. "'Devstvuiushchaia tserkov' Khristova na Severe' o. Simeona—pamiatnik sovremennoi staroobriadcheskoi literatury." *Obshchestvennoe soznanie i literatura XVI–XX vv.: Sbornik nauchnykh trudov.* Novosibirsk, 2001. Pp. 274–91.

———. "Staroobriadcheskii pisatel' Afanasii Murachev: Novye sochineniia na evangel'skie siuzhety." *Istoricheskie istochniki i literaturnye pamiatniki XVI–XX vv. Razvitie traditsii.* Novosibirsk, 2004. Pp. 286–307.

Zol'nikova, N. D. *Sibirskaia prikhodskaia obshchina v XVIII v.* Novosibirsk, 1990.

———. *Soslovnye problemy vo vzaimootnosheniiakh tserkvi i gosudarstva v Sibiri (XVIII v.)* Novosibirsk, 1981.

———. "Sovremennyi pisatel'-staroobriadets s Eniseia." *Traditsionnaia dukhovnaia i material'naia kul'tura.* Pp. 283–88.

Index

Aleksandr, Bishop of Viatka, 41–42
Aleksei Mikhailovich, Tsar (1645–1676),
    33, 36, 38, 45, 58, 66, 72, 75, 93, 179
Alexander I, 109–11, 159–60
Alexander III, 110–11
alleluia (double or triple), 39, 42, 79–83
Amvrosii, Old Believer bishop, 101–2
Anna of Kashin, 44
Antichrist, 50–51, 60–61, 120–22, 163,
    179–80
*Antifeodal'nyi protest uralo-sibirskikh
    krest'ian staroobriadtsev v XVIII v.,*
    172–74
archeographic expeditions. *See* research
    expeditions
Arsenius (Arsenii), 78, 89
Artem'ev, Tereshka, 105
Avraamii, 41–43, 48, 72–91, 93–96, 119;
    Christian's Secure Shield of Faith,
    41, 74–75, 80, 89
Avvakum, 10, 12, 25, 33, 37, 40–42, 47–49,
    53, 55, 57, 71–75, 80, 84, 87–89, 91–96,
    119, 130, 133–34

Baidin, Viktor Ivanovich, 177
Bakhtin, Mikhail, 18
Barsov, Elpidifor Vasil'evich, 120
beglopopovtsy, 101
beguny, 10, 24, 116, 184–85, 189
Belaia Krinitsa. See *Belokrinitskaia
    hierarchy*
Belokrinitskaia hierarchy (Belokrinitsy),
    101–2, 109, 162
bespopovtsy, 7, 14, 20, 123, 185, 192
Billington, James, 13
bogadel'nia (bogadelennye doma)

(charitable institution, almshouse), 105,
    109–14
Bogdanov, Sila, 40–41, 45
Borisov, Andrei, 24, 135–219: "life" of
    Andrei Denisov by, 137, 143–8, 151;
    sermons of, 137, 148–51
Bubnov, Nikolai Iur'evich, 71, 73–75, 89
Bushkovitch, Paul, 87, 95–96
Bynum, Carolyn Walker, 95

Catherine II, 21, 109–10, 139–40, 153,
    158–9, 161
cenobitic (monastic community), 100,
    103–9, 117, 131
charitable institution. See *bogadeln'ia*
chasovennye, 102–3, 109, 116–17, 176–77,
    187, 189
Cheremshan, 108–9
Cherniavsky, Michael, viii–x, 11,179
Chistov, Kirill Vasil'evich, 184
Chubykinsk (Old Believer community, St.
    Petersburg), 112–13
Chumicheva, Ol'ga Valer'evna, 181–82, 186–87
confessionalization, 32, 38, 40, 44–46
Councils of 1666–1667, 69, 74
cross, sign of (two-finger vs. three-finger),
    39–42, 63–64, 71–73, 78–82, 89, 92
cultural system, 22–23, 68–77, 79–84, 119,
    159

D'iakonovy Otvety, 144, 183
Danilov, Vasilii, 138, 143
Dashkov, A. V., 141, 162
Demkova, Natal'ia Sergeevna, 105, 190
Denisov brothers, 48, 105, 119–35, 140,
    143, 148, 180

Denisov, Andrei, 105, 120–21, 124–26,
137–38, 143–48, 151, 153
Denisov, Semen, 49, 54, 91, 94, 119–27,
130–34, 182
Denisova, Solomoniia, 127
Diderot, Denis, 154–55
Dmitrii, Metropolitan of Rostov, 54
Don Cossacks, 20–21, 46, 116
Druzhinin, Vasilii Grigor'evich, 72–73,
137, 146
Duffy, Eamon, 41
dukhovnye stikhi (spiritual verses), 23,
50, 70–71

ecclesiastical historiography, 8–14, 69,
157–58, 174–75, 187–88, 191
edinoglasie, 35, 39
edinoverie (edinovertsy), 108, 161–62, 177
Ekaterinburg, 14, 169, 177–79
Elizabeth, Empress (1741–1762), 161
Emel'ianov, Vasilii, 141–42, 151–53
Ephraem Syrus (Efrem Sirin), Saint, 61,
79
Epifanii, 41–42, 71–72, 74, 88, 91, 93–96
Evfimii (founder of *beguny*), 184–85
Evfrosin (Old Believer polemicist), 47–49,
54, 57

fasting, 43, 59–61, 126–27, 136
Fedor, Deacon, 41–42, 71–76, 81–82, 89,
94–95, 119, 136
Fedoseevtsy, 101, 109, 112–14, 137,
140–41, 185
Feodosii Vasil'ev, 102–3
Fedotov, G. P., 120
Filippov, Ivan (historian of Vyg), 49, 105,
120, 126–27, 130–31, 134, 143–44,
181–82
Filippovtsy, 101, 116, 140–41, 179, 184
Filipp, elder, 161
Florence Council of, 39, 75, 77
Freemasonry. See *Masons*
Freeze, Gregory, 25, 50

Galanin, Miron Ivanovich, 188

Geertz, Clifford, 15, 68–69
Gerasim Firsov, 81, 181
Ginzburg, Carlo, 20, 53
Golubinskii, Evgenii Evstigneevich, 9
Goriacheva, Tat'iana Dmitrievna, 112–14
government policy toward the Old Believ-
ers, 45–47, 50–51, 160–64
Grammatika of 1595, 81
Grebenshchikovskaia Obshchina (Riga),
115–16
Griboedov, Fedor, 134
Guchkov, F. A., 114
Gur'ianova, Natal'ia Sergeevna, xi, xiii, 13,
179–84, 187–89
Gurevich, Aron Iakovlevich, 18

hagiography, 85–88, 91–96, 122, 133
Hildermeier, Manfred, 13
historiography of Old Belief. *See*
ecclesiastical historiography; populist
historiography; western historiography

Ignatii, Metropolitan of Siberia, 54, 57
Ilarion, Archbishop of Riazan', 43, 45, 59
Ioasaf, Patriarch, 34–35, 38
Irgiz, 107–9, 116, 161
*Istoriia o ottsekh i stradal'tsekh
Solovetskikh,* 120, 182
Iukhimenko, Elena Mikhailovna, xi, xviii,
106, 112, 133, 180, 182, 191
Ivan Alekseev, 102–3

Jesuit. *See* Ukrainian scholarship/influence
Jesus prayer, 133–34
Joseph of Volokolamsk, 76, 122–23

Kapiton, 12, 43, 48, 52–66, 125–26
Kapitonovshchina, 14, 44, 52–67
Kapterev, Nikolai Fedorovich, 9
Kerzhenets, 49, 91, 102, 106, 160, 176
Kirillova kniga, 79, 81, 183
kladbishcha (cemeteries), 110
Klibanov, Aleksandr Il'ich, xi, 53, 184
Kniga o vere, 79–81, 183
Koliada, 35

Kormchaia kniga, 76, 81
Kornilii (early leader of Vyg), 56, 105, 120, 124
Kovylin, Il'ia, 110–13, 185
Kuandykov, Lev Kabdenovich, 104–5, 180
Kurenevsk, 109

L'vova, Stepanida, 43, 62–63
Lazar', 41–42, 71–73, 94
Leksa, 50, 104–7, 124, 127, 137–41, 148–51, 162
Leonid (disciple of Kapiton), 43, 59–62
Levin, Eve, 31, 44
Liubopytnyi, Pavel, 137–38, 140, 143, 156
Lyzlov, Andrei, 134

Macarius, Metropolitan, 8
Maksim Grek, 74, 76, 81–82, 143, 172
Mal'tsev, Aleksandr Ivanovich, 185–87
Malyshev, Vladimir Ivanovich, viii–x, 6, 73, 117–18, 168–69, 182, 190
Mariia (Morozova's companion), 92–93
marriage, Old Believer debates on, 100–101, 109–10, 112, 142–43, 151, 163
martyrdom, 80, 87–96, 121–24, 130, 133–34
Masons, 152
Matveev, Daniil, 137–38
Mazunin Aleksandr Ivanovich, 91
Melaniia (Morozova's confessor), 93–94
meshchane (urban lower middle classes), 21
Michels, Georg, 7, 13, 32, 40–41, 45–46, 192
Mikhail Romanov, Tsar (1613–1645), 57
miracles (miraculous), 88–96
mnogoglasie, 34, 55
monastic rule in Old Believer communities, 100, 103–7, 113, 124, 180
Moninskaia molennaia (Moninsk), 109–10
Morozova, Boiarynia, 44, 47, 74–75, 85, 87–88, 90–96, 127
Muchembled, Robert, 19
Murachev, Afanasii Gerasimovich, 177–78, 188

Nasedka, Ivan, 182–83
nastoiatel' (bol'shak), 103, 138
Neronov, Ivan, 33–34, 40–42, 74
Nicholas I (1825–1855), 8, 108, 114, 158–9, 161–63
Nikita Dobrynin "Pustosviat", 41–42, 46, 72–73, 81–82
Nikon, Patriarch (1652–1667), 9, 12, 18, 26, 33, 38–42, 44, 49, 53–60, 64, 67–71, 74–82, 89, 92, 120–21, 130–42, 135, 182
reforms of, 7, 9–12, 15, 20, 32–33, 38, 42–46, 53–58, 65, 70–82, 86, 89–90, 92, 101, 119–22, 130–33, 135, 174–75
Nil Sorsky, 76, 122–23
Nizhnii-Novgorod, 34–36, 43, 49, 62–63, 102, 144, 146, 160
Novgorod, 33, 38, 48, 53, 55, 102–3, 133, 145–46
Novosibirsk, 14, 54, 166–91

Old Belief, comparative perspectives on, 15–6; definitions, 6–7; geographical distribution of, 21–22, 116, 166–67; intelligentsia within, 22, 42–43, 70–72, 85–86, 137–38, 142–56; militant/radical currents within, 47–67, 122, 172, 177–82, 184–86; social origin of adherents, 25–26, 177–78
Old Believer communities, structures of, 99–118
Oparina, Tat'iana Anatol'evna, 182–83

Paert, Irina, 192
Paleostrovskii Monastery, 46–48, 105–6, 122
Pascal, Pierre, 12–14, 169
Paul, Bishop of Kolomna, 40, 130
Pentikäinen, Juha, 23
Peter I (1689–1725), 8, 10, 50–51, 129, 160–61, 174, 179
Petrov, Manuil, 146–47
Petrozavodsk, 140, 144, 147, 169
Philotheus of Pskov, 76
Pokrovskii, Nikolai Nikolaevich, 20, 26, 54, 103, 116–17, 166–89

Polotskii, Simeon, 7, 41, 76
Pomorskie otvety, 120, 147–48, 183
Pomortsy, 101–3, 109, 137, 141–42,
    152–53, 185
popovtsy, 7, 14, 20
popular religion/popular religious move-
    ments, 17–21, 24–27, 53–54, 166–69,
    177, 189
populist historiography, 8–14, 69, 157–58,
    168, 174–76, 180–81, 184, 187–89
Potapov, Ustin Sergeevich, 137, 139–40,
    153
Potemkin, Spiridon, 41, 71–73, 76
Pozdeeva, Irina Vasil'evna, 118, 169
prayer, Old Believer teachings on and
    practice of, 119–28; disputes over
    prayers for the ruling monarch, 137,
    140–41, 163, 179
pre-Christian (pagan) folk rituals, 33–36, 55
Preobrazhenskoe Kladbishche (Preobra-
    zhensk), 109–15, 161, 163
Prikaz Tainykh Del, 59, 66–67
Pudozh, 47
Pustozersk, 71–74, 80, 84, 122, 127
Puteshestvie za redkimi knigami, 172,
    175–76, 186

Raeff, Marc, x–xi
raskol'nik (pejorative legal term for Old
    Believers), 139–40
Razin, Stenka, 10
research expeditions, 169–72, 175–76,
    179–80, 186
Riabushinskii circle, 156
Robson, Roy, 13, 115–16
Rogozhskoe Kladbishche (Rogozhsk),
    109–15, 161
Rollin, Charles, 154–55
Romme, Gilbert, 152–55
Romodanovskaia, Elena Konstantinova,
    178–79
Rousseau, Jean-Jacques, 154–55
Rtishchev, Fedor Mikhailovich, 33, 38
Rumiantseva, Vera Mikhailovna, 32,
    53–54, 65

Rusalii, 35
Ryndziunskii, Pavel Grigor'evich, 112

sacred history, Old Believer interpretations
    of, 76–79, 131–35, 182
saints' lives. *See* hagiography
Sakalov, Artemii (Altai peasant), 26, 186
self-immolation, 33, 46–48, 51, 54, 60–64,
    105, 120, 160, 173
Shchapov, Afanasii Prokop'evich, 9–10,
    174–76, 183
skit (skity), 100, 106–8, 116–18
skomorokhi (folk entertainers), 35–36
Skrizhal, 41, 81
Slavophiles, 12
Smirnov, Petr Semenovich, 8–9, 120, 175,
    185
Sokolovskaia, Marina L'vovna, 104, 106–7
Solovetskii Monastery (Solovki), 20, 46,
    63, 71–4, 103–5, 120, 122–24, 130–33,
    180–81; petitions to the tsar from, 72,
    78, 81–82
Sophia (Regent, 1682–1689), 8, 46, 160
spirituality, 119–28
Stalin, 115, 171
Starodub, 41, 49, 107
staropechatnye knigi, 111
Stock, Brian, 22, 69
Stoglav, 35, 77, 81–82, 130, 143
stranniki. See beguny
Subbotin, Nikolai Ivanovich, 8–9, 89

Tara, 121–22, 174, 186–87
textual community, 22–23, 26, 49, 69,
    176–77
Tikhomirov, Mikhael Nikolaevich, 170–72
Turner, Victor, 15

Ukrainian scholarship/influence, 24, 38,
    42, 119, 128, 134, 143, 146, 152–53,
    182–84
Uliianiia Lazarevskaia (Osor'ina), Tale
    of, 93, 95
Urals, 14, 21–22, 102, 116–17, 166, 171–73,
    176, 178–79

Urusova, Princess, 92–93, 127
Uspensky, Boris A., 15, 192

Vavila (disciple of Kapiton), 43, 59–62
Vetka, 49, 106–7, 161
Viazniki, 43–45, 58–63, 66
Vikulich, Daniil, 48, 105
Vinograd rossiiskii, 91, 120, 122, 130,
    133–34
Vologda, 43–44, 62–66
Voltaire, 154–55
Vonifat'ev, Stefan, 33–40
Vyg community, 13, 22–24, 48–51, 64,

70, 73, 91, 102–13, 116, 119–56,
    158–64; literary and artistic school
    of, 24, 142–43, 183–84; plans for an
    academy at, 152–53; role of liturgy in,
    123–25; scholarship in, 142–48; western
    historiography of Old Belief, 11–13

Zavoloko, Ivan. Nikiforovich, x, 115, 190
Zealots of Piety, 12, 25, 33–36, 38, 50, 67
zemstvo, 10
Zenkovsky, Serge, 11–14, 168
Zol'nikova, Natal'ia Dmitrievna, 116–17,
    176–78, 187, 189

Chronological History of the Chapters

1988

8—The Spirituality of the Vyg Fathers. Source: First published in *Church, Nation, and State in Russia and Ukraine,* ed. Geoffrey A. Hosking (Macmillan, 1991), 23–37. Republished with the kind permission of the School of Slavonic and East European Studies, University of London.

1988

4—Religious Radicalism in Seventeenth-Century Russia: Reexamining the Kapiton Movement. Source: First published in *Forschungen zur osteuropäischen Geschichte* 46 (1992): 172–85. Republished with the kind permission of Otto Harrassowitz Verlag.

1990

9—The Historical Framework of the Vyg Fathers. Source: First published in Russian in *Traditsionnaia dukhovnaia i material'naia kul'tura russkikh staroobriadcheskikh poselenii v stranakh Evropy, Azii i Ameriki: Sbornik nauchnykh trudov* (Novosibirsk, Nauka. Sibirskoe otdelenie, 1992), 90–96.

1991

11—Interpreting the Fate of Old Believer Communities in the Eighteenth and Nineteenth Centuries. Source: First published in *Seeking God: The Recovery of Religious Identity in Orthodox Russia, Ukraine, and Georgia,* ed. Stephen K. Batalden (Northern Illinois University Press, 1993), 144–59. Republished in slightly abridged form with the kind permission of the publisher. The historiographical introduction of the original article has been shortened considerably. For a more detailed discussion of these issues, see chapter 1 of this volume.

1992

5—The Origins of the Old Believer Cultural Systems: The Works of Avraamii. Source: First published in *Forschungen zur osteuropäischen Geschichte* 50 (1995): 121–38. Republished with the kind permission of Otto Harrassowitz Verlag.

1993

2—Old Belief as Popular Religion: New Approaches. Source: Published in *Slavic Review* 52 (1993), 700–712. Republished with the kind permission of the American Association for the Advancement of Slavic Studies.

1993

6—The Miracle of Martyrdom: Reflections on Early Old Believer Hagiography. Source: First published in *Religion and Culture in Early Modern Russia and Ukraine*, ed. Samuel H. Baron and Nancy Shields Kollmann (Northern Illinois University Press, 1997), 132–45. Republished with the kind permission of Northern Illinois University Press.

1994

1—Past and Current Interpretations of the Old Belief. Source: Published in *Russia's Dissident Old Believers 1650–1950* (Minnesota Mediterranean and East European Monographs, number 19), ed. Georg B. Michels and Robert L. Nichols (University of Minnesota Press, 2009), 39–51. First presented at the conference titled Russia's Dissident Old Believers, 1650–1950: An International and Interdisciplinary Conference and Exhibition, at St. Olaf College, Northfield, MN, in October 1994. It reflects that state of the literature at that time. Republished with the kind permission of the University of Minnesota and its Modern Greek Studies Program.

1995

10—The Cultural Worlds of Andrei Borisov. Source: First published in *Forschungen zur osteuropäischen Geschichte* 54 (1998): 135–57. Republished with the kind permission of Otto Harrassowitz Verlag.

1998

3—Ecclesiastical Elites and Popular Belief and Practice in Seventeenth-Century Russia. Source: First published in *Religion and the Early Modern State: Views from China, Russia, and the West*, ed. James Tracy and Marguerite Ragnow (Cambridge University Press, 2004), 52–79. Republished with the kind permission of Cambridge University Press.

2003

7—**Old Believer Communities**: Ideals and Structures. Source: Presented at the Workshop on the History of the Russian Orthodox Church at Yale University, September 20–21, 2003.

2011

12—**The Novosibirsk School of Old Believer Studies**. First published in this volume.

2011

Preface and Afterword—First published in this volume.

Lightning Source UK Ltd.
Milton Keynes UK
UKHW011257300721
387961UK00001B/38

9 780875 806501